Migrants and Migration in Modern North America

D0932815

Migrants and Migration in Modern North America

Cross-Border Lives, Labor Markets, and Politics

Dirk Hoerder and Nora Faires, eds.

Duke University Press *Durham and London* 2011

© 2011 Duke University Press
All rights reserved.

Printed in the United States of America
on acid-free paper ∞
Typeset in Arnhem Blond with Magma display
by Tseng Information Systems, Inc.

Library of Congress Cataloging-in-Publication Data
appear on the last printed page of this book.

"Undone by Desire: Migration, Sex across Boundaries,
and Collective Destinies in the Greater Caribbean,
1840–1940," by Lara Putnam, originally appeared
in *Connecting Seas and Connected Ocean Rims*,
edited by Dirk Hoerder and Donna R. Gabaccia,
forthcoming, by Koninklijke BRILL NV.

Dedicated by Nora Faires:
To all those whom I love and who have supported me in my journey

Dedicated by Dirk Hoerder:
To my friends across North America

Contents

List of Maps

Preface

Dirk Hoerder and Nora Faires

If we step back from nation-state perspectives and take a continental view, what happens to our understanding of people and their movements within, between, and among Canada, the Caribbean, Mexico, and the United States over the last two centuries? How much more do we know about the processes of migration? How does what we previously accepted become revised when we adopt this broader geographic and societal perspective while keeping individual lives in the forefront of analysis? These questions prompted us to develop this volume. The perspective presented here is continental, not continentalist: contributing scholars do not present a brief for some form of North American integration, but seek to place the population movements and historical memory about them both within and beyond national narratives.

The goal of the volume is to provide an integrated history of North American migration. We seek to put forward a nuanced understanding of continental trends, countering the continued fragmentation of research along national lines. Scholars from several disciplines discuss the state of the art in the many research fields involved and place contemporary developments in long-term historical context. Contributors delineate the shifting demographics of North America and examine multifaceted movements of population across the continent with regard to changing cultural, political, and economic patterns. Crossing disciplinary boundaries, the volume attends to cultural regions (notably bilingual French-English Québec and the Spanish-English Hispanic-Anglo region) as well as nation states and to diverse populations. Perspectives range from the macro-level, placing North American migrations in global context, to the micro-level, discussing the aspirations and agency of particular groups and individuals. As the subtitle for the volume indicates, we are interested in the various means by which people in the past and present have fashioned cross-border lives, and for whom this fashioning has proved most difficult; in the ways in which shifting labor markets have facilitated or hindered women's and men's movements across borders; the making of borderlands economies, societies, and cultures; and the place of formal and informal politics in these processes and in diverse migrants' lives. These accounts include the experiences of many actors, revising those narratives that focus on only one country (often the most powerful one) or that assume that migrants' lives are of interest only when they reach their destination.

In particular, this book aims to foster awareness regarding:

— synthetic analyses of overall migration patterns within the continent and the Western Hemisphere from the period before Native-European contact through the present;
— the extensive body of research investigating the Mexican-U.S. borderlands, the migrations of Mexicans and Latina/o migrations, and the changing settlement patterns and economic activities of these migrants;
— the smaller body of comparable work on the Canada-U.S. borderlands and the enduring patterns of population movement from Canada to the United States;
— the scholarship on selective crosscurrents of migration from the United States to Mexico and Canada;
— the emerging work on connections to and from the Caribbean to diverse mainland sites; and
— studies of such topics as the black experience in Canada, migration from Central America to all three major North American nation-states, and the relationship of migration to foreign relations.

Conceptual Frameworks

An implicitly U.S. historical perspective holds that North America is framed by the Atlantic Coast and, in the nineteenth century more an afterthought, the Pacific Coast. Yet in Canada (except for the Maritime Provinces) until well into the nineteenth century the St. Lawrence River rather than the distant coast counted and since the British East India Company in a transpacific move from its Asian domain colonized the Pacific Northwest (named "British Columbia") early, the Pacific achieved a presence in policymakers' minds. No similar narrative emerged in the United States because when New England ministers and writers established the foundational stories, the Pacific Coast was part of the Spanish Empire and the Russian realm. When Spanish and Russians had to leave in a shift of global power, their historical memory went with them. Newly arriving U.S.-socialized local and regional historians developed a new Anglocentric story. New Spain's and Mexico's perspectives hardly enter English-language narratives. What became the Great Southwest of North America and California was a traditionally bilingual region. The historical memory of Spanish-speakers needed to be silenced by those speaking English only, by many "national" scholars who chose not to learn a second language.

The Mexican isthmus was bicoastal. The European self-styled "conquistadors," or "aggressors" in English, arrived from the Iberian Atlantic through the world of the Caribbean Islands and quickly developed a transpacific galleon trade to the Southeast Asian section of the Spanish empire, with Manila as entrepot, and to the trade networks of the diaspora of Chinese merchants based in China's southern ports. Between Mexico and Europe was not only the Atlantic but the many island societies of the Caribbean. The gaze both of Europeans and of scholars in the Atlantic World is drawn toward the impressively large, in terms of geography to the North American continent and in terms of polities to the United States. Small entities are easily overlooked. This was not so when the Caribbean islands' European-imposed plantation regime produced sugar and immense profits while the North American segment of the dual continent had little to offer and constituted a drain on imperial treasuries. Perspectives were and are different for the people who live on the continent and for those of the island societies that form their communities and life-worlds and are connected to other segments of the globe.

Size counts when human beings, of which scholars are a subspecies, establish frames of reference and anchor-points for analysis. We have accepted this. We have thus not begun with the landscapes and societies, the narratives and socioscapes of the First People, often still called "Indians" because the first European newcomers who named them had no idea where they had arrived. When Europeans realized that they were not in India, those in the Caribbean amended the terminology slightly: "West Indians" as opposed to the "East Indians" in South Asia. Those immigrants narrowly clinging to the Atlantic seaboard could not be bothered by such detail and continued to call the resident peoples "Indians." Having only one God, they did not understand complex spirituality and added as marker of Otherness and inferiority "heathen" to "Indian." Finally, alien to the landscape and ways to subsist in it but filled with a single-track belief in their own superiority, they labeled the residents "primitives" to hide their own limitations. We know that several of the colonizing attempts collapsed because the newcomers lacked knowledge and adaptability and obstinately refused to learn from those who had the funds of knowledge to live in the natural environment and develop complex societies.

In this volume we attempt to show both continuities and discontinuities, exchange and conqueror-imposed violence, that mark the transition from a world of many Native, or First, Peoples to the takeover by the immigrants from

Europe, the Second Peoples. Just as the life-worlds of the many First Peoples were interrelated, the European-background peoples, all "Americans" once the continent had thus been named, were highly differentiated. The chapters of this volume deal with continental North American and Caribbean Sea societies as many-cultured and interactive but also as bordered by political boundaries, divisions between men's and women's roles, racist lines of separation, and power hierarchies in all of these. We have attempted to be careful with our language: to many the word "migrant" conjures up a male image. Our mental hard drives run a disastrous software called "mother tongue" embedded in unidentifiable background programs providing connotations in the 0.1 version of "mother tongue spoken in a father land" or the more recent 0.2 "national language as embodiment of national culture and identity." "Canadian" as national designation may refer to a French-speaking one, to an Anglophone one (of British or Guianese or Hong Kong background), to Native culture in its present version, or to people of some two hundred other backgrounds. An "American," on a first level the matching categorization of "African," "European," or "Asian" but in North America usually meaning a U.S. citizen, can be a Midwestern or Southwestern person, a Californian, Oklahoman, or New Yorker. And a Mexican can be a woman from Mexico City or a peasant man from Oaxaca. Nation-state designations, considered the foundation rocks of American History 101, are muskegs in which analysis sinks and is smothered by moss.

Again, this volume cannot escape from the terms, discourses, and connotations of our time. Thus its title refers to both North America and the states and regions. We place North America in a larger perspective: the often evoked Atlantic World, South America, to which the Caribbean and Mexico can be a link, the Pacific Ocean across which migrants came from Asia. Once mariners had developed shipping technology in Europe's North Sea and Atlantic port cities capable of ocean crossing, the Atlantic Ocean's rims step by step became an Atlantic World to which Africans, given the power relation and under far more difficult and constraining conditions, added the African diaspora or Black Atlantic. (Such connectivity had been achieved by mariners in the Indian Ocean, Southeast Asian and East Asian seas a millennium or two earlier.) On the western rim of the Americas no similar "Pacific World" emerged. The expanse of this ocean was separating rather than connecting, though specific sea-lanes did develop and bring men and women to the Americas.

The subtitle of the volume, "Cross-Border Lives, Labor Markets, and Politics," refers to Canada, the Caribbean, Mexico, and the United States and would suggest in terms of theorization a transnational approach. However, the nation-state perspective focuses on the sizable, the big structures, the master narratives. It deprives the people in the societies of voice, makes them invisible, symbolically annihilates them. Starting from the nation-states, a transnational approach can point to frames: It is states which regulate border-crossings of human beings, goods, and capital. It is statewide societies which provide structures, processes, and cultural guidelines on how to express oneself, how to be an agent in one's own life. Thus states, societies, and ideologies of nation—as well as of religion—may not simply be cast aside. They are part of the stories that the chapters in this volume trace.

Yet borders, like structures, are porous and permeable. Around the turn of the twentieth century, state bureaucrats erected the Great Wall of exclusion legislation against the Oriental masses that racists claimed threatened white dominance. Facing the paperwork of legislation and administration, many immigrants from Asia's cultures adopted the host-hostile country's discourse and created paper children who could cross the paper wall. In the present, the states of the capitalist world (or free world in times of the Cold War) see their borders crossed by unimaginable masses of capital flows, moved by highly remunerated bankers in global cities, which threaten common people in all of these states, hindering them in earning a livelihood. To the category "state" the category "global" needs to be added. Contrary to some pundits' pronouncements, scholars know globalization is not a new phenomenon. In the colonial period of North America and the Caribbean, the fur trade was globalized in the northern hemisphere (capitalized and coordinated in cities with global outreach such as London, Paris, Amsterdam, and Moscow); the cotton economy of the U.S. South was part of the plantation belt circling the globe and dependent on African forced labor; Mexico's silver, then New Spain's, affected currencies and volume of trade in Southeast Asia and the Chinese Empire.

In this volume the place of North America and the Caribbean in the globe is touched upon only occasionally. We are more interested in the level of regions within states or transborder areas. Migrants move between particular localities, from a Ukrainian village to a specific place in the Canadian prairies around 1900, from a Hong Kong neighborhood to a Metro Vancouver one in the present; from specific places of origin in Vietnam or Guatemala to neighborhoods in new gateway cities in the United States; from Latin American societies, particularly when dictatorial regimes are in power, to Mexico and further north. When they cross geographies they are guided by networks of information flows and relationships. Facilitators or exploitative smugglers of human beings may help or hinder their journey. In the twenty-first century, the Ford Motor Company, which produces in Mexico, the United States, and Canada, has installed a camera system at the border checkpoints its supply trucks have to cross. The company's logistics personnel can thus redirect truck routes if obstacles such as delays at one checkpoint threaten their intricate, just-in-time production processes. Migrants and travelers would appreciate to be moved with as much care and speed. This is why the European Union, attempting to encourage a European citizenship, has abolished its internal borders (while fortifying its perimeter).

For migrants, the connections thus are localities and regions with economies that offer jobs suitable for their skills and with multilingual guides and translators that may help insertion into an economic niche, segment, or larger labor market at the destination. To permit empirical accuracy in data collection and interpretation, the conceptual framework thus needs to be translocal and transregional, rather than transnational or—generically speaking—transcultural. While "nationals" or, simply, locally resident and unmoving people, can make do with one local cultural frame, migrants need at least two and perhaps more. They need to negotiate cultural difference, to translate everyday patterns of life and values so that they may be understood by themselves and their neighbors, co-workers, or classmates. Since the transcultural approach had to overcome constraining localism, the approach is developed into a Transcultural Societal Studies in the Introduction. The interpretive frame developed there has not been imposed on other contributors to the volume but helps to understand the specific angles and perspectives on North American migration.

Overcoming or transcending localism, like globalism, is not a distinctive feature of modern times. Native Peoples developed macroregional, perhaps transcontinental exchange networks. Objects of everyday usage and ceremonial artifacts signifying spiritual expression were exchanged over great distances. The "primitive" or "prehistory" discourse collapses when scholars and teachers look at information available for a long time but which certain discourses and ideological blindfolds prevented analysts of the dominating societies from seeing. Thus the chapters in this volume attempt to move research and teaching beyond the frames of the nation-state or Western Civilization. Migrants hoped that crossing borders led them to better options. Similarly, we hope that crossing language, terminological, and disciplinary borders provides a fascinating range of new perspectives. A quotidian example makes the point: How does international migration relate to food history? Nationalist histories have it that migrants move internationally to Canada, America, or Mexico. Food history, not a worthy topic for historians of institutions and statesmen, has added a different, cross-border approach. Ketchup was allegedly once the particularly tasty tomato sauce of the German-background grandmother of a third-generation German American who built a commercial empire on tomato sauce. Mexican tacos are achieving global reach in the present. Migrants from eastern and southern Europe, in their own many languages, which most Anglophone historians of the immigrant saga cannot read, said about their trajectory, "We are going to bread," or "We are following the stomach to bread." This is what Senegalese villagers arriving in New York, Chinese rurals in Vancouver, Vietnamese in Atlanta, and Mexican day laborers in Arizona are doing today. They connect their local places of origin with places elsewhere, whether within their state of birth or across an international border, to increase their options, to feed themselves and families, or to perhaps provide schooling to children. They move transculturally in legal frames (or avoiding these frames' discriminatory restraints) imposed by states that, once ideologized as nations, have become multicultural.

Organization

This book is divided into four parts. In the Introduction Dirk Hoerder provides a sweeping overview of North American societies in the Atlantic world, examining how people have moved across shifting and permeable borders over centuries, and setting forth the transcultural approach to migration sketched above. This Introduction develops in greater detail the Transcultural Societal Studies approach combining attention to the local, regional, national, and transnational. As Hoerder demonstrates, this framework serves as a mechanism for escaping the national perspectives inherent in terms such as "multicultural."

Part I, "Intersocietal Migrations," features analyses of movement across major national borders, the traditional state-centered approach to international migration, and departure from and entry into specific sectors and regions of internally differentiated societies during the nineteenth and twentieth centuries: that between Mexico and the United States (by Jaime R. Aguila and Brian Gratton); Canada and the United States (by Bruno Ramirez); and the Greater Caribbean and the United States (by Lara Putnam).

Part II takes a closer look at aspects of these borders, examining the theme of "Connecting Borderlands, Littorals, and Regions" from different disciplinary locations and perspectives. Nora Faires examines U.S.-Canada relations through the lens of migration. Carlos G. Vélez-Ibáñez, with Dirk Hoerder, analyzes "Greater Southwest North America" in a *longue-durée* perspective focusing on interactions. Melanie Shell-Weiss traces Caribbean-North American migrations and the migrants' insertion into urban contexts, while Delia González de Reufels and Dirk Hoerder look closely at movements to and within Mexico, contextualizing northward cross-border moves within a history of interregional moves. Two final chapters in this part turn to the borders themselves, emphasizing the construction of boundaries and their changing legal, social, and cultural meanings. Angelika E. Sauer surveys the building of a North American perimeter at the beginning of the twentieth century and Omar S. Valerio Jiménez considers the border between Mexico and the United States as a material and cultural barrier.

While the essays in the first three parts attend to complexity and the changing nature of patterns of migration as related to individual life projects, experiences, and itineraries, the contributions to part III, "Complicating Narratives," focus on the stories of particular migrants and migrant groups. Susan E. Gray traces a multigenerational Odawa family story; Dan Killoren discusses the Gila River Pima at the time of the imposition of the border between the United States and Mexico and the arrival of Anglos in ever-increasing numbers; James N. Gregory assesses the relationship between producers of knowledge on migration and the mass media; and Sarah-Jane (Saje) Mathieu examines the black experience in Canada. This part also includes essays by Yukari Takai on Asian-origin migrants crossing the land-borders and by John Mason Hart on U.S. capitalists in Mexico and resulting development and associated migration.

Part IV, "Contemporary and Applied Perspectives," turns to issues of special salience in the current era, when questions of migration and migration policy are at the forefront of local, regional, national, continental, and global debates. María Cristina Garcia demonstrates how concerns about Central American migrants have shaped refugee policy; Rodolfo Casillas-R. analyzes responses to Central Americans who traverse Mexico in their movements further north; and Kerry Preibisch evaluates a Canadian seasonal agricultural workers program that has attracted interest among policymakers in the United States and other nations. In the final chapter Angelika Sauer and Catherine O'Donnell suggest ways to revise the teaching of the U.S. history survey at the college and university level so that it becomes the study of continental North American history.[1]

Together the contributions to this book illuminate the sweeping yet intricate movements of people that have taken place in the North American continent for centuries. In the present as in the past, controversies regarding the economic, political, and cultural consequences of population movements rage within and across the nations and regions discussed in this volume, fostering policies with significant consequences for migrants, the societies they leave, and the societies they enter. We hope to inform a broad readership on these pressing policy concerns, for they are serious issues too often debated without substantive foundation.

WE EXTEND heartfelt thanks to the authors in this volume for their cordial collaboration in this project. Nora Faires expresses her gratitude for the support provided by the Burnham MacMillan Fund of the Department of History and the Office of the Vice President for Research at Western Michigan University. Dirk Hoerder expresses his gratitude to Deborah Losse, Dean of Humanities, and the North American Center for Transborder Studies, Arizona State University, for their support, as well as to the Canadian Embassy, Washington, for helping to bring together some of the authors in a workshop in April 2008.

IN SADNESS I also extend my thanks to my co-editor and friend Nora Faires, who had been fighting cancer for many years and had hoped to see this volume to completion. She died in February 2011. Her dedication of this volume to her friends was written with the knowledge that she was losing the fight. We all will miss her probing, analytical mind and her courageous personality.

Note

1 The editors' attempt to provide similar perspectives for high school courses expanded beyond the frame of this collection and has been published separately as an issue of the *OAH Magazine of History* (fall 2009).

Migration, People's Lives, Shifting and Permeable Borders

The North American and Caribbean Societies in the Atlantic World

Dirk Hoerder

The image of North America on maps of physical geography seems unambiguous: the northern part of the double continent. However, the continent is "the Americas": a plurality of geographic regions and human spaces, of cultures and societies. In public perception only *one* superpower makes up its northern half though there are *three* states—Canada, the United States, and Mexico. In a less state-centered view, North America consists of five cultural-political regions: French-Canada, once extending from Nouvelle France on the St. Lawrence along the Mississippi to Nouvelle Orléans; Anglo-Canada with its many regions; the United States of America with multiple cultures; the United States of Mexico—Estados Unidos de Mexico—also divided into many cultures; and, fifth, the highly differentiated World of the Caribbean.

In this chapter, I will first place the settlement of the macro-region "North America" in a long-term perspective. I will, second, discuss the emergence of states out of colonies in the Ages of Revolution and of Romanticism, both European periodizations, and question the concept of nation-states. Third, I will place these societies in the context of the nineteenth-century Atlantic World, especially as regards migration, and touch briefly upon the transpacific connection. Fourth, I will discuss migrations within the North Americas and the imposition of borderlines. Fifth, I will indicate how transborder perspectives were developed by scholars in the 1920s and 1930s, and, in conclusion, suggest a transcultural approach that combines the transregional with the translocal and the transnational.

Writing the history of macroregions with many peoples requires—as all historiography does—a careful examination of terminologies and their connotations, of concepts and their relations to cultural context, of the interdependence of knowledge and interest. The *longue-durée* history of Native People over twenty to thirty thousand years is not merely pre-history to the five hundred years of European presence as white terminology has it. Euro-American events and processes are not necessarily confined by a state's borderlines. "People, ideas, and institutions do not have clear national identities. Rather, people may translate and assemble pieces from different cultures. Instead of assuming that something was distinctively American [or Canadian, Mexican, Jamaican, Cuban, . . .], we might assume that elements of it began or ended somewhere else."[1] History needs to be written in a way that all actors—slave and free, women and men, resident and migrant, on each side of a border—may recognize themselves. Finally, human beings are actors in their own lives, but they make history under conditions not of their own making.

The Re-peopling of the North Americas in a Longue-durée Perspective

Anglo-European arrival, when labeled "The Peopling of British North America," misreads the empirical evidence. Its *re*-peopling involved expulsions of First Peoples, "refugee generation" in modern terms. Choosing Plymouth Rock as a starting *place* and the pilgrim fathers', mothers', children's, and servants' arrival as the starting *time* is arbitrary even for newcomers from Europe. Centuries earlier, Norsemen and Norsewomen crossed the Atlantic in their hemispheric migrations extending from Scandinavia westward to North America (not yet named), eastward to the Moskva River, and southward to the Mediterranean cultures. Next Iberian-origin people, sometimes called "Spaniards" but, in fact, Andalusians, Extremadurans, and Castilians, with Jewish-Christian *conversos* and Moriscos of Muslim-North African background among them, came first to the Caribbean Isles and mainland Mexico, then to Florida, the Carolinas, and New Mexico.[2] Only from the early 1600s, people of other languages—English, French, German—defining themselves by religion as Puritans, Anglicans, Protestants, Catholics, or other came from Europe's Atlantic littorals. All were subjects of dynasties bent on expanding their states into empires. England had reduced Ireland to the status of a colony (1603) and had annexed Wales (1536) and Scotland (1707). The Parisian French dynasty had annihilated religio-cultural diversity and difference in the realm's south. In addition to the Europeans, departing under severe economic constraints and religious persecutions, men and women from West Africa were forcibly migrated first under indentures but soon as slaves. To the 1830s more Africans reached the Americas than Europeans. Along the continent's northern Pacific Rim, people from Russia arrived via Siberia and Alaska.[3]

Beginning the history of the Americas with the arrival of European conquerors and settler migrants (i.e. Second Peoples) expunges from collective memory or symbolically annihilates First Peoples. From the Inuit and Dene in the north to the Mexica (Aztec) and other indigenous groups in the south, these cultures comprised more than sixty major languages and language families.[4] Natural landscapes framed First People's lives: riparian agriculture where possible, big game hunting, collecting of food, and water's edge living. To overcome natural constraints, peoples in arid regions developed large-scale techniques of irrigation. Others expressed spirituality in mound building, which required planning and collective labor. Geographic frames could be changed by human agency. In the Greater Southwest the northern Ancient Pueblo (or Anasazi or Hisatsinom) cultures attained their apogee in the two centuries before 1130, while the southern Mexica founded Tenochtitlán in 1325. Trade and cultural exchange connected these societies: copper and parrots from Mexico, shells from the Pacific Coast and the Gulf of California, other products from several neighboring cultural groups. In the Northeast, the Iroquois Confederacy was negotiated in 1451. Peoples migrated and, since the continent was settled, "bumped into each other" (Vélez-Ibáñez). Negotiation and coexistence could result. But so could warfare. Migrating peoples carried "funds of knowledge" (Haury) with them that permitted adaptation to new ecologies and formation of new viable communities.[5] Such societies required highly sophisticated observation of nature and techniques of adaptation for survival.

The European intruders' funds of knowledge, on the other hand, were inadequate or their application too dogmatic for the new surroundings. The Norse established agricultural settlements, but rather than negotiate with the resident peoples, fought them—in view of numbers and length of supply lines a self-defeating strategy. Basque and Bristol fishermen, perhaps with women for fish processing, summered along the coasts of Newfoundland. Columbus, a migrant from the declining Mediterranean urban economy to the rising Atlantic seaboard, began the decimation of the Caribbean peoples. The conquistadors relied on firepower rather than on funds of knowledge, and the germs they carried killed millions. As regards chronology, in New Mexico Spanish men and women arrived in the 1540s, in the St. Lawrence Valley fur traders from France around 1600. The English Virginia settlers, coming in 1585 and 1606, hardly survived because they lacked agricultural expertise. The Puritans (arriving 1620), high on dogma and low on applicable knowledge, had to ask the resident "primitives," as they viewed them, the Massachusets, for food to avoid starvation. The founding narrative is one of food handouts from Native Americans to and of warfare and violence by immigrant Europeans.

The North Americas became part of global trading and colonization networks. The northern fur trade, dependent on commercial capital in London,

Amsterdam, Paris, and Moscow, encompassed Scandinavia and Siberia. While it permitted First Peoples to acquire iron tools that facilitated women's work in food and hide preparation, the trade involved competition and undercut the relation to nature: They depleted the stocks of fur-bearing animals. In the south, the port of Acapulco connected the Spanish colonizers with their acquisitions in the Philippines. On this transpacific route, free and enslaved men and women from several Asian cultures came to New Spain. First Peoples had developed transcontinental trading networks, second arrivals developed transoceanic ones. In the Plains and the Southwest, horses, introduced by the Spanish in an unintended exchange of material culture, made First Peoples like the Dakota and Apache more mobile, and this "transportation technology" increased raiding and warring.

In the sixteenth century the St. Lawrence Valley fur trade involved exchange between equals. To the last inter-imperial war, 1754–63, the European belligerents treated First Peoples as independent nations. Negotiations involved cultural evaluation: English officers in Cherokee towns could not understand gender roles; they considered the agency of Cherokee women "petticoat-government." Some of the Cherokee could not understand Christian beliefs: The Bible "seems to be a good book—strange that the white people are not better, after having had it so long."[6] Historians need to be aware of the many viewpoints.

The North American-Caribbean cultural macroregion was segmented into connected and shifting regions by First Peoples; it was segmented differently by the Second People's European dynasties. First Peoples' borders were cultural and economic-ecological; they involved regions of contact, and they shifted.[7] Trade across cultural borders required interpreters whether between First Peoples or between specific First and specific Second Peoples; contact zones, cohabitation, or conflict could emerge. The newcoming Europeans' concept of territories with fixed, arbitrary borderlines, drawn straight across complex landscapes, stood diametrically opposed to borderlands emerging from usage. As Edgar W. McInnis noted, none of North America's "political divisions explain themselves," no physical features "explain why the division lies where it does—or, indeed, why there is a division at all." When the British-Spanish-French-American peace commissioners in 1782 selected the 49th parallel as the border from the Lake of the Woods to the Mississippi, they did not know what they were doing: The 49th parallel runs far north of the river's source. Any of the First Peoples residing in the region could have told them.[8]

The lines drawn between the United States and British North America in the grass of the prairies in 1846 and in the sands of the Sonoran desert in 1848 and in 1853 had little local meaning. The former was negotiated between Wash-

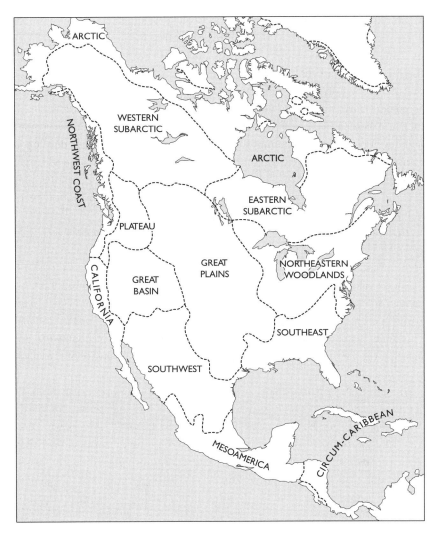

Geographic and cultural regions of North America

ington and London, the latter imposed after aggression by the United States against the Republic of Mexico. The power relationship between the United States and the Estados Unidos de Mexico resembled the hierarchies between Britain and Ireland or Germany and Poland. In each case the more powerful state, whether dynastic or republican, imposed dividing lines and, over time, would require many of the vanquished to migrate in search of jobs: Poles to the German Reich, Irish to England and Scotland, Mexicans to the United States. In the Caribbean the colonizer powers had staked regions and claims

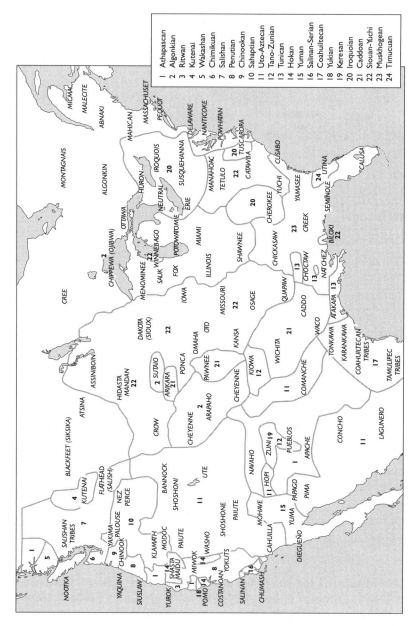

First Peoples' settled spaces at the time of contact: Cultures, languages, nations

1	Athapascan
2	Algonkian
3	Ritwan
4	Kutenai
5	Wakashan
6	Chimikuan
7	Salishan
8	Penutian
9	Chinookan
10	Sahaptian
11	Uto-Aztecan
12	Tano-Zunian
13	Tunican
14	Hokan
15	Yuman
16	Salinan-Serian
17	Coahuiltecan
18	Yukian
19	Keresan
20	Iroquoian
21	Caddoan
22	Siouan-Yuchi
23	Muskhogean
24	Timucuan

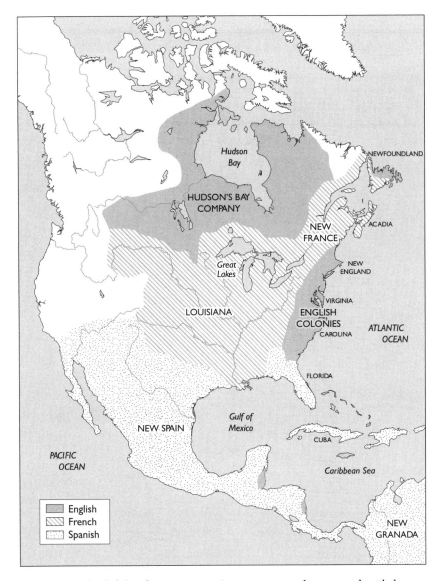

European empires' claimed spaces, 1713: Contact zones and spaces and settled areas

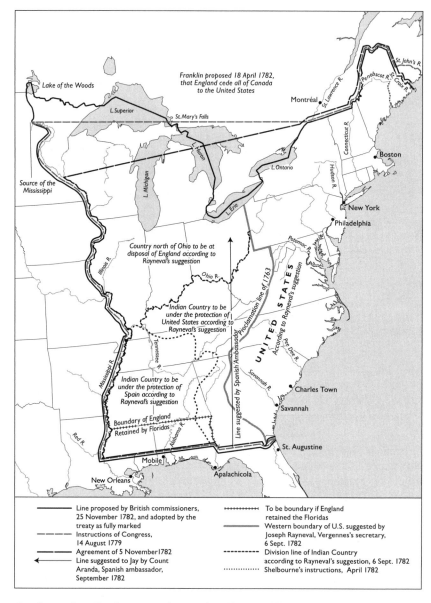

The change from lived spaces to invented and imposed lines: Boundaries proposed in the Great Britain-U.S. peace negotiations of 1782

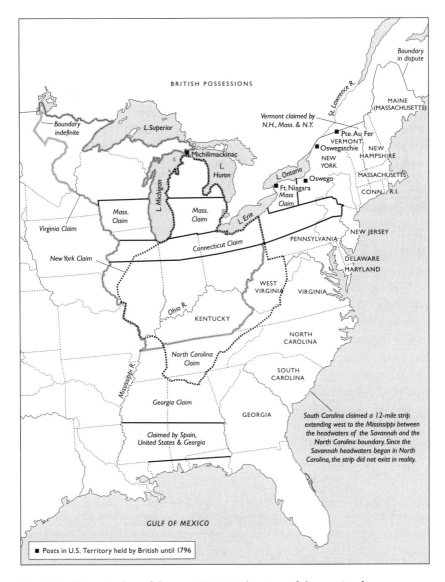

Acquisitive lines: Borders of the new U.S. states' western claims, 1783, drawn without knowledge of geography or consultation with the settled First Nations

to islands during the pre-state buccaneer period and, as gunpowder empires (Andrews), retained territories as possessions and people as subjects longer than on the continent.[9] Interest determined possessions: after losing one more inter-imperial war in the Atlantic World,[10] the French dynasty, having to compromise with the British one in the negotiations for peace in 1763, traded in its French-settled, Catholic, and white Quebec colony in order to retain the more profitable multireligious and multilingual African and Mulatto sugar-producing colonies of Martinique and Guadeloupe. Economics and revenues counted rather than cultural affinities or color of skin.[11]

The Emergence of Independent Societies and States

The Euro-Creole societies of the North Americas, as colonies or after independence, were never self-contained. Their histories developed in the frame of Europe's empires. Caribbean plantation economies produced profits for European investors while the continental colonies hardly paid for themselves. Thus the British attempt in 1765 to tax the colonies. Similarly, dynastic France regulated the colony on the St. Lawrence to a degree that the British takeover in 1763 appeared as economic liberation until a later generation developed a legend of conquest in the 1840s.[12]

The emergence of nation-states in the (North) Americas occurred in the context of European Enlightenment concepts of human rights and political agency, the rationalist aspect, and, as emotional aspect, Romanticism's postulate of affective attachment to a "national" culture of dynastic states undergoing change to middle-class republican states. On the American side, the contexts included the Iroquois Confederacy and the societal structures of First Peoples, whether participatory as in the case of the Cherokees and Pima, dynastic-hierarchical as in the case of the Mexica and Toltecs, or masculine aggressive as in the case of the Apache. Self-liberated African slaves established state-like societies (maroon or cimmarone communities) whether participatory or hierarchized.[13] All peoples in the Americas, long settled or newly arrived, had experience with social structuration and government. But intellectual elites came to hold the power of definition and the control over public memory. They wrote the agency of "indigenous" peoples, of slaves, free Africans, and of Euro-origin women and the lower classes out of history texts, conjured it out of public memory. In nineteenth-century nation-state narratives, the respective author's nation usually appears at the top of human evolution or, at the least, better than the neighboring nations. This was the case in U.S., British, French, and German historiography. Anglo-Canadian and Hispanic Mexican historians, on the other hand, in a kind of mental self-colonization,

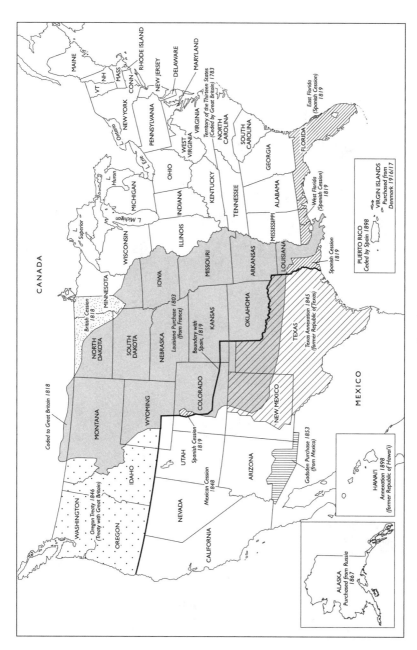

U.S. expansion 1783–1853, 1867, 1898, and 1917, including acquisition of the territories' societies and peoples

Within the map:

CANADA

MEXICO

MAINE
NH
VT
MASS
RHODE ISLAND
CONN
NEW YORK
NEW JERSEY
DELAWARE
MARYLAND
PENNSYLVANIA
WEST VIRGINIA
VIRGINIA
Territory of the Thirteen States
(Ceded by Great Britain) 1783
NORTH CAROLINA
SOUTH CAROLINA
GEORGIA
East Florida (Spanish Cession) 1819
West Florida (Spanish Cession) 1819
FLORIDA

L. Ontario
L. Erie
L. Huron
L. Michigan
L. Superior

OHIO
MICHIGAN
INDIANA
KENTUCKY
TENNESSEE
ALABAMA
MISSISSIPPI
WISCONSIN
ILLINOIS
IOWA
MISSOURI
ARKANSAS
LOUISIANA
Spanish Cession 1819

MINNESOTA
British Cession 1818
NORTH DAKOTA
SOUTH DAKOTA
NEBRASKA
KANSAS
OKLAHOMA
TEXAS
Texas Annexation 1845
(former Republic of Texas)

Louisiana Purchase 1803
(from France)
Boundary with Spain, 1819

Ceded to Great Britain 1818
MONTANA
WYOMING
COLORADO
Spanish Cession 1819
NEW MEXICO

Oregon Treaty 1846
(Treaty with Great Britain)
WASHINGTON
OREGON
IDAHO
UTAH
Mexican Cession 1848
NEVADA
ARIZONA
Gadsden Purchase 1853
(from Mexico)
CALIFORNIA

PUERTO RICO
Ceded by Spain 1898

VIRGIN ISLANDS
Purchased from
Denmark 1916/17

HAWAI'I
Annexation 1898
(former Republic of Hawai'i)

ALASKA
Purchased from Russia
1867

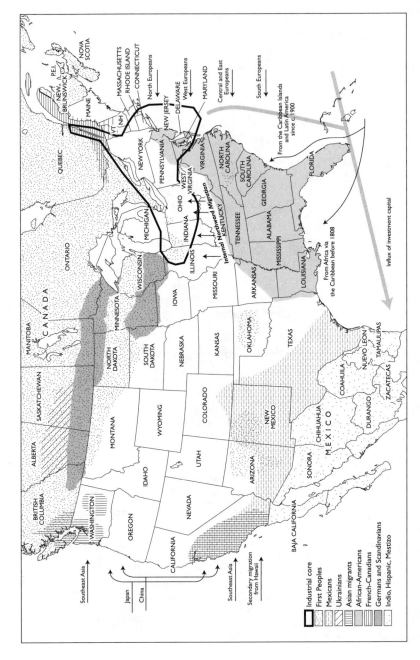

The cultural regions of North America: Migration and bicultural spaces

Legend:
- Industrial core
- First Peoples
- Mexicans
- Ukrainians
- Asian migrants
- African-Americans
- French-Canadians
- Germans and Scandinavians
- Indio, Hispanic, Mestizo

Labels on map:
NOVA SCOTIA, P.E.I., NEW BRUNSWICK, MAINE, VT, NH, MASSACHUSETTS, RHODE ISLAND, CONNECTICUT, North Europeans, West Europeans, DELAWARE, MARYLAND, Central and East Europeans, South Europeans, From the Caribbean Islands and Latin America since c.1900, QUEBEC, NEW YORK, PENNSYLVANIA, NEW JERSEY, VIRGINIA, NORTH CAROLINA, SOUTH CAROLINA, FLORIDA, ONTARIO, MICHIGAN, OHIO, WEST VIRGINIA, KENTUCKY, Internal Northward Migration, TENNESSEE, GEORGIA, ALABAMA, From Africa via the Caribbean before 1808, Influx of investment capital, INDIANA, ILLINOIS, WISCONSIN, MISSISSIPPI, LOUISIANA, ARKANSAS, MISSOURI, IOWA, MINNESOTA, NORTH DAKOTA, SOUTH DAKOTA, NEBRASKA, KANSAS, OKLAHOMA, TEXAS, CANADA, MANITOBA, SASKATCHEWAN, ALBERTA, BRITISH COLUMBIA, WASHINGTON, OREGON, IDAHO, MONTANA, WYOMING, COLORADO, UTAH, NEVADA, CALIFORNIA, ARIZONA, NEW MEXICO, BAJA CALIFORNIA, SONORA, CHIHUAHUA, COAHUILA, NUEVO LEON, TAMAULIPAS, DURANGO, ZACATECAS, MEXICO, Southeast Asia, Japan, China, Southeast Asia, Secondary migration from Hawaii

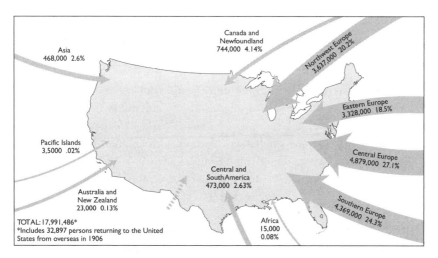

Contrast: The master narrative's view of an orphan nation filled by European immigrants

looked to Spain and Britain as models of high culture and saw themselves as secondary or derived.[14] The many oral traditions, the counternarratives, and the subaltern views did not find a place in heroic foundational tales of nation-building written by white men.

When thirteen of the British colonies in North America moved toward independence, some activists knew of earlier attempts to defy oppressive rulers, for example in Naples in 1647, and they had to unify the different governmental structures, feelings of belonging, and local affinities. The British-origin creoles' proud "we as Englishmen" had to be metamorphosed into "we as colonized, we as Americans." During the war between the colonies and the "mother country," tens of thousands of "American Englishmen" who wanted to remain loyal to Great Britain had to flee. Those going to the Canadian colonies constructed themselves as British, and most were anglophone, but included families of Dutch, German, Swiss, Indian, African, or Jewish cultural background. In the era of romantic nationalism, Noah Webster labored to change the new states' British English language into an American variant. The Federal legislature and white settlers in many localities moved to deprive the First Nations of their territories and independence. Slice by slice and patch by patch the new nation-state acquired its continental possessions: Napoleonic France sold Louisiana in 1803; Spain was forced to cede Florida and other bits and pieces of land in 1819;[15] the northern border was delineated by treaties with Britain in 1818 and 1846; Texas was annexed in 1845; and the aggression against Mexico expanded the territory in 1848 and in 1853 by purchase to its present borders.[16]

The men and women of the First Nations who had survived the unwittingly or intentionally introduced germs and U.S. exterminating wars were removed and reduced to concentrated settlements in undersupplied and underserviced reservations.

The result was not an "e pluribus unum" nation but a territorial state whose many cultures grew constantly by migrants and immigrants. Several major bicultural regions emerged: the Afro-European South, the Hispanic-American Texas and Southwest, the small Asian-European urban and rural settlements along the Pacific Coast, the German-Scandinavian-English-Ukrainian transborder belt from Wisconsin to Montana and Alberta, and the French Canadian-New England textile-producing region. The slave-holding societies of the U.S. South had more in common with the Caribbean and circum-Caribbean societies than with the commercialized mid-Atlantic states, and the U.S. Southwest had more in common with the Mexican Hispanic societies than with Protestant New England.

The trajectory of the Spanish- and Portuguese-held Americas to nation-states was different and related to intra-European power struggles, the reactionary dynastic states' wars to contain the democratizing impulses of the French Revolution as well as Napoleonic imperial expansion eastward (parallel to the early phases of U.S. westward expansion). These struggles weakened the colonizer states, and when Napoleon invaded Spain and Portugal, the Spanish-origin Creole elites in Mexico seized the opportunity and achieved independence after a protracted civil war, 1810–21. The Mexican population was still 60 percent Indian and 10 percent each Indo- and Afro-Mestizo. The 20 percent Iberian-background "Whites" and socially distinguished Mestizos would write Mexico's master narrative—as the New England intellectuals had done in the United States. While the United States expanded by force of arms, Mexico shrank. First, the southern United Provinces of Central America separated,[17] then it lost almost half its remaining territory to the rapacious northern neighbor.[18] The Mexican Catholic middle classes and elites, in contrast to the Protestant Anglo-North American ones, did not develop a commercial or industrial investment ethos.[19] Thus internally financed economic development lagged, and from the mid-1850s on, U.S. capitalists attempted to gain control over some of the Central American states with the help of filibusters like William Walker. In Mexico, French, British, and German entrepreneurial capitalist and business-class in-migrants joined the exploitation (see chapter 15). Mexico's political development was hampered by foreign aggressions, such as the European-French invasion, 1861–67, and turmoil between political and military factions under a practice of caudillismo, which involved some 250 revolts before 1857.[20] The liberal land reforms of the 1850s, meant to break the power of the church, dispossessed First Peoples of much of their corporately held land. This and the Hispanic society's disdain for the culture of the "Indios" segregated these into an underclass forced to migrate in search of a living (see chapter 7). Not only were no working-class migrants from Europe or Asia needed, but men and women from the underclasses would have to migrate to the United States where their labor was needed but their culture was unwanted.

The third and last continental region to gain—if only partial—independence was Canada. In 1867 Dominion status provided self-administration but left foreign policy under British control. The state comprised two nations, the French- and English-Canadian ones, the latter more numerous, more powerful, and with better access to the British government. To retain their tithe-payers, Quebec's Catholic bishops prevented emigration from the overpopulated St. Lawrence Valley to agricultural regions in the west. They also hindered industrialization and thus more than half a million Quebecois migrated to New England's textile economy since the 1840s. Out of touch with reality, the bishops began to dream of an independent Catholic New France-New England state. First Peoples were reduced to reservations by a series of treaties. The Manitoba Métis, descendants of French-language Indian women and Quebec men in the fur trade, intended to continue their self-government once the new Canadian state had purchased "Rupert's Land" from the British Hudson's Bay Company. But immigrant Anglo-Ontario merchants and land speculators labeled such self-government "rebellious," and obligingly, the Federal government intervened militarily. This West, separated from Canada East by the Canadian Shield and the Great Lakes, was at first accessible only through the United States: from Windsor, Ontario, via the *détroit* (narrows) to Detroit, Chicago, and St. Paul, to Winnipeg. In British Columbia settlers and business-people—like their counterparts in California—realized the transpacific potential of Asia as well as, in the context of the British Empire, the competition of New Zealand's agriculture. The Canadian state needed immigrants not only to expand its population but to settle the Prairies with European-origin people and thus connect its two Euro-Canadian segments, the Atlantic and Pacific Coast provinces.

In the Caribbean, Europeans' debates about human rights and enslaved Africans' views of their humanity merged. French revolutionary demands for abolition of slavery reached Whites, Mulattoes, and—unintendedly—Africans. From 1794 to 1804, Africans in French-held Haiti (the western part of the island Hispaniola, also known as Saint-Domingue) liberated themselves from slavery and achieved independence. While France's revolutionary Assembly had abolished slavery, Napoleon, connected to the interests of the Creole planter class, reinstituted it in 1802. Haiti's independence led to large-scale flight of Whites with (some of) their slaves to other parts of the Greater Carib-bean. In multicultural Nouvelle Orléans they would strengthen the French ele-ment—French by claim of the former Bourbon dynasty, by settlement, and by the arrival of French-language Acadians deported from Nova Scotia in 1755. The Caribbean and Canada were also connected: Britain transported Jamai-can Maroons, self-liberated and self-governing Africans, after their defeat in 1796 to Halifax, where free African sailors from the British merchant marine had already formed a community. In the Caribbean of the early 1800s, the planter classes, in response to debates about abolition, began to experiment with recruitment of cheap, temporarily bound European and Asian laborers. When Europeans refused to accept the working conditions, large-scale impor-tation of Asian indentured workers[21] began: In the 1830s the British Empire did abolish African slavery but imposed a contract labor system on British-India and through Chinese middlemen on the southern provinces of Imperial China.[22]

With abolition of slavery, first in (French) Haiti and last in (Spanish) Cuba in 1880/86,[23] inter-island migrations increased (see chapter 3). Traditional small migratory contacts to the coasts of Mexico and Florida continued. All of the smaller islands remained colonies. Of the larger islands Cuba remained a Spanish colony to 1898, only to be entangled in new political and economic dependencies afterward; Jamaica remained British until 1958/1962. From the mid-nineteenth century on the United States extended a quasi-colonial reach over several islands and circum-Caribbean states, including a protectorate over Cuba and annexation of Puerto Rico in 1898. The capital investments and working-class contacts induced migrations to and from the United States.[24] All societies and states forming themselves in North America, the Caribbean included, were part of the white and the black Atlantic worlds and, to a very limited degree, of the transpacific migratory circuits. All were many-cultured. African-origin men and women were few in Canada but outnumbered Euro-origin whites by a large ratio in the Caribbean societies.

In 1867, not usually considered a pivotal date, North America achieved its final political-territorial shape: Mexico expelled the French invaders, and President Juárez began his, at least partially, socially inclusive policies. The United States began reunification and Reconstruction after coming apart in a bloody war. It also acquired its last continental possession, Alaska, by pur-chase from the tsar. Canada advanced from colony to Dominion and took its territorial shape by purchase of Rupert's Land.

The new societies, following a European intellectual and constitutional innovation of the late eighteenth and early nineteenth centuries, considered themselves nation-states. Europe's middle classes, to distinguish themselves from the transeuropean, always exclusive and often oppressive nobility, had begun to refer to themselves as the cultural nation and had often buttressed their claim with references to the cultures of allegedly soil-rooted yeomen peasants. This new emphasis on "*the* people" involved a corollary of vast impact: Those of different cultures were excluded from belonging to the one and single nation—Bretons in France and Basques in Spain, for example. They came to be labeled "minorities," though majorities in their regions. While, in absolutist but flexible dynastic states all inhabitants were equally subjects of the ruler and negotiated their status according to religion, craft, language, urbanity, or other criteria, the absolute primacy of the nation in the new republican-democratic polities reduced other cultures to lesser rights. A "nation" was the ethnic group with the power to impose hegemony and rule on less powerful ethnicities living in the same territory: It replaced absolutist states' negotiated diversity by imposition of absolute cultural homogeneity. The emergence of *exclusive* cultural nations paralleled the emergence of *inclusive* republican or democratic states. Thus the "nation-state" involved a contradiction in terms: Sovereignty of a republican people postulated that each and every person was equal before the law while the nationality-principle postulated inequality between people of different cultures within the polity. Like resident minorities, migrants and immigrants of different culture lost their right to distinctiveness and faced discrimination as regards access to societal resources, whether education, labor markets, or governmental services. In Europe nation-states marginalized those not deemed worthy to assimilate (Jews and Slavs for example). In the North American context, English-background Anglo-Americans and Anglo-Canadians as well as Iberian-background Mexicans placed themselves over all other cultural groups. French-Canadians challenged such arrogance from the start, and in the Caribbean societies the small numbers of Euro-Caribbeans made the assertion of White hegemony more difficult.

All states in the Atlantic World were historically and are presently many-cultured. Even the dominant groups defining themselves as the nation are regionally diverse and segmented by class and gender. White New Englanders are culturally different from white Texans, people in Canada's Maritimes from those in Ontario and Saskatchewan, Sonorans from inhabitants of Mexico City or Oaxaca. Territorial borderlines thus do not demarcate lines between different cultures, rather their expansion or contraction indicate power relations and the change from national consciousness to aggressive national chauvinism. Prairie farmers in Canada and the United States had more similarities between them than each group had with Ontarians (not to mention Quebecers) or New Yorkers (not to mention Southerners). In the Greater Southwest, local people had more in common among them than with people living either in Washington or Mexico City. In the Caribbean, cultural differences between islands were obvious to the inhabitants but not necessarily to those who gazed from the outside. Thus meso- and micro-regional specifics and inter-regional migration characterized the heterogeneous North American-Caribbean macro-region.

The North Americas in the Atlantic World: Connections and Migrations

In the realm of economies and power, through the nineteenth century the Caribbean economies remained under the control of the European cores; Anglo-Canada traded mainly with Great Britain but increasingly with the United States. In contrast, Quebec's extremely dogmatic Church abhorred the political reform, industrialization, and urbanization that made France a modern state. Under the concept of "two Frances," a contaminated European one and a purer Quebec one, intellectuals attempted to construct the province as the hegemonic center for all of francophone North America—a stance unacceptable to Canada's Métis as well as French-speaking Caribbeans. As regards economic exchanges, the United States, to some degree, kept out European imports through protective tariffs, but after the 1870s it developed an export industry. At the time, free trade was not a panacea from the view of U.S. governments. Since it serves mainly developed industrial states with a naval military presence across the seas, Great Britain would have benefited. As to power politics, the United States intervened repeatedly in the Caribbean and circum-Caribbean and established dominance though President Theodore Roosevelt's crude late-nineteenth-century "big stick" policy.

As regards cultural connections, Anglo-Canadian writers remained mentally dependent on Great Britain, Mexican intellectuals on Spain. These were processes of self-colonization rather than impositions from the European side. The Atlantic World's center of cultural innovation, Paris of the 1920s, attracted Mexicans as well as Afro-Americans and some Euro-Americans. The smaller Caribbean societies, still under colonial rule, could take less initiative. Only in the 1930s and later did the islands' *and* Africa's cultural presence come to be recognized in the Atlantic World through the anti-colonialism of Aimé Césaire (Martinique), the concept of *négritude* (Leopold Senghor, Senegal), French-language discussion of colonized subjects' identities, and English-language analysis by Eric Williams (Trinidad and Tobago) of capitalism, slavery, and the plantation regime.

As regards migrations, once Europe's revolutionary, counter-revolutionary, and imperialist wars ended in 1815, departures for the North Americas resumed, propelled in the southwestern German-language emigration region by famine conditions.[25] The region's traditional emigration to the South Russian Plains was curtailed by Tsarist authorities who began to prefer Slavic-cultured migrants. Thus the peasant families turned westward via the Rhine River and Dutch ports to the U.S. East. From the 1820s out-migration from Europe, at first from the societies of the Atlantic littoral, grew continuously but stagnated with each major depression since too few economic options to gain a livelihood would be available after arrival. The history of migration to the five cultural regions in the North Americas varied widely. Determining factors included labor regimes, images of the societies of destination current in Europe, demographic factors, and immigration policies.

The French-language regions in the North Americas received but few migrants. In Catholic France, couples pursued a procreation strategy of few children only, the church's pro-natalist dogma notwithstanding, and thus no surplus population had to depart, and neither the French-Caribbean nor the French-Canadian population grew by free migration. The small numbers of French-speakers in the Mississippi Valley, with the exception of the New Orleans community, lost their French-First Nations dual culture when Anglo-American settlers and the U.S. Army took over. Only Martinique-Guadeloupe-Haiti as well as Quebec remained major French-language clusters. Migration from the Caribbean societies to France began in the 1930s, from Haiti to Quebec only in the 1960s.

French, British, and Spanish (as well as later-immigrated U.S.) plantation owners in the Caribbean decided to defy their governments' ban on the slave trade, 1807–8 and generalized in 1815, but extended to Brazil only in the 1860s. Almost two million enslaved African men and women were forcibly migrated to the labor regimes of the Caribbean plantations and Brazil in the decades before the 1870s. By the standards of international politics and treaties, the western societies' slave-trading elites were a criminal cartel. Unexpectedly, the commodified and traded Africans brought religious beliefs and cultural practices, adapted them to the new environment, and thus developed a resource for resistance.

Mexico's history of in-migration and attitudes to foreigners differed widely from those of the Anglo–United States and Anglo-Canada (see chapters 1 and 7). Though little immigration occurred, anti-foreigner feelings ran high. The first target was the European-born Spanish, who had monopolized lucrative offices in the colonial period and opposed independence. Next, invading Yankees seized half of Mexico's territory. From 1862 to 1867 the invading French added themselves to the list. The Mexican government's invitation to U.S. farmers and ranchers to settle Texas resulted in these immigrants severing Texas from Mexico in 1836. While Mexican public opinion thus already had good reasons for hostility, the attitude was reinforced by the conduct of a lengthening list of foreign capitalists who took advantage of the Mexican upper class's lack of entrepreneurship and whose attitude to Mexican labor was one of racialized exploitation (chapter 15). By the end of the dictatorship of Porfirio Díaz, in 1910, three-quarters of the largest Mexican companies were owned by foreign capital. Investors brought foreign skilled personnel of miners, railroad engineers and skilled workers, oil technicians, and others, and especially U.S. companies, paid their immigrant U.S. workers far better than Mexicans and did not permit skilled Mexicans to accede to skilled jobs.[26] At the same time, Mexico offered refuge to many: Confederate cotton traders and army officers after their defeat in the nineteenth century, Mennonites, Russian revolutionaries, Spanish Civil War refugees, Jewish refugees from Fascist Germany, Cold War refugees from the United States, Guatemalan refugees from the right-wing dictatorship, and Lebanese in the twentieth century. Mexican political exiles in turn sought refuge in Europe and the United States (where arms traders were happy to outfit them for return).[27] In the rigorously stratified Mexican society, the majority of the population—"Indios" and Afro-Mexicans—were excluded from education, some Liberal educators' plans and promises notwithstanding. They remained mere objects of exploitation by native capitalists who would not participate in the Atlantic World's culture and labor markets and by foreigners.

Both the United States and Canada attracted millions or tens of millions of migrants from Europe's emigration regions, which expanded from the Atlantic littoral to West Central (German-language) and North Europe and, from the 1880s, to East Central and South Europe. In the East, from the Tsarist Empire, only Jews and Ukrainians departed to escape cultural persecution and economic oppression. Canada pursued a policy of "preferred immigration," a euphemism for a racially motivated British-only policy that was, however, adapted pragmatically to admit Icelanders, Russian-German Mennonites, and others. By the mid-1890s, when ever fewer migrants came from the British Isles, the minister for immigration mitigated the policy's racist undertones and constructed Ukrainians as similar to English yeomen farmers: "Stalwart peasants in sheepskin coats, born on the soil, whose forefathers have been farmers for ten generations with stout wives and a half-dozen children."[28] Canada's open-door policy continued into the 1920s, since both industrial laborers and settlers for the West were still needed. However, radicals and paupers were not accepted.[29]

The United States of America became "America" in European potential migrants' imagination, a mythical place in which cheap land and jobs were available, in which trains ran over the roofs of houses (an "expanded version" of New York's el-trains), and in which everything was fast, faster than at home, and great, greater than at home. When a mining shaft in Europe was brought down particularly fast, it was done "the American way"; when a particularly large tenement bloc was built, it was named "little Chicago." Such images succeeded each other: At the turn to the nineteenth century constitutional government enamored Europe's intellectuals; to the 1870s the "free land" image held sway; thereafter the "dynamic industrial society and jobs" image took over. In these images neither First Peoples nor the Hispanic Southwest appeared. Read as a paean to the United States, the image was in fact a critique of the migrants' own hierarchical societies. Men and women did not depart under such cliché-like, otherworldly images of perpetual bliss: they relied on information from earlier migrating kin and friends, people they knew and whose veracity they could trust: 94 percent of all migrants from Europe went neither to a mythical "America" nor transnationally to the actual United States but, according to their declarations at Ellis Island, to kin and friends in a translocal move from the place of birth to the social space where their correspondents lived—a transcultural move. Few waxed lyric about a "home" society: they left because difficult and unjust conditions offered no prospects, perhaps not even sufficient food.

The United States, both as a state and as a society, was not always welcoming. Nativism in the 1850s targeted Germans and Irish as well as Mexicans in the Californian gold fields; in 1875 the Page Law and in the 1880s exclusionism took aim at Asian peoples. Such racism, including a so-called scientific variant, popularly expressed in Madison Grant's *The Passing of the Great Race, or The Racial Basis of European History* (1916), was translated into exclusion laws in the 1920s: European laborers were no longer needed because African-American men and women finally began to leave the lynch-law-infested southern states for jobs in the northern urban industries, and Mexicans came on their own or were recruited. "Negroes" and "greasers" could be segregated more easily than "olive" or "dark" Europeans. With the onset of the Great Depression in-migration came to a standstill, and from this period the Atlantic migration system stagnated. It came to an end in the 1950s. Only Portuguese and Italians continued to migrate to Canada's urban construction industries—like Mexicans to the United States. Thus a century after the end of the Black Atlantic's forced migration system, the White Atlantic's migrations, voluntary within a frame of severe economic constraints, also ended.

By the mid-1980s, in the third phase of the transpacific migration system, more people reached the North Americas from Asia. Migration from Asia had developed differently both as regards chronology and numbers. It had involved a first phase of partly forced migrations from Manila to New Spain in the sixteenth and seventeenth centuries. In the 1790s the globally operating British East India Company sent Chinese sailors and craftsmen across the Pacific to Vancouver Island to compete with the transatlantic Hudson's Bay Company's fur trade, and in the mid-1840s U.S. merchant families returning from China brought Chinese servant women to California. The gold rushes in California and, ten years later, in British Columbia attracted pioneer migrants from Guangdong province, the only region to send migrants to North America. Next, when both in the United States and in Canada transcontinental railroad construction required workers, Chinese men were recruited for the western segments. The prospects of trade with Asia, China in particular, made Chinese merchants welcome.[30] From the 1880s Japanese men and women came and, after 1900, Punjabi Sikhs arrived through the British imperial connection. With U.S. annexation of the Philippines as a colony, Filipinos and Filipinas also arrived. Numbers of migrants from the several Asian cultures remained small, but anti-Asian racism manifested itself early. By 1882 the United States excluded Chinese workers from entry. Migrants crossed the cruelly racist legislators' and bureaucrats' legal paper walls by using sophisticated paper identities. They had no reason to consider themselves inferior to Euro-Americans. While the Canadian government pursued a similarly exclusionist policy, the Mexican government, as in all migration matters, pursued its own course. No anti-Asian immigration restrictions were passed before the 1930s, even though outbreaks of animosity and violence had occurred. Since the U.S. and Canadian barriers concerned seaside entry-ports and not yet landside borders, Chinese and Japanese entered Mexico and Canada and then moved on to the United States—for them the North Americas were one migration region (see chapter 14). A fourth region with different migration patterns was the Caribbean plantation societies. From the 1840s Chinese as well as workers from India were brought as contract labor to many islands, Trinidad and Tobago and Cuba in particular. Their freely migrating compatriot families, so-called passenger migrants, established businesses and cultural communities. From this base the Caribbean Asians inserted themselves into politics and achieved far more influence than in the exclusionist continental polities. Following this same course, from the Pacific side, were the Asian migrants settled in Hawai'i after the islands' annexation by the United States.[31]

The North Americas thus were part of global labor migrations, and the traditional immigration paradigm implied that conditions in the Americas were so attractive that no one wanted to leave. However, life-courses and family strategies were different—many migrants come only temporarily. Around 1900 one-third of the European migrants arriving in the United States returned to their society of origin; Canada experienced both return to Europe and transit migration to the United States. In Mexico, where supply of (dispossessed) Native workers surpassed demand and industrialization lagged, few migrants arrived even though the government had tried to draw immigrants, especially from Europe. Migrants selected destinations carefully; they knew how and where to find labor markets (or, earlier, rural settlement areas), and U.S. capital kept both land borders open to the beginning of the Great Depression to be able to draw on an integrated pool of reserve labor.[32]

Migrations in the North Americas and the Imposition of Borderlines

The political borders of the three continental states, imposed, surveyed, and mapped by the mid-nineteenth century, had little meaning for resident people whose living spaces, landscapes, and socio-scapes they arbitrarily divided. Where economies were similar on both sides there was no reason to disrupt agriculture, commerce, or fisheries just because far-off national governments had established a nation-state division. Economic-societal delimitations created very different and changing maps of the North Americas.

The trope of intra-continental migration, "westward ho" to the "frontier," mythologizes one single development and usually refers to the U.S. Prairies and European settlers only. In the Americas three other major frontier societies existed: Canada, Brazil, and Argentina.[33] The "advance of civilization" cliché hides the refugee migrations imposed on First Peoples and, in the United States and Brazil, the forced migrations imposed on slaves. It overlooks that all rural settlement was accompanied by commercial migrations to small-town nodes of exchange, that farmers demanded market access and railroad laborers came, and that once market access was achieved, merchants and land speculators came with financial resources. Patterns of migration toward the Canadian Prairies were similar and yet different. The uninhabitable and to some degree untraversable Canadian Shield prevented access. For the United States the Atlantic port of arrival, New York's Ellis Island and the Statue of Liberty, became the gateway in the public mind. In Canada Winnipeg's railroad sheds, in the middle of the country, became the gate to the Prairies. Canada's economic historians, not prone to booster rhetoric, at first labeled the West "a hinterland." While this was not fully justified, it kept the financially and intellectually powerful metropoles, Toronto and Montreal, and thus intrastate hierarchies in the analysis.

In both countries farming families' sons and daughters from Ontario and New England migrated westward because of land shortages in their region of birth. In more densely populated Mexico migrations since colonial times were

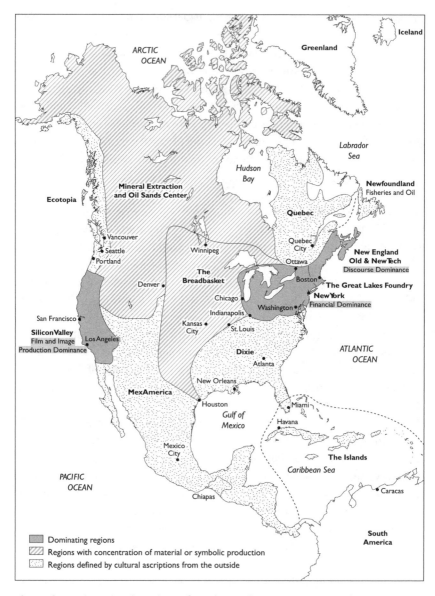

The twelve socioeconomic regions of North America, a 1960s perspective

multidirectional and often followed a south-north trajectory. The federal government's mid-nineteenth-century policy to break up large landholdings of corporations (i.e. the Catholic Church) and to liberalize economic exchanges forced people into migration. It deprived Native communities of their commonly held village lands, labeled "corporate" holdings. Since peasants were too poor to acquire family plots, the declamations about a redistribution of church lands remained empty. Instead the (urban) Mexican upper classes became latifundia owners. At the time of independence in 1821 villagers held about 40 percent of the arable land, after the mid-nineteenth-century "reforms" only half as much, and in 1910—when peasants accounted for 80 percent of the population—less than 5 percent. The legislation created an impoverished ethno-class, a landless proletariat of potential migrant workers at a time when lagging industrialization did not provide jobs. The dispossessed men and women, mostly of Native cultural background and thus despised as "Indios," became the reservoir for the vast intra-Mexican rural-urban migrations, for the future northward migrations to the United States, and after the end of the twentieth century, to Canada (see chapters 7 and 18).

In the nineteenth century several major regionally specific migration patterns emerged. In the U.S. South—part of the global plantation belt—soil exhaustion and the beginning of steamship transport on the Mississippi in 1817 led to a shift of the cotton economy with its slave-based labor regime westward from the Atlantic seaboard to the Mississippi valley. Slaves were migrated westward and, if considered refractory, forcibly migrated down the river through sale to the harsher regimes of exploitation. To increase agricultural output in Texas and populate hitherto unused land, the Mexican government in 1825 had invited American settlers, calling for families of Catholic faith. When those who did come, mainly Protestants, brought slaves, the Mexican Congress in 1830 prohibited further importation. In response the invited Americans engineered secession, and the U.S. Congress annexed the state in 1845, creating a precedent for annexation of California. In the West the minerals in the Canadian and U.S. Rocky Mountains attracted miners; the gold rushes in California and British Columbia attracted Americans, Europeans, Mexicans, and Chinese. No settlement frontier moved across the continent. Islands of economic activity attracted people who were entrepreneurs of their own lives.

Sizable in-migration in some regions was paralleled by large out-migration in others. In the 1840s (U.S.) settlers rushed to Oregon on the Pacific Coast. In the 1870s families in Canada's Maritime Provinces had to leave because of the decline of the shipbuilding industry and of mining. The out-migration from rural Quebec (see chapter 2) lasted for decades. Whenever couples in a family farm economy raised more than two children, harvests could not feed all, and younger sons and daughters had to migrate to new land or urban jobs. Thus from the mid-nineteenth century westward migrations were accompanied by rural-urban migrations, often eastbound to the big cities but on the whole manifold and multidirectional. Migrant rural laborers from Europe, without funds to buy land, stayed in the mining regions and industrial cities of the region circumscribed by New York, Philadelphia, Pittsburgh, Toronto, and Chicago, moved within the region, or returned to Europe. Migration along the Pacific Coast, both to agriculture and horticulture and to port cities like Mazatlán, Los Angeles, San Francisco, Seattle, and Vancouver, involved native-born merchants, traders, dockworkers, and men and women in other urban professions and services rather than immigrants as in the East. Like the transoceanic migrations, the internal ones resulted from unsatisfactory or unacceptable conditions in the region of birth.

Building the east-west and south-north railroads, which could also be viewed as west-east and north-south connections, was the task of migrant railroad workers. They were completed between 1869 and 1883 in the United States, in 1885 in Canada, and in the later 1880s between Mexico City and the northern border. The last, from Ciudad Juárez-El Paso, connected to Kansas City and Chicago.[34] In Mexico the charters granted to foreign companies seriously impeded the development of a functional mass transportation system. Companies used different (i.e. unconnectable) gauges; others never commenced construction. Mexican railway workers recruited to the United States moved northward and westward along the lines from El Paso just as Italian workers moved westbound along the lines beginning in Montreal. Railroad workers, as much as pioneer migrant farming families, remained mobile, moved back and forth, brought in families, and introduced other migrants to the transportation network. Railroads provided market connections for small towns and farmers, but they also made the newly connected regions a market for goods produced more cheaply elsewhere. Such "internal imports" might force local families out of business and into further migration. Shipping connections to the Caribbean societies, at first mainly by fishing boats, were sped up by the coming of steamships. Migrations like those from the Cayman Islands to the coast of Florida and to British Honduras had a long history; others emerged under the impact of new investments and new labor markets.

From the mid-nineteenth century to the beginning of the Great Depression in 1929, borderland migrations and long-distance cross-border migrations grew in volume. Migration in either direction between Canada and the United States created little public debate, though. To Canadians "Americans" sometimes appeared as rowdy, and when sporting the U.S. flag in Canada, somewhat too nationalist. Migration between Mexico and the United States, on the other hand, was often intensely debated—in the United States with racist undertones, in Mexico first with fears of a massive drain of population and then with worries about the fate of Mexicans who were moving back and forth. Their European-Spanish background notwithstanding, Mexicans were not considered white, and the North Americans would stress their mixed descent, which made them "mongrels." In Mexico Americans appeared as arrogant and bossy. Migrations extended from the northern Canadian mining regions to southern Mexico. The first recorded Mexican settlers—rather than workers—arrived in Minnesota in 1860, and by the 1920s Spanish-speaking Mexicans competed with French- and English-speaking Canadians for jobs in automobile factories in Detroit and mines in northern Michigan. Canadian firms investing in Mexico sent personnel. The connection of the eighteenth century from the Caribbean to Nova Scotia had ended, and new northbound migration from the Caribbean along the U.S. East Coast's cities emerged in the 1920s. It accelerated under wartime labor recruitment in the 1940s, and assumed large proportions in the 1960s. As regards Canada, at first the British Commonwealth frame still played a connecting role.[35]

In the northern borderlands, both as spaces immediately adjacent and as larger regions, people from the Maritimes migrated to Maine and New England, and some New Englanders moved north. Quebec, which had received Loyalist settlers from the emerging United States in the 1780s and American investors in the 1920s and 1930s, sent worker families into New England and beyond. To the 1860s fugitive or, better, self-liberated U.S. slaves reached Ontario. Montreal, for long the main Canadian port of arrival for European migrants, was a transit place for Italians and others moving south to New York or arriving from New York via the Hudson River corridor. English-Canadians migrated south, and Americans moved to Toronto and the industrializing cities along Lake Ontario, crossed by numerous ferries. English- and French-Canadians worked in Michigan lumbering and mining. Political allegiance was of no importance to decisions about where to work and live. In the Prairies the Minnesota-Manitoba settlement belt expanded regardless of the dividing line. Small entrepreneurs as well as settler families moved, worked, and owned land on both sides of the border. On the Pacific Coast, Seattle was home to many Canadians, and Vancouver to many Americans.[36]

In the south, with the annexation of the Greater Southwest and Texas, a Spanish-speaking Mexican population of some 50,000 Mexicans and 100,000 Natives (with Mexican citizenship) had been incorporated into the United States. As in Europe's internecine struggles, the border was moved over nonmigrating people. From one day to the next they found themselves in another

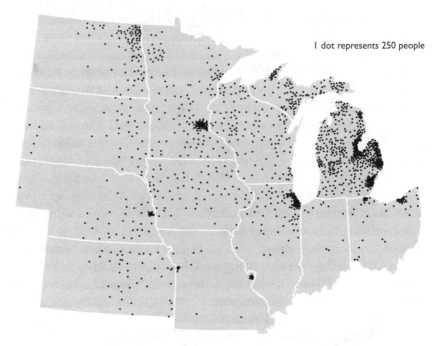

I dot represents 250 people

A Canadian-born persons in the north central states of the United States, 1890

I dot represents 250 people

B Canadian-born French-language persons in New York and New England, 1900

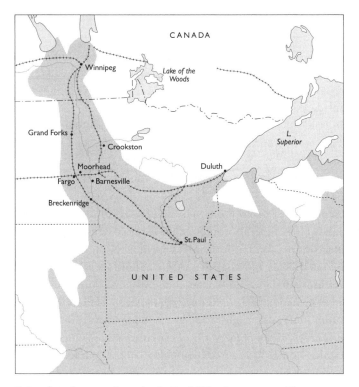

C Rural settlement along the St. Paul–Winnipeg route, 1881

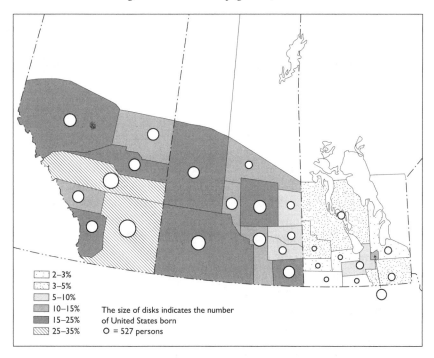

D U.S.-born persons in Canada's Prairie Provinces, 1911

country with no more than paper guarantees for their property, identities, and citizenship. Among those annexed were Native Peoples who in Mexico had citizenship but in the United States were reduced to wards of the government or were considered enemies. The new borderline posed no hindrance to movement: during the U.S. Civil War, 1861–65, the Confederate side used the Tamaulipas and Nuevo León provinces for cotton shipments; the Union side supported President Juárez against the French invasion, 1862–67. Confederate refugees moved to Mexico's cities; exiles from the many Mexican internal political struggles moved to El Paso, St. Louis, or Chicago. From the mid-1860s skilled U.S. workers entered the upper echelons of the Mexican labor force, and from the 1880s Mexican workers moved north, if at first in small numbers. The unsettled conditions of the Mexican Revolution induced some 700,000 to 800,000 or more to move north—of whom perhaps 200,000 stayed (see chapter 1). Reasons for the Revolution, a liberation movement against Porfirio Díaz's regime, included the Old Regime's support for U.S. capitalist oppression of its Mexican workers and the sellout of huge tracts of land to U.S. development companies. When the new capitalist landowners sent surveyors to measure and stake for sale farming and ranching lands occupied by Mexicans of Spanish and Indian descent—or "mestizos"—these rebelled, just as French-speaking resident "Métis" in Manitoba had rebelled in 1871 and 1885 when, on instigation of land jobbers of Ontario origin, the Canadian government had sent surveyors into the Red River valley, the site of the future Winnipeg, to expropriate them.[37]

All three continental colonial regions and, as of 1776–83, 1821, and 1867, independent states were connected by migration to the Caribbean Islands. Through the British Empire's shipping connections free African-Caribbean sailors had settled in eighteenth-century Halifax. Migration to the circum-Caribbean societies from the Guyanas via the Isthmus to Louisiana had a history dating back at least to Haiti's independence. Beginning with U.S. interests, military interventions, and investments in the Caribbean societies, migration to the United States began. Since in the British colonies all inhabitants regardless of skin color were British subjects (of the respective monarch), they could migrate to the United States even after the restriction law of 1921. But the next law, in 1924, excluded them as being of the wrong color (see chapter 3). From the 1950s migrations to the North American East Coast and the cities of the interior increased massively. Canadians and U.S. citizens moved to the islands for business or the winter months.

Within particular countries internal migrations included the African-American out-migrations from the South to northern cities from the early 1900s and, in larger numbers, from the years of the First World War. They turned dependent sharecroppers into independent wage laborers. The dust-bowl migration from Kansas and Oklahoma westward to California turned independent farming families into migrant harvest laborers. It had its Canadian equivalent during Saskatchewan's dry years. At the same time the Mexican government repatriated migrants from the United States and distributed land. The Depression years induced U.S. transborder deportations of Mexican migrants and—given the racism of some sheriffs' forces—Mexican-American citizens to Mexico. Earlier, during the Red Scare (or White Fear) of 1917–21, the U.S. government had shipped alleged and committed radicals of European origin back across the Atlantic. In the 1920s and 1930s Canada deported or threatened to deport immigrants liable to become public charges, including pregnant women. During the Depression numerous migrants returned to their European and Mexican societies of origin, where they could rely on family networks, small agricultural plots, or incipient public social security provisions. Such return migration shifted the cost of unemployment to the societies of origin. Political machinations in the state of Sonora, where by 1904 already 45 percent of all the Chinese living in Mexico resided, led to anti-Chinese measures and expulsion from the state (but not from the country) in the 1930s. Baja California, Sinaloa, and Chihuahua as well as Yucatán on the Caribbean coast hosted major Chinese communities, which also suffered because of political changes.

Border controls and the general introduction of passport papers along land borders were an innovation of the late nineteenth century. Until then circulation and migration across borders had been a "great natural phenomenon," as an observer of the 1940s called it.[38] Pacific seaports were controlled first to prevent Asian migrants from entering. On the Atlantic Coast European migrants were screened for the presence of "undesirables," but only 2 to 3 percent were rejected. However, since shipping companies were liable to transport back migrants rejected for reasons of health, they themselves screened migrants in Italy's ports of departure and at the German Reich's eastern borders. In an imperial expansion of borders, U.S. controls and other controls inspired by them were thus extended into Italy and to the western borders of the Romanov and Habsburg Empires. Actual control of the U.S. land borders by—a very few—agents began in 1924 pursuant to a basically unused Sec. 24 of the act of 1888 to control Asian immigration. Border control was directed against Mexicans, not Canadians.

While the exclusion laws of 1917, 1921, and 1924, aimed at East and South Europeans, closed the "front doors," as they have been called from a Eurocentric perspective, the "back doors"—a racialized term—to Mexico remained ajar because workers were still needed. The Second World War ended migration from Europe that had been interrupted by the Depression and, after the arrival of wartime displaced persons in the late 1940s, Europe's economic recovery ended transatlantic migration in the 1950s. The demand for manpower during this war threw the southern door, for Mexicans the front door, wide open.[39] From 1942 to 1947 and through program extensions to 1964, the U.S. government recruited almost five million workers across "the border that joins."[40] They were called "braceros," because strong arms were in demand but not human beings with minds and hearts who would stay and call for their families to join them. The war also became the excuse for another forced migration: Tens of thousands of Japanese immigrants, Japanese-American citizens as well as Japanese-Canadians, were deprived of their property and sent to relocation camps: those in the desert of Arizona were like concentration camps.[41]

Transnational Perspectives in Scholarship of the 1920s and 1930s

People of all classes crossed borders when it was in the interest of their lives and plans. They did so in translocal, transregional, and transnational moves. Cultural theories based on empirical data need to reflect such interaction and heterogeneity, mobility and constant evolution; political science focusing on statewide structures and institutions often overlooks it. National historians composing master narratives obliterated heterogeneity from public memory, but those writing local his-and-her stories or regional narratives usually kept the many-cultured migrants in the story. Establishing a master narrative was easiest in the United States, with New England's intellectual hegemony, monolingual elites, and school systems designed to produce national clones. It was more difficult in bilingual English-French Canada and Spanish-Nahuatl Mexico[42] and in the Caribbean states in which white historians wrote for tiny Euro-Creole minorities. Monolingualism may facilitate communication across a society, but it is conceptually confining and may be self-defeating.

Some scholars of the 1920s to the 1940s studied their complex societies comprehensively and thus understood the many-cultured composition of states. Helen MacGill Hughes and Everett Hughes, who lived and formed their thought in bicultural Montreal, argued that according to the empirical data no state offered just one model of assimilation or acculturation to newcomers. In Cuba, Fernando Ortiz studied the sugar plantation economy and its hierarchically placed agents originating in Europe, Africa, and China. He argued that the habitus of a society emerges from processes of "transculturation."[43] In Mexico the *indigenistas* pursued a program to incorporate the First Peoples, "Indios," into the state's history. However, racial and ideological blinders prevented the development of data-based analyses, and José Vasconcelos constructed a new "cosmic race," emerging from *mestizaje* of Europeans, America's Natives, Africans, and Asians, as a tool to counter the Yankees' exclusive claim to a master race, racial superiority, and manifest destiny. Other scholars developed an archeological approach to emphasize the ancient civilizations of the Mexica and Maya and the European input and stress the existence of a high culture before the advent of the Spaniards. This turn to the precontact past conveniently helped them avoid implementing cultural equality and equal rights for First Peoples living at the time of the conceptualizations.[44]

The U.S. scholarly record is different: the Chicago school of sociology's narrow concept of assimilation and, subsequently, Oscar Handlin's catchword of migrant uprootedness emerged as reigning paradigms.[45] Variations like the "nation to ethnic enclave" version of migrant travels between rigorously bordered ethnic communities, or the "cultural baggage" approach, which had migrants begin their lives at Ellis Island and deposit their culture-filled suitcases somewhere, were the products of scholars who had no language other than English. Some scholars and public intellectuals were aware of cultural differentiation. The Chicago ethnologist William I. Thomas, an internal migrant from a small rural community via a southern university town to the metropolis of Chicago, felt that on his way he had traversed three centuries. With the Polish philosopher and sociologist Florian W. Znaniecki, trained in Polish-language ethnology, he analyzed cultural transfer, and both understood the continuities involved in migration between societies. Caroline F. Ware, in a sensitive community study of Greenwich Village, New York, pointed to generational differences and the funds of knowledge that helped migrants to reestablish communities after migration.[46]

Thus on the marketplace of ideas and data, the information and concepts for transborder cultural continuities were available since the 1920s, but most nation-state socialized scholars followed the received opinion of migrant inferiority and, like fast-food addicts, never tasted differentiated interpretations based on ingredients produced by empirical research. The minority, like the Hugheses, Ortiz, or Ware, understood migrant agency and the creation and adaptation of societal structures through myriad cultural exchanges. Public intellectuals in the United States, like Randolph S. Bourne, clearly stated as early as 1916 that "America is coming to be, not a nationality but a transnationality, a weaving back and forth, with the other lands, of many threads of all sizes and colors." No democratic society needs to "fly into panic at the first sign" of migrants' self-determination and cultural expressions. And according to Horace Kallen's conceptualization of "cultural pluralism," states were federations of nationalities rather than the monocultural entities that state-imposed curricula and media-created billboards imposed.[47]

An integrated perspective on North America was self-evident to numerous scholars of the 1920s, 1930s, and 1940s. They dealt with economic interactions, cultural influences, and migrations between Canada, the United States, Mexico, and the Caribbean. As regards educational institutions, Canada was part of the Carnegie Foundation's continental approach to civic virtue and self-improvement. In the 1920s the U.S. foundations supported social science projects since, from their perspective, Canada was still a kind of laboratory in which social developments could be studied *in statu nascendi*. In the United States—not to talk of Europe—patterns were assumed to be more fixed. This approach hypothesized that an early diagnosis of social problems would prevent internal conflict and international warfare. The foundations had "a vested interest in the present organization of society"; they protected "their gains by alleviating disruptive elements." In their view the concepts of free and of capitalist societies were congruent, provided capitalist philanthropy "help[ed] solve some of humanity's most pressing problems" to "enhance social stability" along lines of middle-class values. The philanthropists were "sophisticated conservatives" among whom critical stances were fully acceptable.[48]

From the 1920s through the 1940s the Carnegie and Rockefeller foundations provided some $19 million (U.S.) to Canadian institutions for education, the social sciences, and research on U.S.-Canadian relations. Immigrant settlement in the Prairies received as much attention as social problems in the big cities, Montreal in particular. The Carnegie Endowment for International Peace's Division of Economics and History funded "The Relations of Canada and the United States," a series with a total of twenty-five volumes published. While the studies on politics and economics have become outdated, the seminal studies of transborder migrations in both directions by Marcus Lee Hansen and John Bartlet Brebner, by Leon E. Truesdell, and by Robert H. Coats and Murdoch C. MacLean are still being cited.[49] Brebner was at Columbia University, where Caroline Ware and several other scholars of migration and anthropology of the period worked. Franz Boas was the most famous and Manuel Gamio the specialist for Mexico-U.S. migrations. In addition, scholars close to the Canadian border, the "Minnesota School," looked at continuities of cultures from Europe's regions to North America's Plains and Prairies. None of these succumbed to rhetoric about nations or about uprootedness of migrants.

In their foreword to *The Mingling of the Canadian and American Peoples* the authors note that they refused "to be deceived by political frontiers" and traced the migrations "in continental terms": The agricultural and urban expansion of U.S. and Canadian settlement was not parallel but "integral," undertaken "by eager land seekers who thought much of fertility and markets [as well as of jobs and of business opportunities] and little of political jurisdiction." From an Atlantic base settlers and speculators moved inland, Loyalists and their land-jobbing successors moved northward, the northern timber economy attracted workers, men threatened by the U.S. Civil War draft moved to Canadian cities, industries attracted younger men and women from the rural regions, railroad corporations facilitated movement, U.S. branch companies moved into Ontario, and Canada's slower development led to southward migration. "[I]nternational boundaries have been disregarded ... for almost two centuries" by "men and women, responding to pressures generated by their own numbers, by the proportions of young and old among them, or by new tides of immigration." Their movement dissolved as well as created "states and systems of community life."[50]

In the south the permeability of the border along the Rio Grande and in the Sonoran Desert was as high, yet its meanings were different. Annexation of lands settled for two centuries—in addition to First Peoples—by migrants from New Spain and, since the 1820s, by Mexicans, exposed these to Anglo-American racism. They saw their ways of life destroyed and their identities mocked. The major historian of California, Hubert H. Bancroft, sent field workers to interview the Spanish-speaking Californios only to contort or suppress their stories. He saw their memories "as his property to be used or not as he saw fit."[51]

The Mexican migrations were studied in the 1920s and 1930s by the foremost Mexican anthropologist, Manuel Gamio, and the U.S. political economist Paul S. Taylor.[52] They also caught the attention of U.S. writers and of the photographer Dorothea Lange. However, in contrast to the northern "mingling of peoples," the southbound migrations of U.S. citizens were not studied, and discrimination rather than interweaving was diagnosed.[53] The studies showed that northbound migrants came from as far south as Michoácan and Pueblo and were going as far north as Chicago and the Mesabi Range, though concentrated in the U.S. part of the Greater Southwest and along the northbound railroad lines. Gamio, who worked with Franz Boas and had published a study of the people of the Teotihuacán Valley from the Mexica to modern times (1922), interviewed more than a hundred migrants in 1926 and 1927. His work was funded by the U.S. Social Science Research Council's Committee on Scientific Aspects of Human Migration (chaired by Edith Abbott, an economist and specialist on migrants from Europe). Taylor studied the insertion of migrants in the (political) economy of the United States, investigated race relations, for example in Nueces County, Texas, and analyzed living conditions and social networks in a community of origin of migrants in Jalisco. He too used interviews but relied mainly on economic and social data.[54]

In the interviews most migrants described the border crossings as easy, the officers at the checkpoints as unconcerned about the transborder movements, and return frequent. Some wanted to stay in the United States; others moved back and forth. Of the latter some were saving money to settle permanently in agricultural colonization communities sponsored by the Mexican government. Some had English or deliberately learned it; others remained monolingual Spanish or perhaps had Nahuatl or another indigenous language in addition. Several were bitter about discrimination; others did not mention it. All seemed strongly committed to retain their Mexican citizenship. This latter finding would require verification: after his return to Mexico, Gamio became a central personage in the movement to construct a *mestizo* Mexican national identity. Thus the phrasing of the respective questions may have suggested this answer. Experience of discrimination also leads people to emphasize their culture of origin, since they have no reason to consider themselves inferior. They may in fact be more accommodative and open than the racists who have discriminated against them. Finally, first-generation migrants, regardless of European, Asian, or Latin American background, often value their *culture* of origin (and childhood socialization) but neither their *state's* political conditions nor the *labor market's* prospects experienced in their adult lives. The deep class cleavages and machismo politics in Mexican society lead to unsupportable lives for many. Societies need to guarantee sustainable lives.

In the mid-1930s Dorothea Lange, a Farm Security Administration photographer who worked mainly in California, cooperated with Paul S. Taylor. She had portrayed the internal environmental refugees from the Dust Bowl region as well as external transpacific Filipino and other Asian labor migrants. Lange and Taylor formed an ideal team, since they both carefully recorded personal and economic data about the working people in their photographs; he had used illustrations in his studies. Jointly they published *An American Exodus* in the series "American Farmers and the Rise of Agribusiness." Lange documented the migration to California's war industries in the 1940s.[55] Other American writers, like Katherine Anne Porter, and photographers, like Edward Weston and Charis Wilson Weston, explored Mexican cultures. The Mexican muralists Diego Rivera, David Alfaro Siqueiros, and José Clemente Orozco, and the painter Frida Kahlo, were well received by progressive circles in the U.S. although they were highly critical of American capitalism and mainstream culture and used their art to express this criticism. Thus cultural exchanges were always part of the relations between the two United States.

The "culture-migration-color of skin-working class" connection manifested itself in other ways important for innovative and inclusive scholarship often connected to Columbia University. Frank Tannenbaum, an Austrian immigrant and labor activist on the fringes of the intellectual and artistic seed-bed of Greenwich Village, became a student and a specialist on Mexico, Latin America, and slavery in the Americas. In the tradition of W. E. B. Du Bois, he connected the study of bound and free labor with racism in the U.S. South and economic structures. He worked on landholding patterns and land re-form in Mexico and their consequences for human migration; he integrated economic approaches, societal change, slavery, agrarian reform, and migra-tion.[56] In intellectual proximity, in Harlem in the 1920s and 1930s, the pres-ence of Caribbean migrants influenced research and artistic creation. Baha-mian songs were part of the Harlem Renaissance, and under the guidance of Franz Boas, Bronislaw Malinowski, Edward Sapir, Ruth Benedict, and Robert Redfield, Zora Neale Hurston, Katherine Dunham, and Eleanora Deren under-took anthropological research on African-inspired culture, including voodoo and folktales in Caribbean societies, Florida, and British Honduras in the 1930s and 1940s.[57]

As regards disruptive hierarchies and resulting mobility internal to the United States, the Carnegie Foundation supported the Swedish sociolo-gist Gunnar Myrdal's research on race and social inequality. His perceptive look from the outside, *An American Dilemma: the Negro Problem and Modern Democracy* (1944), was far ahead of U.S. scholarship. The foundation's person-nel came from the enlightened elites in search for stable internal and exter-nal peace, and it called for dispassionate analyses of societal problems from new perspectives to make them amenable to change. This systematic curiosity (Hurston) was cut short by the Cold War repression. U.S. intellectuals had to flee to Mexico. Others would migrate to Canada in the 1970s. Scholars and foundations from the 1920s to the 1940s pursued macro-regional perspectives rather than the views confined by the nation-state of the 1950s and after. Only in the 1990s would the international perspectives be reclaimed.[58] In contrast, Hollywood's film corporations had long produced cross-border films—from red-light Tijuana to romantic and titillating Niagara Falls.[59]

Transcultural Societal Studies:
Placing People's Agency in Societal Processes and Structures

In the many-cultured societies of the Americas, all of them former colonies with culturally stratified populations and remnants of mental dependency on the European colonizer cultures, scholars had thus begun to analyze social interaction in terms of many cultures and of *métissage* from the 1930s on. Since then diversity between regions, cultural backgrounds, and economic practices across borders in past and present has been theorized as distinct whole ways of life (Raymond Williams) and as transcultural mixing, *métissage*, *mestizaje* (Ortiz). While interaction and awareness of connectivity was part of people's lives, the curiosity for the Other was deliberately exorcized from mainstream scholarship under nation-centeredness. Postulates of enmity and actual power hierarchies during the Cold War, often brutally imposed, lives and cultures remained inextricably entwined.[60]

In North America's societies the semi-colonial dependency, the struggles to sever such dependency relationships, and the interactions between First Peoples, people of African origin, European origin, and Asian origin, and people who would claim descent of all of these groups, cultural elements, and practices led to multiple and competing layers of discourse and scholarly approaches. Internal diversities between genders, classes, regions, life-cycle phase and generation, urban and rural ways of life, and plantation and free agriculture led to a lack of one single discourse about national identity, of one single theory of society, one single methodology of studying it, and perhaps most important, one national gatekeeper-discourse-based curriculum into the confines of which all young people, including future scholars, were corralled. Anglo-British gatekeepers in Canada attempted to impose one British mold onto Canadian experiences; Mexican anthropologists in the 1920s attempted to develop one national identity that combined Mexican Spanishness with the pre-contact Mexica and Maya cultures; the American studies movement of the 1930s postulated its integrative role. U.S. scholars were aware that they dealt with myths and symbols, whether as encompassing as the frontier or as local as Washington's cherry tree. Still women, Afro-Americans, Chicanos, and Asian-Americans had to struggle to insert themselves into the narrative and showed a "hunger of memory."[61] When Canada in the 1960s officially recognized its biculturalism and bilingualism, the immigrants of many cultures protested and demanded inclusion. Recognition of multicultural ways of life and memory was the result. In Mexico, in contrast, the social reform policies of the 1930s attempted to include the descendants of First People, but the national narrative remained Mexican-Hispanic. National narratives hide cultural diversity and migrants' mobility.[62]

Diversity of experiences within societies and across borders, constantly changed by continuing interaction and migration, resulted in diversity of public memories and, especially since the 1960s and 1970s, brought new theoretical approaches to scholarship. The arena of production of memory could no longer be claimed by "national" historians, who by excluding women, the working classes, immigrants, "minorities," and young people from the narrative wrote a 5 percent version of societies' histories: 95 percent of the citizens were being excluded as irrelevant from this great-white-men version developed by small white minds. While the archeology ("great ruins") and Euro-Hispanic model of Mexican studies and the self-centered model of American studies—which as an integrated interpretation of U.S. culture and history was an advance over separate literary and historical readings—remained limited, Canadian studies early began to look at societal development in a comparative perspective, at Native peoples' worlds, at the political economy of international trade, and from the 1960s on, at the diversity of the population and at the colonial mental dependency of previous generations of British-origin and French-origin Canadians. This recognition repeated what Ortiz had developed for Cuban society in the 1940s, a transculturation perspective. Migrants to all the North American societies had undertaken such analyses for long: They had comparatively evaluated social institutions, economic options, and life projects in the frame of their society of birth and of their destination. Miscalculation they could not afford.

From Canadian Studies and postcolonial as well as subaltern perspectives, a new integrative and comprehensive "Transcultural Societal Studies" may be derived. It integrates the traditional discourse-based humanities, the data-based social sciences, the habitus-centered behavioral approaches, the normative disciplines of law, ethics and religion, the life sciences, and the environmental sciences, as well as other fields. It provides a transdisciplinary approach to whole societies rather than to particular fragments of them—workers, women, men, New Yorkers and Vancouverites, Oaxacans and Sonorans, New Englanders and Quebecois. Cultural transfer has often been understood as occurring in hierarchies, from nationals to immigrants, from (mature adult) parents to (immature) children, and, in a variation, from men to women by the legal construction common in the western world to the 1960s that a married woman's national or ethnic identity is derived from that of her husband regardless of her culture of birth. Such views of transfer assume an unmediated, straight passing on or handing *down*—note the hierarchy—with neither resistance nor adaptation as well as demarcated, internally homogeneous cultural(-genetic) groups. Cultural theory, however, points to an encoding of cultural preferences, a transmission of these messages, and a process of receiving and decoding by the less powerful—whether immigrants, women, or youths—in their own terms of reference.

Transcultural societal studies capture the diversity of human lives and the diversity in every human being's life. They reach out globally to the diversity of origins of some 180 cultural groups in Canada and the United States, perhaps fewer in the Caribbean and Mexico. They include Amerindian cultures not counted in this figure. Acknowledging regional and local diversity, they study relations, interactions, and networks rather than essentializing or even geneticizing identities and social slots of ethnicities, classes, or genders. They look at peoples' lives and their roles in creating ever-new social expressions and structures; they study processual structures and structured processes as well as caesura, conflicts, and clashes. The stability posited by ideologues of national homogeneity is often but stagnation—or even less, the limited vision of its proponents. Diversity of cultures means diversity of options, creative energies, and development. People who combine multiple cultural capabilities increase their individual and social capital. This adds to the assets available in society as a whole.

Notes

The maps in this chapter and additional ones may be downloaded from http://nacts .asu.edu/Knowledge_Center/North_American_Migration (as of March 2010).

1 David Thelen, "Of Audiences, Borderlands, and Comparisons: Toward the Internationalization of American History," *Journal of American History* 79 (1992), 432–62, quote p. 436.

2 Before the "Founding" Puritans arrived in New England, the Spanish settled St. Augustine, Florida, in 1565 and Santa Fé, New Mexico, in 1598.

3 Bernard Bailyn, *The Peopling of British North America: An Introduction* (New York: Random House, 1986). Cole Harris understood the displacement: *The Resettlement of British Columbia. Essays on Colonialism and Geographical Change* (Vancouver: University of British Columbia Press, 1997). See also Dirk Hoerder, *Cultures in Contact: World Migrations in the Second Millennium* (Durham: Duke University Press, 2002), chapters 2.3, 5.3, 8, 9.

4 William C. Sturtevant, ed., *Handbook of North American Indians*, vol. 17, "Languages" (Washington: Smithsonian Institution, 1996), 4–8.

5 Carlos G. Vélez-Ibáñez, *Border Visions. Mexican Cultures of the Southwest United States* (Tucson: University of Arizona Press, 1996), 5; Emil W. Haury, "Thoughts after Sixty Years as a Southwestern Archeologist," *Emil W. Haury's Prehistory of the American Southwest*, ed. J. Jefferson Reid and David E. Doyel (Tucson, University of Arizona Press, 1986), 435–63.

6 Quotes in Duane King with Ken Blankenship and Barbara Duncan, *Emissaries of Peace: The 1762 Cherokee and British Delegations: Exhibit Catalogue* (Cherokee, N.C.: Museum of the Cherokee Indian, 2006), 51, 52.

7 Helen Hornbeck Tanner, ed., Janice Reiff, John H. Long, Dirk Hoerder, Henry F. Dobyns, associate eds., *The Settling of North America: The Atlas of the Great Migrations into North America from the Ice Age to the Present* (New York: Macmillan, 1995), 29.

8 Edgar McInnis, *The Unguarded Frontier: A History of American-Canadian Relations* (New York: Doubleday, 1942), 1, 74–75.

9 Kenneth R. Andrews, *Trade, Plunder and Settlement: Maritime Enterprise and the*

Genesis of the British Empire, 1480–1630 (Cambridge: Cambridge University Press, 1984).

10 The British and American colonists called this the "French and Indian war."

11 In the case of the Acadians, acquired by treaty in 1713, the British had summarily and brutally deported most of them from Nova Scotia at the beginning of the next inter-imperial war, in 1755. After acquisition of Quebec's French-language and Catholic population, the British monarchy, in contrast, accepted pluralism: the Quebec Act (1774) permitted Quebecers to use the French language and legal system, remain Catholic, and govern themselves.

12 The best analysis of Quebec history is Paul-André Linteau, René Durocher, Jean-Claude Robert, and François Ricard, *Histoire du Québec contemporain*, 2 vols. (Montréal: Boréal, 1979, 1991), Engl. as *Quebec: A History, 1867–1929*, trans. Robert Chodos (Toronto: Lorimer, 1983), and *Quebec since 1930*, trans. Robert Chodos and Ellen Garmaise (Toronto: Lorimer, 1999).

13 Richard Price, ed., *Maroon Societies: Rebel Slave Communities in the Americas* (Baltimore: Johns Hopkins University Press, 1979; revised edition 1996); Gad Heuman, ed., *Out of the House of Bondage: Runaways, Resistance and Marronage in Africa and the New World* (London: Frank Cass, 1986); Herbert Aptheker, *American Negro Slave Revolts* (New York: Columbia University Press, 1943); Eugene D. Genovese, *From Rebellion to Revolution: Afro-American Slave Revolts in the Making of the Modern World* (Baton Rouge: Louisiana State University Press, 1970).

14 Dirk Hoerder, "The Long History of Area / Country Studies: Canadian Studies as Model or Special Case of Societal Studies," *Lendemains* 122–23 (2006), 62–76. In the United States the writing by the nationalist-literary historians George Bancroft and Francis Parkman are cases in point; the Canadian equivalent has been called "promotional history." Hoerder, *To Know Our Many Selves: From the Study of Canada to Canadian Studies* (Edmonton: Athabasca University Press, 2010), 65–109. Mexican historiography emerged as the imperial perspective of Hispanophile Conservatives, added the "providential nation" perspective of Hispanophobe Liberals, and became criollo patriotism without mention of living First Peoples.

15 States, which within Europe fought bitter wars over tiny parcels of land, bartered away huge chunks of land on other continents.

16 In addition, the United States purchased Alaska from Russia in 1867; annexed Puerto Rico in 1898 after a war against Spain; annexed the Republic of Hawaii in 1898; and bought the Virgin Islands from Denmark in 1917.

17 These dissolved into several states, 1849–50.

18 The Pan-American Congress, assembled in 1826 by Simon Bolívar to bring together the republics of the Americas, was not attended by the United States. Lester D. Langley, *The Americas in the Age of Revolution, 1750–1850* (New Haven: Yale University Press, 1996).

19 Isabelle Vagnoux, *Les États-Unis et le Mexique* (Paris: L'Harmattan, 2003). The Catholic Church hierarchy in Quebec also opposed economic development, though lay elites did not always accept such constrictions.

20 See Hubert Howe Bancroft, *Vida de Porfirio Díaz: Reseña histórica y social del pasado y presente de México* (México: Compañía Histórica, 1887), 231.

21 The term "coolie" for self-indentured or kidnapped laborers came to symbolize cheap and despised men and women among white capitalists and working-class organizations alike. The word meant "bitter strength" in Chinese and "wage for menial work" in Tamil.

22 Hugh Tinker, *A New System of Slavery: The Export of Indian Labour Overseas, 1830–1920* (London, Oxford University Press, 1974); David Northrup, *Indentured Labor in the Age of Imperialism, 1834–1922* (Cambridge: Cambridge University Press, 1995).

23 In Brazil liberation came even later, in 1888.

24 The—mostly African-origin—cigar makers of Ybor City, Florida, and Havana, Cuba, migrated in both directions.

25 No united German state existed. The multitude of dwarf states had been reduced through reorganization by Napoleon, but the duality of the two major dynasties, Hohenzollern and Habsburg, prevented unity even after the establishment of the German Reich in 1871.

26 In the latter decades of the nineteenth century intellectuals of the Científicos group opined that in the global racial struggle for survival—a vulgarized social Darwinism—Mexico was disadvantaged and needed to recruit European immigrants to "whiten" the Mexican genetic stock. This ideology was also propagated in other Latin American countries by European-background technocratic elites. Richard Graham, ed., *The Idea of Race in Latin America, 1877–1940* (Austin: University of Texas Press, 1990).

27 Dolores Pla, Guadelupe Zárate, Mónica Palma, Jorge Gómez, Rosario Cardiel, and Delia Salazar, *Extranjeros en México (1821–1990): Bibliografía* (Mexico City: INAH, 1994).

28 Quoted in John W. Dafoe, *Clifford Sifton in Relation to His Times* (Toronto: Macmillan, 1931), 142. On the racialization of East Europeans see Donna Gabaccia, "The 'Yellow Peril' and the 'Chinese of Europe': Global Perspectives on Race and Labor, 1815–1930," *Migrations, Migration History, History: Old Paradigms and New Perspectives*, ed. Jan Lucassen and Leo Lucassen (Bern: Lang, 1997), 177–96.

29 Jean R. Burnet and Howard Palmer, *"Coming Canadians": An Introduction to a History of Canada's Peoples* (Toronto: McClelland and Stewart, 1988); Roger Daniels, *Coming to America: A History of Immigration and Ethnicity in American Life* (New York, Harper Collins, 1990); Ronald Takaki, *A Different Mirror: A History of Multicultural America* (Boston: Little, Brown, 1993).

30 Hoerder, *Cultures in Contact*, chapters 8.2, 15, 19.5.

31 For Afro-Caribbeans see Cindy Hahamovitch, *The Fruits of Their Labor: Atlantic Coast Farm Workers and the Making of Migrant Poverty, 1870–1945* (Chapel Hill: University of North Carolina Press, 1997); Ronald Takaki, *Pau Hana: Plantation Life and Labor in Hawaii, 1835–1920* (Honolulu: University of Hawai'i Press, 1983).

32 David R. Smith, "Structuring the Permeable Border: Channeling and Regulating Cross-Border Traffic in Labor, Capital, and Goods," *Permeable Border: The Great*

Lakes as Transnational Region, 1650–1990, by John J. Bukowczyk, Nora Faires, David J. Smith, and Randy W. Widdis (Calgary: University of Calgary Press, 2005), 120–51; Randy W. Widdis, *With Scarcely a Ripple: Anglo-Canadian Migration into the United States and Western Canada, 1880–1920* (Montreal: McGill-Queen's University Press, 1998).

33 Walter Nugent, *Crossings: The Great Transatlantic Migrations, 1870–1914* (Bloomington: Indiana University Press, 1992).

34 Donna Gabaccia, "Constructing North America: Railroad Building and the Rise of Continental Migrations, 1850–1914," *Repositioning North American Migration History: New Directions in Modern Continental Migration, Citizenship, and Community*, ed. Marc S. Rodriguez (Rochester: University of Rochester Press, 2004), 27–53.

35 From the late 1940s Jamaican workers on their own initiative moved to Britain by the boatload. Canada recruited the first Caribbean ("British West Indies") domestic workers and caregivers in 1955. Christiane Harzig, "'The Movement of 100 Girls': 1950s Canadian Immigration Policy and the Market for Domestic Labour," *Zeitschrift für Kanada-Studien* 19, no. 2 (1999), 131–46.

36 Dirk Hoerder, *Creating Societies: Immigrant Lives in Canada* (Montreal: McGill-Queen's University Press, 1999), chapters 11–15.

37 The border city Paso del Norte was later renamed Ciudad Juarez because President Juarez had briefly made it his official seat during the French invasion.

38 James T. Shotwell, Introduction, *The Mingling of the Canadian and American Peoples*, by Marcus L. Hansen and John B. Brebner (Toronto: Ryerson, 1940), v.

39 During the First World War France and Britain had relied on about one million Asian indentured workers to support their troops in Europe, but in the Versailles peace negotiations they denied independence to the workers' societies of origin.

40 Manuel García y Griego, *The Importation of Mexican Contract Laborers to the U.S., 1942–1964: Antecedents, Operation, and Legacy* (La Jolla: University of California, San Diego, 1981), repr. in *The Border That Joins: Mexican Migrants and U.S. Responsibility*, ed. Peter G. Brown and Henry Shue (Totowa, N.J.: Rowman and Littlefield, 1983).

41 Roger Daniels, *Concentration Camps, North America: Japanese in the United States and Canada during World War II* (Malabar, Fla.: Krieger, 1981); Richard Drinnon, *Keeper of Concentration Camps: Dillon S. Myer and American Racism* (Berkeley: University of California Press, 1987). In view of the doubtful legality of the act, the Army impounded all photos of the deportations made by as renowned a photographer as Dorothea Lange. They were rediscovered and released only much later. Linda Gordon and Gary Y. Okihiro, eds., *Impounded: Dorothea Lange and the Censored Images of Japanese American Internment* (New York: W. W. Norton, 2006).

42 The "pioneer Spanish" of the early decades of New Spain's development was a Spanish-Nahuatl creole language.

43 Everett C. Hughes, "The Study of Ethnic Relations," *Dalhousie Review* 27 (1948), 477–82; Hughes and Helen MacGill Hughes, *Where Peoples Meet: Racial and Ethnic Frontiers* (Glencoe, Ill.: Free Press, 1952). Fernando Ortiz, "Del fenómeno de la transculturación y su importancia en Cuba," *Revista Bimestre Cubana* 27 (1940), 273–78,

trans. Harriet de Onís as *Cuban Counterpoint: Tobacco and Sugar* (1947; repr. Durham: Duke University Press, 1995). Gilberto Freyre argued that Brazilian society was African and European (as well as Native), though he overemphasized the peacefulness of Euro-Brazilian planters' paternalism.

44 José Vasconcelos, *La Raza Cósmica: Misión de la Raza Iberoamericana* (Paris: Agencia mundial de librería, 1925); Justo Sierra equated Mexican national identity with the mestizo: *The Political Evolution of the Mexican People* (1900–1902).

45 Robert E. Park, Herbert A. Miller, and Kenneth Thompson, *Old World Traits Transplanted: The Early Sociology of Culture* (New York: Harper, 1921); Robert E. Park, "Human Migration and the Marginal Man," *American Journal of Sociology* 33 (1928), 881–93; Oscar Handlin, *The Uprooted: The Epic Story of the Great Migrations that Made the American People* (Boston: Little, Brown, 1951); Rudolph J. Vecoli, "The *Contadini* in Chicago: A Critique of *The Uprooted*," *Journal of American History* 51 (1964), 404–17.

46 William I. Thomas and Florian Znaniecki, *The Polish Peasant in Europe and America*, 2 vols. (Chicago: University of Chicago Press, 1918–20); Caroline F. Ware, *Greenwich Village, 1920–1930: A Comment on American Civilization in the Post-war Years* (Boston: Houghton Mifflin, 1935; repr. Berkeley: University of California Press, 1994), and *The Cultural Approach to History* (New York: Columbia University Press, 1940).

47 Randolph Bourne, "Trans-National America," *Atlantic Monthly* 118 (1916), 86–97; Horace M. Kallen, "Democracy versus the Melting Pot: A Study of American Nationality," *Nation*, February 1915.

48 Based on Dirk Hoerder, "Canadian Universities and U.S. Foundations, 1920s–40s," *To Know Our Many Selves*, 144–45; Charles R. Acland and William J. Buxton, *American Philanthropy and Canadian Libraries: The Politics of Knowledge and Information* (Montreal: McGill University Graduate School, 1998); Theresa Richardson and Donald Fisher, eds., *The Development of the Social Sciences in the United States and Canada: The Role of Philanthropy* (Stamford, Conn.: Ablex, 1999), quotes pp. 7–8, and esp. 75–93. Coordination was undertaken by the U.S. Social Science Research Council (established 1923) and, considerably later, the Canadian Social Science Research Council (established 1940).

49 Marcus L. Hansen and John B. Brebner, *The Mingling of the Canadian and American Peoples* (Toronto: Ryerson, 1940); Leon E. Truesdell, *The Canadian Born in the United States: An Analysis of the Statistics of the Canadian Element in the Population of the United States, 1850 to 1930* (New Haven: Yale University Press, 1943); Robert H. Coats and Murdoch C. MacLean, *The American-Born in Canada: A Statistical Interpretation* (Toronto: Ryerson, 1943).

50 *The Mingling of the Canadian and American Peoples*, by Marcus L. Hansen and John B. Brebner (Toronto: Ryerson, 1940), quotes ix–x, 1–3.

51 Genaro M. Padilla, *My History, Not Yours: The Formation of Mexican American Autobiography* (Madison: University of Wisconsin Press, 1993), esp. 77–108, quote p. 107; Samuel Truett and Elliott Young, eds., *Continental Crossroads: Remapping U.S.-Mexican Borderlands History* (Durham: Duke University Press, 2003).

52 Of the large number of publications of Gamio and Taylor only a few can be listed here. Gamio, *Mexican Immigration to the United States: A Study of Human Migration and Adjustment* (Chicago: University of Chicago Press, 1930), and *The Life Story of the Mexican Immigrant: Autobiographic Documents*, ed. Robert Redfield, trans. Robert C. Jones, introduction by Paul S. Taylor (New York: Dover, 1971) [orig. publ. as *Mexican Immigrant: His Life-Story*, Chicago: University of Chicago Press, 1931]; Taylor, *Mexican Labor in the United States*, Univ. of Calif. Publications in Economics, vols. 6–7 (Berkeley: University of California Press, 1928–32; repr. New York: Johnson, 1966), and *Migration Statistics* (Berkeley: University of California Press, 1933–34; repr. New York: Johnson, 1968).

53 John M. Hart, *Empire and Revolution: The Americans in Mexico since the Civil War* (Berkeley: University of California Press, 2002).

54 Taylor, *An American-Mexican Frontier, Nueces County, Texas* (Chapel Hill: University of North Carolina Press, 1934), and *A Spanish-Mexican Peasant Community: Arandas in Jalisco, Mexico* (Berkeley: University of California Press, 1933).

55 John Raeburn, *A Staggering Revolution: A Cultural History of Thirties Photography* (Urbana: University of Illinois Press, 2006), 158–64; Lange and Taylor, *An American Exodus: A Record of Human Erosion* (New York: Reynal and Hitchcock, 1939; repr. New York: Arno, 1975). Charles Wollenberg, *Photographing the Second Gold Rush: Dorothea Lange and the East Bay at War, 1941–1945* (Berkeley: Heyday, 1995).

56 Helen Delpar, "Frank Tannenbaum: The Making of a Mexicanist, 1914–1933," *Americas* 45, no. 2 (October 1988), 153–71.

57 Hurston, *Dust Tracks on the Road: An Autobiography* (New York: Lippincott, 1942; rev. New York: Harper Perennial, 1996), esp. 143–92; Dunham, *Journey to Accompong* (1946) and others; Deren, *Divine Horsemen: The Living Gods of Haiti* (1953).

58 Thomas Bender for the Organization of American Historians and New York University, *The LaPietra Report: Project on Internationalizing the Study of American History: A Report to the Profession* (September 2000).

59 Dominique Brégent-Heald, "The Tourism of Titillation: Film and Cross-Border Tourism in Niagara Falls and Tijuana," *Journal of the Canadian Historical Association* 17 (2006), 181–205.

60 Raymond Williams, *Culture and Society, 1780–1950* (New York: Columbia University Press, 1958). Clifford Geertz, *The Interpretation of Cultures: Selected Essays* (New York: Basic Books, 1973); James Clifford and George E. Marcus, eds., *Writing Culture: The Poetics and Politics of Ethnography* (Berkeley: University of California Press, 1986); Arjun Appadurai, "Global Ethnoscapes: Notes and Queries for a Transnational Anthropology," *Recapturing Anthropology: Working in the Present*, ed. Richard Fox (Santa Fe: School of American Research Press, 1991), 191–210; Allen F. Roberts, "La 'géographie processuelle': Un nouveau paradigme pour les aires culturelles," *Lendemains* 31, nos. 122–23 (2006), 41–61.

61 See for one view of Mexican living in the United States: Richard Rodríguez, *Hunger of Memory: The Education of Richard Rodríguez: An Autobiography* (Boston: Godine, 1982).

62 Gene Wise, "'Paradigm Dramas' in American Studies: A Cultural and Institutional History of the Movement," *American Quarterly* 31 (1979), 292–337, 305–7; Linda K. Kerber, "Diversity and the Transformation of American Studies," *American Quarterly* 41 (fall 1989), 415–31; Alan Knight, "Racism, Revolution, and *Indigenismo*: Mexico, 1910–1940," *The Idea of Latin America, 1870–1940*, ed. Richard Graham (Austin: University of Texas Press, 1990), 71–113; Guillermo Bonfil Batalla, *México Profundo: Reclaiming a Civilization* (1987), trans. Philip A. Dennis (Austin: University of Texas Press, 1996); Gary Nash, "The Hidden History of Mestizo America," *Journal of American History* 82 (December 1995), 941–62.

PART ONE

Intersocietal Migrations

CHAPTER ONE

Mirando atrás

Mexican Immigration from 1876 to 2000

Jaime R. Aguila and Brian Gratton

The study of Mexican immigration to the United States has been *au courant* since the start of the twentieth century, when government officials on both sides of the border, concerned about the status of labor conditions, began investigating cross-border movements. Even at this early date, each nation recognized the growing interdependence. Economic and human exchange grew still more across the century, and the constant flow of Mexican immigration has had more than economic effects, becoming part and parcel of domestic issues in both countries.

After a brief review of contemporary immigration conditions within the United States, this chapter uses new research sources to study the period from the late nineteenth century to the first half of the twentieth. It begins by explaining how Mexico became the primary sending nation of immigrants to the United States and how this affected the demographic profile of the American Southwest. The Mexican perspective on these demographic events is then analyzed, a view often ignored in treatments of Mexican immigration. Mexican public policy sought to address the causes of a massive exodus of the country's working-age population. Officials initially believed that the loss of a significant portion of its population had a negative impact on Mexico's strength as a nation. From the late 1800s to the 1930s officials tried to dissuade the exodus and to encourage the return of those already in the United States. Such objectives continue to manifest themselves in the twenty-first century as Mexican leaders search for a way to manage the Mexican migration stream. In concluding remarks the same issues are reviewed from the perspective of U.S. immigration policy and its relationship with evolving political, economic, and social factors.

The Current Scene

Today Latin America is the largest sending area for immigrants to the United States; however, the size of the Latino population represents just one element of a complicated story of immigration and settlement. The U.S. Census Bureau estimates that there are 31 million Latinos (including all generations) in the United States, about 11.2 percent of the national population.[1] The Census concluded that this number exceeded that of African Americans for the first time in 2002.[2] The March 2000 Current Population Survey reported that only two of five Latinos were foreign born and, given that a quarter of these were naturalized, only 30 percent were not U.S. citizens. The geographical distribution of Latino groups remains true to the basic history of Latino settlement: Almost half reside in California and Texas. However, one out of eight residents of Illinois is Latino, and the most recent striking trend in Latino settlement has been their arrival in regions in which they had not previously had a presence.

Mexico is the most important source for both legal and illegal Latino immigrants, a circumstance that has held true for nearly ninety years, proving Mexico's intimate linkage to the U.S. labor force. Undocumented immigrants tend to be concentrated in the working-age population and make up about 5 percent of the labor force, mostly in farming, domestic housework, and construction. In 2006 Mexicans represented 30.8 percent of the documented foreign-born population in the United States or over 11.5 million. Although no exact figures for the undocumented exist, estimates claim that Mexicans represent nearly 60 percent of approximately 10.3 million persons.[3] Consequently, a conservative estimate of the total Mexican-born population in the United States is 17.5 million; such a figure implies that a tenth of the population of Mexico lives in the United States.[4] As the Mexican writer Carlos Fuentes stated in 2006, "[w]hat is happening now with the Mexican worker cannot be called 'migration' anymore . . . It is an exodus. Millions of our people are leaving us . . . Out of 120 million, 50 million are unemployed. Poverty forces them to emigrate."[5]

The enduring relationship between the Mexican labor force and the U.S. economy has not dampened controversy over the rights of Mexicans in the United States and that society's responsibility for their social welfare. Since the first mass arrival in the early twentieth century, significant hostility to their presence has been evident in sporadic attempts to restrict their admission and to expel them. While much has been written about nativist reaction to Mexican immigrants, less attention has been given to the impact of immigration on the Mexican/Mexican American community itself, which has created significant advantages and disadvantages for its members. The long duration of Mexican immigration separates the experience of this community from most other ethnic groups in the United States.[6] Although there was a sharp inter-ruption during the 1930s, immigration has refreshed the *Mexicanidad* of the community regularly, in contrast to every other immigrant group. Moreover, their geographical concentration in areas of the Southwest is greater than the case for most ethnic groups. As a result, foreign-born Mexicans coexist along-side Mexican Americans who have lived in the United States for multiple gen-erations.

Concerns about the Mexican population's foreignness appeared in the re-action of many Americans to the massive pro-immigrant demonstrations throughout the United States in 2006. These manifestations revealed the mag-nitude of the population and its deep location within not simply the economy, but American society. The use of Mexican flags and the manifest demands for rights for persons who were neither citizens nor legally resident, but who were laboring hard in its factories, hotels, and fields, provoked, instead of sympa-thy, a negative reaction. This empowered anti-immigrant leaders who touted the massive protests as additional proof that more stringent border regulation was required. The former Colorado congressman Tom Tancredo, perhaps the most prominent restrictionist, stated: "All these folks who are here illegally know they can protest brazenly. It's really a mockery of our immigration sys-tem." Even moderates such as Senator John Cornyn of Texas believed that the marches would only inflame the issue.[7]

The marches, like the recent reaction against anti-immigrant legislation in Arizona and other states, were just the most recent statement in the long de-bate over whether or not civil and social rights ought to extend to all people who contribute and labor on behalf of our society, regardless of their legal status or citizenship. The debate over "what to do" with Mexican immigrants, especially those who have arrived illegally, has been a vexing one for decades, as a review of earlier periods reveals.

Immigration, 1900 to 1930

One major crisis over Mexican immigration occurred in the early 1930s, when the Great Depression led to public schemes to repatriate Mexicans, as well as extensive voluntary repatriation on the part of Mexican immigrants. This crisis had as its demographic foundation an equally massive and unprecedented im-migration between 1900 and 1930. Before 1900 most growth in the Mexican-origin population in the United States had come from a natural increase in the population long resident in the Southwest, such as the major centers of South

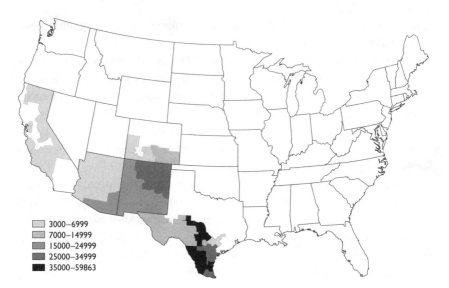

Persons identified as Mexican by IPUMS, 1900

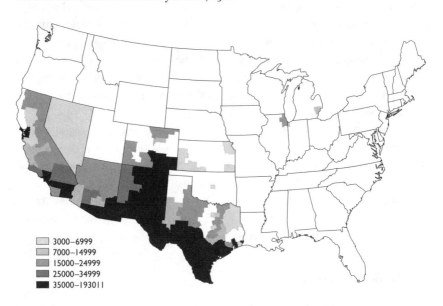

Persons identified as Mexican by IPUMS, 1930

Texas and Northern New Mexico. Map 1.1 shows the limited settlement areas and small density of this ethnic group.[8]

But by the turn of the century a powerful process was under way that led to a much greater increase in the Mexican-origin population and its settlement in almost all sections of the Southwest. Immigration was the chief engine of this broader transformation. In the late nineteenth century fewer than five thousand immigrants from Mexico arrived in the United States per year, largely, and ironically, because of the lack of economic development in Mexico. As was the case with Europe, immigrants tended to come from regions opened up to transportation systems and economic opportunity. At the turn of the century, mining, commercial agriculture, and the railroad networks needed to serve these enterprises had arisen simultaneously under the Porfirian regime in northern Mexico as well as in the southwestern United States, creating a unified economic system. Both sides of the border saw a dramatic rise in migration as poor agricultural populations sought better income; substantially higher wages in the United States made the northern side more alluring.[9] Formal and informal mechanisms emerged to move labor across the border, systems quite like those for European immigrants to the United States.[10] After 1910 annual immigration rates exceeded twenty thousand Mexicans per year and, during the First World War, regularly exceeded forty thousand per year. Figure 1.1 shows the modest level of immigration from Mexico in the late nineteenth century, the clear upward trend after 1900, and the acceleration after about 1910.[11]

During the 1920s Mexicans became the largest foreign group still entering the United States, with an average of about 57,000 per year from 1924 to 1929.[12] While the Mexican Revolution had some effect in pushing workers north, even more critical was the disruption of European immigration streams, first by the First World War and next by the success of nativist restrictions, which prohibited most European sources while excepting Mexicans from the law. Congressmen representing the economic system that had arisen in the Southwest provided their votes for European restriction so long as Mexicans were not affected. Heavy immigration led to rapid increases in the Mexican-origin population, and a strong shift toward foreign birth. In the late nineteenth century, most of the growth in the Mexican origin population in the United States had been by natural increase, but after 1900, immigration drove it. Between 1900 and 1910 the population jumped from 400,000 to nearly 640,000, and in 1920 it stood close to one million. In 1930 it was 1,789,000. The proportion born in Mexico rose from 32 percent in 1900 to 36 percent in 1910 and to 50 percent in 1920. This proportion fell across the 1920s to about 35 percent, revealing, as will be shown below, more permanent settlement patterns.

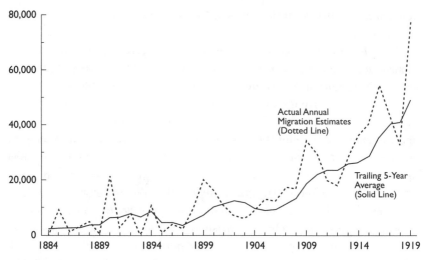

Figure 1.1 Raw and smoothed estimates of Mexican migration to the United States by year, 1884–1919

Not only were these migrants born in Mexico, but they followed routes that native-born Americans and European immigrants had been taking, routes that did not lead toward traditional Hispanic settlements. Like migrants and other immigrants, they sought regions of economic development and high-wage urban settings. For example, Mexican immigrants largely ignored the once imposing Hispanic zone of Northern New Mexico. As map 1.1 shows, persons of Mexican origin rapidly filled in the once-vacant spaces, and now had a visible presence in nearly all of California, all of Arizona and New Mexico, most of Colorado, and nearly everywhere in Texas.

By 1930 the impact of immigration was manifest; Mexican origin persons now had a presence in nearly all regions in the Southwest, and had established significant outposts in Kansas, Nevada, Missouri, Illinois, and Michigan. In certain areas they had become a very large part of the population. In parts of South Texas the group was not only the majority, but also constituted more than two-thirds of the total population. Thus not only had the absolute population risen over time, but the relative proportion of the Mexican-origin population increased as well, rising from about 7 percent of the five southwestern states in 1900 to 16 percent in 1930.

Moreover, like other immigrants Mexicans sought high-paying jobs away from traditional agriculture. In 1920, when immigrants made up 50 percent of the entire Mexican-origin population of the Southwest, they were 65 percent in the Phoenix area, 56 percent in the Los Angeles region, and 63 percent in San

Francisco. In contrast, in the northern New Mexico homeland they were less than 10 percent. In 1880, 14 percent of foreign-born Mexicans lived in urban places (defined as those with 2,500 or more residents), well behind the national average of 24 percent. In 1910, as immigration from Mexico began to rise, 29 percent lived in urban places, and 10 percent lived in the central core of metropolitan areas. By 1950 the majority of immigrants and their children lived in metropolitan areas, and nearly a third resided in the central city. Measures of occupational status confirm that they sought places where better jobs were offered. Northern and southwestern New Mexico, which immigrants avoided, had low occupational ratings, joined by the poor agricultural regions in the Rio Grande Valley of Texas. Cities in Arizona and California, conversely, offered ethnic Mexicans better job prospects, as did El Paso and San Antonio in Texas. Better wages were found in cities, and better wages attracted immigrants. The eminent scholar Manuel Gamio chronicled the same phenomenon in his pathbreaking studies of immigrants in the 1920s. His maps on remittances provide very similar evidence of the geographical and occupational choices Mexican immigrants made in the United States (for example, indicating high levels of remittances from high-wage states like Illinois), while also suggesting that most of the immigrants in this period had homes not in the northern parts of Mexico but came from west central states such as Michoacán.[13]

After 1930 immigration stalled, not to resume in a major way again until the 1970s, except for the guest workers in the Bracero Program. But in that year, their presence made itself felt in a new racial category in the U.S. Census. The sudden appearance of Mexican immigrants in new places in the early twentieth century, their direct competition with native-born Mexican-American and other workers, and a rising racialized antipathy led to their identification as the new immigrant threat. Although the precise reason for the institution of a Mexican racial category in the 1930 U.S. Census has yet to be identified (nor have we a good explanation of its equally sudden removal), it likely reflected the belief among many Americans that Mexicans constituted a racial problem.[14] Evidence for such attitudes can also be seen in the brief repatriation campaigns of the early 1930s, when local governmental authorities, joined by private charities, service organizations and, curiously, the Mexican government itself, urged Mexicans to return to their home country and provided financial assistance to do so. On the whole, however, repatriation was voluntary, following a common practice among Mexican migrants in previous eras and, in fact, the customary practice of most immigrants in the early twentieth century. Large numbers of Mexicans left between 1930 and 1934, although the total numbers of returnees has been greatly exaggerated by some scholars.[15] Alanís Enciso, in an incisive argument, provides the best analysis using

Mexican government records.[16] Alanís suggests that repatriation in the critical period between 1930 and 1934 amounted to about 350,000.

Few Mexicans, or immigrants of any nationality, entered the United States in the remainder of the 1930s, and the Second World War interrupted immigration again, save for the Bracero Program discussed earlier. This meant that the resident Mexican-American population in the United States after 1930 was based largely upon the immigrants of the period 1900–1930 without subsequent replenishment from Mexico. As Arturo Rosales has shown, the immigrant population of the early twentieth century, the *México Lindo* generation, differed strikingly from the original settlers in the nineteenth century, and differed as well from its children and grandchildren, who came of age in the 1950s and 1960s.[17] Many of the characteristics he identifies — such as intense attachment to homeland and hoped for and achieved return to the homeland — are the characteristics of Italians, Poles, and other immigrants in the same period. But, as we have shown, their children became intensely American, and intensely conscious of their rights and privileges as American citizens.

Mexican Emigration Policy, 1876–1930s

Porfirio Díaz's thirty-five-year dictatorship, from 1876 to 1911, modernized and disrupted traditional conditions and eventually provoked the Mexican Revolution. When the populist president Lázaro Cárdenas peacefully transferred power to his successor, Manuel Avila Camacho, Mexico became a one-party state. Mexican emigration public policy orientation reflected these major social and political shifts. From 1876 to 1915 policies were inconsistent and reactive to economic and political conditions. After 1916 emigration policy became more assertive. Mexican government officials promoted the ideals of the post-Revolutionary state, but also hoped to exploit the resources of the expatriate community and, when necessary, to protect that community, including assisting in repatriation.

Less than one year after coming to power in 1876, Díaz's regime displayed an interest in the social welfare of the compatriots in the north, largely as a way to expand the reach of the state.[18] On October 2, 1877, the minister of foreign relations, Ignacio Vallarta, critically reminded consuls along the border that their duties included monthly updates about the social welfare of their compatriots and that caring for the interests of the Republic required protecting its citizens. He was most concerned about his office's lack of information concerning crimes against Mexican citizens and their property by Americans.[19]

Porfirian officials inconsistently discouraged emigration while simultaneously encouraging plans intended to populate the sparse northern territories of the Republic. Although the primary objective of the Public Land Act of 1883 was to survey public land in order to facilitate its transfer to private commercial ownership, it included provisions for encouraging the repatriation and settlement of emigrants in barren regions. The executive branch financed the process, allocated the public land, encouraged the purchase of additional tracts, and even furnished tools for colonizers. All Mexican citizens in the United States were eligible. By 1910 a total of 198,327 colonists took advantage of this law, and of those, 31,658 were Mexican repatriates.[20]

Nonetheless the lure of high wages in the United States increasingly attracted emigrants despite official policy and considerable criticism of emigration in newspapers and other popular media.[21] The recession of 1907 led many Mexicans in the United States to seek assistance from the Mexican state to return home. These petitioners included seasonal workers who normally returned to Mexico after a few months' stay, but also some long-term residents who found themselves in distress. This was the first government-assisted repatriation drive and foreshadowed future repatriation programs during similar periods of economic crisis.

From December 1907 to March 1908 more than two thousand Mexicans returned on trains, many aided by the same railroad companies that had employed them.[22] Antonio Lomelí, the El Paso consul for Mexico, advised the federal government to distribute information about the declining employment opportunities in the United States throughout the states of Zacatecas, Guanajuato, Aguascalientes, Querétaro, Michoacán, and Jalisco, where the majority of emigrants originated.[23] As would always be the case, limited government funds could be applied to repatriation, but the more important factor in the lack of permanent return was that seasonal workers simply returned the following year when the American economy again demanded their labor. In 1909 2,562 Mexicans passed through El Paso into the United States, and in 1910, 10,146 more emigrated.[24]

The Mexican Revolution

The chaos of the Mexican Revolution prevented any significant policy reform until the ascendance of Venustiano Carranza to the presidency in 1916. Nonetheless, during the period 1910–15 two interim leaders, Francisco I. Madero and Victoriano Huerta, considered emigration policy. After his election on October 1, 1911, Madero blamed the exodus on the nation's limited labor opportunities, which he believed the government could prevent with agricultural cooperatives for unemployed workers.[25] In addition, socially conscientious *Maderistas* such as Luis Cabrera, a member of the Chamber of Deputies, supported the restitution of *ejidos* (communal village property) to prevent further emigration.[26]

In November 1911 Madero created the Department of Labor within the Ministry of Development to improve working conditions. The unit collected data regarding labor conditions, arbitrated disputes between employers and labor, and monitored wage agreements. According to Alan Knight, the department "epitomized the Maderista concern for social cohesion, for stable economic development, and for progress."[27] The Department of Labor devised a national system of employment offices that matched employers' needs with unemployed workers. Inspectors assessed national working conditions and made recommendations. Another presidential mandate allowed workers to quit their jobs when they wished arguing that such freedom would allow *braceros* (*bracero*, Spanish for "arm," had become the generic term for Mexican workers in the United States) to migrate to areas with labor shortages within the nation rather than to the United States.[28]

Madero's administration was cut short by Victoriano Huerta's counterrevolution, which resulted in the president's assassination on February 21, 1913. The coup renewed the social chaos of the revolution. Manuel Gamio claimed that this period's violence not only increased the number of people exiting, but unlike economic factors, also prevented them from returning seasonally.[29] While the effect of the revolution on increasing immigration has been exaggerated, and John Womack found that the economy continued to expand despite the violence, it did add another factor during a crucial and formative era of Mexican immigration in the United States.[30] Huerta's administration considered emigration policies within the framework of violence and refugee flight. In September 1913 many families along the border between Coahuila and Texas were in a state of panic because of the fighting between federal troops and Venustiano Carranza's forces. Nearly ten thousand refugees had crossed into Eagle Pass, Texas, from Ciudad Porfirio Díaz.[31] Consular officials reported that the refugee flow showed no signs of dissipating and asked federal officials for additional assistance.[32] Overwhelmed by the growing exodus, consular staff lamented the loss to their nation: "a valuable labor resource is being denied our nation's agricultural sector where they were greatly needed. It also makes our job as consuls extremely difficult because on daily basis immigrants ask for intervention with their problems."[33] The Huerta administration's response was unimaginative and futile. The Ministry of State asked the governors of the major migrant-sending states to curtail emigration. But there was little that state officials could accomplish, as the governor of Zacatecas commented: "Article 11 of the 1857 Constitution, among other rights, gives

citizens the prerogative of entering and leaving the territory of Mexico freely
. . . in addition the laborer contracts that are used, according to the terms in
which they are understood, do not violate the 5th article of the same constitution; in whose virtue this government is not able to do anything to impede
emigration, as harmful as it is for the country's welfare."[34] Huerta's inability
to either curtail the emigration flow or exploit it contributed to his eventual
demise. On March 5, 1914, the consul in Del Rio, Texas, warned the military
commander in Ciudad Porfirio Díaz that many unemployed peasants from
Coahuila were joining Carranza's forces along the border. Military reports
concluded that the only beneficiaries of the peasants' miserable condition
were the *Carrancistas* who persuaded them to take up arms on both sides of
the border against the federal government. Military advisors recommended
that the federal government intervene to alleviate the hardships of the rural
population in order to prevent them from joining rebel armies.[35] But such
advice, whether accurate or not, was irrelevant after Huerta's regime fell in
August 1914.

With the promulgation of the Mexican Constitution in 1917, and a measure
of stability, Mexican public policy took on a more proactive stance. Revolutionary Nationalism, promoted in Carranza's administration (1916–20), rested
on his understanding that his political success depended on alleviating the
suffering that plagued Mexico and led to emigration. Mexican officials, especially the executive and the Ministry of Foreign Relations (Secretaría de Relaciones Exteriores, or SRE), provided immigrants in the United States with legal
assistance and advised them during labor negotiations. However, the most
common and costly form of aid was repatriation.

Under Article 123 of the 1917 Constitution, as with the 1857 Constitution,
Mexicans were free to exit the nation when they pleased. However, Articles 25
and 26 empowered the federal government to regulate the exit process, truly
an innovation. On this basis the Ministry of State prohibited emigration unless the citizen had a valid contract outlining the length of employment and
pay scale. This new law aimed at the most common complaints of employer
abuse: low wages and failure to fulfill contracts.[36]

However, Mexican reforms did little to improve conditions abroad, where
employers used Mexicans as scabs to break railroad and agricultural strikes.
American unions opposed Mexican *braceros*, and they experienced violent
opposition. American employers violated labor contracts that *braceros* had
signed with labor recruiters. Furthermore, reports surfaced that the U.S. Army
was drafting *braceros* against their will causing some Mexican males to abandon jobs and, in some cases, families and return to Mexico. In March 1918
President Venustiano Carranza responded by breaching the constitutional

right of exit, prohibiting the issuing of passports to citizens seeking employment abroad, even if they had contracts.[37]

In trying to stop Mexicans from emigrating and urging their return, Mexican officials resorted time after time to strategies producing no results.[38] Ineffective as they were, the nationalistic characteristics of Carranza's administration became an integral element of public policy and rhetoric in subsequent administrations, a recognition that the emigrant community was a significant part of the Mexican body politic.

The 1920s

After 1920 Mexican administrations introduced more aggressive policies. Because of the political instability engendered by Carranza's violent 1920 demise, Adolfo de la Huerta's interim presidency could not fashion a useful response to the 1920 postwar economic recession. Upon assuming office on December 1, 1920, Alvaro Obregón encouraged consulate offices to anticipate problems, expand protective services, and increase interaction with Mexican immigrants within their jurisdictions. By 1922 his office claimed to have repatriated more than 150,000 Mexicans.[39] Although officials may have overestimated the number, Obregón recognized that conditions of the emigrant community in the United States sparked public scrutiny in Mexico. An editorial in *El Excelsior* declared, "since the Revolution forced them to emigrate, it is only just that the government born out of this Revolution provide them with the resources to return to their homeland."[40]

On February 16, 1921, Obregón ordered consuls to repatriate "all those Mexicans who were in a state of poverty or unemployed" and transferred 250,000 pesos to the SRE. Indeed, Obregón declared publicly that regardless of the cost, he was going to repatriate all Mexicans living in the United States. The government spent 1,500,000 pesos repatriating 1,500 Mexicans in the spring of 1921 alone.[41] By October Obregón considered conditions in the United States stable enough to end the emergency repatriation drive, and, as would occur in the Great Depression, little consideration was given to repatriates' needs in Mexico.[42]

Consuls were charged with and in many cases tried to inform Mexicans of U.S. immigration laws; they intervened in civil disputes, investigated deaths, advised workers about their labor contracts, and helped them obtain compensation for work-related injuries. Fourteen of the fifty-nine consulates served about 80 percent of Mexican migrants, all but the Chicago agency located in the Southwest.[43] In 1923 President Obregón created the Department of Repatriation within the SRE and made consulates directly responsible for processing repatriation requests. Federal officials lauded these reforms, although consular budgets were only modestly increased. Obregón also created two mutual aid organizations, the *Comisiones Honoríficas Mexicanas* (*Comisiones*) and the *Brígadas de la Cruz Azul Mexicana* (*Brigadas*), which became formal conduits between migrants and the consulates as well as tools for promoting Mexican nationalism among expatriate communities.[44]

The *Comisiones'* attachment to the consulates extended the reach of the Mexican government and demonstrated to critics that it was concerned for the emigrants' well-being. The emerging stable relationship created a relatively inexpensive and effective means to expand protection services. Some communities in Arizona had never before seen a representative of the Mexican government in person.[45] The *Comisiones* were instrumental in organizing communities throughout the United States and aiding consular personnel into the 1930s.

Upon assuming the presidency in 1924, Plutarco Elías Calles inherited a more stable nation and a more systematic program of emigrant aid than Obregón had in 1920. However, the Mexican economy was still incapable of keeping its workforce at home. Government resources were insufficient and opportunity abroad too alluring. By 1928 policymakers resorted to rhetorical appeals in the media, a weak defense against the high wages and ready employment across the border. Some protection could be offered to those who left through official ports, but those who left illegally—violating both Mexican and U.S. law—did so at their own risk, a problem that still plagues Mexico today.

During a speech before Congress on September 1, 1925, Calles described emigration as a bane to the Republic, but also to the emigrants themselves: they "were wickedly exploited and incapable of protecting themselves." Now that peace had been restored, it was the duty of the Mexican leadership to encourage their return and to keep them from leaving again.[46] The *Boletín Comercial*, an SRE publication, maintained in the mid-1920s that the only jobs readily available in the United States were low paying and limited to the building and upkeep of railroads. Mexicans obtained these jobs because Europeans and Americans avoided them due to their dangerous nature and low pay.[47]

Newly established migration offices in Torreón and Saltillo, Coahuila, two of the busiest points of departure for the United States, limited the sale of railroad passages, trying to compel emigrants to follow a procedure that provided them information about U.S. immigration laws, their rights, and how to contact the nearest consulate.[48] Furthermore, a law that became effective on December 26, 1926, required proof from emigrants that they met the receiving nation's minimum requirements for legal emigration, otherwise they would be denied a passport.[49] It required an identification card for both Mexicans and foreigners entering Mexico, which replaced the passports issued before the promulgation of the Constitution of 1917. Consuls were responsible for issuing the identification abroad, and the Department of Migration had the responsibility domestically. The card did not automatically permit legal departure; an emigrant still had to fulfill other regulations such as having a valid work contract.[50] It also restricted immigration to Mexico: requiring skills and resources that would benefit the Republic, making literacy and health requirements more rigorous, and preventing European and Asian migrants from using Mexico for entry into the United States (see chapter 14).[51]

After 1927 Calles's administration aggressively discouraged Mexicans from leaving while reducing government-sponsored repatriation, in concert with a plan to lessen the government's role, placing more responsibility on the individual who left for the United States. Migration offices enforcing the new regulations found that limited financial resources and personnel resulted in lengthy periods for processing paperwork and the emigrant's inability to meet all the requirements. Emigration without documents was more expedient.[52] Calles's administration deregulated the system for protecting emigrants, leaving only a rhetorical appeal to keep workers from leaving and protecting them when they still left. Government critics lamented the loss of human capital and argued that the escalating antagonism to Mexicans within the United States contributed to the abuse of Mexican emigrants: "The nation's gravest affliction is the outpouring of its greatest energy source, its people. . . . The Mexican government should not allow Americans to restrict Mexican citizens from entering the United States, but should instead restrict its citizens from leaving for the United States."[53]

The Mexican Response to the Great Depression

Even as Calles reduced the Mexican government's role, a storm rose on the horizon that tested that government's capacity to respond to emigrants' needs. Calles, who had demonstrated keen Machiavellian tactics with the creation of the Partido Nacional Revolucionario[54] after the assassination of President-elect Obregón, was unprepared for the severity of the Great Depression. By 1930 the Mexican consular system, including the *Comisiones* and *Brigadas*, was instrumental in implementing an unprecedented repatriation drive as the only means of protection available for their compatriots. Unfortunately, once in Mexico the repatriates found themselves without additional relief from their government. Many repatriates did not receive sufficient arable land or support such as agricultural credits that were absolutely necessary for their livelihood.

The administration of Lázaro Cárdenas (1934–40) was committed to implementing the goals of the Constitution of 1917 and sought to include the welfare of citizens in the United States as part of its developmental agenda. According to the plan Sexenal de Gobierno (1935), encouraging the compatriots in the United States to return, would help fulfill the objectives formulated at the Querétaro Convention. Ironically, policymakers determined that Mexico's sparse population was one of its most significant problems. The plan called for the return to relieve migrants of their misery abroad and for steps to prevent departures in the future.[55] Of course these goals were tied to the Cardenista agrarian reform program, which distributed 54 million acres of land to rural families and villages. However, by the end of Cárdenas's administration in 1940 it was clear that the *ejido* cooperatives such as that at Laguna and the henequen plantations in Yucatan were failures because of their declining production. Reasons were multiple and unfortunately not unfamiliar to Mexicans today: unresponsive bureaucracy, corrupt local officials, parcels of land that were too small and infertile, and lack of modern technology and implements.

United States Immigration Public Policy from the 1930s to the Present

The Great Depression

The Great Depression was not the first economic crisis that precipitated immigration troubles, but it lasted a decade; Mexican, and secondarily Canadian, immigrants felt its effects. Both had enjoyed free access to the United States even after the First World War and restrictive immigration legislation had curtailed arrivals from Europe. The open doors of the 1920s had allowed Mexicans to become more significant contributors to the U.S. economy and, at the same time, their remittances became an essential component of the Mexican economy. Because of the public's hostility toward immigrants, expressed in the 1920s quota acts, those who used Mexican labor or countenanced their arrival had to argue for their distinct traits. One of the common arguments, which actually fit the basic intentions of most Mexican immigrants, was that they were birds of passage, relatively submissive and docile, and inclined to return to Mexico rather than to settle permanently in the United States.[56] Their voluntary cycle of return was however often not seen as sufficient. Especially in times of economic crisis, various patriotic groups such as the Veterans of Foreign Wars and the American Legion led demands in some areas that Mexicans be "repatriated." The National Club of America for Americans called on all Americans to pressure their government to deport all Mexicans and close the border to all Latin Americans.[57] However, such outrageous demands by overly vocal fringe groups rarely had any real impact on public policy.

Nonetheless, as unemployment rose in 1929, President Herbert Hoover increased consular control over immigration from Mexico and the number of visas for entry declined—he followed the same policy in Canada and Europe. Although his administration, unlike that of his successor Franklin D. Roosevelt, did not seek to end local repatriation efforts, neither administration sought special laws to deport Mexicans or Canadians. The Great Depression, not public policy, minimized the northbound migration. Xenophobia may have driven many Mexicans and their Mexican American children home, but unemployment and dwindling economic opportunities were the primary causes of this mass exodus.

The Bracero Program

From 1942 to 1964 the United States and Mexico engaged in a series of bilateral agreements allowing for *braceros* to temporarily work in the United States for up to six months. Immediately following U.S. entry into the Second World War, agricultural employers throughout the Southwest claimed that labor shortages threatened the war effort. Mexican officials were initially reluctant to take part in another temporary labor program because of the harsh treatment Mexicans faced in the United States during the Great Depression, particularly in Texas. Ultimately, the administration of Manuel Avila Camacho, seeking improved relations, foreign loans, and investments, agreed to support another temporary worker initiative and, because it held the cards at the beginning of the arrangement, was able to shape early policy. After complaints about discrimination, for example, for a time it prohibited application of the program in Texas.[58]

The Bracero Program experienced three phases with Public Law 45 initiating Phase I from August 1942 until December 1947. During this period 250,000 *braceros* participated. Leaving aside the minority of guest workers from other regions, such as the Caribbean (chapter 6), and those from Mexico employed for railroad work only during the war, the typical *bracero* was a single male from rural west central Mexico who was either unemployed or severely underemployed, illiterate, and who spoke few words of English. Phase II, 1948–51, took place outside legal parameters as local officials, employers, and Mexican immigrants continued on despite the expiration of Public Law 45; there was no legitimate program during these three years. Two-thirds of the Mexican workers in the United States were originally undocumented workers, apprehended by officials from the Immigration and Naturalization Service (INS) and then transported to processing centers along the border. This phase was yet another example of lax legal enforcement that directly benefited U.S. employers, although it went unnoticed by the general public. A second agreement between the two nations introduced Phase III in 1951, after the Korean War prompted both governments to again formalize the process with Public Law 78. During this thirteen-year period 4.21 million *braceros* participated. These were older than the original cohort and more likely to have families.[59] After the war the Mexican government had much less influence over policy, since the United States did not face a war emergency labor shortage—instead those in favor of the program faced considerable public and union opposition. Mexico hoped, however, to continue both the income advantages of the wages and remittances of *braceros* and the political release it gave since these workers might in fact be unemployed and discontent in Mexico.

The McCarran-Walter Act (1952)

In the 1950s controlling the border and regulating the undocumented immigration process evolved into competing domestic and foreign policy objectives for the first time since the 1930s. The Bracero Program encouraged increased flows of both documented and undocumented migrants into the United States, which conditioned employers to depend on inexpensive field labor from Mexico.[60] Within the context of the Cold War, U.S. policymakers had to mediate between employers' demands for continued access to Mexican labor and having to maintain the appearance of secure borders. Furthermore, divisions within the Mexican American community also reflected the complexity of this struggle. According to David Gutiérrez, "many Mexican American organizational spokesmen seemed to have succumbed to the increasingly common cold war notion that communists were somehow slipping into the country with illegal aliens from Mexico and other Latin American nations."[61] Pro-labor groups (including Mexican American organizations such as National Agricultural Workers' Union) argued that Mexican immigrant labor lowered wages and created unfair competition for low-skilled employment.

In 1951 President Truman complained to his Mexican counterpart about the growing illegal immigration problem: "I am anxious to see progress made toward improving working conditions and living standards for our own citizens and for the contract workers from Mexico who are employed on our farms . . . But if these things are to occur the governments of the United States and Mexico must take steps to shut off the stream of Mexican citizens immigrating illegally into the United States."[62] Truman's ability to secure the support of President Miguel Alemán was partly based on the goodwill he had gained by helping settle a dispute between the U.S. Railroad Retirement Fund and the Mexican government. During the Second World War 160,000 Mexican railroad workers had contributed $6 million into the fund, and after the war Mexican officials requested that their workers' share be paid. "It took the direct intervention of President Truman to return the money, with 3.5 percent interest."[63]

Nonetheless, the Bracero Program had inadvertently reignited additional components of the large-scale Mexican migration stream, including workers who overstayed their work permits and clandestine border crossers. U.S. policymakers failed to assess which offense was the more significant violation: undocumented immigration, illicit employer hiring practices, or labor smuggling. Still, public policy allowed the three components to coexist for the sake of the economic health of Southwestern employers dependent upon Mexican labor and the political health of politicians dependent upon these employers.

As is the case today, employers argued that disrupting the flow of exploitable labor could damage the economy, particularly in the Southwest. Raising wages and formal recognition of the undocumented population would not be cost effective. Truman and Eisenhower had to control the U.S. border from a real or imagined potential communist threat, while simultaneously allowing for an adequate labor supply for U.S. employers.

Despite attention to undocumented immigration, it did not figure greatly in immigration policy. Playing on communist fears and on the continued hostility of Americans to immigrants and refugees, Senator Pat McCarran and Congressman Francis Walter designed an act that continued the ethnically biased quota system erected in the 1920s for all countries, while trying to evade charges of racism by extending small quotas to Asian countries. Mexico and other Western Hemisphere countries continued to enjoy most-favored-nation status in that there were no statutory limits on their immigration. The act addressed illegal immigration by imposing draconian penalties: "Importing, transporting and harboring" undocumented immigrants became felony offenses, and the INS could search private property, but not homes, for undocumented workers.

For employers the most important provision was the Texas Proviso, which protected them from prosecution for hiring undocumented workers. The only major initiative against Mexican undocumented workers was Operation Wetback (1954), which authorities claimed "expelled over one million undocumented immigrants." It is doubtful such massive expulsion occurred, and it is highly probable that most of those deported quickly returned. But some argue that its basic result was to cause fearful immigrants to accept the poorest working conditions and lowest-paying jobs.[64]

The Hart-Celler Act (1965)

The Hart-Celler Act terminated the racist quota system that had been in place since 1921, replaced it with equal opportunity to persons from any country or region, and prioritized family reunification. The quota laws had to be abolished, according to most commentators, because, as Senator Edward Kennedy stated, they had been "conceived in a period of bigotry and reaffirmed in the McCarthy era."[65] But the new law's most critical provision for the *creation* of mass illegal immigration was that it established national and hemispheric quotas and an overall annual immigration level. Though Italians, for example, were no longer limited to 5,645 persons per year (as dictated by the revisions made in 1952 of the 1921 quota bills), the Eastern Hemisphere could, in sum, provide only 170,000 and no one country more than 20,000 of these. Such limits would not in fact have much effect on Italy, since by the 1960s few Italians intended to immigrate to the United States.

But for Mexico these provisions made illegal immigration highly probable, since it had never had a quota. Moreover, Mexican workers had just lost the opportunity to migrate as official guest workers. The struggle between growers using this labor and union forces and their liberal allies over the Bracero Program ended in 1964 with the end of the program.[66] At the time Mexican American workers competed with these *braceros*, evidenced by the opposition of Cesar Chavez's United Farm Workers (UFW) to Mexican immigration, into the 1970s. This competitive condition would dissipate as Mexican Americans moved into higher-paying jobs—one result would be the decline in Mexican American opposition to Mexican immigration.

The Bracero Program's termination, the Hart-Celler Act and its country limits, and ironically the success of Mexico in improving public health, evident in a sharply rising population, created the conditions of mass illegal immigration. While the Mexican economy had shown significant growth in the mid-twentieth century, Mexico's high birthrate ensured a rate of population growth that exceeded job creation in the economy—as had happened in Catholic Quebec a century earlier. Wages remained four and five times higher north of the border. These factors largely guaranteed that the number of persons strongly desiring to enter the United States would exceed the number legally allowed.

While prioritizing family reunification, immigrants with exceptional abilities, and labor for occupations with labor shortages, some provisions of Hart-Celler had nonetheless "proven inadequate, others had triggered unanticipated consequences, and new issues emerged with which the existing system proved unable to cope."[67] The U.S. Border Patrol registered 110,371 apprehensions in 1965 and 1,348,749 in 1985—the sixth year since 1977 that apprehensions exceed one million.[68] Although estimates for the size of the undocumented migration stream are difficult to verify, some studies claim that for every illegal immigrant captured, two to three others enter successfully, the majority being Mexican or Central American.[69]

As stated earlier, the law of 1968 placed a ceiling of 120,000 on immigration from the Western Hemisphere, and in 1976 an annual ceiling of 20,000 was added for each Western Hemispheric nation. Given the characteristics noted before, Mexicans dominated the number of applicants for legal entry: in 1974, for example, 45,364 persons applied for legal entry. The numerical ceiling was clearly out of touch with demand. In 1976 alone there were 300,000 applicants per year and a two-and-a-half-year backlog for approval.[70] Consequently, in the mid-1980s U.S. policy had to once again realign immigration policy to address the unexpected consequences of the current legislation while focusing on protecting the health of the economy and addressing prevailing societal sentiment regarding race and ethnicity.

The Immigration Reform and Control Act (1986)

The Immigration Reform and Control Act (IRCA), which represents the last major revision of the Immigration Act of 1965, contained three principal provisions: sanctions for employers who knowingly hired or recruited undocumented workers, increased enforcement measures along the border, and an amnesty program for undocumented workers who could prove that they had completed at least ninety days of farm work in 1985–86 or for illegal aliens who had continuously resided in the United States since 1982. For the 2.3 million Mexican immigrants who obtained legal status, IRCA was a success. For immigrants such as Apolonia Calderon of Palm Desert, California, amnesty doubled her wages, protected her from abuse on the job and in the street, and allowed her to obtain U.S. citizenship in May 2006.[71]

Unfortunately IRCA's long-term consequences drastically disrupted the seasonal migration process, encouraging permanent residence in the United States.[72] The amnesty provision attracted further undocumented arrivals and encouraged other Mexicans to think that further reprieves might be enacted, although to date it has been the only major amnesty. "Of the IRCA applicants, about 1.8 million were in the 245A program, and about 1.2 million were in the SAW (Special Agricultural Worker) program. While the numbers in the first program were somewhat lower than predicted, those in the SAW program were two and three times higher than expected."[73] Amnesty recipients and other undocumented immigrants who succeeded in obtaining papers had a cumulative effect larger than their own numbers. Over three-fourths of all U.S. legal admissions are a product of the family reunification provisions stemming from the Hart-Celler Act: each legal immigrant had the right to sponsor immediate family members, including spouses, children, and siblings. The multiplying effect leads to growth in the immigrant population based on the size of the most recent to arrive, in this case Latinos (largely Mexican) and to a lesser degree Asians. Employer sanctions in the 1986 act were never applied—the "knowingly" clause was a powerful form of protection that employers made sure was part of the act, since courts were unlikely to rule an employer guilty as long as its workers provided some form of legal identification. Employers did not have to verify the documents required to legally work in the United States, which in turn led to a large market for fraudulent documents. Even if wary about the increased documentation demands, employers could and did resort to subcontractors to fulfill their labor demands, allowing them to avoid prosecution for hiring undocumented workers. Moreover, neither Republican nor Democratic administrations devoted much attention or resources to internal enforcement.

Indeed, despite the act's rhetoric, border enforcement actually fell after its implementation (arrests along the border fell from 1.6 million in 1986 to 830,000 in 1989). As a result of the promise of amnesty and the emptiness of any punishment for employers or for illegal arrival, seasonal migrants simply quit crossing back and forth, because the amnesty program required that they stay in the United States while their legalization process was resolved and because they were required to take English and civics classes. In the 1990s border enforcement began to constitute an actual threat to crossers (for example with Operation Gatekeeper), and the "coyotes" who arranged clandestine trips began charging higher fees. As a result, according to Jorge Durand, Douglass Massey, and Emilio Parrado, seasonal migration fell sharply. They argue, and many agree, that undocumented immigrants simply tried repeatedly to cross until they succeeded, and then did not risk a return. As a result, the population of permanent illegal immigrants began to rise, which also meant a stronger impetus for women and family members to cross and join men now committed to the United States.[74]

In addition to promoting the growth of the Mexican population, amnesty and legalization programs also allowed undocumented workers to come out of the shadows of work available to them and enter more lucrative economic sectors. Agricultural workers left the fields with their legalized status in hand and pursued urban employment. Legalization meant that new opportunities for the formerly undocumented created even greater labor shortages for commercial growers. This change in employment was another cause for more permanent stays in the United States rather than seasonal migration. Urban non-seasonal jobs offered limited time for travel to Mexico, and even those who remained in seasonal agricultural jobs were now eligible for unemployment compensation in the United States.[75]

The politics of the 1986 act also proved the near complete shift away from hostility toward a welcoming of Mexican immigrants—legal or undocumented—among Mexican American leaders and organizations. Drawing first on the civil rights agitation of the 1960s, especially by Chicano activists, and on a subsequent broad identification of racial unity proclaimed by organizations like La Raza Unida Council, the tenor of Mexican American comment on immigration shifted toward acceptance of all Mexicans as co-ethnics and consequently to strong approval of amnesty programs. From this point forward, such organizations would form a major political force in congressional activity in immigration, seeking tolerant immigration laws and paths to citizenship for undocumented immigrants.[76]

Conclusion

During the twentieth century Mexican immigration to the United States became a fundamental component of the U.S. and Mexican economies. The intimate relationship has transcended world wars, governmental changes, depression, economic policies, the Cold War, and the rise of global terrorism. The century has seen other developed nations confront mass immigration induced by similar factors: sharp differences in average wages, foreign policy, legacies of colonial periods, globalization, and refugees' demands have all led to mass movements across national boundaries. But none of these movements possesses a tradition as long as that between Mexico and the United States. Although the intake of large numbers of migrants has presented significant challenges for receiving countries, their presence has also provided many benefits, most importantly inexpensive labor. Mexicans working in the United States constitute one such example, which along with their posterity finalized that contribution, becoming citizens of the United States and forming a large part of the population.

As we have seen, Mexico's emigration is not primarily driven by a poor, undeveloped economy. According to Durand and Massey, "international immigration does not arise from a lack of economic development, but from development itself."[77] The origins of mass emigration from Mexico lie in the initial industrial and transportation development in Mexico in the late nineteenth century, and it grew even during the era of the "Mexican Miracle," 1940–70, when the Mexican "economy grew at a rate of over 6 percent per year, a rate superior to all other Latin American countries except Brazil."[78] Mexicans continued migrating to the United States as temporary workers, undocumented workers, and legal immigrants.

Recent debates in the United States about illegal immigration from Mexico have largely ignored the long history. While the volume of undocumented or illegal migration is the result of particular conditions after 1965, the Mexican immigration, migration, repatriation, and settlement have been part of the history of both countries for more than a century. Current disputes often focus only on illegality or on segments of the U.S. or Mexican societies, rather than on larger structural issues such as shared histories, free trade commitments, and international accords. The many Mexican-origin persons concentrated in the Southwest have become an integrated part of the region's population—they claimed this region from before the Mexican-American war, and they have been a formidable part of its population since the early twentieth century. In the last third of the twentieth century Mexicans settled in other parts of the country and thus became ever more similar to other immigrant groups with a long history, such as Italians. Policy changes present but new chapters in an old history. Hardly ever was the intense interchange between the two societies interrupted and, one imagines, the interchange will persist even after the pronounced economic downturn provoked by the financial collapse of September 2008.

Notes

1 "'Hispanic' or 'Latino' refer to persons who trace their origin or descent to Western Hemisphere countries colonized by Spain, where Spanish is the primary language. Origin can be considered as the heritage, nationality group, lineage, or country of birth of the person or the person's ancestors. People who identify as Hispanic or Latino may be of any race." "About the Hispanic Population of the United States," U.S. Census Bureau, http://www.census.gov/.

2 "Hispanic Population Reaches All-Time High of 38.8 Million, New Census Bureau Estimates Show," *U.S. Census Bureau News*, June 18, 2003. http://www.census.gov.

3 "Statistical Portrait of the Foreign-Born Population in the United States, 2006," Pew Hispanic Center, http://pewhispanic.org, January 23, 2008, table 3; and Jeffrey S. Passel, "Unauthorized Migrants: Numbers and Characteristics," Pew Hispanic Center, June 14, 2005, http://pewhispanic.org/.

4 CIA World Fact Book, June 22, 2007, https://www.cia.gov.

5 Jorge Ramos, "The Mexican Election: A Talk with Carlos Fuentes," July 12, 2006, http://www.jorgeramos.com.

6 Irish immigration has almost as long a history, beginning in the 1840s and persisting, though at a greatly diminished rate, into the early twentieth century. For Ger-

mans, the largest single ancestry group, large-scale immigration lasted for about fifty years, and for Italians, Poles, and others in the early twentieth century less than thirty years.

7   "Are the Immigration Protests Creating a Backlash?" *Time*, March 29, 2006.

8   Maps and other data presented in this section are Brian Gratton's calculations from data drawn from the Integrated Public Use Samples of the United States Censuses (IPUMS). Steven Ruggles, Mathew Sobek, Trent Alexander, Catherine A. Fitch, Ronald Goeken, Patricia Kelly Hall, Miriam King, and Chad Ronnander, Integrated Public Use Microdata Series: Version 4.0 [machine-readable database] (Minneapolis: Minnesota Population Center, 2008), http://usa.ipums.org/usa.

9   Daniel D. Arreola and James R. Curtis, *The Mexican Border Cities: Landscape Anatomy and Place Personality* (Tucson: University of Arizona Press, 1993).

10 Gunther Peck, *Reinventing Free Labor: Padrones and Immigrant Workers in the North American West, 1880–1930* (Cambridge: Cambridge University Press, 2000); F. Krissman, "Sin Coyote Ni Patrón: Why the 'Migrant Network' Fails to Explain International Migration," *International Migration Review* 39, no. 1 (2005), 4–44.

11 Maps and figures from Myron P. Gutmann, Robert McCaa, Rodolfo Gutiérrez-Montes, and Brian Gratton. "Los efectos demográfios de la revolución Mexicana en Estados Unidos," *Historia Mexicana* 50, no. 3 (2000), 145–65.

12 Ibid.

13 Manuel Gamio, *Mexican Immigration to the United States: A Study of Human Migration and Adjustment* (Chicago: University of Chicago Press, 1930). To review these maps go to http://nacts.asu.edu/the-north-american-migration-project.

14 E. K. Merchant, Brian Gratton, and Myron P. Gutmann, "Race and Deportation: Mexicans in the 1930 and 1940 Censuses" (paper presented at Social Science History Association, Miami, October 2008).

15 Francisco E. Balderrama and Raymond Rodriguez, *Decade of Betrayal: Mexican Repatriation in the 1930s* (Albuquerque: University of New Mexico Press, 2006), 151, states: "it is reasonable to estimate that the total number of repatriates was approximately one million."

16 Fernando Saúl Alanís Enciso, "¿Cuántos fueron? La repatriación de mexicanos en los Estados Unidos durante la Gran Depresión: Una interpretación cuantitativa 1930–1934," *Aztlán: A Journal of Chicano Studies* 32, no. 2 (2007), 65–91, and *Que se queden allá: El gobierno de México y la repatriación de mexicanos de Estados Unidos, 1934–1940* (México: Colegio de la Frontera Norte, 2007).

17 F. Arturo Rosales, *¡Pobre Raza!: Violence, Justice, and Mobilization Among México Lindo Immigrants, 1900–1936* (Austin: University of Texas Press, 1999), 5–6.

18 Díaz entered Mexico City on November 23, 1876, after defeating his last major opposition at the battle of Tecoac. He was elected president on May 5, 1877.

19 Minister of Foreign Relations to Consuls on the Border, October 2, 1877, Archivo Histórico de la Secretaría de Relaciones Exteriores, 2-1-1785.F. 2–4, in Angela Moyano Pahissa, *Protección consular a Mexicanos en los Estados Unidos, 1849–1900* (Mexico City: Archivo Histórico Diplomático Mexicano, 1989), 137–38.

20 Moisés González Navarro, *Los extranjeros en México y los mexicanos en el extranjero, 1821–1970*, 3 vols. (Mexico City: El Colegio de México, 1994), 2:125; and *La colonización en México, 1877–1910* (Mexico City: Talls. de Imp. de Estampillas y Valores, 1960), 1–6.

21 "Solicitan replantear el programa de repatriación humana," *La Red del Norte*, November 6, 2008, http://www.masnoticias.net/id.pl?id=10877&relax=&pub=Congreso%20Estatal&mensub=Politica; and Arturo Rentería, "Apoyan con trabajo a 90 repatriados," *El Mañana*, November 30, 2008. http://www.elmanana.com.

22 Friedrich Katz, *The Life and Times of Pancho Villa* (Stanford: Stanford University Press, 1998), 49.

23 *El Imparcial*, February 6, 1907.

24 González Navarro, *Los extranjeros en México*, 2:380.

25 Lawrence Cardoso, *Mexican Emigration to the United States, 1897–1931* (Tucson: University of Arizona Press, 1980), 31; Francisco I. Madero, *La sucesión presidencial en 1910*, 3rd ed. (Mexico City: Editora Nacional, 1974), 211–21.

26 Cardoso, *Mexican Emigration*, 55–56.

27 Alan Knight, *The Mexican Revolution: Porfirians, Liberals and Peasants*, vol. 1 (Lincoln: University of Nebraska Press, 1990), 433.

28 González Navarro, *Los extranjeros en México*, 3:80.

29 Gamio, *Mexican Immigration to the United States*, 159–69.

30 John Womack, "The Mexican Economy during the Revolution, 1910–1920: Historiography and Analysis," *Marxist Perspectives* 1 (1978), 80–123.

31 Now Piedras Negras.

32 Consul in Eagle Pass, Texas, to the Consulate Inspector in San Antonio, Texas, September 30, 1913, Archivo Histórico de la Secretaría de Relaciones Exteriores LE-842, f. 113-R-13, 56; and Consul in Eagle Pass, Texas, to the Consulate Inspector in San Antonio, Texas, October 2, 1913, Archivo Histórico de la Secretaría de Relaciones Exteriores LE-842, f. 113-R-13, 100, cited in Douglas Richmond, ed., *La Frontera: México-Estados Unidos durante la epoca revolucionaria, 1910–1920* (Saltillo: Gobierno del Estado de Coahuila, 1996), 23–24.

33 Subsecretario de Gobernación to Secretario de Fomento, October 3, 1913, Archivo General de la Nación, Departamento de Trabajo (hereafter cited as AGN-DT), 1913-8-31.

34 Ibid.

35 Military Commander in Ciudad Porfirio Díaz to Governor of Coahuila, March 10, 1914, Archivo General del Estado de Coahuila, Saltillo LE-335, exp. 48, cited in Richmond, *La Frontera*, 24.

36 Article 123 of the 1917 Constitution, "Proyecto de Ley Sobre Reforma del Articulo 123," October 6, 1921, AGN-DT volume 322-exp. 4–6.

37 Oficial Mayor SRE to All Migration Inspectors Along the Border, March 20, 1918, Records of the Department of State (RDS) 812.111/36 (0080–81), roll 107, cited in Douglas Richmond, "Mexican Immigration and Border Strategy During the Revolution, 1910–1920," *New Mexico Historical Review* 57, no. 3 (1982), 269–88, 276.

38 *Diario Oficial*, March 21, 1918, circular no. 9, cited in Richmond, "Mexican Immigration," 279.

39 Lawrence A. Cardoso, "La repatriación de braceros en época de Obregón, 1920–1923," *Historia Mexicana* 26, no. 4 (1977), 576–95, 589.

40 Linda B. Hall, "Alvaro Obregón and Mexican Migrant Labor to the United States, 1920–1924," *La ciudad y el campo en la historia de México: Memoria de la VII reunión de historiadores Mexicanos y Norteamericanos* (Oaxaca: Universidad Nacional Autónoma de México, 1992), 764.

41 Hall, "Alvaro Obregón and Mexican Migrant Labor," 763; Informe oficial al Presidente Alvaro Obregón, June 10, 1922, Archivo General de la Nación, vol. 711 exp. M-30; Informes de las repatriaciones autorizadas en el més de enero de 1922, Archivo Histórico de la Secretaría de Relaciones Exteriores 36-16-318.

42 Manuel Gamio, *Quantitative Estimates: Sources and Distribution of Mexican Immigration into the United States* (Mexico City: Talleres Gráficos Editorial and the "Diario Oficial," 1930), table III.

43 Francisco E. Balderrama, "México de afuera y los consulados mexicanos, 1900–1940," *Revista Mexicana de Ciencias Políticas y Sociales* 27 (1981), 104–5, 175–85, 179.

44 Jesús Franco, *El alma de la raza: Narraciones históricas de episodios y la vida de los Mexicanos residentes in los Estados Unidos del Norte América: la repatriación. La vida y origen de las Comisiones Honoríficas Mexicanas y la Cruz Azul Mexicana* (El Paso: La Patria, n.d.), 7.

45 Memorandum from Mexican Consul in Phoenix, Arizona, Renato Cantú Lara, to Consul General in El Paso, Texas, December 29, 1931, Archivo Histórico de la Secretaría de Relaciones Exteriores IV-339-23.

46 *Diario de los debates de la Cámara de Diputados*, September 1, 1925, cited in Moisés González Navarro, *Los extranjeros*, 3:32–33.

47 *Boletín Comercial*, April 10, 1925.

48 Ibid.

49 Secretaría de Gobernación, *Ley de Migración de los Estados Unidos Mexicanos* (Mexico City: Talleres Grafícos de la Nación, 1926), article 17.

50 Ibid., articles 14–15.

51 Ibid.

52 *El Universal*, May 19, 1927.

53 Ibid., May 16, 1927.

54 The Partido Nacional Revolucionario, founded in 1929, was the precursor to the Partido Revolucionario Institutional, the party name since 1946.

55 Andres Landa y Piña, *Política demográfica estatuida en el Plan Sexenal* (Mexico City, 1935), 3–4.

56 Mae M. Ngai, *Impossible Subjects: Illegal Aliens and the Making of Modern America* (Princeton: Princeton University Press, 2004), 50, and Camille Guerin-Gonzales, *Mexican Workers and American Dreams: Immigration, Repatriation, and California Farm Labor, 1900–1939* (New Brunswick: Rutgers University Press, 1994), 25–47.

57 Balderrama and Rodriguez, *Decade of Betrayal*, 68.

58 David G. Gutiérrez, *Walls and Mirrors: Mexican Americans, Mexican Immigrants, and the Politics of Ethnicity* (Berkeley: University of California Press, 1995), 160.

59 Matt S. Meier and Feliciano Rivera, *Mexican Americans/American Mexicans: From Conquistadors to Chicanos* (New York: Hill and Wang, 1993), 184.

60 Paul Ganster and David E. Lorey, *The U.S.-Mexican Border into the Twenty-first Century* (Lanham, Md.: Rowman and Littlefield, 2008), 118–19.

61 Gutiérrez, *Walls and Mirrors*, 162.

62 Harry S. Truman to Miguel Alemán, July 14, 1951; Migratory Labor Folder 17, Mexican Labor, 1951 [3 of 4], Truman Papers, Truman Library.

63 William G. MacLean to Harry S. Truman, July 19, 1946, Truman Library, official file 146, cited in Stephen R. Niblo, *War Diplomacy and Development: The United States and Mexico, 1938–1954* (Wilmington, Del.: Scholarly Resources, 1995), 251.

64 Ibid., 132, and Roger Daniels, *Guarding the Golden Door: American Immigration Policy and Immigrants since 1882* (New York: Hill and Wang, 2004), 120–21.

65 Edward M. Kennedy, "The Immigration Act of 1965," *Annals of the American Academy of Political and Social Science* 367 (1966), 137–49, 137.

66 Vernon Briggs, *Immigration Policy and the American Labor Force* (Baltimore: Johns Hopkins University Press, 1984), 101.

67 Briggs, *Immigration Policy*, 61.

68 U.S. Department of Justice, *Statistical Yearbook of the Immigration and Naturalization Service, 1996* (Washington: U.S. Government Printing Office, 1997), 173.

69 U.S. Congress, House, Committee on Appropriations. Subcommittee on Departments of State, Justice, Commerce, the Judiciary, and Related Agencies Appropriations for 1981, *Hearings Before a Subcommittee of the Committee on Appropriations*, 95th Cong., 2nd sess., 1980, 32, and Briggs, *Immigration Policy*, 134.

70 Briggs, *Immigration Policy*, 67.

71 "86 Amnesty Frames Immigration Debate," *Los Angeles Times*, June 3, 2006.

72 Briggs, *Immigration Policy*, 61.

73 David North, "Lessons Learned from the Legalization Program of the 1980s," Center for Immigration Studies, January 2005, http://www.cis.org; Philip L. Martin, "Good Intentions Gone Awry: IRCA and US Agriculture," *Annals of the American Academy of Political and Social Science* 534 (1994), 44–57, 48–49.

74 Jorge Durand, Douglas S. Massey, and Emilio Parrado, "The New Era of Mexican Migration to the United States," *Journal of American History* 86, no. 2 (1999), 518–36, 524.

75 Ibid., 698.

76 Gutiérrez, *Walls and Mirrors*, 181–82.

77 Jorge Durand and Douglas S. Massey, "Borderline Sanity," *American Prospect* 12 (2001) 17, 28.

78 Douglas W. Richmond, *The Mexican Nation: Historical Continuity and Modern Change* (Upper Saddle River, N.J.: Prentice Hall, 2002), 315.

CHAPTER TWO

Through the Northern Borderlands

Canada-U.S. Migrations in the Nineteenth and Twentieth Centuries

Bruno Ramirez

When the decennial U.S. census figures from 1900 were made public, they showed the number of Canadian-born living in the United States as 1,179,922, or 22 percent of Canada's entire population. Adding their U.S.-born children, the number more than doubled, equalling 54.8 percent.[1] At roughly the same time the Canadian census of 1901 was showing that 13 percent of the Dominion's population that year consisted of foreign-born people, some from the United States, the majority from Europe. These rather simple figures are very suggestive of what Marcus Hansen and John Brebner called "the mingling of the Canadian and American peoples," while simultaneously capturing a striking aspect of the history of North Atlantic and intracontinental migration and in particular the role that Canada played in the international circuits of labor and migration.[2]

Migration from British North America (which later became the Canadian Dominion) into the American republic has marked continental history throughout much of the nineteenth and twentieth centuries. As early as the 1830s British colonial authorities expressed deep concern for "the exodus of young people from Lower Canada," and soon French Canadian elites employed the expression "exode" to denounce the conditions that pushed many thousands of their young people to work in the United States.[3] The same expression would later resound in many districts of Atlantic Canada, as county after county was depopulated.[4] In many ways this continental southward flow of population and labor can be best understood by adopting a regional scale of observation.

Migration from French Canada

Throughout much of the nineteenth century French Canada remained an agrarian society, despite the growing importance of proto-industrial activities and a few commercial centers such as Quebec City, Three-Rivers, and Montreal. The coexistence of commercial and subsistence agriculture proved insufficient to sustain the natural growth of this rural population, whose birthrate was one of the highest in the western world.[5] Moreover, in the absence of adequate public policies to encourage the settlement of largely forested hinterland regions, rural French Canadians began to overflow from the old parishes toward commercial centers and increasingly across the border into the United States. By mid-century the southward population movement seemed irreversible, as ascertained by a public inquiry in Quebec in 1857. While the majority crossed into rural districts of neighboring states, and a few joined the expanding agricultural frontier in the American Midwest, a growing number migrated seasonally to work in canal and railroad construction and logging, thus providing a significant labor input to the initial phase of industrialization associated with antebellum America.[6]

Despite the multidirectional nature of these cross-border flows, two sections in the United States acted as major magnets: the Great Lakes region, owing—at least initially—to the previous existence of French Canadian enclaves that had survived the decline of the fur trade; and New England, on account of the geographical proximity of its expanding labor markets. On the eve of the Civil War Michigan, Illinois, and Wisconsin had become the destination for nearly half of all French Canadians residing in the United States. Of these, Michigan soon rose as the leading pole of French-Canadian settlement. One key factor was the pull exerted by the forestry industry, whose rapid development by the 1860s had made Michigan the major producer state in the union. Many French-Canadian lumberjacks had followed the industry in its continental move from east to west; others, encouraged by improvements in fluvial and rail transportation, joined in Michigan as enclaves and communities started to multiply. By 1885 French Canadians made up 13 percent of the valley's population, with more than half of their labor force employed in logging operations and sawmills, thus making them the largest immigrant group within the valley's forestry industry.[7]

In the northern section of Michigan, known as the Keweenaw Peninsula, French Canadians began to arrive in the 1850s. To a large extent their early arrival and subsequent influx were related to the rapid growth of copper mining and its centrality in the region's economy. So acute was the labor shortage in this sector that on many occasions employers sent recruiting agents across the border to entice Canadians with the promise of higher wages. By the end of the century French Canadians made up 12 percent of the peninsula's population and had created a stable institutional network. Not surprisingly, mining-related work became the leading single sector of occupation among French Canadians, followed by logging and a variety of service-related occupations.[8] Among the manufacturing centers of the Midwest, Detroit exerted the most important pull for French Canadians. By 1900 they had become the leading immigrant group after the British, the Anglo-Canadians, and the Polish and were engaged primarily in unskilled and semiskilled occupations.[9]

Despite the importance of this westward movement, by the end of the century, for every French Canadian migrating to Great Lakes states four more were choosing New England as their destination. It was mostly after the Civil War that hard-pressed rural French Canadians began to discover the opportunities of the New England textile mills. Geographical proximity and the integration of Quebec into the region's railway network were key contributing factors. Although this integration had begun in the 1850s, it was primarily after the postwar railroad boom that it reached the major centers of the province. Now French Canadians only had to travel to the closest rail junction to reach any major urban center in New England in less than a day. These factors help explain the rapid redirection of the migration flows that had linked Quebec to New England. In fact, while during the antebellum era the main destinations were the rural districts of neighboring states (in 1850 65 percent of all French Canadians in New England resided in Vermont), during the last third of the century the majority migrated farther south, to Massachusetts, Rhode Island, and New Hampshire, to the textile industry's heartland.[10]

Textile manufacturing was the first industrial sector to experience mechanization on a large scale, and the first that from the very beginning relied on cheaper wages paid to women and children.[11] It was the ideal context for various family members to access waged work. Arriving in Fall River in 1899 with her parents and siblings, Elmire Boucher recounted how often French Canadians lied about their children's ages so that they could work: "Arriving families would bring their children to the mills and just say they were fourteen years old. I know some who have gone to work at the mills at the age of ten, my own husband among them. They did not ask you for any certificate."[12] Such practices were quite frequent and suggest the extent to which textile manufacturing enabled these migrants to rely on the earnings of various family members.

Findings drawn from the state of Rhode Island illustrate how the migration of families and entire kinship networks became the predominant pattern. In 1880 80.4 percent of French-Canadian children aged eleven to fifteen were employed, while 8.5 percent attended school. The manuscript census schedules do not specify the sectors of employment, but they clearly indicate that the majority of French Canadians who went to Rhode Island chose cities such as Woonsocket and Pawtucket, the state's main textile centers.[13] A similar scenario emerges from studies of the other New England textile-production states.[14] Not surprisingly, children were a major component of this population flow, with the family acting as a key vehicle of spatial mobility. In Rhode Island in 1880 about 30 percent of French-Canadian immigrants were children aged fourteen and younger, with 81 percent of this population composed of nuclear families.[15] But while textile manufacturing was the main factor setting off and sustaining this regional cross-border migration flow, French Canadian immigrants, especially adult males, accessed a variety of other employment sectors, as the more accurate twentieth-century data indicate.

Migration from the Maritimes

For much of the nineteenth century the timber trade and shipbuilding were the two sectors responsible for inserting the Maritimes' economy into some of the major routes of international trade. These sectors created a sort of symbiotic relationship with a mostly rural population practicing subsistence farming. A similar relationship existed with the third-most important sector of activity: fishing. Though never a major industry, fishing was the main activity in most coastal villages and was practiced in combination with subsistence farming. In many ways farmer-fishermen were perpetuating a way of life that had become a century-old tradition.[16]

Much of the early migration from this region grew out of the mobility patterns engendered by these three main sectors of the local economy. As the perimeter of that mobility enlarged, it became increasingly frequent for Nova Scotians to take up work on U.S. fishing vessels, for naval craftsmen to join building crews in the yards of Rhode Island, or for New Brunswick farmers to seek better wages in lumber camps in Maine. Soon, however, the region would enter a period of important economic change that disrupted long-established ways of life and work. The 1860s to the 1890s could be characterized as a period of economic reconversion that entailed the restructuring of some sectors, the creation of new ones, and the elimination or disappearance of others. Its overall effect was continued growth, which also engendered considerable dislocations, namely by changes in the utilization and processing of natural resources, the introduction of new technologies, the penetration of factory-produced consumer goods into the countryside, and most importantly the localization of new productive activities.[17] Many local labor markets were disrupted and long-established occupational patterns undermined.

Despite new opportunities and development, the economy proved unable to absorb the vast population on the move. For many Maritimers this was a step in an ongoing migration that ultimately took them outside their region; for the majority this meant the United States. While the available sources do not distinguish migrations that ended (if temporarily) in a nearby district or province from those that ended in the United States, it is very likely that step-migration characterized these mobility patterns: first toward commercial and industrial districts, then farther away, beyond the region's border to Ontario, the Canadian West, and most importantly the United States. From 1871 to 1901 the Maritimes would lose approximately a quarter of a million people to the United States, much of it during the 1880s and 1890s. During each one of these two decades the losses corresponded to 10.5 percent of the region's total population, the highest in those years in Canada.[18]

The trend toward cross-border migration had already become visible in the early stages of the exodus when in 1880–81 three out of four Maritimers residing outside their region were in the United States. By then the largest proportion of Maritimers had chosen industrial New England. Much as for Quebeckers, the rapid growth of the textile and leather industries after the Civil War provided ample job opportunities for young Maritime women, whose role in the household economy was increasingly undermined by cheaply produced consumer goods. But it was the greater Boston district that became by far the leading destination. The New England metropolis had long been a crucial reference point both for its economic opportunities and cultural attraction. As the exodus intensified, craftsmen and tradesmen put their skills to profit in Boston. Soon they became the dominant force in the local building industry, in the shipyards as carpenters, making inroads in commercial activities, and in a variety of white-collar sectors. Equally important, Boston afforded ample opportunities to Maritime women, who generally migrated in larger numbers than men. The majority found employment as domestics, but for many others the New England metropolis offered opportunities in nursing, sales, and office work.[19]

Migration from Ontario

Ontario too lost a significant portion of its population to the migration movement toward the United States, especially during the last third of the century. Much as in the other two regions, outmigration was part of wider, complex population movements sparked by rapid and profound changes encompassing much of Ontario's economic base and society. During the last third of the century the region that in earlier decades had been "the granary of two continents" had to face new challenges from developments in international trade and, increasingly, the domestic market. The most momentous development was the abrogation in 1866 of the Reciprocity Treaty with the United States, resulting in the loss of what for over a decade had been the major market for Ontario's agricultural products. This, coupled with a period of severe instability in the international price of wheat, spelled the end of the "wheat boom era."[20]

Along with the decline of wheat trade, crop failures, soil exhaustion, and the scarcity of new land also brought chaos and insecurity to many rural counties and districts. However, this did not prevent farmers with sufficient capital and other means from turning to mechanization, which significantly reduced the need for farm labor and became one of the main factors contributing to rural depopulation.[21] The growing scarcity of arable land also caused population pressures. By the 1850s the Ontario farming frontier had been pushed to its physical limits, with only a few tracts of marginal Crown land left for settlement. Rural Ontario's relatively high fertility rate, coupled with the constant arrival of land-seeking immigrants, made land availability a major problem. It touched both long-established farming districts and areas of new settlement, making it difficult for farmers to establish their sons on the land. These economic transformations also affected the largest stratum of the province's agrarian population, the smallholders. In the absence of an easily marketable cash crop, and faced with the unequal competition from commercial farmers, most smallholders' only alternative was wage labor; increasingly, that meant moving to where jobs could be found.[22]

The extent of rural depopulation at the province-wide level emerges eloquently from census statistics. During the last three decades of the century, despite a population increase from 1.6 million to 2.5 million, the total number of rural Ontarians remained constant from one decade to the other, yet its proportion declined to 57.1 percent in 1901 from 78 percent in 1871. When proper weight is given to the rates of natural growth and rural inmigration, it is clear that the increase the rural population would have normally experienced from 1871 onward was taken away by outmigration.[23]

Equally important in this evolving scenario are the transformations taking place in the manufacturing sector. As agriculture entered its new age of commercialization and diversification, the myriad of villages and small commercial towns throughout the province's countryside incorporated more specialized and technically advanced forms of industrial production. This, and the particular spatial configuration of industrialization in Ontario, not only contributed to the making of an industrial working class but also shaped patterns of mobility and the range of opportunities available to outmigrants in their own region.[24] In Ontario more than in the Maritimes, and much more than in Quebec, farmers' children, clerical workers, and experienced crafts-men and industrial workers did not have to travel very far to find the wages and career opportunities they sought. For many of them their search could go on in nearby districts or take them beyond their province—to a town or an industrial center south of the border.

Not surprisingly, a fast-growing industrial district such as Detroit, just across the Detroit River, would become the most important destination for Ontarians and Anglo-Canadians from other provinces.[25] In 1860 they made up 14.5 percent of the city's foreign born; twenty years later that figure rose to 23.6 percent, making them the third-largest foreign-born group, after the Germans and the British. By 1880 Ontarians' presence was firmly established in the urban universe of the city.[26] By the end of the century Ontarians were present in virtually all the major industrial centers of the Midwest, particularly in neighboring states like New York, Ohio, and Michigan. In several of those regional labor markets Ontarians would rub shoulders with other, mostly European immigrants, but soon also with the first contingents of Mexicans whose migration project had pushed them further north to industrial centers like Detroit, Chicago, and the mines of the Mesabi Range.[27]

The Twentieth Century and Border-Crossing Data

As the twentieth century began, and both Canada and the United States entered into an unprecedented era of economic growth and industrial expan-sion, immigration and cross-border outmigration kept feeding regional labor markets, transforming the landscape of many cities and industrial districts from coast to coast. Although migration from Canada to the United States declined somewhat compared to the years 1860–1900, it remained a persis-tent feature of continental life. In fact, until the Great Depression drastically interrupted the movement, Canada's net population contribution to its south-ern neighbor surpassed the one-million mark. During years of labor shortage, such as that caused by the Great War, Canada was the leading labor donor to the U.S. economy. Thanks to a new system of border control and inspection instituted by U.S. immigration authorities in the early 1900s, the social, demo-graphic, geographic, and occupational data from that century are much more precise. Consequently, one can now reconstitute as accurately as possible the various profiles of Canadian outmigrants, the variety of migration patterns in-volved, and the local and regional dimensions of this continental migration movement.[28]

From a spatial perspective the twentieth-century migration movement was continental in scope, involving virtually all Canadian provinces and U.S. states along the northern belt. As with the cross-border flow of previous decades, the twentieth century can best be understood in a regional context. Thus Maritimers kept migrating predominantly to the New England states, Ontarians to the Great Lakes region and northwestern New York districts, and Canadians from the prairies and British Columbia largely to U.S. western and Pacific states. As for Quebec outmigrants, though an important proportion kept heading to Michigan, the predominant destinations were now along the southern corridor, from New York State and Maine, through the various northern New England States, down to Connecticut and Rhode Island. Much as in the late nineteenth century, the textile labor markets of southern New England continued to exert a major pull for French Canadians despite child labor reforms and the gradual move of textile manufacturing toward southern states.

Two striking features of Canadian migration at this time were the fairly equal participation of males and females and the presence of virtually all age groups. The proportion of children and young adults combined represented well over half the migrating population. This demographic feature helps to explain, at least in part, some of the movement's prevailing patterns. Some Canadians, in fact, left while young and unmarried, while others left in family units. Still others practiced repeat migration—a pattern that was partially prompted by the proximity of the two countries and by the extensive social networks within which most of these migrants moved. One of these repeat migrants was David Watkins, a fifty-three-year-old fisherman from Nova Scotia. He had worked and lived in Massachusetts from 1914 to 1915, and two years later he headed there again. Similarly, when William Baily—a young unmarried machinist from Kingston, Ontario—migrated to Detroit in 1911, this was his second migration experience, as he had previously worked and lived in Massachusetts.[29] These are not isolated cases. In fact, if we exclude children aged fourteen and under, well over one-third of the Canadian population migrating during the years 1906 to 1930 had already migrated to the United States at least once.

Equally significant was the occupational composition of the migrating Canadian labor force. The social profile of Canadian immigrants that emerged from the massive Dillingham inquiry (1909–12) placed them at the top of the overall immigrant population in terms of schooling, proficiency in English, skill composition, and premigration work experience, especially in the manufacturing sectors. The border data enrich that profile, showing the wide occupational spectrum to which Canadian migrants belonged. While the majority had been associated with agricultural and manufacturing activities at the time of their migration, nearly 20 percent of the male adults outmigrating were businessmen, professionals, supervisors, and miscellaneous white col-

Table 2.1 Anglo-Canadian and French-Canadian Migrants, by Type of Relationship with the Reference Person(s) at Destination (in Percent)

	Anglo-Canadian	French-Canadian
Spouse, son, daughter	11.2	11.3
Parents, brother, sister	26.5	29.7
Other kin (uncle, aunt, cousin, in-laws)	19.4	27.4
Friend	12.6	8.5
Board, hotel	1.1	0.4
Institutions (including companies)	4.9	3.3
Other	0.9	0.9
Undetermined	23.4	18.5
N	1,449	4,224

lars as well as students. An even larger proportion included skilled production workers and independent craftsmen. Even more significant was the occupational composition among women, with as many as 48 percent belonging to occupational groups such as professionals and supervisors, nurses, miscellaneous white collars, and students. One can thus safely say that Canada was contributing to the U.S. economy the most varied workforce of any migrant-sending country. Moreover, a significant component of this workforce was equipped to adjust quickly to the growing technological and administrative transformations that the U.S. economy was undergoing during the first third of the twentieth century.

Whether migrating for the first or the second time, whether doing so as single men or women or as members of a family group, and regardless of their occupational skills, the majority of both Anglo-Canadians and French-Canadians moved within networks that had grown from long-established migration traditions. As table 2.1 shows, a majority of Canadians did the move under the auspices of family members and various types of kin. For another small but significant minority, the destination contact was a friend. Even when well-delineated migration fields had not emerged, or are not always visible through the available data, for nearly four out of five Canadians their migration project rested on the important role played by close social relations. These data invite us to look beyond the mere economic dynamics of migration and appreciate its character of social process based on personal loyalty, solidarity, and willingness to share a positive experience with less fortunate townspeople—be they siblings, relatives, or friends.

The representative experience of George Marion reveals the extent to which the migration project rested on enduring social webs that extended across the border. When in 1921 he left his Quebec parish for Fall River, Massachusetts, he moved with his two parents, who had previously lived there and were now remigrating. Moreover, both his mother and his father had parents living in that same city. For three generations Fall River had thus been a crucial part of the Marion family's life. When a few years later both his parents returned to Quebec, George was hardly left alone. He went to live with his paternal grandparents, though he could have chosen one of several uncles living in the city.[30] By then Fall River had a French-Canadian population of about 28,000, representing a quarter of the entire city's population. Besides the mere size of the French-Canadian group, the chain migration of the past forty years had produced a very elaborate institutional network similar to those found in most large New England textile centers. As of 1909 Fall River's French-Canadian immigrants and their children were served by six parishes, eleven parish schools, a college, and more than 150 societies and associations ranging from mutual-benefit societies to religious congregations to cultural and leisure organizations.[31]

The need to preserve their language and religion—the two foundations of French-Canadian culture—was the pivotal factor that fueled the rich associational life characterizing most *petits Canadas*, whether in New England or in Midwestern districts. This explains why hardly any equivalent of this urban phenomenon could be found among Anglo-Canadian immigrants in the United States. In his historical study of Detroit's evolving social and ethnic structure during a period of massive Canadian immigration there, Oliver Zunz found no major residential clusters among the many Anglo-Canadians working and living there. The few small clusters he did find were in areas largely populated by native white Americans and, to a lesser extent, by British immigrants. Nor were Anglo-Canadians that visible as a group in the city's public and social spheres. The intermarriage patterns he observed provide evidence of the tendency among Anglo-Canadians to associate with mainstream American life. In fact, only one of five Anglo-Canadian males chose a spouse within the same group. A larger proportion chose native white Americans as spouses, and the remaining proportion married women belonging to British and other ethnic groups. Zunz's book is one of the rare existing historical inquiries on the presence of Anglo-Canadians in urban America.[32] Yet it is very likely that the residential choices as well as the patterns of incorporation that he described for Detroit are similar for most areas of Anglo-Canadian settlement in the United States.

The Postwar Era

As peace returned and Canadian authorities lifted wartime regulations discouraging workers to leave the country, thousands of Canadians rushed to U.S.

consulates to seek visas. In the last six months of 1945 as many as 8,767 visas had been approved, and many more were pending.[33] In the following months and years, as the new Republican-dominated Congress debated restrictions on a wide range of European nations and retooled the country's racial and ideological fences, Canadians continued to head south in ever-increasing numbers, soon making Canada the leading donor country along with Germany—a role maintained until the revocation of the quota laws in the mid- to late 1960s.

Once again, what is striking about this cross-border migration movement—beyond its mere magnitude—is its occupational composition, making it one of the most qualified workforces to flow into the U.S. economy. During the previous industrialization era Canadian immigrants had contributed to the growth of virtually all U.S. manufacturing sectors. Now, in the postwar era, marked by ongoing mechanization, rapid technological transformations, and the growing role of the service sector, Canadians made up some of the most skilled and educated sectors of the population, including an important cross-section of technicians, engineers, and intellectual workers. As in past years, health-care professionals (nurses in particular) were among the most important professional groups. A survey done in the 1950s concluded that "Canada was . . . the number-one provider of immigrant scientific and engineering talent for the United States, followed by the United Kingdom and Germany." A Canadian government statistical study was more precise; it found that during the same decade Canada had contributed 27 percent of all professional immigrants to the United States.[34] The expression "brain drain" had barely entered the public jargon, but it is likely that Canada was among the advanced industrial societies to experience that phenomenon most acutely.

The long-established tradition of transborder migrations, the contiguity of labor markets between the two economies, the ongoing communication occurring in trade and professional channels across the border, and Canadians' affinity with American society and its institutions are among the major factors that facilitated the migration project for hundreds of thousands of Canadians, turning those newcomers "from the North" into a major economic and social asset and into highly valued candidates for civic and cultural incorporation.

The Re-emigration Movement

Any discussion of Canada's role in intracontinental flows of population and labor would be limited if one left out those hundreds of thousands of border-crossers who were not Canadians, but rather Europeans who had first migrated to Canada and subsequently remigrated to the United States.[35] Saverio Varteo was one of this large cohort of border-crossers. A thirty-four-year-old Italian-born laborer, he had first migrated to Canada in 1906. Three years later he was in Edmonton, Alberta, from where he remigrated to Boston. Similarly, Beatrice Pritchard, a native of Wellington, England, had migrated to Canada in 1912 and two years later she left the city where she lived—Winnipeg—and remigrated to Lancaster, Minnesota.[36]

Although during the twentieth century Britons such as Beatrice continued to remigrate across the border, by that time remigration from Canada to the United States had become a practice for a variety of European immigrants who had been part of the unprecedented surge in immigration to the Dominion. The vigorous expansion that the Canadian economy experienced at the end of the century and through the Laurier era—centered mostly on natural re- sources, railroad construction, and manufacturing—forced Canadian authori- ties to turn to non-British sources of European immigration. By 1901, in fact, the latter component accounted for 18 percent of the entire immigrant popu- lation, and it continued to grow.

The rich variety of information contained in the cross-border manifestos (*Soundex Index*) allows us to draw a very accurate profile of the remigrant population for the years 1906 to 1930.[37]

Much like the migration of Canadians, remigration was a continent-wide phenomenon. If less frequent in the Maritimes, it is because their share of im- migration was proportionately much lower than that of the other Canadian re- gions. Spatially, it articulated itself within regional contexts, with nearly two- thirds of remigrants moving to a U.S. border state. Much like their Canadian counterparts, they departed from various socioeconomic settings: metropoli- tan areas, middle-sized cities, small frontier towns, and agrarian districts.

Remigrants belonged to all age groups. However, when compared to Cana- dian migrants, they included a much higher proportion of fifteen- to twenty- nine-year-olds. If men and women aged thirty to thirty-four are added, these two age groups (prime working age) represented nearly 90 percent of the en- tire remigration movement. But perhaps a more striking feature was the over- whelming presence of men (four out of five), and most of them unmarried. These are typical attributes that suggest a highly mobile population that could adjust its migration according to perceived opportunities. This hypothesis is reinforced somewhat by the occupational structure that characterized this population.

An analysis of the occupation declared at border crossing reveals that vir- tually all categories of labor, including white-collar and professional employ- ment, were represented and that consequently the remigration movement fed virtually all sectors of the U.S. economy. Yet within this wide spectrum, the most important occupation was "laborers" (nearly one out of two male

Table 2.2 European-born Remigrants, by Major Group
and Country of Origin, 1906–1930 (in Percent; $N = 4,632$)

British Isles		29.4
England	48.4	
Scotland	26.2	
Ireland	16.8	
Other and undetermined	8.6	
Western Europe		8.7
Germany	34.5	
Belgium	25.4	
France	15.8	
Netherlands	12.6	
Other	11.7	
Central-eastern and southern Europe		49.8
Russia	34.9	
Italy	26.8	
Austria	16.3	
Hungary	3.9	
Poland	3.6	
Romania	3.2	
Other	11.3	
Scandinavia and Finland		12.1
Sweden	38.6	
Norway	26.5	
Denmark	9.5	
Finland	25.4	

remigrants), and the largest proportion was found among remigrants from central-eastern and southern Europe, where they made up two-thirds of all occupations.

Next to laborers and agriculturalists, the other most frequent occupations can be grouped into three categories: white-collar workers, small independent producers, and factory-related workers. Whereas the latter two categories were found in varying degrees in all four European groups, white-collar remigrants were most frequently Britons and to a lesser extent western Europeans. No doubt language proficiency and forms of training comparable to those practiced in North America are the key factors explaining the stronger white-collar presence among these two groups of European remigrants.

A small but significant minority of women were part of the remigration movement. Even if the majority of them (53 percent) declared no occupation or simply that of "housewife," several others were considered wage earners. Thus a discussion of the occupational configuration of this movement would not be complete without taking into account the role of working women. Given the relatively small number of wage-earning women, their occupational range was considerably narrower than that of men. Still, some clear tendencies emerge from the data. The most conspicuous one was the significant presence of domestics—nearly one out of two. By far the largest concentration was to be found within the British and the Scandinavian and Finnish groups. Also significant was the minority (17 percent) of remigrant women involved in white-collar occupations, particularly within the British and western European groups, with nursing the most frequent occupation. Equally significant were occupations associated with the clothing and dressmaking sectors, though it is difficult to assess the extent to which these occupations were practiced in a factory or as independent trades. Occupations such as "garment worker" or "mill-hand," for instance, clearly denoted a factory setting, whereas other occupations such as "embroiderer" or "seamstress" were most likely self-employment.

The Reverse Flow: Migrating from the U.S. to Canada

Apart from the American Loyalists who moved and settled in British North America during the revolutionary era, the nineteenth and twentieth centuries witnessed a constant and sometimes dramatic movement of Americans into Canada. Yet since Hansen's and Brebner's seminal work, which locally and regionally situated a variety of movements of Americans into Canada, very little systematic attempt has been made to study this important development in continental history, and this movement has not found its way into the migration literature.[38] Much like the Anglo-Canadians in the United States, Americans in Canada did not behave as ethnic minorities, and hence they exhibited little cultural and institutional visibility within Canadian civil society. This may have been compounded by the composition of the American immigrant group, the largest component of which was made up of "returnees" (former Canadian immigrants in the United States, along with their U.S.-born children). In most cases they returned to their provinces where they resumed their life and work, most likely in their original communities. One must also note the limitations of the data: because for much of the historical period in question no official records of this cross-border movement were made, and the estimates offered occasionally are fragmentary and not always reliable.

Starting with the first confederate decennial census (1871), the mention of the place of birth of the enumerated Canadian population allows researchers to identify the number of U.S.-born residing in Canada. Limited as this information is to grasp the dynamics of the movement during the intercensus

Table 2.3 U.S.-Born Individuals Residing in Canada by Census Year, as Percentage of Total Canadian Population

1871	64,613	1.8	1921	374,024	4.3
1881	77,753	1.8	1931	344,574	3.3
1891	80,915	1.7	1941	312,473	2.7
1901	127,899	2.4	1951	282,010	2.0
1911	303,680	4.2	1961	283,908	1.6

years, it is the only reliable information that can provide an initial sense of the magnitude of the American presence within the Canadian population. Note the progressive growth of the American presence through the last three decades of the nineteenth century, followed by a dramatic rise during the first decade of the twentieth. This surge was largely the result of the massive migration of Americans who took up farmlands in the Canadian Prairies—a regional movement that will be discussed later. As shown in table 2.3, the peak census year was 1921, when the U.S.-born made up 4.3 percent of Canada's total population—a presence that remained above the 300,000 level until 1941. (A U.S.-born person enumerated, for example, in the Canadian census in 1921 will reappear again in the ensuing censuses as long as the person is alive.)

The following series of analytical observations offer a global view of the historical significance of this reverse movement within the continental migration equation. Four major historical contexts seem to have produced the conditions leading Americans to move across the northern border.

Agrarian Migrations

The profile of the agrarian American cross-border migrant diverges from that of a typical migrant seeking higher wages in the receiving country; it suggests an agriculturalist intent on exploiting the availability of land and the farming conditions in Canada at specific conjunctures. In the nineteenth century the most significant migration of American agriculturalists occurred in Quebec's Eastern Townships (south of the St. Lawrence River) and involved New Englanders who sought a solution to demographic pressures and the hardening of agrarian life. Though most of these agriculturalists sought new opportunities in the Ohio Valley, a minority headed northward, as the Eastern Township region became open to colonization. Adopting a land-grant system similar to that in use in New England ("leader and associates"), between 1792 and 1809 about fifty groups of American settlers obtained land grants and began populating the region. This process was slowed by the war of 1812–14, and in subsequent years Britons and Canadians joined in the settlement of the region.

Still, over the years the presence of the original American settlers attracted a stream of New England agriculturalists, and by 1840 Americans made up nearly two-thirds of the entire population of the region, particularly in townships contiguous to Vermont.[39]

Much more dramatic and historically significant was the massive migration of American agriculturalists to the Canadian prairie region during the Laurier era—more than half a million from 1897 to 1912. The social and political impact on the region during the ensuing years and decades was also significant. As Harold Troper shows, this massive migration grew out of an exceptional economic and continental conjuncture: the official closing of the American farming frontier and nearly a decade of economic hardship and political defeat among American farmers coincided with the massive efforts made by Canadian authorities to develop the resource-rich western provinces. One corollary was the extensive network of recruitment—involving hundreds of agents—set up by the Canadian Immigration Branch to attract American farmers.[40]

Whether looking at the latter western case, or the earlier one of New England and Quebec, Canada's natural resources and socioeconomy were a safety valve for American populations and regions caught in the grips of an agrarian crisis of historic proportions.

Entrepreneurs, Managers, Technicians

Though difficult to quantify, a variety of historical sources in business and entrepreneurial history, as well as in biography and local history, shed light on the presence of this group within American migration. This presence extends from the early stages of industrialization to the more mature economy of the twentieth century, when American direct investments—along with their subsidiaries and branch plants—increasingly marked the Canadian economic landscape.

As Paul-André Linteau's recent systematic historical exploration regarding the Province of Quebec shows, a significant number of American artisans and entrepreneurs contributed to the early industrial development of the province when they brought capital and new technologies in a variety of key sectors: foundry and hardware, marine engines, mills, refining, shoes and leather, and logging.[41] With the industrial expansion that marked the American economy during the last third of the nineteenth century, Canada became the leading target for U.S. direct investments by many large manufacturing corporations. By 1936 these American establishments were concentrated in Ontario (66 percent of the total), followed by Quebec (16 percent). Equally important was the presence of these enterprises in the natural resource sectors, such as mining and forestry.[42]

Linteau shows that the predominant tendency was the migration of executive and managerial cadres who often brought engineering and technical personnel from the United States. The several examples cited are all from Quebec, but one may assume the other provinces had the same tendency. This will remain a constant feature of American emigration well into the postwar era and beyond.

Canadian Returnees and Their U.S.-Born Children

Very likely the largest component of the reverse cross-border flow to Canada—certainly during the first half of the twentieth century—was Canadian immigrants who moved back to Canada with their U.S.-born children. The Bournival family is representative of this widespread pattern. After migrating twice to New England they decided to return permanently to Quebec in 1930. The family now included three children who were born in the United States and who were formally considered by the Canadian census authorities as U.S. immigrants.[43] As we shall see, the classification assigned to parents varied according to changing census criteria.

Historians and demographers have pointed to the difficulties of quantifying this movement, owing largely to the limitations of the official statistics and to the divergent ways—on the part of Canadian government agencies—to classify Canadian returnees and "American immigrants." As we have seen, Canadian migration to the United States was marked by temporary sojourning that led to return migration and repeat migration. Geographical proximity undoubtedly enhanced this cross-border mobility, but in addition, return to the homeland led Canadian authorities and private organizations to implement specific initiatives and programs.

As far as the late nineteenth century is concerned, a partial measure of the repatriation movement can be obtained from the official figures reported by Canadian authorities, ranging from 8,971 in 1873 to 26,152 between 1880 and 1890.[44] From 1925 on the Canadian Department of Immigration published yearly data on Canadian repatriation. In addition, the federal censuses of 1931 and 1941 included within the immigrant population "Canada-born individuals who had resided abroad"; the latter census also specified the country of last residence. Using these three sources, the historical demographer Yolande Lavoie estimates the total number of Canadian returnees from the United States at nearly half a million during the years 1901 to 1941—the decades when this movement was most intense. This reverse population flow

Table 2.4 Provincial Distribution (in Percent) of Immigrant Population
Originating from the United States, 1941

Prince Edward Island	0.5	Manitoba	4
Nova Scotia	3	Saskatchewan	19
New Brunswick	3	Alberta	21
Quebec	17.5	British Columbia	7
Ontario	24		

Source: 1941 Canadian Census, vol. 4, table 24.

was augmented by the U.S.-born children of Canadian migrants; as of 1931 they amounted to over 150,000.[45]

The census of 1941 provides additional statistical information on Canadian returnees from the United States. This latter group was somewhat arbitrarily subdivided into those who had resided in the United States for one year and over ("immigrants") and for less than a year ("repatriated"). Following this classification, the number of "repatriated" as of 1941 amounted to 140,044.[46] The 1941 census also breaks down this population movement at the provincial level, indicating the province of birth before migration to the United States and that of residence after return to Canada. Thus, as to the repatriated group, 68 percent had originated in Ontario and Quebec, and 24 percent in the Maritime Provinces. Moreover, the majority of the repatriated went on to reside in their province of birth. Quebec showed the highest rate, with 92 percent of Quebec-born repatriated returning to Quebec, while Nova Scotia, New Brunswick, Ontario, and British Columbia registered rates ranging from 83 to 88 percent.[47] As to the "immigrant" category, table 2.4 shows their provincial distribution in 1941.

Professional and Intellectual Workers, Managers, and Political Resisters

The period between the end of the Second World War and the late 1960s witnessed a particularly intense migration between the two northern neighboring countries. Not only did Canada become the leading donor country to the United States, but by 1971 the United States was the leading source of immigrants to Canada, moving up from second place in 1968.[48]

During the postwar period up to 1963, at a time when Canada experienced a major economic expansion and technological change, two-thirds of all the professional workers migrating into Canada came from Britain and the United States—eloquently suggesting both the place that Canada still held within the British Commonwealth and its place within the North American socioeconomic system. In the ensuing years professional workers continued to be a major component of U.S. immigration, mostly attracted by opportunities in the expanding tertiary sector of the Canadian economy. Their weight within the northbound migration must be assessed along with another key component: managerial personnel. As the trend toward direct investments intensified and the two economies became more integrated, managerial personnel, especially in manufacturing, finance, and insurance, increasingly became part of cross-border migration.

One Canadian institutional sector that experienced a major expansion and was responsible for attracting significant numbers of U.S. intellectual workers was the university system. Writing in the early 1970s, a leading student of immigration to Canada estimated that during the previous decade or so "the inflow of university teachers from the U.S. to Canada had been roughly three times as great as the outflow"—a development which at the time intensified the fears of U.S. cultural domination.[49]

This historical overview would not be complete without briefly mentioning the social movements of the 1960s and the Vietnam War. Most estimates have placed the total number of draft resisters who moved to Canada at about 100,000. Though this was largely a political migration that did not result in massive permanent residence, it stands to remind us of the historical role that Canada played as a safe haven for fugitive slaves and later for Afro-Americans who sought to free themselves from an oppressive racial system.

Conclusion

Seventy years have passed since the historians Marcus Hansen and John Brebner published what became the seminal work on the history of cross-border population movements between Canada and the United States from a continental perspective.[50] Yet except for one short section set in the industrialization era, the migrants discussed in that text moved predominantly across a North American agrarian universe where farmlands constituted the main poles of attraction and settlement.

Since then the United States and Canada have undergone profound transformations typical of postindustrial societies, while also becoming major players in the new global economy. More importantly, through the enforcement of free trade agreements in 1988 and 1994 (which included Mexico), the two neighboring countries have strengthened their positions as each other's most important trading partners. Direct investments, along with the constant flow of natural resources, goods, and services in both directions, could have hardly occurred without the transfer of technical and managerial personnel and their families, whether temporarily or permanently. This reconfigured

North American economic landscape has forced momentous changes in immigration policies and significantly shaped cross-border mobility trends and the spatial distribution of American and Canadian immigrants. For instance, the U.S. census in 2000 revealed the growing presence of Canadian immigrants in North Carolina, South Carolina, Georgia, and Tennessee—southern states that historically have been outside Canadians' range of destinations.

At the same time, partly in response to the threat of international terrorism, the border separating and uniting the two countries has become more guarded than ever, bearing little resemblance to the one studied by Hansen and Brebner. Yet as in the previous century, tens of thousands of Americans and Canadians keep crossing it daily either to go to work or to visit family and friends. Economic necessity, emotional concerns, and the sharing of an interwoven mass culture continue to make the two countries overlap, certainly in those northern borderlands (see chapter 4).

Notes

1 Leon E. Truesdell, *The Canadian Born in the United States* (New Haven: Yale University Press, 1943), 10, 16, 57.

2 Marcus L. Hansen and John B. Brebner, *The Mingling of the Canadian and American Peoples* (New Haven: Yale University Press, 1940).

3 Gerald M. Craig, ed., Introduction to *Lord Durham's Report* (Ottawa: Government Printer, 1964), 136.

4 Alan A. Brookes, "The Exodus: Migration from the Maritime Provinces to Boston During the Second Half of the Nineteenth Century" (Ph.D. diss., University of New Brunswick, 1979).

5 Robert Armstrong, *Structure and Change: An Economic History of Quebec* (Toronto: Gage, 1984).

6 *Report of the Special Committee on Emigration*, Journals of the Legislative Assembly (Toronto: Lovoll, 1857), appendix N, 47.

7 Jean Lamarre, *The French Canadians of Michigan: Their Contribution to the Development of the Saginaw Valley and the Keweenaw Peninsula, 1840–1914* (Detroit: Wayne State University Press, 2003), esp. chapter 3; Gregory S. Rose, "The Origins of Canadian Settlers in Southern Michigan, 1820–1850," *Ontario History* 79, no. 1 (1987), 31–52.

8 Lamarre, *The French Canadians of Michigan*, 117–51.

9 Olivier Zunz, *The Changing Face of Inequality: Urbanization, Industrial Development, and Immigrants in Detroit, 1880–1920* (Chicago: University of Chicago Press, 1982).

10 Ralph Vicero, "The Immigration of French-Canadians to New England, 1840–1900" (Ph.D. diss., University of Wisconsin, 1966).

11 Thomas Dublin, *Women at Work: The Transformation of Work and Community in*

Lowell, Massachusetts, 1826–1860, 2nd edition (New York: Columbia University Press, 1993).

12 Oral history interview, in Jacques Rouillard, *Ah les États!* (Montreal: Boréal, 1985), 90.

13 Bruno Ramirez, *On the Move: French-Canadians and Italian Migrants in the North Atlantic Economy, 1860–1914* (Toronto: McClelland and Stewart, 1991), 120–25.

14 Bruno Ramirez, "French-Canadian Immigrants in the New England Cotton Industry: A Socioeconomic Profile," *Labour/Le Travail* 11 (spring 1983), 125–42. On specific New England textile towns see also Frances Early, "The French-Canadian Family Economy and Standard of Living: Lowell, Massachusetts, 1870," *Journal of Family History* 7 (June 1982), 180–99; Yukari Takai, *Gendered Passages: French-Canadian Migration to Lowell, Massachusetts, 1900–1920* (New York: Lang, 2008); Tamara Hareven, *Family Time and Industrial Time: The Relationship between the Family and Work in a New England Industrial Community* (Cambridge, Cambridge University Press, 1982).

15 Ramirez, *On the Move*, 120–22.

16 Brookes, "The Exodus," 32–36; Ian McKay, "Class Struggle and Merchant Capital: Craftsmen and Labourers on the Halifax Waterfront, 1850–1900," *Constructing Modern Canada*, ed. Chad Gaffield (Toronto: Prentice-Hall, 1994), 33–34; D. A. Muise, "Parties and Constituencies: Federal Elections in Nova Scotia, 1867–1896," *Annual Report of the Canadian Historical Association*, 1972, 83–101.

17 Eric Sager, "Dependency, Underdevelopment, and the Economic History of the Atlantic Provinces," *Acadiensis* 17, no. 1 (1987), 117–37; T. William Acheson, "The National Policy and the Industrialisation of the Maritimes, 1880–1910," *Acadiensis* 1, no. 2 (1972), 3–18.

18 Brookes, "The Exodus," 72–75; Patricia A. Thornton, "The Problem of Out-migration from Atlantic Canada, 1871–1921: A New Look," *Acadiensis* 15, no. 1 (1985), 3–34.

19 Frederick A. Bushee, *Ethnic Factors in the Population of Boston* (New York: Arno, 1970); Alan A. Brookes, "Out-migration from the Maritime Provinces, 1860–1900: Some Preliminary Considerations," *Acadiensis* 5, no. 2 (1976), 26–55.

20 See Randy William Widdis, *With Scarcely a Ripple: Anglo-Canadian Migration into the United States and Western Canada* (Montreal: McGill-Queen's University Press, 1998), esp. chapter 5, for a discussion of the impact of these developments on depopulation in southeastern Ontario.

21 D. A. Lawr, "The Development of Ontario Farming, 1870–1914: Patterns of Growth and Change," *Ontario History* 64, no. 4 (1972), 239–51.

22 David Gagan, *Hopeful Travellers: Families, Land, and Social Change in Mid-Victorian Peel County, Canada West* (Toronto: University of Toronto Press, 1981), 126–42; Gordon Darroch, "Class in Nineteenth-Century Central Ontario: A Reassessment of the Crisis and Demise of Small Producers during Early Industrialization," *Class, Gender and Region: Essays in Canadian Historical Sociology*, ed. Gregory Kealey (St. John's, Nfld.: Committee on Canadian Labour History, 1988), 49–72.

23 Terry Crowley, "Rural Labour," *Labouring Lives: Work and Workers in Nineteenth-*

Century Ontario, ed. Paul Craven (Toronto: University of Toronto Press, 1995), 57. See also Widdis, *With Scarcely a Ripple*, esp. 87–114.

24 Terry Crowley, "Rural Labour," 57. See also Widdis, *With Scarcely a Ripple*, esp. 87–114.

25 For a broader historical analysis of the Great Lakes region that sheds light on the structural content of cross-border migrations see John J. Bukowczyk, Nora Faires, David R. Smith, and Randy W. Widdis, *Permeable Border: The Great Lakes Basin as Transnational Region, 1650–1990* (Pittsburgh: University of Pittsburgh Press, 2005).

26 Zunz, *The Changing Face of Inequality*, 106.

27 Manuel Gamio, *Mexican Immigration to the United States: A Study of Human Migration and Adjustment* (Chicago: University of Chicago Press, 1930).

28 The archival source used, the *Soundex Index to Canadian Border Entries*, is part of the records of the U.S. Immigration and Naturalization Services, Record Group 85. For a detailed discussion of this source see the appendix in Bruno Ramirez (with Yves Otis), *Crossing the 49th Parallel: Migration from Canada to the United States, 1900–1930* (Ithaca: Cornell University Press, 2001). Unless otherwise specified, all the quantitative data presented in this section are computations made by the author and based on a representative sample of border crossers derived from the *Soundex Index* and presented in greater detail in *Crossing the 49th Parallel*.

29 Ramirez, *Crossing the 49th Parallel*, 129.

30 Oral history interview, Projet d'Histoire Orale, Université de Montréal.

31 L. J. Gagnon, ed., *Guide officiel des Franco-Américains, 1916–1946* (Fall River, Mass.: Belanger, n.d.).

32 Zunz, *The Changing Face of Inequality*, 32.

33 *Time*, April 1, 1946.

34 Department of Labour, Economics and Research Branch, *The Migration of Professional Workers into and out of Canada, 1946–1960* (Ottawa: Department of Labour, 1961); *Canadian Business*, March 1955, 46. For a broader contextualization of this postwar trend see Donald H. Avery, *Reluctant Host: Canada's Response to Immigrant Workers* (Toronto: McClelland and Stewart, 1995), 177–78.

35 In other contexts and circumstances—as in the case of Poles traveling through Germany and then to the United States or Canada—"transit migration" is more appropriate. The movement discussed here, however, entailed a "remigration" (to the United States) after a relatively lengthy stay in Canada.

36 Ramirez, *Crossing the 49th Parallel*, 148.

37 For a more extensive analysis see Ramirez, *Crossing the 49th Parallel*, chapter 5.

38 Hansen and Brebner, *The Mingling of the Canadian and American Peoples*.

39 G. F. McGuigan, "La concession des terres dans les cantons de l'est du Bas-Canada," *Recherches sociographiques*, 4, no. 1 (January–April 1963), 71–89; J. I. Little, *Ethnocultural Transition in the Eastern Townships of Quebec* (Ottawa: Canadian Historical Association, 1989).

40 Harold Troper, *"Only Farmers Need Apply": Official Canadian Government Encouragement of Immigration from the United States, 1896–1911* (Toronto: Griffin, 1972).

For a more recent discussion see Randy W. Widdis, "American-Resident Migration to Western Canada at the Turn of the Twentieth Century," *Prairie Forum* 22, no. 2 (1997), 237–62.

41 Paul-André Linteau, "Les migrants américains et franco-américains au Québec, 1792–1940: Un état de la question," *Revue d'histoire de l'Amérique Française* 53, no. 4 (spring 2000), 561–602.

42 Linteau, "Les migrants américains et franco-américains," 578.

43 Oral history interview in Rouillard, *Ah les États!*, 113–19.

44 Yolande Lavoie, "Les mouvements migratoires des Canadiens entre leur pays et les États-Unis au XIXe et au XXe siècles," *La population du Québec: Études rétrospectives*, ed. Hubert Charbonneau (Montreal: Presses de l'Université de Montréal, 1973), 79; Gilles Paquet, "L'émigration des Canadiens français vers la Nouvelle-Angleterre, 1870–1910: Prises de vue quantitatives," *Recherches sociographiques* 5, no. 3 (September–December 1964), 338–41.

45 Lavoie, "Les mouvements migratoires," 82, 85.

46 Census of Canada, 1941, vol. 4, table 24.

47 Census of Canada, 1941, vol. 4, table 24 (computed by the author). See also Lavoie, "Les mouvements migratoires," 83. A wide variety of cross-tabulations from Canadian census statistics are provided in David D. Harvey, *Americans in Canada: Migration and Settlement since 1840* (Lewiston, N.Y.: Mellen, 1991).

48 Freda Hawkins, *Canada and Immigration: Public Policy and Public Concern*, 2nd ed. (Montreal: McGill-Queen's University Press, 1988), 41.

49 Freda Hawkins, *Canada and Immigration*, 40.

50 Hansen and Brebner, *Mingling of the Canadian and American Peoples*.

CHAPTER THREE

The Making and Unmaking of the Circum-Caribbean Migratory Sphere

Mobility, Sex across Boundaries,
and Collective Destinies, 1840–1940

Lara Putnam

The populations and social systems of the Caribbean basin have been shaped by each of the great global migrations of the modern era. In the seventeenth and eighteenth centuries forced migration carried some 4.6 million Africans into this region. In the generations after emancipation in 1838, over 400,000 South Asian indentured migrants traveled to the British Caribbean. Nearly 180,000 Chinese immigrants reached the region in the same era.[1] Meanwhile the last decades of the nineteenth century saw the creation of a system of circular migration in which hundreds of thousands of Afro-Caribbeans left the British territories for work in the booming export economies of the Spanish-speaking rimlands and islands, a movement that reached its heyday after the First World War. Caribbean migration to the United States—to Harlem, most of all—soared in the same era.

Unprecedented steps by the hemisphere's receiving societies in the 1920s and 1930s to exclude potential migrants on the basis of racial "unassimila-bility" ruptured the circum-Caribbean migratory sphere and, in doing so, profoundly shifted the twentieth-century trajectories of British Caribbean colonies, Spanish American republics, and the North American continent alike. These macropolitical changes reflected a heightened interest by states in the biopolitics of borders—a belief that demography was destiny—which itself responded to the enacted micropolitics of intimate life around the region. Interracial sex had become a key topic for experts and activists writing about the Caribbean, both on the islands and beyond. Some sought to abstract the lessons that the contemporary "science of racial difference" held for Caribbean peoples; others sought to use Caribbean examples to push debates within the international "science of race." This chapter places those learned and political debates over race-mixture alongside the traces of actual boundary-crossing sexual contact preserved in judicial testimony, allowing us to observe the everyday interactions through which expressions of intimate desire sometimes underlined, sometimes undermined, group boundaries in the Greater Caribbean. Some immigrant group identities became folded into others; some acquired a retroactive stability they had never known in the era of migration. Both in rhetoric and in practice, collective destinies were shaped by the contours of intimate desire.[2]

Population and Migration in the Gran Caribe, 1800–1900

At the eve of the era of Atlantic revolutions, largely autonomous black, part-black, and indigenous populations dotted the fringes of empire, along the continent's coastline from Veracruz east to the peninsula of Yucatán, south to Portobello, and east to the Guianas. Over the preceding centuries Spanish, British, French, and Dutch rivalries had provided these heterogeneous populations with useful allies and prevented any colonial state from asserting control over vast stretches of land between the imperial powers' essential ports. Meanwhile the ports themselves were peopled by *negros*, *mulatos*, and *pardos*, mostly freepeople working as artisans, shipbuilders, muleteers, and militia members.[3] Euro-mestizo settlement, in contrast, centered on cities and towns in the fertile valleys of the inland mountain ranges. Around the Caribbean's rim indigenous populations far outnumbered creole Spaniards and *mestizos*. The demographic catastrophe of European disease and dislocations had finally abated, and indigenous communities had seen steady growth since the early 1700s. Plantations growing cacao in Venezuela and eastern Costa Rica and sugar in southern Mexico, Guatemala, and Demarara employed Afro-descended slaves—thousands in Venezuela and Demarara, a few hundred in Costa Rica.

News of the slave revolt in 1789 in French Saint Domingue reverberated across this vast region. Fears of a similar African-led conflagration on the British sugar colonies encouraged parliamentary passage of the Amelioration Acts in 1798 and abolition of slave trade aboard British ships in 1807. The refusal of the enslaved on British islands to acquiesce in the fiction that "amelioration" made slavery tolerable and ongoing abolitionist pressures within Great Britain led to passage of apprenticeship legislation in 1833 and to final emancipation in 1838. This did not end the arrival of Africans into the British Caribbean. In the half-century after abolition of the British slave trade, British ships seized scores of thousands of the hundreds of thousands of enslaved Africans still en route to Cuba, Brazil, and elsewhere. Ten thousand were shipped under contract of indenture to Jamaica, fourteen thousand to British Guiana, and eight thousand to Trinidad.[4] The coloured population of Jamaica (those claiming mixed African and European ancestry) was 68,000 in 1844 and had surpassed 120,000 by 1891; the white population hovered between 15,000 and 13,000 over the same half-century.[5] Trinidad's population of 85,000 in 1861 included a large minority of French creoles whose residence predated British acquisition of the territory; arrival from Venezuela and Portugal as well as Britain continued over the nineteenth century.[6] In 1858 there were some 35,000 Portuguese in British Guiana.[7]

In Spain's remaining insular possessions, technological shifts allowed Cuban sugar production to expand rapidly to fill demand left by Saint Domingue's drop in production. Some 550,000 Africans were transported to Cuba as slaves between 1811 and 1865.[8] Wary of Saint Domingue's fate, Havana's *Junta de Fomento* in 1796 urged "white colonization in the rural districts" as a balance to the growth in numbers of the enslaved.[9] Hundreds of thousands of Galicians and Canary Islanders arrived over the following two generations; the 1861 census found that 116,000 stayed.[10] Transport of indentured workers from China to Cuba began in 1847; some 142,000 men arrived over the following quarter-century, most from southern Guangdong province. Forced recontracting meant that most served sixteen years of indenture on the sugar plantations before they moved into more profitable occupations in cities or other regions.[11]

In 1870 Spain passed the Moret Law, promising gradual abolition and imposing restrictions on owners' authority over those left in their "care." Ongoing pressure by the *patrocinados* (apprentices) rendered the system unsustainable; the *patronato*—and with it unfree labor for those of African ancestry—ended in Puerto Rico in 1873 and in Cuba in 1886.[12] Spanish efforts to increase the numbers of loyalists on the island were hardly successful. Between 1882 and 1894 224,000 Spaniards traveled to Cuba and 142,000 returned home, and in 1894 Cuban insurgents launched their ultimately successful war to end Spanish imperial control.[13] Throughout the years of civil unrest, continuous migration linked Cuba to Tampa, where the cigar industry flourished, and southern Florida more broadly. Cayman Islanders and others from nearby British West Indian islands also circulated continuously to and through these ports. The 1890 census counted over twelve thousand souls born in "Cuba or the West Indies" living in the state of Florida.[14]

Indentured South Asian migration from British-controlled India to the British Caribbean began simultaneously with the migration of indentured

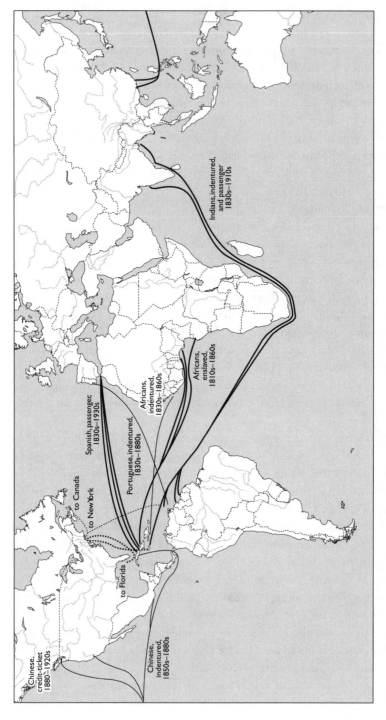

Migratory movements into and out of the Caribbean, 1810s–1930s

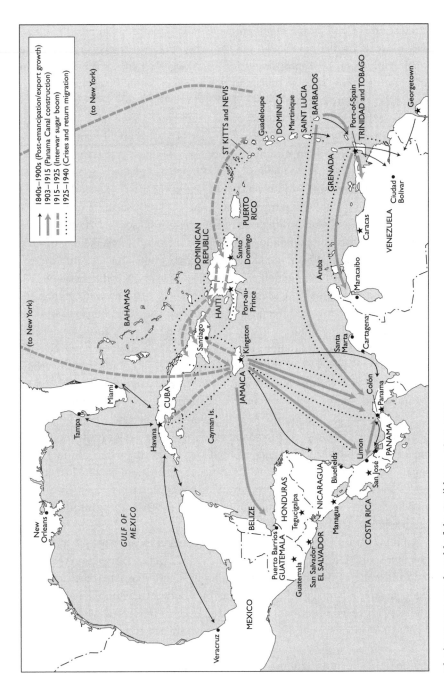

The interconnected world of the Caribbean, 1840–1940

Legend:
- 1840s–1900s (Post-emancipation/export growth)
- 1903–1915 (Panama Canal construction)
- 1915–1925 (Interwar sugar boom)
- 1925–1940 (Crises and return migration)

(to New York)

New Orleans
Veracruz
MEXICO
GULF OF MEXICO
Tampa
Miami
BAHAMAS
Havana
CUBA
Cayman Is.
Santiago
Kingston
JAMAICA
BELIZE
Puerto Barrios
GUATEMALA
Guatemala
San Salvador
EL SALVADOR
Tegucigalpa
HONDURAS
Managua
NICARAGUA
Bluefields
COSTA RICA
San José
Limón
PANAMA
Panamá
Colón
HAITI
Port-au-Prince
DOMINICAN REPUBLIC
Santo Domingo
PUERTO RICO
ST KITTS and NEVIS
Guadeloupe
DOMINICA
Martinique
SAINT LUCIA
BARBADOS
GRENADA
TRINIDAD and TOBAGO
Port-of-Spain
Georgetown
VENEZUELA
Ciudad Bolívar
Caracas
Aruba
Maracaibo
Cartagena
Santa Marta
(to New York)

Chinese into Cuba. Some eighteen thousand indentured Chinese "coolies" reached the British Caribbean in the late nineteenth century, and the label would soon be appropriated for a far larger stream of migrants from British India. More than 36,000 indentured Indian "coolies" reached Jamaica before the system was finally abolished in 1917. But it was the southeastern rimland colonies that most eagerly subsidized the arrival of indentured Asian workers in these years. Nearly 240,000 Indians traveled under contracts of indenture to British Guiana, another 145,000 to Trinidad.[15] In the nearby French islands of Martinique, Guadeloupe, and French Guiana, where slavery was abolished in 1848, some 87,000 Indians were serving terms of indenture by 1885. Another 35,000 would travel from India to Dutch Surinam over the following generation, alongside 22,000 indentured Javanese.[16] By the start of the twentieth century the population of Trinidad included some 150,000 of African or part-African origin, 90,000 East Indians, 5,000 Chinese, and around 50,000 whites of British, French, Spanish, Portuguese, and other descent.[17]

In the same years the descendants of enslaved Africans were taking advantage of their newfound freedom of movement in shorter hops around the eastern Caribbean. Sojourners from the Virgin Islands, St. Kitts, Nevis, and Antigua traveled to Puerto Rico and the Dominican Republic in small but ongoing migration after 1880, harvesting sugar and creating distinctive creole-speaking barrios within capitals and major ports. Barbadians circulated to Trinidad and Guiana, Brazil and beyond: departures totaled over fifteen thousand from 1863 to 1870 alone.[18] Bustling Port of Spain had whole neighborhoods filled with immigrants from Barbados, Grenada, St. Vincent, and Dominica. Other Windward Islanders crossed the seven-mile-wide channel that separated Trinidad from Venezuela's Paria peninsula and established themselves as cacao farmers and small traders. Many thousands labored on the gold fields and rubber-gathering camps deep in the Orinoco rainforest before heading on or heading home.[19]

In the western Caribbean the first two generations after British abolition saw increasing temporary and longer-term movements. Circulation of turtlemen and traders from small English-speaking islands like San Andres and Providencia strengthened the longstanding links between the British islands and outposts and Mesoamerica's rain-forested eastern lowlands. When the California Gold Rush created an isthmian transport boom in 1849, hundreds of Jamaicans rushed to Panama. Over a thousand of them were contracted by a U.S. company to build a railroad across the isthmus, working alongside a similar number of indentured Chinese laborers.

Panama by 1855 had acquired a cosmopolitan population, arranged in a clear occupational hierarchy according to race and national origin. "The railroad officials, steamboat agents, foreign consuls, and a score of Yankee traders, hotel-keepers, billiard markers and bar-tenders comprise all the whites, who are the exclusive few," one visitor wrote. "The better class of shop-keepers are Mulattos from Jamaica, St. Domingo, and the other West Indian islands, while the dispensers of cheap grog, and hucksters of fruit and small wares are chiefly negroes. The main body of the population is made up of laborers, negroes from Jamaica, yellow natives of mixed African and Indian blood, and sad, sedate, turbaned Hindoos, the poor exiled Coolies from the Ganges."[20] Those Chinese workers who survived the horrendous conditions of railroad construction usually moved on to the Pacific coastal destinations—from Peru in the south to California in the north—drawing large numbers of their countrymen in the same years, or headed from Panama's Atlantic railroad terminus to the main ports of the western Caribbean: Havana, Santiago de Cuba, and Kingston (where they were among the first Chinese arrivals).[21] Afro-Jamaican workers too were more likely to move on than to head home.

A western Caribbean labor market emerged as projects like the *Ferrocarril al Atlántico* in Costa Rica drew thousands of English-speaking black migrants. A thousand indentured Chinese, contracted by the railroad boss Minor Keith in California, Honduras, and Macao in 1872–73, labored on the Costa Rican railroad project alongside several thousand Afro-Caribbeans and nearly two thousand Italians (the latter's arrival arranged by Keith and subsidized by a Costa Rican state eager to introduce, in Keith's phrase, "select breeding stock").[22] Over the following generation a few thousand Spaniards, Italians, and Germans would dock at Central America's Caribbean ports and head to the highlands, where they became overseers, managers, and merchants in the burgeoning coffee sector.

The efforts of Ferdinand de Lesseps of France to build a sea-level canal across the isthmus of Panama from 1881 to 1889 drew on these well-established migratory connections and created new ones. Thousands of men and women from French-speaking islands of the eastern Caribbean sailed west to seek work. Labor recruiters advertised in the Jamaican press and hired on the docks of Kingston. Still, most British Caribbeans headed to Colón without contract, from Port Limon (Puerto Limón), Bocas del Toro, or Montego Bay.[23] Recruiters aimed to sign on workers who would stay put, but Western Caribbeans preferred to cycle through. Jamaican departures for Panama topped 24,000 in 1883; over eleven thousand returned in the same year. Such was the demand generated by the massive influx of mostly male workers that washerwomen from Kingston picked up laundry in Colón to wash, starch, and press on the island and return on the next steamer.[24] In all some fifty thousand British islanders reached Panama in these years.[25] The new cycle of isthmian prosperity also drew Chinese immigrants whose second eight-year term of indenture in Cuba was just ending.[26] By 1890 the Chinese population of Panama numbered around three thousand.[27]

The Heyday of U.S. Investment and Intraregional Migration, 1900–1930

U.S. intervention in the Cuban War of Independence in 1898 brought Puerto Rico into permanent colonial status and Cuba into a more partial and punctuated political subordination. The new Panamanian state rewarded U.S. aid to the independence effort with the concession "in perpetuity" of a ten-mile wide strip of land to complete the canal abandoned by the French. Workers arriving under contract to the U.S. government's Isthmian Canal Commission (ICC) included 20,000 Barbadians, 7,500 from the French colonies of Guadeloupe and Martinique, 8,000 Spaniards, 2,000 Italians, and 1,000 Greeks.[28]

However, personal networks mobilized many more migrants than labor recruiters did. By 1907 the number of potential workers reaching the docks of Colón on their own—mostly British West Indians—was more than double the number arriving under contract.[29] The 20,000 Barbadian contract workers were matched by another 25,000 men and women who paid their own passage from Barbados. Tens of thousands from smaller islands of the eastern Caribbean joined them. But as before, it was Jamaicans who dwarfed all other migrants to Panama; some 80,000 to 90,000 made the journey in the era of construction.[30] The 1912 census found 389 men (and one woman) born in India residing in the Canal Zone, but several times that number surely resided outside of U.S. territory, in the Republic of Panama.[31] Chinese immigration, putatively illegal, continued apace.[32] A new program of forced registration of Chinese men in 1913 found some 7,300 in residence on the isthmus.[33]

Beyond Panama agricultural and extractive exports expanded across the Greater Caribbean as U.S. direct foreign investment, already well established in Cuba, spread. The United Fruit Company (UFCo), born in 1898, was by far the largest single plantation employer of men (and on the islands, women). Along the coastal lowlands of eastern Guatemala, northern Honduras, and northern Colombia, United Fruit took over existing regional systems of smallholder production; in British Honduras, northern Nicaragua, southeast Costa Rica, and western Panama, it claimed and cut vast tracts of tropical rainforest. Now stevedores and passengers circulated from the Greater Caribbean through New Orleans, United Fruit's main port of entry for bananas from Central America. Nevertheless the total numbers of Cuban- or West Indies–born residents of Louisiana was never more than a few hundred in this period.[34]

Rising U.S. investment redoubled the long-established pattern in which overseas capital underwrote dense populations of coerced workers and intensive monocrop production. United Fruit Company banana and citrus plantations in Jamaica employed thousands by the 1920s. U.S. capital and trade preferences fueled a steady expansion of sugar plantations in Cuba and the Dominican Republic, which boomed when the disruption of European beet-sugar production during the First World War sent prices sky-high. The harvest season of 1920 brought over 27,000 Jamaicans and 36,000 Haitians to Cuban shores in a single year.[35] All told, sugar plantations in eastern Cuba drew hundreds of thousands of workers from Jamaica and Haiti; plantations in the western Dominican Republic relied on Haitian seasonal migrants, while those in the south employed tens of thousands from the eastern British Caribbean. In the early 1920s several thousand British West Indians entered the Dominican Republic for each harvest.[36] Some ten thousand British West Indians, mostly Jamaicans, reached Haiti in the same years, and 1932 found three to four thousand still resident there, hungry and unemployed.[37]

Meanwhile Chinese entry to Cuba, restricted in 1899, was permitted again as sugar production boomed. Cuba's Chinese population had dropped from over 40,000 in 1877 to just over 10,000 in 1919, but rose to nearly 25,000 by 1931.[38] Dwarfing all other migrant streams, immigration from Spain accelerated continuously. More than 800,000 Spaniards entered Cuba between 1902 and 1931, over 94,000 of them in 1920 alone.[39] In 1931 the population of Cuba included 250,000 persons born in Spain. The same census registered 102,000 blacks born outside Cuba.[40]

Export production also expanded in the eastern Caribbean, although British rather than U.S. capital predominated. Trinidad's East Indian population, 120,000 strong, remained the mainstay of that island's sugar labor force.[41] Meanwhile hard-up neighborhoods of Port of Spain swelled with migrants from nearby small islands where economic opportunities were even scarcer. By 1946 the population of Trinidad included 12,000 Barbadians and 36,000 Windward Islanders.[42] The first commercial oil well began producing in Trinidad in 1902, and by the 1920s more than ten thousand men, Trinidadians and small islanders, had traveled to work on the oilfields. Some ten thousand eastern Caribbeans found work on the oilfields of Maracaibo, Venezuela, after production began there in 1916; a generation later the population of Trinidad would include over three thousand people born in Venezuela in this era.[43] In turn, new refineries in Curaçao and Aruba drew thousands from Trinidad and Barbados beginning in the interwar years. Venezuela's ports and cities continued to attract traders and tradesmen, and Afro-Antillean entries into Venezuela totaled from six to eleven thousand annually throughout the first three decades of the twentieth century.[44]

In sum, the expansion of export production on the islands and rimlands of the Greater Caribbean had created both new opportunities and new constraints for the region's working people. On the one hand, new plantations and extractive enterprises offered new wage sources from which remittances could be sent home, whether home was a few parishes or many islands away. Ports grew, and with them service economies and attendant opportunities for independent entrepreneurship, often in women's hands: boardinghouses, sidewalk vending, laundry, prostitution. Expanded banana plantations in areas not previously under intensive cultivation (like northeast Honduras, eastern Nicaragua, southern Costa Rica, and western Panama) encroached on lands crucial to indigenous populations' subsistence. But as locals lost autonomy along the rimlands, newcomers gained it. In contrast, on the far more densely populated islands the expansion of fruit plantations made peasant smallholds ever harder to sustain, increasing land pressure and driving up taxes.

The circum-Caribbean migratory system drew the grandchildren of British Caribbean freedmen and freedwomen out of rural island communities to rimland jungles and docks in the first decades of the twentieth century and then spun those migrants' children and grandchildren onward in turn, now to urban employment: on the islands of their grandparents' birth, in the Spanish American republics of their own birth, and in the industrialized economies of Europe and North America. By 1906 to 1912 movement from the Caribbean to New York reached a pace nearly equaling the well-established flow to Florida, and by the 1920s surpassed it.[45] Some seven thousand black immigrants to the United States in the first three decades of the twentieth century gave Central America as their last region of residence.[46] The number of British West Indians who reached the United States via Cuba was doubtless many times greater. Black immigration from the Caribbean to the United States averaged 3,500 per year from 1903 to 1913, climbed to 5,000 per year from 1914 to 1923, and surpassed 10,000 in 1924 alone. All told over 100,000 Afro-Caribbeans entered the United States in the first quarter of the twentieth century, and many stayed. The 1930 census recorded 74,500 "Negroes" of West Indian birth.[47]

Small numbers of Afro-Caribbeans also traveled to Canada in the first decades of the twentieth century: women to work as domestic servants under a short-lived contracting scheme, men laboring in mines in Nova Scotia and elsewhere. Dense shipping lanes linked the eastern Caribbean to Newfoundland and thus made it possible for individual trajectories to tie eastern Canada into the circum-Caribbean circuits described above.[48] In 1912–15 annual West Indian entry into Canada totaled around two hundred people; it would not top those numbers until policies and prospects were remade after the Second World War.[49] Even on the basis of the very small-scale interwar movement, in the Maritimes, Toronto, and Montreal communities formed and institutions were built, including churches, chapters of the United Negro Improvement Association, and fraternal lodges.[50]

Breachable Boundaries in a Heterogeneous World

Using the broadest strokes, contemporary authors described migrant flows with reference to their territories of origin, continental ancestry, color, and imperial filiation. Yet these broad collectives were both crossed by individuals and redrawn over time. Fundamental to both the maintenance and the remaking of social boundaries were matters of sex. Ultimately it was the intimate encounters between migratory men and women that determined the contours of collective identities over time. In this sense any analysis of Caribbean migration demands attention to both the micro- and macro-politics of desire.

One factor shaping patterns of kinship and sexuality within and between groups in the Caribbean was the demographic composition of migrant streams. Overall the larger the distance between origin and destination, the greater the predominance of men. Women were fewest in the earliest years of a new migratory movement; the number of women and children then increased over time; more women migrated to cities than to rural areas. Exceptions occurred when employers or public officials dictated specific gender criteria. Migrants contracted to labor on the Panama Canal were exclusively male. East Indian migrants traveling under indenture to Trinidad, Guyana, and Jamaica included a relatively high proportion of women because British imperial officials went to great effort to recruit women, hoping to increase the number of South Asian migrants who remained past their term of indenture. Because of the strictures of indenture, East Indian women's patterns of residence were just as rural as East Indian men's, and even after indenture ended they were significantly more likely than Afro-Caribbean women to be directly employed on plantations.[51]

In the early years of migration to Panama, Central America, and Cuba, British West Indian settlements might include eight or ten times as many men as women. Conversely, the migrant flows that were largest in volume, most urban in destination, least shaped by employers' recruitment, and most enduring included the largest number of women. One can see the impact of recruitment, for instance, in the fact that Barbadians living in the Canal Zone in 1912 numbered 7,400 men and only 1,500 women, while Jamaicans in the same census had 12,000 men and 8,000 women. The same dynamic dictated that the Chinese population of Cuba was almost exclusively male, while Chinese populations elsewhere (the product of individual migration rather than indentured contracting), though still heavily male, contained a few more women. Cuba's Chinese population was from 97 to 99 percent male in every census from the start of indenture through 1943.[52] Guatemala's total Chinese population in 1940 comprised 629 men and 41 women; in Honduras in 1930 the numbers were 265 men and 13 women; in Costa Rica in 1927 it was 580 men and 153 women.[53]

The population of the Republic of Panama in 1930 included 9,900 foreign whites, 26,900 foreign blacks, 4,900 foreign *mestizos*, 1,300 foreign *mulatos*, and 3,000 foreigners of "yellow" race. Men outnumbered women 10 to 1 among "yellow," but only 1.5 to 1 among whites and only 1.3 to 1 among blacks.[54] Costa Rica's 29,000 foreign-born in 1927 included 11,000 whites, 11,000 blacks, 5,800 *mestizos*, 800 *mulatos*, and 480 of "yellow" race. Foreign-born men outnumbered women by 1.8 to 1 among whites, 1.7 to 1 among blacks, 1.5 to 1 among *mestizos*, and over 10 to 1 among the "yellow" population.[55] But these national figures masked huge regional variations. British West Indian women were most numerous in Colón, Panama City, the Canal Zone, Santiago de Cuba, Havana, and Port Limon. The same ports drew Spanish-speaking *mestizas* from small towns and the countryside farther inland, beyond the plantation zone.[56]

In the banana zones and bustling ports of Central America, sex was structured by a wide array of arrangements: some involving long-term expectations of support, many not; some involving the immediate exchange of cash, many not; some preceded by formal church or state sanction, many not; some involving outright violence, many not. Categories in use at the time termed these relations consensual partnership, prostitution, marriage, or rape. One can find examples of each of these enacted between men and women of the same origin, and between men and women separated by gulfs of language, nationality, ancestry, wealth, and power as well. "Things was rugged in them days," one Yankee old-timer recalled in 1933, describing life a quarter-century earlier when United Fruit was just opening operations in Puerto Barrios, Guatemala, "but you could get a gal for a fishhook, and fishhooks was two for a nickel in the commissary."[57] U.S. banana men's reminiscences from the 1920s and 1930s also record the existence of established couples: a "white Jamaican" overseer and "his 'woman'," a "good-looking and very pleasant black Jamaican, [like him] born in Costa Rica," living together in Chiriquí, Panama; a German overseer, Charley Lanz, and "Maria, at best half Indian who had had other protectors before she acquired Charley," raising their twin boys on a Honduran plantation.[58]

Other tales leave no doubt that in the *zona bananera* forced sex was common and female consent a fungible concept.[59] However, women were not automatically or inherently disempowered in heavily male settings. To the contrary, the very fact of male demographic predominance created a seller's market for traditionally female services, including laundry, meals, and sex. The British author Winifred James, living in Bocas de Toro in 1913, wrote with amusement that her husband "picked up a letter one day which turned out to be from one of the best known ladies of pleasure in the town. Every week a contingent of them go up the line in the pay train. It was to her 'sweet-man' telling him about her profits that week-end and adjuring him not to fret for she was 'thinking of him all the time.' The world is a quaint place."[60] James smiled at the notion that sex work could be compatible with an ongoing conjugal partnership, but the historical record makes clear that romance was integral to the lives of sex workers in Caribbean Central America.[61]

Just what a given intimate partnership entailed in terms of economic and extended family obligations could be a matter of contention. Therese Jones, from Trinidad, traveled to Panama on her own some time around 1908 and set up a *cantina* in Portobello. She moved in with the Barbadian George Springer in 1910 and later agreed to marry him. In February 1913 Springer went to Barbados to visit his ailing mother; Therese gave him 230 *pesos* in silver for the round-trip passage. When he ran through that money before buying passage home, Therese sent along another 30 *pesos* in gold. Once back in Colón, Springer refused to seek work. He told Therese to open another *cantina* like the one she had had in Portobello; she replied that he should try to get hired at the Canal Commission. When he ignored her and continued to expect her to cover their rent and expenses she decided to separate, start a new business in Bocas del Toro, and find a new (Trinidadian) man.[62]

Folks in polyglot ports like Limon, Colón, and Bocas clearly thought about sex in terms of race: to be accused of "whoring with Chinese" was a commonly hurled insult among Spanish-speakers and English-speakers alike in Port Limon, and occasioned no end of civil suits over "damaged reputation" and injured pride.[63] Sexual intimacy with Chinese was evidently regarded as particularly transgressive.[64] But while racial boundaries mattered in thinking about sex, which boundaries counted as racial was never fixed.

Discussing "sex across boundaries" in the context of migration risks reifying the very divides we wish to question. Divisions between Hindu and Muslim South Asians, between French-creole- and English-creole-speaking islands within the British Caribbean were vitally important but—just like those between *"trinitarios"* and "true Venezuelans" or between *"afroantillanos"* and "native Panamanians"—never as eternal as those who insisted on them supposed. As Aisha Khan points out, there was never an original moment of unmixed purity for any migrant group in the Caribbean. Categories acquired retroactive homogeneity only as certain differences were silenced or redefined as insignificant.[65]

To narrate the story of migration and settlement in the Caribbean it is necessary to use categories, and simplest to use the categories of collective identity that appear most basic in the present. But the resulting tautology obscures the fact that current lines of division are the *result* of past choices regarding alliance, avoidance, and self-definition, rather than the *cause* or explanation of them. Even divisions based on continent of origin, for which we use labels thought of as racial (black, white, East Indian, Chinese) are the results. Over the first half of the twentieth century Caribbean Jews went from being routinely categorized as Oriental to being routinely categorized as white.[66] The division between French-speaking islanders and English-speaking islanders was jealously guarded at some migrant destinations, only to be erased not only from practice but from memory a few generations later.[67] And in some places East Indians started off black and became *afrodescendientes*.

With our perceptions guided by late-twentieth-century racial constructs, it seems obvious that Afro-Caribbeans were black, because African, and East Indians were brown, because Asian. Yet Costa Rican journalist Antonio Zambrano, describing the rail line just south of Port Limon in 1895, noted the "crops of the *coolies*, the yucca clusters, the plantings of yam and beans, of sugar cane and of the many other things that the East Indian black [*el negrito de las Indias Orientales*] cultivates to supply the Limon market" and went on to rave about the "girls of brilliant ebony in whose breasts nubility trembles" who made up this (East Indian) community's youth.[68]

The racial coordinates of South Asian immigrants—their degree of distance from Afro-descended British West Indians in particular—were just not that clear in Limon. Across the British Caribbean the term "coolie" (also "cooley-man" or "cooley-gal") was applied to South Asian migrants, the terms "china-man" or "chiney" to the Chinese. In 1912, the Costa Rican president outlawed all further entry into Costa Rica by "individuals of the 'cooli' class." But whose arrival, exactly, had been forbidden? The central government consulted local medical professors and the published works of German ethnographers. The governor of Limón tried to help too: "By their special physiognomy they are easily recognized at first sight: of copper color, they speak not English but a dialect; they are filthy in their dress to the extreme that they exhale an unsupportable stench; it is their custom not to bathe, but instead grease their whole body with coconut oil." They arrived in small groups, under the command of a boss who translated and signed contracts; sometimes they all wore a towel wrapped around their heads; others who arrived separately wore velvet caps and dedicated themselves to peddling. They refused to work with either machete or axe, preferring to live from theft and arson.[69]

Yet despite these supposed bodily, sartorial, and characterological markers, coolies did not form a group apart in Limon. References to "*culis*" appear occasionally in judicial testimonies from the first decades of the twentieth century in Limon, but so do references to "jamaicanos" born in "Indostan." A Jamaica-born "Jhon Gupi (culi)" was accused in 1911 of causing one "Mari Hall, Culi" to die of fright in Cieneguita (the community Zambrano had described as the center of East Indian settlement fifteen years earlier). The witnesses against Gupi included Joseph Nish Foley, born in "Indostan," and Foley's son Charles Bennet, "jamaicano."[70] "Coolies" and "Jamaicans" overlapped at the level of daily life as well as at the level of rhetoric. In 1906 the Afro-Jamaican Joaquin Thompson Porkins killed his consensual partner, a "cooli woman."[71] References to "coolies" also appear occasionally in the English-language press of Port Limon as late as the 1930s, when an irate letter from "Mr. Ramsay Dosha, an East India planter" long established in the region, explained that the label "coolie" was "detestably insulting" to his people.[72] Every indication from newspaper references is that East Indians were fully integrated into the heavily Jamaican social world of English-speaking black Limon, attending weddings and parties alongside other members of the port's fiercely respectable middle class. Today Costa Ricans profess no knowledge that immigrants from South Asia ever reached their shores; no academic account of Limon's past mentions their presence; and the tag *negro culí* is identified by some aging highlanders as referring to "a really dark-skinned negro; you know, the ones who are almost blue-black."[73]

In Panama in the first years of the twentieth century "babú" rather than "coolie" became standard slang for South Asian immigrants, perhaps because the term "coolie" was already in use among North Americans on the isthmus for the many Chinese immigrants there. Ideas about Chinese migrants drawn from other Pacific settings certainly shaped perceptions of race in Panama. The Canal Zone census taker Harry Franck reported in 1913: "Almost every known race mingles in Panama city, even to Chinese coolies in their umbrella hats and rolled up cotton trousers, delving in rich market gardens on the edges of the town or dog-trotting through the streets under two baskets dancing on the ends of a bamboo pole, till one fancies oneself at times in Singapore or Shanghai."[74] Notably larger than Costa Rica's South Asian population from the start, Panama's self-described *hindostanos* chose to build difference rather than blend in, founding temples and mosques; Hindu, Muslim, and mixed cricket clubs; and a Sociedad Hindostana de Panama, inaugurated on the occasion of Indian Independence in 1947, which remains active to this day—

a stark contrast to the "negritos de las Indias Orientales" just up the coast in Port Limon, whose choice of Afro-Antillean partners both reflected and hastened the dissolution of the line separating East from West Indian there.[75]

While export economies were booming and immigrants welcomed across the region, some observers offered optimistic visions of the role that difference and desire would play in shaping the Americas. "Now that the emigration of our people is creating so much attention," wrote the pseudonymous "Mountain Man" in the Kingston *Daily Gleaner* in 1917, "It would seem as if there must eventually be a fusion of all the races in America, and a race of super-man evolved. The Jamaican young women in emigrating in such large numbers to the States, may be obeying an instinct which we do not at present understand, and the effects of which will be powerfully felt in the centuries to come. Who knows?"[76] But ultimately this hopeful vision of the fusion of immigrants into a single "race of super-man" would find scant support, whether on islands or rimlands, in Havana or Washington. The spirit of the coming era was captured instead in a letter adjacent to Mountain Man's, from a pseudonymous "AUSTRALIAN" who attacked "Oriental" immigration to Jamaica and concluded, "We must turn the flood of Chinese into another channel. Let them try Cuba or Puerto Rico, so that we may see and get an object lesson as to how the Americans handle such problems. For the sake of our future population we might pass a law requiring every Chinaman coming here in future to bring his Chinese wife with him. This would avoid another 'colour problem' in the future."[77] Within this paradigm sex across boundaries was the problem, not the solution: and race-based immigration restriction the proper antidote.

The Science of Difference and Desire and Its Policy Implications

For contemporary observers the claim that racial groupings reflect cultural constructs rather than biological entities would have seemed absurd. The early-twentieth-century Atlantic world saw the zenith of scientific racism as a paradigm for understanding collective difference. Group boundaries were understood to reflect biological divides that sexual intimacy breached literally and irreversibly. While some early-twentieth-century authorities agreed with Mountain Man that the biological fusion of races as a result of migration and sex could be a good thing, more voices insisted along with "AUSTRALIAN" that breeding and interbreeding by immigrants threatened receiving societies at their very core. Thus debates over the contours and consequences of sexual intimacy became central to policy debates in the interwar Atlantic, particularly regarding immigration policy.

The Caribbean became a privileged place to observe the impacts of race

Figure 3.1 U.S. eugenicists sought to document and quantify the results of "mixing" "B[lack]," "R[ed]," "Y[ellow]," and "W[hite]" "racial stocks" through studies of Caribbean people.
Source: Harry H. Laughlin Papers, Truman State University, Lantern Slides, Black Case, section 7,1736; Dolan DNA Learning Center Image no. 943. Original title: "Mixed race Jamaican school children."

crossing. In 1908 the statistician Karl Pearson of University College, London, began corresponding with Isaac Costa, a doctor in Jamaica.[78] Pearson sought empirical evidence to reconcile the Mendelian model of plant hybridity to the world of humankind, where the unitariness of black and white races seemed self-evident but outcomes refused to conform to expectations. Pearson's questions poured forth: "Mulatto + white gives a quadroon. Is this again a blend? Our theorists would say it must consist of half whites and half mulattos in number. I should have thought that the quadroon was lighter in skin than the mulatto. . . . and that pure white skins did not occur in 50% of quadroons." "Mulatto + mulatto. Is this usually a mulatto in colour? Our theorists say 25% are pure white skins, 25% pure black skins, and only 50% mulattos." Dr. Costa replied with the disdain of an elevated insider, calling the ideas of the theorists "ridiculously incorrect." "There are now and then slight variations from the usual mulatto brown or mulatto-yellow," he reported, "but you may be quite certain that no pure black skins or pure white skins come from mulatto + mulatto. You can state this dogmatically."[79] When Pearson published "A Note on the Skin-Colour of Negro and White Crosses from Information Received from the West Indies" in *Biometrika* the following year, photos and letters from Costa were his only data.[80]

Caribbean politics as well as Caribbean bodies were read for data on the impact of race mixing. Pearson's contemporary Harry Johnston cheered on the influx of Spaniards into Cuba circa 1910, without which the island "had a considerable chance in the near future of developing into another Haiti or a San Domingo." Were it not for Spaniards' arrival and enfranchisement "the 'coloured' vote would soon have amounted to a third of the total, and before long to a half, and finally have preponderated over the white element—with what effect on public order or efficiency it is difficult to say, since the Cuban negro . . . has not yet been sufficiently tried in positions of responsibility and public trust to have established a racial character, good or bad."[81]

A contrasting set of claims about the political outcomes of interracial sex animated one of the most widely debated works on imperial rule in its day, Sydney Olivier's *White Capital and Coloured Labour* (1910). Olivier was an Oxford-educated Fabian Socialist, longtime Colonial Office official, and governor of Jamaica from 1907 to 1913. The book is an extended brief against "colour-prejudice and race antagonism" and the "negrophobist theory of exclusion."[82] Yet Olivier's is an antiracism that reifies race at every turn, as he attributes political and social processes of all kinds to the ancestral inheritance of those involved. Hence "the future of the relations between White Capital and Coloured Labor depends so largely on the possibility of Race-fusion either by the bodily process of blending by intermarriage, or by some alternative psychical process of establishing sympathetic understanding, that we must establish what . . . has been done in this direction in those communities in which people of European and African races have been forced into social contact."[83] In other words, the future of modern capitalism and colonialism depended on lessons drawn from a past of sex across boundaries in the Caribbean.

For Olivier, relying on the West Indies as his constant example, it was indisputable that "a colony of black, coloured, and whites has far more organic efficiency and far more promise in it than a colony of black and white alone."[84] Other observers drew opposite conclusions. One traveler, A. Hyatt Verrill, informed his readers that within the Jamaican middle class, those of "both races and all colors . . . are all socially equal and . . . freely intermarry." For Verrill this arrangement must be inherently unstable, given that "the primitive negro strain is far more virile than the white, and there is a constant tendency for offspring of mixed blood to revert to the African rather than to the Anglo-Saxon type. . . . And it is an established biological fact that, should the intermarriage of the two races continue, the result would be, not the absorption of the negro race by the Caucasian, but the annihilation of the Caucasian by the negro, with a wholly colored community as the ultimate result."[85] As Verrill's passage underlines, questions about the individual biological consequences of "interracial" unions and the society-wide political consequences of race-mixing were inextricable. The essence of race in the eugenicist paradigm was that it represented the point of fusion of individual and collective destinies.

Thus as demography and population dynamics came to the fore in prescriptions for national progress, the question of who might have sex with whom and with what results was always at issue in debates over migration control. This is evident in the testimony by the Princeton economist Robert Foerster before the U.S. House of Representatives Committee on Immigration and Naturalization in March 1925. The topic was "The Racial Problems Involved in Immigration from Latin America, the West Indies, and Canada," an exploration of the implications of the decision embodied in the Johnson-Reed Act (1924) to leave immigrants to the United States from all "American republics" outside the quota system, that is, their volume of entry subject to no numerical cap. Like many before him, Foerster found that "the most notable racial aspect of Latin America doubtless has been the crossing of races."[86] Profoundly worrisome, then, that although "provisions drastically limiting the immigration of oriental peoples prevent the immigration into the United States of Chinese, Japanese, and some other peoples . . . no law has been enacted imposing any similar restriction upon the immigration of the races which constitute the dominant stocks in the Latin American countries"—that is, Indians, Negroes, and "Mixed Stocks."[87]

Where Sydney Olivier had seen in sexual contact the possibility of blending and harmony, Foerster saw disharmony, asymmetry, and a need for utmost caution. "The effects of race mixture are still far from being understood. . . . [D]espite the fact that important studies are today being pursued in various parts of the world, the difficulties in ascertaining race elements in parentage and of distinguishing environmental or social influences from hereditary or physical influences are such that exact knowledge, except of limited aspects, is likely to remain scanty." Yet there was no need to let this state of scholarly ignorance put the brakes on policy advising. State-of-the-art science left no doubt: hybrids at best would be inferior to the superior strain and at worst even less fit than the inferior strain.[88] Radical restriction of immigration from Latin America and the Caribbean was essential to the future stability and harmony of the United States.

Prominent among the "important studies" of race mixing under way was that conducted in Jamaica by Charles Davenport, head of the Eugenics Record Office, and his research associate Dr. Morris Steggerda. Financed by the Carnegie Institution and published in 1929, *Race Crossing in Jamaica* included anthropometric surveys, intelligence testing, and psychological evaluations of adolescent students at Mico College. Steggerda and Davenport reported that the "mulattos" among their subjects suffered dangerous physical disharmonies, and insisted that statistics showing coloured subjects' success on intelligence tests masked the unusual frequency of "muzzle-headedness" they had observed among these experimental subjects.[89]

Even at the time such views were contested. W. E. Castle mocked Davenport's and Steggerda's Jamaican research in *Science* in 1930, particularly their stress on a half-centimeter differential in mean leg length minus mean arm length. Castle concluded, "We like to think of the Negro as inferior. We like to think of Negro-white crosses as a degradation of the white race. We look for evidence in support of the idea and try to persuade ourselves that we have found it even when the resemblance is very slight. The honestly made records of Davenport and Steggerda tell a very different story about hybrid Jamaicans from that which Davenport and Jennings tell about them in broad sweeping statements."[90] Davenport fired back a fierce defense of the significance of his team's statistical findings and of the biological reality of race.[91] Hybrids do not harmonize; stock determines psyche; demography is destiny.

These were the messages that Davenport and his deputy Harry Laughlin carried to the Pan American Conferences of Eugenics and Homiculture in Cuba in 1927 and in Buenos Aires in 1934, along with new "Model Immigration Law" templates and an implicit threat of future U.S. restrictions on immigration from Spanish American republics. While representatives from some of the larger South American nations called such diagnoses and prescriptions into question, those from the Spanish-speaking republics of the circum-Caribbean did not. Representatives from Panama and Cuba spoke vehemently in favor of Davenport's proposals, insisting on a distinction between their nations' "own" populations of partial African ancestry and the undesirable recent immigrants of color who could not and should not be assimilated.[92] Davenport's proposals regarding premarital screening and prevention of reproduction by the "unfit" proved too controversial for the Latin American delegates to countenance, but his proposed language regarding immigration restriction was adopted whole cloth—and made patent that the issue at stake was reproductive crossing, that is, sex with natives. "The nations of America will issue and apply laws of immigration with intention to bar the entry into their territory of individuals from races whose association with the natives may be considered biologically undesirable."[93]

Declarations by Hispanic Caribbean delegates at the Pan American Conference, like the contemporaneous speeches of populist politicians back home, ignored the long history of circum-Caribbean migration and mixing; and proclaimed the United States responsible for having introduced "alien" and "undesirable" populations into their territories in the first place.[94] The muckraking progressive journalist Carleton Beals echoed in 1931 the anti-imperialist arguments made by these *mestizo* populists: the "Negroes who swarm out of overpopulated Haiti, Jamaica and Trinidad . . . are the breeders of this vast circle of ocean, island, and sky. . . . [T]he Negro brought even greater love and lust than the natives . . . So his kind have multiplied and continue to multiply in a frenzy of fertility and magic."[95] Ultimately, "The Caribbean is an enormous black incubator," whose swarming offspring have been harnessed to the interests of U.S. capital. Corporate activities "disseminat[ed] the Negro race" ever more widely in a process that brings "growing denationalization and cultural chaos," pushing islands "to fall under self-perpetuating tyrannies completely servile to American interests."[96]

Thus the late 1920s and 1930s saw Spanish American republics drawn into dialogue with northern eugenicism precisely as populist nativism intensified in response to regional economic crisis. As reformist middle-class politicians struggled to wrest control of nation-states from the old oligarchies, nonwhite immigrants and their descendents became the targets of racist invective and legislative exclusion across the Greater Caribbean. New laws restricted black entry, employment, and naturalization at site after site. They also added new penalties to the restrictions on "Asiatic," "yellow," "Mongolian," and Middle Eastern immigration that had been legislated a generation earlier. New anti-black legislation was passed in Honduras in 1923 and 1926, in El Salvador in 1925, in Guatemala in 1936, in Panama in 1926, 1928, and 1941, in Costa Rica in 1942, in Cuba in 1933, and in Venezuela in 1929. Movement from the British Caribbean to the United States was similarly barred after 1924, the Johnson-Reed act made to function as a ban on British West Indian migration despite its race-neutral language.[97]

Extralegal violence by police and others toward nonwhite non-citizens rose markedly as well, especially in Cuba, Venezuela, and the Dominican Republic—where the scapegoating of black migrants reached its nadir with the slaughter of some fifteen thousand Haitians and Dominicans of Haitian ancestry in the border region, on the orders of the country's dictator Rafael Leonidas Trujillo in 1937.[98] As doors slammed shut across the region, once-proud working-class emigrants hunkered down in ethnic enclaves within increasingly hostile lands, or headed back to their islands of origin, some penniless, some physically disabled by hard labor or abuse. The multigenerational saga of migrants who expanded transnational kin networks and created new routes to partial prosperity reached a grim denouement of falling wages and state racism, lean pickings nearby, and no easy way out. For earlier generations the borders of nation and empire had been extraordinarily porous in this region of islands and littorals, small craft and steamers. But in the 1920s and 1930s statesmen and scholars collaborated to impose borderlines based on skin color, birthplace, and assumed genetic heritage in a region that had been built out of mixing. Like all borders these supposed divides were in fact permeable; yet that truth did not stop states from transforming the seductive fiction of difference into the most rigid barriers they could build.

Notes

An earlier version of this chapter appeared in Donna Gabaccia and Dirk Hoerder, eds., *Connecting Seas and Connected Ocean Rims: Indian, Atlantic, and Pacific Oceans and China Seas Migrations from the 1830s to the 1930s* (Leiden: Brill, 2011). The editors are grateful to Lara Putnam and Brill Publishers for permission.

1 Walton Look Lai, "The Chinese Indenture System in the British West Indies and Its Aftermath," *The Chinese in the Caribbean*, ed. Andrew Wilson (Princeton: Markus Wiener, 2004), 4.

2 Cf. Ann Laura Stoler, ed., *Haunted by Empire: Geographies of Intimacy in North American History* (Durham: Duke University Press, 2006).

3 See Lowell Gudmundson and Justin Wolfe, eds., *Blacks and Blackness in Central America: Between Race and Place* (Durham: Duke University Press, 2010).

4 George W. Roberts, *The Population of Jamaica* (Cambridge: Cambridge University Press, 1957), 109–10.

5 Roberts, *The Population of Jamaica*, 65.

6 Bridget Brereton, *Race Relations in Colonial Trinidad, 1870–1900* (Cambridge: Cambridge University Press, 1979), 12. Nearly half the island's population in 1891 had been born elsewhere.

7 Sr. M. Noel Menezes, "The Madeiran Portuguese and the Establishment of the Catholic Church in British Guiana, 1835–98," *After the Crossing: Immigrants and Minorities in Caribbean Creole Society*, ed. Howard Johnson (London: Frank Cass, 1988), 62; G. W. Roberts and J. Byrne, "Summary Statistics on Indenture and Associated Migration Affecting the West Indies, 1834–1918," *Population Studies* 20, no. 1 (July 1966), 125–34.

8 Francisco Scarano, "Labor and Society in the Nineteenth Century," *The Modern Caribbean*, ed. Franklin Knight and Colin Palmer (Chapel Hill: University of North Carolina Press, 1989), 76.

9 Duvon Corbitt, "Immigration in Cuba," *Hispanic American Historical Review* 22, no. 2 (1942), 280–308, quote p. 286.

10 Rebecca Scott, *Slave Emancipation in Cuba: The Transition to Free Labor, 1860–1899* (Pittsburgh: University of Pittsburgh Press, 2000), 217.

11 Kathleen Lopez, "'One Brings Another': The Formation of Early Twentieth-Century Chinese Migrant Communities in Cuba," *The Chinese in the Caribbean*, ed. Wilson, 94–95.

12 Slavery was ended in Spanish Hispaniola in the context of the Haitian invasion in 1821; the lands east of Haiti attained definitive independence as the Dominican Republic in 1865.

13 Corbitt, "Immigration in Cuba," 304.

14 Historical census data calculated through the Historical Census Browser of the University of Virginia, Geospacial and Statistical Data Center, http://fisher.lib.virginia.edu/collections/stats/histcensus.

15 Roberts, *The Population of Jamaica*, 128.

16 Bonham Richardson, "Caribbean Migrations, 1838–1985," *The Modern Caribbean*, ed. Franklin W. Knight and Colin A. Palmer (Chapel Hill: University of North Carolina Press, 1989), 208.

17 Harry Johnston, *The Negro in the New World* (New York: Johnson Reprint, 1969 [1910]), 317.

18 Basil Maughan, "Some Aspects of Barbadian Emigration to Cuba, 1919–1935," *Journal of the Barbados Museum and Historical Society* 37 (1985), 263.

19 Winthrop R. Wright, *Cafe con leche: Race, Class and National Image in Venezuela* (Austin: University of Texas Press, 1990), 77–78; National Archives of the United Kingdom [PRO], Colonial Office [CO] 295/423: Correspondence [re: Venezuela] with Foreign Office, 1903.

20 Cited in Elizabeth Maclean Petras, *Jamaican Labor Migration: White Capital and Black Labor, 1850–1930* (Boulder: Westview, 1988), 77.

21 Roberts, *The Population of Jamaica*, 132; Li Anshan, "Survival, Adaptation, and Integration: Origins and Evolution of the Chinese Community in Jamaica (1854–1962)," *The Chinese in the Caribbean*, ed. Wilson, 42.

22 Moisés León Azofeifa, "Chinese Immigrants on the Atlantic Coast of Costa Rica: The Economic Adaptation of an Asian Minority in a Pluralistic Society" (Ph.D. diss., Tulane University, 1988), 65–78; Watt Stewart, *Keith y Costa Rica*, trans. José B. Acuña (San José, Costa Rica: Editorial Costa Rica, 1991), chapter 6; Carmen Murillo Chaverri, *Identidades de hierro y humo: La construcción del Ferrocarril al Atlántico, 1870–1890* (San José, Costa Rica: Porvenir, 1995), quote p. 85; Steven Palmer, "Racismo intelectual en Costa Rica y Guatemala, 1870–1920," *Mesoamérica* 31 (June 1996), 99–121.

23 David McCullough, *The Path between the Seas: The Creation of the Panama Canal, 1870–1914* (New York: Simon and Schuster, 1977), 161, 191–235; Petras, *Jamaican Labor Migration*, 97–100; Omar Jáen Suárez, *La población del istmo de Panamá del siglo XVI al siglo XX* (Panamá: Impresora de la Nación, 1979), 451–58; Lara Putnam, *The Company They Kept: Migrants and the Politics of Gender in Caribbean Costa Rica, 1870–1960* (Chapel Hill: University of North Carolina Press, 2002), chapter 2.

24 Olive Senior, "The Colon People," *Jamaica Journal* 11, nos. 3–4 (1978), 62.

25 Richardson, "Caribbean Migrations," 209.

26 Indentured Chinese emigration to Cuba was cut off in 1874 in response to repeated abuses; 142,000 Chinese men had reached the island under indenture over the course of the preceding quarter-century. See López, "One Brings Another," 94.

27 Ramón Mon, "Procesos de Integración de la Comunidad China a la Nación Panameña," *Este País, Un Canal: Encuentro de Culturas*, ed. Ileana Gólcher (Panama: CEASPA, Naciones Unidas, 1999), 83.

28 Jáen Suárez, *La población del Istmo*, 459.

29 Michael Conniff, *Black Labor on a White Canal: West Indians in Panama, 1904–1980* (Pittsburgh: University of Pittsburgh Press, 1985), 27.

30 Velma Newton, *The Silver Men: West Indian Labour Migration to Panama, 1850–1914* (Jamaica: Institute for Social and Economic Research, 1984); Bonham Richardson,

Panama Money in Barbados, 1900–1920 (Knoxville: University of Tennessee Press, 1985), 125.

31 U.S. Isthmian Canal Commission, *Census of the Canal Zone*, February 1, 1912 (Mount Hope, C.Z.: I.C.C., 1912), 40–41.

32 Kingston continued to be a crucial way station. For instance, in 1908 it was reported that "of the last two batches of Chinese who arrived here there are not three left in Jamaica now. . . . [T]hey have all left for Bocas del Toro, Colon and Bluefields." "Chinese Depart?," *Kingston Daily Gleaner*, June 1–2, 1908, p. 3.

33 Mon, "Procesos de Integración," 85.

34 Figures calculated through the Historical Census Browser of the University of Virginia, Geospacial and Statistical Data Center, http://fisher.lib.virginia.edu/collections/stats/histcensus.

35 Cuba, Secretaría de Hacienda, Sección de Estadística, *Informe y movimiento de pasajeros . . .* (Havana, 1921).

36 Patrick Bryan, "The Question of Labor in the Sugar Industry of the Dominican Republic in the Late Nineteenth and Early Twentieth Centuries," *Between Slavery and Free Labor: The Spanish-Speaking Caribbean in the Nineteenth Century*, ed. Manuel Moreno Fraginals, Frank Moya Pons, and Stanley Engerman (Baltimore: Johns Hopkins University Press, 1985), 239.

37 PRO, CO 318/406/2: Immigration of British West Indians to Central and South America.

38 Lopez, "One Brings Another," 94–95.

39 Imre Ferenczi and Walter Willcox, eds., *International Migrations*, vol. I: *Statistics* (New York: National Bureau of Economic Research, 1929), 525–27; Alejandro de la Fuente, *A Nation for All: Race, Inequality and Politics in Twentieth-Century Cuba* (Chapel Hill: University of North Carolina Press, 2001), 101.

40 Cuba, *Censo de 1943* (Havana: P. Fernandez, 1945), 888–89.

41 Roberts, *Population of Jamaica*, 131.

42 Malcolm J. Proudfoot, *Population Movements in the Caribbean* (Westport: Greenwood, 1970), 101, 94–96.

43 Miguel Tinker Salas, "Relaciones de poder y raza en los campos petroleros venezolanos, 1920–1940," *Asuntos* 5, no. 10 (Caracas: CIED, 2001), 77–103; Proudfoot, *Population Movements in the Caribbean*, 96.

44 Wright, *Cafe con leche*, 77–78.

45 Historical census data calculated through the Historical Census Browser of the University of Virginia, Geospacial and Statistical Data Center. http://fisher.lib.virginia.edu/collections/stats/histcensus/.

46 From statistics in Winston James, *Holding Aloft the Banner of Ethiopia: Caribbean Radicalism in Early Twentieth-Century America* (New York: Verso, 1998), 356–357.

47 James, *Holding Aloft the Banner*, 356–357; Bonham Richardson, *The Caribbean in the Wider World, 1492–1992* (New York: Cambridge, 1992), 140; Proudfoot, *Population Movements in the Caribbean*, 89.

48 Archivo Nacional de Panamá (ANP), Crim 2445 c141 RPAM, Sección Jurídica, Juzgado

Tercero Circuito, exp. 4876, iniciado el 18 de diciembre de 1916 en la corregiduría de Santa Ana.

49 Agnes Calliste, "Race, Gender and Canadian Immigration Policy: Blacks from the Caribbean, 1900–1932," *Journal of Canadian Studies* 28, no. 4 (1993–94), 131–48.

50 Brian Douglas Tennyson and Roger Flynn Sarty, *Guardian of the Gulf: Sydney, Cape Breton, and the Atlantic Wars* (Toronto: University of Toronto Press, 2002), 418 n. 54; Robin W. Winks, *The Blacks in Canada: A History* (Montreal: McGill-Queen's University Press, 1971) 325, 334, 354, 414–20.

51 Lara Putnam, "Migración y género en la organización de la producción: Una comparación de la industria bananera en Costa Rica y Jamaica (1880–1935)," *Memoria del IV Simposio Panamericano de Historia del Instituto Panamericano de Geografía e Historia* (Mexico City: Instituto Panamericano de Geografía e Historia, 2001). The official target for indentured departures from India was set at forty women per hundred emigrants in 1913. It was rarely met. Still, by the end of indentureship in 1921 Indians in Jamaica, for instance, numbered 10,203 men and 8,407 women.

52 Lopez, "One Brings Another," 95.

53 Guatemala, Secretaría de Hacienda y Crédito Público, Dirección general de Estadística, *Quinto Censo General de Población, levantado del 7 de abril de 1940* (Guatemala, 1942), 862; Honduras, Dirección General de Estadística, *Resumen del Censo General de Población levantado el 29 de junio de 1930* (Tegucigalpa, 1932), 31; Costa Rican 1927 census data analyzed through Centro Centroamericano de Poblacion, http://censos.ccp.ucr.ac.cr.

54 Panama, Secretaria de Agricultura y Obras Públicas, Dirección general del Censo, *Censo Demográfico de 1930* (Panama: Imprenta Nacional, 1931), 17. Total population was 467,000.

55 Data analyzed through Centro Centroamericano de Población, http://censos.ccp.ucr.ac.cr.

56 Douglas W. Trefzger, "Making West Indians Unwelcome: Bananas, Race and the Immigrant Question in Izabal, Guatemala, 1900–1929" (Ph.D. diss., University of Miami, 2006).

57 Clyde Stephens, comp., *Bananeros in Central America: True Stories of the Tropics, History and Anecdotes of a Bygone Era* (Fort Meyers, Fla.: Clyde Stephens, 1989), 37.

58 Stephens, comp., *Bananeros in Central America*, 107–8, 60–63.

59 See the discussion of sexual abuse of indigenous women in the context of UFCo expansion in Lara Putnam, "Work, Sex, and Power in a Central American Export Economy at the Turn of the Twentieth Century," *Gender, Sexuality, and Power in Latin America*, ed. Katherine Bliss and William French (Lanham, Md.: Rowman and Littlefield, 2006).

60 Winifred James, *Out of the Shadows* (London, 1924), 57.

61 See Putnam, *The Company They Kept*, chapter 3.

62 ANP, Archivo Judicial, Caja Primero Municipal de Colon, Juzgado Primero de Colon, no. 95, 28-5-1915.

63 See Putnam, *The Company They Kept*, chapter 5.

64 See Lara Putnam, "Contact Zones: Heterogeneity and Boundaries in Caribbean Central America at the Start of the Twentieth Century," *Iberoamericana* [Ibero-amerikanisches Institut, Berlin] 6, no. 23 (September 2006), 113–25.

65 Aisha Khan, *Callaloo Nation: Metaphors of Race and Religious Identity among South Asians in Trinidad* (Durham: Duke University Press, 2004).

66 Cf. "Rambles in Jamaica," *Sunday Inter-Ocean* [Chicago], January 13, 1895, 31; "Jewish Race" *Daily Gleaner*, April 28, 1914, 14.

67 On "patua" negroes see ANP, Caja Primero Municipal de Colon, Juzgado Primero Municipal de Colon, September 6, 1917.

68 Antonio Zambrano, "Crónica de la visita del señor presidente Rafael Iglesia al Puerto de Limón," *El Heraldo de Costa Rica*, July 14–August 2, 1895, repr. in Fernando González Vásquez and Elias Zeledon Cartín, comps., *Cronicas y relatos para la historia de Puerto Limón* (San José, Costa Rica, 1999), 200.

69 ANCR, Policia 06112 (correspondence with the governor of Limon, 1912).

70 ANCR, Limon Juzgado del Crimen 218 (homicidio, 1911).

71 ANCR, Limon Juzgado del Crimen 150 (homicidio, 1906), and for further cases the Limon Juzgado del Crimen for 1911 and 1912.

72 "What Is a Coolie?," *Limon Searchlight*, November 15, 1930 (National Library of Costa Rica, microfilm, "Periodicos de Limon," roll 1).

73 Personal interview, E.P.S. and M.P.S., San Pedro de Montes de Oca, Costa Rica, March 2002.

74 Harry A. Franck, *Zone Policeman 88: A Close Range Study of the Panama Canal and Its Workers* (New York: Century, 1913).

75 Rosita Shahani, "La Comunidad Hindostana de Panamá," *Este País, un Canal: Encuentro de Culturas*, ed. Ileana Gólcher (Panama: CEASPA/Naciones Unidas, 1999), 167–68.

76 "Migration to America," *Daily Gleaner*, November 6, 1917, 13.

77 "The Chinese Traders," *Daily Gleaner*, November 6, 1917, 13.

78 The last name Costa suggests Sephardic Jewish ancestry. Correspondence makes clear that this wealthy and well-educated doctor considered himself both European and white.

79 "Isaac Costa letter to Karl Pearson, about race mixing in Jamaica with reference to mulatto 'just under your nose' (10/3/1908)," image 1949, Image Archive of the American Eugenics Movement, Dolan DNA Center, Cold Springs Harbor Laboratory, http://www.eugenicsarchive.org.

80 "*Biometrika* abstracts (vol. 6:4 [1909]), including Karl Pearson's notes on Jamaica race mixing based on observations provided by Isaac Costa," image 1999, Image Archive of the American Eugenics Movement, Dolan DNA Center, Cold Springs Harbor Laboratory, http://www.eugenicsarchive.org.

81 Johnston, *The Negro in the New World*, 59.

82 Sydney Olivier, *White Capital and Coloured Labour* (Westport: Negro Universities Press, 1970 [1910]), 19.

83 Olivier, *White Capital and Coloured Labour*, 29.

84 Olivier, *White Capital and Coloured Labour*, 38.

85 A. Hyatt Verrill, *Jamaica of Today* (New York: Dodd, Mead, 1931), 135–36.

86 Robert F. Foerster, "The Racial Problems Involved in Immigration from Latin America and the West Indies to the United States," *Hearings of the Committee on Immigration and Naturalization, House of Representatives, March 3, 1925* (Washington: U.S. Government Printing Office, 1925), 329.

87 Foerster, "The Racial Problems Involved in Immigration from Latin America and the West Indies to the United States," 304. Cf. Mae Ngai, "The Architecture of Race in American Immigration Law: A Reexamination of the Immigration Act of 1924," *Journal of American History* 86, no. 1 (1999), 67–92.

88 Foerster, "The Racial Problems Involved in Immigration from Latin America and the West Indies to the United States," 330.

89 Charles B. Davenport and Morris Steggerda, *Race Crossing in Jamaica* (Washington: Carnegie Institution, 1929).

90 W. E. Castle, "Race Mixture and Physical Disharmonies," *Science*, new series 71, 1850 (June 13, 1930), 605–6.

91 C. B. Davenport, "Some Criticisms of 'Race Crossing in Jamaica,'" *Science*, new series 72, 1872 (November 14, 1930), 501–2.

92 *Actas de la Primera Conferencia Panamericana de Eugenesia y Homicultura de las Repúblicas Americanas, celebrada en la Habana, Cuba, desde el 21 hasta el 23 de diciembre de 1927* (Havana, 1928); Harry Laughlin, "The Codification and Analysis of the Immigration-Control Law of Each of the Several Countries of Pan America, as Expressed by Their National Constitutions, Statute Laws, International Treaties, and Administrative Regulations, as of January 1, 1936" (mimeographed, Eugenics Record Office, Carnegie Institution of Washington, October 1936); Nancy Leys Stepan, *The Hour of Eugenics: Race, Gender, and Nation in Latin America* (Ithaca: Cornell University Press, 1991), chapter 6; Lara Putnam, "Eventually Alien: The Multigenerational Saga of British West Indians in Central America, 1870–1940," *Blacks and Blackness in Central America*, ed. Gudmundson and Wolfe, 278–306.

93 *Actas*, 323.

94 Aviva Chomsky, "'Barbados or Canada?' Race, Immigration, and Nation in Early-Twentieth-Century Cuba," *Hispanic American Historical Review* 80, no. 3 (2000), 415–62; and Chomsky, "West Indian Workers in Costa Rican Radical and Nationalist Ideology: 1900–1950," *Americas* 51 (1994), 11–40; Lara Putnam, "'Nothing Matters but Color': Transnational Circuits, the Interwar Caribbean, and the Black International," *From Toussaint to Tupac: The Black International and the Struggle for Liberation*, ed. Michael D. West and William G. Martin (Chapel Hill: University of North Carolina Press, 2009); Putnam, "Eventually Alien."

95 Carleton Beals, "The Black Belt of the Caribbean," *Fortnightly Review*, September 1, 1931, 357, 359.

96 Beals, "Black Belt," 366–67.

97 Lara Putnam, "Unspoken Exclusions: Race, Nation, and Empire in the Immigration Restrictions of the 1920s in North America and the Greater Caribbean," *Workers*

across the Americas: The Transnational Turn in Labor History, ed. Leon Fink et al. (Oxford: Oxford University Press, forthcoming 2011); Lara Putnam, "Jazz Age Caribbean Crucible: Migration, State Racism, Popular Culture and Black Internationalism" (unpublished manuscript).

98 See Putnam, "Eventually Alien"; Laughlin, "Codification and Analysis"; Jorge L. Giovannetti, "Black British Subjects in Cuba: Race, Ethnicity, Nation, and Identity in the Migratory Experience, 1898–1938" (Ph.D. diss., University of North London, 2001); PRO, CO 318/417/6: Treatment of British West Indians in Venezuela: Claims for Compensation; PRO, CO 318/436/10: Venezuelan Affairs: Deportation of Foreigners; Richard Lee Turits, "A World Destroyed, A Nation Imposed: The 1937 Haitian Massacre in the Dominican Republic," *Hispanic American Historical Review* 82, no. 3 (2002), 589–635.

PART TWO

Connecting Borderlands, Littorals, and Regions

CHAPTER FOUR

Population Movements and the Making of Canada-U.S. Not-So-Foreign Relations

Nora Faires

The relationship between Canada and the United States has prompted shifting and contradictory assessments that nonetheless invoke recurring themes. Especially common are those that emphasize concord and mutuality, invoking terms such as neighborliness, friendship, and kinship or partnership and alliance.[1] Some stress the differences between these proximate nations, tracing a continental divide that separates the United States, a nation of "fire," from Canada, one of "ice," or, moving to the planetary scale, envisioning the United States as bellicose Mars and Canada as shining Venus.[2] Especially for Canadian writers, asymmetry often provides the main motif: physically massive Canada dominated economically, politically, socially, and culturally by the smaller but wealthier, more populous, much more powerful, often oblivious United States. In an oft-quoted phrase, Prime Minister Pierre Elliot Trudeau of Canada in 1969 likened the relationship to that of a "mouse in bed with an elephant."[3] Several recent analyses echo the theme, calling "life with Uncle [Sam]" increasingly "too close for comfort" for Canada.[4] Yet no trope concerning these nations' relationship is more familiar than that describing their boundary as the "longest undefended border in the world." For at least a century diplomats, politicians, scholars, and journalists have hailed the boundary, 5,525 miles (8,891 kilometers) long, as a symbol of international cooperation.[5]

In 1941 Edgar W. McInnis, noted historian and veteran of the Canadian Expeditionary Force during the First World War, published his classic account of U.S.-Canadian relations, *The Unguarded Frontier*. His slightly reworked trope hints to a twenty-first-century audience of a nascent "borderlands" sensibility.[6] Among other subjects McInnis explored how the unguarded border facilitated the movement of persons between Canada and the United States. Four years later, just months after the end of the Second World War, the American Historical Association produced a pamphlet for the U.S. War Department titled *Canada: Our Oldest Good Neighbor*. Repeating the theme of the open boundary, the pamphlet declared that "for generation after generation, from Atlantic to Pacific, people have moved freely across the Canadian American border," with the result that these nations developed "an international intimacy—there is no other way to describe it—that is quite unique."[7]

This "unique" relationship and its connection to migration found expression in another work of the period more familiar to those interested in population movements, *The Mingling of the Canadian and American Peoples*. Published in 1940 and written primarily by the pioneering historian of immigration Marcus Lee Hansen, the book was completed after Hansen's death by John Bartlet Brebner.[8] Hansen's and Brebner's sweeping narrative, though especially dated in its conceptual debt to Frederick Jackson Turner's thesis of the frontier and consequent neglect of urban and industrial development, nonetheless represents a landmark achievement, documenting a "movement of people to and fro across the Canadian-American boundary" from the seventeenth century through the 1930s and connecting this movement to conditions in both countries.[9] Notably, the book was part of the twenty-five-volume series "The Relations of Canada and the United States," commissioned by the Carnegie Endowment for International Peace as war was declared in Europe and Asia. Accordingly, from its conception *The Mingling of the Canadian and American Peoples* sought to make the process of migration between these nations central to any consideration of their foreign relations.[10] Hansen and Brebner stressed the tremendous duration, scope, and size of this movement, which included both French and English speakers (they had little to say about the many border crossers who spoke other languages); its often regional quality; its "reciprocity"; and its construal as "one of those great natural phenomena . . . taken for granted in the lives of the two nations," as James T. Shotwell, director of the series, proclaimed in the book's introduction.[11] Despite its accomplishments, this work failed to spark sustained interest in the topic from either scholars of immigration or international relations.

Only since the 1990s has a substantial body of work rendered visible this multifaceted migration, rescuing it from what Bruno Ramirez termed "a historiographical desert."[12] The work of Ramirez and others has provided an overarching analysis of the scope and scale of this migration during the last three centuries as well as a charting of the itineraries of individual migrants. Consequently we now know much more about the complexities and intricacies of this vast and diverse crisscrossing of the border.[13] This scholarship has demonstrated that this movement constituted a mass migration across a sometimes quite "permeable border."[14] At the same time, these works have complicated substantially the image of unregulated population flows, demonstrating that both the United States and Canadian governments often acted to forestall the mingling of Métis and Native peoples and the cross-border movements of groups that each nation restricted, including Chinese and Japanese migrants; and that in the early twentieth century Canada prohibited African Americans from immigrating to the prairies provinces, while in 1967 the U.S. Supreme Court ruled that the Immigration and Naturalization Service could deport a Nova Scotian man because of his sexuality.[15] Such studies complement those documenting by far the best-known movement across the Canadian-U.S. border: the Underground Railroad, which operated from the 1830s through the onset of the U.S. Civil War. The dramatic saga of self-emancipating African Americans fleeing a land of chattel slavery for one where the dread institution had become illegal has long been a focus of study. In recent years the subject has drawn great scholarly and tremendous popular attention, evidenced in books, articles, plays, curricula, museums, monuments, heritage tours, and internet sites. Together these efforts to uncover and memorialize the Underground Railroad have significantly advanced understanding of its operation and of those who rode its metaphorical rails across a border saturated with meaning.[16]

Despite the proliferation of this work, literature on the Underground Railroad remains largely divorced from the historiography of other population movements across this boundary and from scholarly work on the U.S.-Canada borderlands. Moreover the study of the Underground Railroad and its participants also remains largely disconnected from analyses of the relations between the two countries, despite its having occurred at a key historical moment offering rich possibilities for plumbing these relations. An exception is Karolyn Smardz Frost's *I've Got a Home in Glory Land: A Lost Tale of the Underground Railroad*, in which she explores a telling example. In 1833, after substantial debate and legal wrangling, the government of what is now Ontario refused to return the fugitives Thornton and Lucie Blackburn to Michigan, from which they had fled after their identity as escapees from slavery became known. This ruling set precedent for decisions in similar cases until the Civil War and has done so more broadly up to the present, Canada continuing to prohibit extradition of those who would be penalized more severely in the United States.[17] Smardz Frost concludes that the "Blackburn incident brought about a genuine crisis in relations between the United States and Canada."[18]

With this insight, we harken back to the motif addressed by Hansen and Brebner, McInnis, and others and recently revisited by John J. Bukowczyk:

the important interplay of borders, border crossing, and international relations between Canada and the United States.[19] In an age of intense public
concern about border regulation in the North American continent and far-
reaching changes in policies governing border crossing, these considerations
seem especially timely. A focus on migration as central to international relations does not ignore or decenter the state, not least because governments
etch the boundary line between nations, enforce the traversal of the border,
and establish policies for commercial and allied exchanges within the international borderland. Instead, such an analysis joins work revitalizing the field
of diplomatic history by examining the state by means of cultural approaches
and considering those outside official channels. This chapter aims to nudge
the topic of those crossing the border between Canada and the United States
closer to the center of the history of these countries' relations.

"Nations of Immigrants"

The heyday of the highly permeable border between the United States and
Canada occurred from the end of the American Revolution (when what became Canada constituted a part of the British Empire) until the 1920s, an era
during which those who fit the receiving country's norms of race, class, and
sexuality traversed this boundary with relative ease.[20] Estimates of the number of "Americans" (those from the United States) to Canada during these years
place the figure at close to 250,000. In contrast, during the century following 1840 some 2.8 million Canadians settled in the United States, accounting
for between 6 and 11 percent of the overall U.S. foreign born. Thus though
the migration between these two nations has been reciprocal, the net flow
has greatly favored the United States, particularly between the late 1830s and
the mid-1890s and between 1915 and the 1920s. Because transatlantic traffic and hence European emigration declined steeply during the First World
War, Canadians accounted for nearly a third of all immigrants to the United
States in these years. At the end of the war a wave of anti-radical and restrictionist sentiment swept across the United States, culminating in legislation
that sharply curtailed immigration. Extending the already formidable barriers against most Asian emigrants, these laws broke with previous policies
regarding European emigration. They limited the number of immigrants admitted and established a "national origins" quota system that greatly favored
those from the north and west of Europe while slamming the "golden door" to
all but a comparative handful from the continent's south and east, precisely
those areas sending the great majority of immigrants. This system remained
in effect until the 1960s.

Like other nations in the Western Hemisphere, Canada was exempted from these laws, the United States continuing its tradition of crafting distinctive policies for the two continents of the "New World" it regarded as its particular domain. Still, border restrictions stiffened for Canadians and other Western Hemisphere nationals during the 1920s and 1930s, especially as the Depression prompted some U.S. officials to worry about potential jobseekers across the northern, and especially southern, border. In spite of tighter immigration controls, tens of thousands of Canadians, with a wide array of economic backgrounds, continued along the well-trodden routes to the United States throughout the era of national quotas, with better rail and road connections facilitating travel.[21]

This chapter does not intend to trace the story of when and why this population flow came forcefully to the attention of one or both nations during the era of high border permeability, or to delineate the rhetoric and policies which ensued. More thorough analysis of the ebbs and flows of concern about migration across the boundary by diverse constituencies in each country would contribute substantially to the neglected realm of binational relations during this period.[22] Suffice it to say by example that Canada's late-nineteenth-century "National Policy," aimed at shielding the Canadian economy from American imports and promoting the development of Canada's infrastructure—an initiative discussed prominently in the literature on Canada-U.S. foreign relations—also sought to stem the flow of labor out of Canada.[23] Tellingly, Liberal critics of the National Policy, championed by Prime Minister John A. Macdonald, claimed that to show that the plan was working, Conservatives drastically undercounted the number of persons emigrating to the United States. Consider the numerical gap at one border crossing: Canadian government statistics indicate that fewer than 7,000 persons left Sarnia, Ontario, for Port Huron, Michigan, in 1880 while U.S. figures show more than 94,000 arrivals.[24]

In some respects this century-old tussle between the Liberals and Conservatives provides an instance of the long-standing practice of Canadian politicians and parties to distinguish themselves by virtue of their relations with and policies toward the United States, part of the larger pattern of constructing the Canadian nation in juxtaposition to the United States and defining "Canadianness" in opposition to "Americanness." That the reverse does not hold true constitutes a crucial quality of the countries' asymmetrical relationship. But an argument over the number of migrants from Canada to the United States also seems to expose a sore spot in the Canadian national psyche.

Both Canada and the United States, despite histories that encompass outbursts of anti-foreign sentiment and nativist legislation, have claimed an identity as a "nation of immigrants." Canada's embrace of this concept reaches back to the nineteenth century and has been expressed through a series of vigorous programs to promote immigration, some quite successful. Yet Walter Nugent's comparative analysis of the transatlantic migrations to the Western Hemisphere from 1870 to 1914 documents that Canada was distinctive among the four major receiving countries (along with Argentina, Brazil, and the United States) for being a nation both of large-scale immigration and emigration.[25] While millions of immigrants poured into Canada, many of them also streamed out, the "land of the second chance" serving as a funnel to the United States.[26] That to a great extent the U.S. government and public, as well as scholars of migration, have neglected this movement might confirm the view that Canada and Canadians barely register in the American consciousness.[27]

Meanwhile Canada, like most sending countries, generally softpedals its history of population loss. There are exceptions. In the nineteenth century Canadian journalists and politicians episodically lamented or decried the flow of population to the United States, while several provincial governments instituted repatriation schemes.[28] Beginning in the 1880s political and clerical leaders in Québec made fervent pleas to French Canadians not to leave their homeland, and in the 1920s voices in English Canada declared that emigration undermined national prosperity and progress.[29] After the Second World War the discourse of the "brain drain" emerged to describe what some Canadian analysts deemed a national problem: the emigration of some of the nation's best and brightest, or minimally those chockfull of Canadian investments in their human capital, to the United States. For Canadian nationalists these highly skilled emigrants carried with them a whiff of defection.

More commonly, the Canadian national story erases emigration. A recent essay collection declares that migration "has been the single most powerful force in shaping the traditions and history of Canada."[30] Yet the volume downplays the crucial role of outmigration, with only two of fifteen essays examining aspects of this pattern.[31] In sharp contrast, emigration from the United States to Canada, so small in comparative numbers, receives substantial scholarly and public attention in Canada and generally hails Canada's role as a destination. In an essay that is a welcome addition to the small body of scholarship on tourism in the Canada-U.S. borderlands (a topic addressed below), Stephen T. Moore offers this concise statement: "Historically, Canada has always been a sanctuary of sorts for refugees fleeing some sort of ill-treatment in the United States."[32] His essay's subjects are Americans who crossed the borderline to slake their thirst during Prohibition, visitors he deems "merely another example (albeit a less persecuted example) of Americans who found that by crossing the border they might avoid, or at least alleviate, the more uncomfortable aspects of being American."[33] For writers in this tradition the list of these refugees includes "British loyalists," "escaping slaves," "Native Americans [fleeing] American troops" (by crossing what some Indians and Metís called the "Medicine Line"), and "Vietnam-era draft dodgers" (referred to as "fugitives from injustice" in another essay in the same volume).[34]

While certainly no consensus exists among Canadian scholars or the Canadian public about which groups of Americans might round out such a roster, some contemporary analysts might add the uninsured seeking healthcare, patients hoping to purchase more affordable prescription drugs, gays and lesbians wishing to marry, advocates of gun control, and opponents of U.S. military interventions. For historians and scholars of migration, any compilation that includes groups as diverse as self-emancipating African Americans, tourists, and war resisters ignores crucial matters of context and chronology, eliding critical distinctions among those crossing the border and obscuring the issue of the border's salience.

For Canadians, reciting a list of Americans who for whatever reason left the United States and moved northward serves an important ideological purpose. In the nationalist narrative of which such recitations form a part, Canada is valorized as a welcoming land to any and all discontented with the nation to the south, the country that projects a self-image as a symbol of liberty and the ultimate destination of choice. Thus by understating its history of massive emigration to the United States and valorizing instances of American movement to Canada (while simultaneously effacing its own history of chattel slavery and mistreatment of Native peoples), Canada not only becomes the "Last Best West" (as the Prairie Provinces announced themselves at the end of the nineteenth century) but attains a self-conception of what might be called the "Last Best Nation" or a "Nation for Emigrants from the Nation of Immigrants."

This nationalist story constructing Canada as a haven for disenchanted Americans dovetails with Canada's postwar self-narrative as less aggressive, more tolerant, more civil, and more civilized than the United States. This view found exquisite expression in the television commercial for Molson Canadian beer ("I am Canadian") that swept Canada in 2000 and rapidly became an icon of popular culture. In the advertisement a character named "Joe" declares Canada "the best part of North America," then proceeds to skewer American ignorance of Canada and of its symbols of national identity, from the "truly proud and noble beaver" to the letter zed.[35] "Joe," the Canadian Everyman, concludes that "Canadians believe in peacekeeping, not policing; diversity, not assimilation"—deft jabs at the stance of the United States toward the rest of the world and to the immigrants in its midst. While "Joe" and his sound bites clearly oversimplify reality, the commercial's pithy phrases resonated with many listeners, including some Americans. Particularly in recent years, an array of U.S. domestic and foreign policies and practices have offered ample fodder for Canada's project to portray itself as the "kindlier, gentler" occupant of North America—the humble, non-predatory, diligent beaver in contrast to the high-flying, sharp-taloned, opportunistic eagle.[36] Belying this humility, however, Canadians apparently believe that a global audience shares much of their self-perception. As the Pew Global Attitudes Project of sixteen countries in 2005 tersely concluded, "Canadians stand out for their nearly universal belief (94%) that other nations have a positive view of Canada." Meanwhile, in that year more than two-thirds (69%) of Americans believed that their country, then waging war on two fronts in the Mideast, was "generally disliked" around the world.[37]

"Mingling" in the Postwar Era

During the last six decades both the United States and Canada have remained major immigrant-receiving countries, their populations enlarged by influxes of the foreign-born.[38] At the beginning of the twenty-first century nearly one in five (18.4 percent) of Canadians were foreign-born; in the United States more than one in nine (11.2 percent). In part because their immigration policies have diverged substantially in this period, the countries have distinctive immigrant profiles. In 2001 Canada's population stood at nearly thirty million persons, of whom 5.5 million were immigrants. Emigrants from European countries accounted for 41.9 percent of those immigrants, those from Asian countries for 36.5 percent. The United States, with a total population of roughly 300 million (ten times larger than Canada's), in 2003 had a foreign-born population of more than 33 million (slightly more than Canada's total population). More than half (52.3 percent) of all immigrants in the United States came from Latin America, Mexico alone accounting for 36.2 percent of all immigrants counted by the U.S. census—a figure universally recognized as substantially below the actual Mexican-born presence. Immigrants from Asian countries made up 27.3 percent of the U.S. foreign born, followed by those from European nations (14.2 percent).

Meanwhile, migration from Canada to the United States has fallen to levels far below that of the years following the Second World War. In the decade after the war the annual number of Canadian emigrants to the United States averaged roughly 30,000 while the number of Americans to Canada averaged some 8,000; between 1977 and 1998 comparable figures were about 13,000 and 7,600.[39] Canadian outmigration increased in the late 1990s as free trade between the nations expanded, the number of Canadians moving to the United

States rising to more than 30,000 in 2001. During the same period the number of Americans settling in Canada decreased, dipping to about 6,000 in 2001.[40] In that year the American-born in Canada totaled 240,000, or 4.4 percent of Canada's overall foreign-born. Canadian immigrants, totaling 820,000 in the United States in 2003, accounted for 2.5 percent of all U.S. foreign-born.

Americans and Canadians thus represent a far smaller share of each other's populations than they did a century ago. Particularly in light of the surges of immigration to both countries from other nations since the Second World War, this diminution in the population exchange between them has undoubtedly contributed to the limited interest in the historic and contemporary mingling of the Canadian and American peoples. Yet for several related reasons, investigating this mingling continues to offer a useful vantage point from which to explore Canadian-American relations.

First, the number of U.S. immigrants now in Canada and of Canadian immigrants in the United States, though low historically, is substantial: together they amount to more than a million people. Second, these current figures represent tips of two very large demographic icebergs. Because of the mass emigration of Canadians to the United States, millions of Americans, with diverse ethnic, racial, religious, and linguistic backgrounds, trace their ancestry to (and many via) Canada. A similar statement could be made, reciprocally, for many Canadians. In other words, many citizens of each nation (and some dual citizens of both) have kin connections which span the border. For some these represent long-ago connections, for others very recent ones, and for still others a combination of the two, older ties across the border renewed by contemporary relations.[41] Icebergs, after all, are floating, not fixed, masses.

Third, intermingling with and further elaborating these kinship ties are bonds of friendship, association, and business. For as long as the border has separated the United States from Canada, people have moved back and forth across it for an array of reasons beyond settlement: seeking work, celebrating holidays, competing in sporting events, joining in worship, taking classes, signing contracts, selling wares, going on school trips, and enjoying vacations—like the more than 1.3 million Canadian "snowbirds" who forsook the "True North" for the United States in the winter of 2002 and the many residents of the U.S. sunbelt, sometimes called "heat refugees," who escaped blistering summer temperatures by traveling to Canada (a topic meriting more research).[42] Since the 1920s easier air and car travel has facilitated short-term moves. Thus in charting the "mingling" of these two populations, we should layer upon our understanding of the historical bedrock of vast migrations between Canada and the United States a consideration of short-term border crossings and investigate how these different types of population exchanges have interacted. Here I do so cursorily, suggesting fruitful avenues for further research by focusing on one leading category of cross-border moves: tourism.

As anyone who has lined up at a major U.S.-Canada border crossing knows, the volume of "nonresident travelers" (as Statistics Canada terms all manner of tourists and visitors) entering Canada from the United States or traveling in the opposite direction can seem staggering.[43] The official figures bear out the view from behind the windshield or from the airport customs line. In 2005 Americans made some 32 million trips to Canada, with American tourists accounting for close to 90 percent of all nonresident travelers to Canada. They came to varied destinations—Cape Breton, Niagara Falls, and Moose Jaw, log cottages and resorts, theme parks and provincial campgrounds, swanky hotels and family farms, the tundra and Toronto—but wherever they traveled, the great majority (89 percent) did so by car. During their time in Canada in 2005, Americans spent 7.5 billion Canadian dollars. Remarkably, in absolute terms as visitors and spenders, Canadians racked up even higher totals. Canadians made 38 million visits to the United States in 2005, where they spent 8.7 billion Canadian dollars.[44]

As with the broad patterns of Canadian migration to the United States, so too do distinct regional patterns emerge with travel. The "snowbird" flight constitutes one clustering of destinations for Canadians. Florida leads the way, followed by California, Nevada, South Carolina, and Virginia, all numbering among the fifteen states that drew the most Canadian visitors in 2005. Significantly, several of these states also rank among those with the largest number of Canadian immigrants. Canadians made over 1.9 million visits to Florida, for example, which counted nearly 100,000 Canadian-born residents. The second cluster of destinations for Canadian travelers also mirrors their migration patterns: border states. From Maine to Alaska, states along the boundary line accounted for all of the remaining ten destinations among the top fifteen states most visited by Canadian travelers. These clusters appear commonsensical but reinforce long-standing trends: when Canadians travel to the United States they tend either to go short distances, which brings them to nearby states, or to take much longer journeys to reach warmer climes. Similarly, residents of border states make up the largest share of American travelers to Canada. These "short-haul" tourists, as industry analysts refer to them, accounted for nearly 60 percent of all U.S. visitors to Canada between 2002 and 2004. During their trips to Canada, Americans from border states spent much less money per capita than those who traveled farther distances north of the border. The most obvious reason for this disparity is that residents of border states hopped across the line to pursue a brief activity—to shop, gamble, go out to dinner, see a play, or go fishing.

"Not-So-Foreign Relations"

For many Canadians, three-fourths of whom live within two hours' drive of the borderline, Americans, including many with Canadian roots and connections, are fixtures of daily life. Canadians, again including those with American kinship and personal ties, are recurrent, routine features of the landscape for many Americans too, but only for those who live in border or "snowbird" states. Through such quotidian population exchanges, whether as a result of migration, tourism, or other forms of travel, many people on both sides of the border consequently have become intertwined through webs of relations which extend far back in time or have been formed only recently. From the perspective of national governments these patterns of interaction and interconnection may be barely discernible. Nevertheless, they constitute a tangible dimension of binational relations for people on both sides of the border. This popular interpenetration, allied with ties of commerce and culture, is a hallmark of the relations between Canada and the United States. It is a relationship of knowledge based on enduring patterns of large-scale population transfers, movements made person by person and relations forged individual to individual, family to family, group to group, not government to government. This knowledge constitutes a vital aspect of the not-so-foreign relations between these two countries.

What does this familiarity portend for future relations between these countries and their peoples? Historically, currently, and perhaps increasingly, the very intimate relationship between Canadians and Americans, and between Canada and the United States, so lopsided in power, engenders discord and dislike as well as harmony and appreciation, both politically and interpersonally: Canadians, it seems, lead the world in finding Americans not only violent but rude.[45] That many Canadians should chafe at the sometimes overbearing U.S. government and the ill-informed or dismissive behavior of some U.S. citizens seems endemic to the relationship. But the recent action by the United States to change its border policy seems to represent a turning point in a key feature of the U.S.-Canada relationship, constituting a rejection of the nations' shared history of minimally regulated movement across this boundary for most of these countries' citizens.

The change came as a result of the passage of the U.S. Intelligence Reform and Terrorism Prevention Act of 2004. As part of new measures to be undertaken by the Departments of State and Homeland Security in accordance with this act, in April 2005 the United States announced the Western Hemisphere Travel Initiative (WHTI), which came into full effect on June 1, 2009.[46] The initiative requires U.S. and Canadian citizens to present a passport or other specified document of identification when entering the United States from land or sea; its first phase of implementation came on January 23, 2007, when these strictures were applied to air travelers.[47] Before the enactment of the WHTI, citizens of the United States and Canada routinely crossed the international boundary by displaying readily available forms of identification such as driver's licenses, with birth certificates also sometimes required.

Shortly after the announcement of the WHTI and with more vigor as the deadline for the first phase of implementation neared, the Canadian government expressed "a number of concerns" about the new regulations for border crossing.[48] The U.S. government largely ignored the Canadian suggestions, despite an estimate by the U.S. Department of State in 2007 that only 27 percent of U.S. citizens and 40 percent of Canadian citizens held passports.[49] In the wake of rising criticism, the United States modified the initiative's provisions: it delayed full implementation; agreed to an initial phase-in for airline travelers (who are more likely to have passports); allowed the development of other valid forms of identification, including "enhanced driver's licenses"; and established provisions for those deemed members of "special groups." Tellingly, these alterations seem largely to have resulted from nationwide U.S. domestic pressures, as citizens, businesses, and representatives from cities and states along the border clamored for changes, their Canadian counterparts joining them.[50]

Critics of the WHTI cite its potential to clog cross-border commerce, the possibility of prolonged delays at border crossings for travelers, and the additional expense to Canadian and U.S. citizens who must secure proper identification, a requirement perhaps especially galling to the nearly twenty-five million Canadians for whom the borderline is proximate.[51] Some Americans and Canadians may also perceive that the act denies centuries of mutual understanding about the "undefended border," rupturing the unique bonds of international intimacy between the nations. Statements by U.S. officials confirm this interpretation, a representative of the U.S. Department of Homeland Security emphasizing: "We're asking people to think of travel in and out of the U.S. [in this hemisphere] in the same way they would travel to and from Europe."[52] The contrast is stark: as citizens of European Union member states move easily within their continent, citizens of the United States and Canada face increasing hurdles to crossing their international borderland. Notably, the WHTI does not require changes in documentation for Mexican citizens seeking to cross the border into the United States because they were already subject to similar restrictions—a testimony to the glaring differences in the histories of these two borderlines and in the nature of U.S. relations with Mexico and Canada. Reflecting on the heightened concern about security on both borders, one scholar concludes: "In a sense there has been a Mexicanization of U.S.-Canada border politics."[53] (On Mexican-U.S. border relations see chapters 1 and 9.)

In the midst of the debate regarding the WHTI the Canadian government took a step toward recognizing the large-scale outmigration of Canadians. Deeming Canada a "diasporic" nation, on Canada Day (July 1) 2005 the ambassador to the United States, Frank McKenna, issued a call to all Canadians resident in the United States to join a network titled "Connect2Canada," a link for which was launched on the Canadian embassy's website.[54] In establishing the network the embassy had intriguing objectives. In general it sought to identify those to whom it might provide services. It also wanted to give Canadians in the United States up-to-date information on U.S.-Canada relations, especially with regard to Canada's cooperation in the quest to combat terrorism. With this information Canadians living in the United States could demonstrate Canada's participation in bilateral efforts to promote security. They could remind Americans, for instance, that none of the terrorists responsible for 9/11 entered the U.S. from Canada, despite a myth which continues to circulate in the United States and which the U.S. secretary of homeland security, Janet Napolitano, repeated in April 2009, provoking outrage from Canadians.[55]

In addition, the embassy hoped that Connect2Canada would link Canadians in the United States and "build and nurture a sense of community" among them.[56] Connect2Canada would show to Canadians and Americans that they could, and did, live together harmoniously. By the time WHTI was implemented about 43,000 people had joined the network, some organizing local chapters and many posting their stories on the Connect2Canada site.[57] Whatever the outcome of this experiment to cultivate a diasporic imagination, the endeavor represents an acknowledgment of the widespread Canadian presence in the United States.

At the same time, officials in Canada seem to understand that the border increasingly is less a gateway between two neighbors and more a checkpoint between two economically interconnected but somewhat wary nation-states. In March 2007 the Canadian ambassador to the United States, Michael Wilson, suggested replacing the iconic phrase for the Canada-U.S. border—the "longest *undefended* border in the world"—with a phrase more reflective of contemporary realities, "the longest *secure* border in the world," the wording now used on the Connect2Canada site.[58] That same year Prime Minister Stephen Harper contended: "[Canada] may be smaller [than the United States] but we're no less fierce about protecting our territory."[59] This emerging climate of vigilance is also expressed in Canadian popular culture. In 2002 the Canadian Broadcasting Corporation (CBC) aired a documentary pointedly titled *The Undefended Border*, which demonstrated "the furious new pace" of Canadian border enforcement units on the "frontlines" of the post–September 11 world. One spur for the documentary was to "defend against Canada's reputation as a 'soft country'"—a charge lodged by both official and unofficial voices in the United States who were "loudly critical of Canada's supposedly lax immigration policing of our 'leaky' border."[60] In 2008 the documentary's producer unveiled a CBC drama titled *The Border*, its plot centering on security issues along the U.S. boundary line.[61]

In the United States, the Mexican, not the Canadian, border commands by far the greatest official and popular attention. Some opinion polls suggest that a majority of Americans endorse the building of a twenty-foot-tall fence all along the nation's southern border, while far fewer endorse a similar structure between Canada and the United States (though in both cases respondents seem unaware of the cost and logistics involved). But at least some Americans committed to enhanced border regulation frame the issue in continental terms. In 2007 Representative Tom Tancredo, Republican of Colorado, a vociferous leader in the fight to restrict immigration, put the issue plainly: "I believe we should defend our borders, secure them, north and south." "[T]hink of it this way: we are only as strong as our weakest link. It makes no sense to secure our southern border and leave our northern border wide open."[62] From this perspective Canada becomes a candidate for the unhappy position of "weakest link" in the defenses of Fortress North America and, perforce, the United States must take unilateral action to secure the borderline.[63]

Admittedly Tancredo holds extreme positions on issues of immigration and border restriction.[64] Yet other Americans, presumably with far less immoderate views, support measures such as the WHTI that purport to strengthen U.S. security. Perhaps some are anxious as they look to the nation to their north. Certainly Canada's official policy of multiculturalism, however far the nation falls short in living up to its creed, stands in stark contrast to views widespread in the United States about the necessity for intensifying assimilation efforts and clamping down on undocumented immigrants. More saliently, Canada's immigration policies since the Second World War have led to a national demographic profile very different from the one that prevailed during the heyday of the permeable border. Not only do immigrants from across the globe currently account for nearly 20 percent of the Canadian population, but Canadian cities now rank among the most diverse spaces in North America. Three of the largest—Montréal, Toronto, and Vancouver—are within an hour's drive of the border.

What does Canada's shifting demographic profile portend for population movements (or would-be movements) across the U.S.-Canada border? In contrast to many of the earlier migrants who traversed this boundary, many of whom were Anglo or French Canadian, "the new transborder travelers," Bukowczyk has suggested, "may be English-speaking Pakistani Canadians, Jamaican Canadians, or Nigerian Canadians."[65] Vibha Bhalla has demonstrated this pattern for the Great Lakes region, where in the last two decades growing numbers of Asian Indian immigrants to Ontario have taken up residence on both sides of the borderline. Like those before them, many recent newcomers to Canada and their children apparently are eager to cross to the United States to travel, take jobs, pursue education, join relatives, relocate temporarily, or emigrate—and wish as well to crisscross this border as they pursue their aims. In so doing they continue and extend the already dense networks that stretch throughout—and beyond—the transnational borderland.[66]

In the early twenty-first century a range of forces is at work affecting the U.S.-Canada relationship. The list is familiar and includes shifting energy markets, divergent social policies, trade and environmental disputes, and U.S. unilateralist tendencies. Government policies, formal institutions, trade agreements, macroeconomic trends, changing security environments—these and other state-centered and capital-centered frameworks, whether explicitly stated as such, are vital parts of the story of bilateral relations. This chapter has argued for integrating analysis of the circulation of population across the U.S.-Canada border into the narrative of these nations' "not-so-foreign" relations. Examining patterns of "mingling"—of migration and cross-border travel and association—adds an important dimension to this account, for these movements are not just of people but of memories, customs, and cultures. In the past and in the present, migration across this border matters in part because it has fostered an imbrication of the diverse peoples of Canada and the United States.

Notes

1 From an expansive literature see for example Jurgen Schmandt and Hilliard Roderick, eds., *Acid Rain and Friendly Neighbours: The Policy Dispute between Canada and the United States* (Durham: Duke University Press, 1985); Janet Kerr Morchain, *Sharing a Continent: An Introduction to Canadian-American Relations* (Toronto: McGraw-Hill Ryerson, 1973); Greg Donaghy, *Tolerant Allies: Canada and the United States, 1963–1968* (Montreal: McGill-Queens University Press, 2002); John Herd Thompson and Stephen J. Randall, *Canada and the United States: Ambivalent Allies*, 3d ed. (Athens: University of Georgia Press, 2002); Robert Bothwell, *Canada and the*

United States: The Politics of Partnership (Toronto: University of Toronto Press, 1992); Norman Hillmer, *Partners Nevertheless: Canadian-American Relations in the Twentieth Century* (Toronto: University of Toronto Press, 1989).

2 Seymour Martin Lipset, *Continental Divide: The Values and Institutions of the United States and Canada* (New York: Routledge, 1990); Michael Adams, *Fire and Ice: Canada, the United States, and the Myth of Converging Values* (Toronto: Penguin Canada, 2003); Jeffrey Simpson, "They're Mars, We're Venus," *Toronto Globe and Mail*, March 21, 2003, § A, 21.

3 Thompson and Randall, *Ambivalent Allies*, 214.

4 Bruce Campbell and Ed Finn, eds., *Living with Uncle: Canada-US Relations in an Age of Empire* (Toronto: James Lorimar, 2006); Maude Barlow, *Too Close for Comfort: Canada's Future within Fortress North America* (Toronto: McClelland and Stewart, 2005).

5 This trope finds expression in a contemporary assessment of Canada-U.S. relations; see Cameron D. Anderson and Laura B. Stephenson, "Moving Closer or Drifting Apart? Assessing the State of Public Opinion of the U.S.-Canada Relationship," Inaugural Research Paper (London, Ont.: Canada-U.S. Institute, University of Western Ontario, 2010), 3, http://uwo.ca/local_files/downloads/20100413-can-us.pdf.

6 Edgar W. McInnis, *The Unguarded Frontier between the United States and Canada* (New York: Doubleday, 1942).

7 A. L. Burt, *Canada: Our Oldest Good Neighbor* (Washington: American Historical Association, 2002 [1946]).

8 Marcus Lee Hansen and John Bartlet Brebner, *The Mingling of the Canadian and American Peoples* (New Haven: Yale University Press, 1940).

9 The quote is from James T. Shotwell, Introduction, *The Mingling of the Canadian and American Peoples*, Hansen and Brebner, v.

10 A similar connection is stressed in the book's two companion volumes: Leon E. Truesdell, *The Canadian Born in the United States: An Analysis of the Statistics of the Canadian Element in the Population of the United States, 1880–1930* (New Haven: Yale University Press, 1943); and R. H. Coats and M. C. McClean, *The American-Born in Canada: A Statistical Interpretation* (New Haven: Yale University Press, 1943).

11 Shotwell, Introduction, *The Mingling of the Canadian and American Peoples*, ed. Hansen and Brebner, v.

12 Bruno Ramirez, "Borderland Studies and Migration: The Canada/United States Case," *Repositioning North American Migration History: New Directions in Modern Continental Migration, Citizenship, and Community*, ed. Marc S. Rodriguez (Rochester, N.Y.: University of Rochester Press, 2004), 21.

13 In this volume see also the Introduction and chapters 2, 8, 10, 13, and 14. Other key works include John J. Bukowczyk, Nora Faires, David R. Smith, and Randy William Widdis, *Permeable Border: The Great Lakes Basin as Transnational Region, 1650–1990* (Pittsburgh: University of Pittsburgh Press, 2005); Benjamin H. Johnson and Andrew R. Graybill, eds., *Bridging National Borders in North America: Transnational and Comparative Histories* (Durham: Duke University Press, 2010); Bruno Ramirez,

Crossing the 49th Parallel: Migration from Canada to the United States, 1900–1930 (Ithaca: Cornell University Press, 2001); Nora Faires, "Going across the River: Black Canadians and Detroit before the Great Migration," *Citizenship Studies* 10 (February 2006), 117–34 [special issue: "Freedom on the Margins"]; Alan Taylor, *The Divided Ground: Indians, Settlers, and the Northern Borderland of the American Revolution* (New York: Vintage, 2007); Sheila McManus, *The Line Which Separates: Race, Gender, and the Making of the Alberta-Montana Borderlands* (Lincoln: University of Nebraska Press, 2005); Betsy Beattie, *Obligation and Opportunity: Single Maritime Women in Boston, 1870–1930* (Montréal: McGill-Queens University Press, 2000); Evelyne Stitt Pickett, "Hoboes across the Border: Itinerant Cross-Border Laborers between Montana and Western Canada," *The Borderlands of the American and Canadian Wests: Essays on Regional History of the Forty-Ninth Parallel*, ed. Sterling Evans (Lincoln: University of Nebraska Press, 2006), 203–21; Elizabeth Jameson and Sheila McManus, eds., *One Step over the Line: Toward an Inclusive History of Women in the North American Wests* (Edmonton: University of Alberta Press, 2008); and *Michigan Historical Review* 34 (spring and fall 2008) [special issue: "Borderlands," ed. Nora Faires].

14 Bukowczyk, Faires, Smith, and Widdis, *Permeable Border.*

15 Marc Stein, "Boutilier and the U.S. Supreme Court's Sexual Revolution," *Law and History Review*, fall 2005, http://www.historycooperative.org (February 7, 2008).

16 Among this vast literature see especially Robin W. Winks, *The Blacks in Canada: A History* (Montreal: McGill-Queens University Press, 1971); Michael Wayne, "The Myth of the Fugitive Slave: The Black Population of Canada West on the Eve of the Civil War," *Histoire Sociale / Social History* 56 (1995), 465–85; Jason H. Silverman, *Unwelcome Guests: Canada West's Response to American Fugitive Slaves, 1800–1865* (Millwood, N.Y.: Associated Faculty Press, 1985); William Henry Pease and Jane H. Pease, *Black Utopia: Negro Communal Experiments in America* (Madison: State Historical Society of Wisconsin, 1963); Sharon A. Roger Hepburn, *Crossing the Border: A Free Black Community in Canada* (Urbana: University of Illinois Press, 2007); and Karolyn Smardz Frost, *I've Got a Home in Glory Land: A Lost Tale of the Underground Railroad* (Toronto: Thomas Allen, 2007). Regarding the establishment of the National Underground Railroad Freedom Center, an especially significant museum which opened in 2004, see http://www.freedomcenter.org.

17 Smardz Frost, *I've Got a Home in Glory Land*, 192–240.

18 Smardz Frost, *I've Got a Home in Glory Land*, 221.

19 John J. Bukowczyk, "The Permeable Border, the Great Lakes Region, and the Canadian-American Relationship," *Michigan Historical Review* 34 (fall 2008), 1–16 [special issue: "Borderlands"].

20 Nora Faires, "Leaving the 'Land of the Second Chance': Migration from Ontario to the Upper Midwest in the Nineteenth and Early Twentieth Centuries," *Permeable Border*, 78–119.

21 K. V. Pankhurst, "Migration between Canada and the United States," *Annals of the American Academy of Political and Social Science* 367 (September 1966), 53–62.

22 See Bruno Ramirez, "Migration and the National Consciousness: The Canadian Case," *Citizenship and Those Who Leave: The Politics of Emigration and Expatriation*, ed. Nancy L. Green and François Weil (Urbana: University of Illinois Press, 2007), 210–23.

23 John J. Bukowczyk, "Migration, Transportation, Capital, and the State in the Great Lakes Basin, 1814–1890," *Permeable Border*, 72–75.

24 David R. Smith, "Structuring the Permeable Border," *Permeable Border*, 128.

25 Walter Nugent, *Crossings: The Great Transatlantic Migrations, 1870–1914* (Bloomington: Indiana University Press), esp. 136–40.

26 Faires, "Leaving the 'Land of the Second Chance.'"

27 Donna R. Gabaccia, "Constructing North America: Railroad Building and the Rise of Continental Migrations, 1850–1914," *Repositioning North American Migration History*, ed. Rodriguez, 40–43.

28 On "depopulation" see "General News," *New York Times*, September 25, 1865, 4; on repatriation efforts see "British North America. Dominion of Canada. Report of Consul-General [Wendell A.] Anderson," *Emigration and Immigration: Reports of the Consular Officers of the United States* (Washington: U.S. Government Printing Office, 1887), 567–72.

29 Ramirez, "Migration and the National Consciousness."

30 Barbara J. Messamore, "Introduction: Canada and Migration: Kinship with the World," *Canadian Migration Patterns: From Britain and North America*, ed. Messamore (Ottawa: University of Ottawa Press, 2004), 1.

31 Ronald Stagg, "The Myth of the Great Upper Canadian Emigration of 1838," 45–50, and Gary L. Hunt and Richard E. Mueller, "International and Interregional Migration in North America: The Role of Returns to Skill," 229–44, quote p. 240, both in *Canadian Migration Patterns*, ed. Messamore.

32 Stephen T. Moore, "Refugees from Volstead: Cross-Boundary Tourism in the Northwest during Prohibition," *Borderlands of the Canadian and American Wests*, ed. Evans, 250–51.

33 Moore, "Refugees from Volstead," 252.

34 Moore, "Refugees from Volstead," 252; Rénee G. Kasinsky, "Fugitives from Injustice: Vietnam War Draft Dodgers and Deserters in British Columbia," *Borderlands of the Canadian and American Wests*," ed. Evans, 270–89.

35 Also known as "the Rant," the commercial is discussed in Gregory Millard, Sarah Riegel, and John Wright in "Here's Where We Get Canadian: English-Canadian Nationalism and Popular Culture," *American Review of Canadian Studies* 32 (March 2002), 11–34.

36 This motif is vividly portrayed on the cover of Barlow's *Too Close for Comfort*.

37 "American Character Gets Mixed Reviews: U.S. Image Up Slightly, but Still Negative," Pew Global Attitudes Project: A Pew Research Center Project (June 23, 2005), 7, 13, http://pewglobal.org (July 25, 2007).

38 The following discussion is based on the author's calculations from Canadian and U.S. census data. See also Betsy Cooper and Elizabeth Grieco, "The Foreign Born

from Canada in the United States," Migration Information Source, http://www
.migrationinformation.org (July 25, 2007).

39 Thompson and Randall, *Ambivalent Allies*, 246; Sterling Evans, Afterword, *Borderlands of the American and Canadian Wests*, ed. Evans, 358–59. The number of U.S.
emigrants to Canada rose to more than 25,000 per year in the early 1970s, dropping
quickly after the end of the U.S. war in Vietnam.

40 Evans, Afterword, 358–59.

41 A survey taken in January and February 2010 of 1,002 Americans and 1,002 Canadians indicated that 62 percent of Canadians had relatives or friends in the United
States, with 16 percent of Canadians reporting they had ten or more family members or friends living there; American percentages were substantial but much lower:
25 percent of U.S. respondents had kin or friends living in Canada. Anderson and
Stephenson, "Moving Closer or Drifting Apart?," 5.

42 Evans, Afterword, 359.

43 The following data derive from tables produced by Statistics Canada, http://www40
.statcan.ca (July 15, 2007).

44 Sarah Hubbard, "Western Hemisphere Travel Initiative: Potential Impact and Congressional Initiatives to Change It," presentation at Joint Michigan-Ohio Canadian Studies Roundtable, Monroe Community College, March 23, 2007; see also
Ed McWilliams, "Changing U.S. Travel Trends to Canada: Findings," Canada Tourism Commission-Industry Presentation (March 2, 2006), http://www.canadatourism
.com (July 15, 2007); and "Tourism Snapshot: 2005 Year Review Facts and Figures,"
http://www.corporate.canada.travel (July 15, 2007).

45 "American Character Gets Mixed Reviews," Pew Global Attitudes Project: A Pew Research Center Project (June 23, 2005), 5, http://pewglobal.org (July 25, 2007).

46 For information see the WHTI website: http://www.getyouhome.gov (June 24, 2009).

47 Valid documents for Canadian citizens in addition to passports include the newly
developed "enhanced driver's licence/enhanced identification card" (issued by
some provinces) and enrollment in a "trusted traveler program." For U.S. citizens
the options include the enhanced driver's license (issued by some states), trusted
traveler enrollment, and a new limited-use "passport card," a cheaper version of the
passport to be used only for land and sea travel. Provisions have been instituted
for both Americans and Canadians who fall into "special groups," including children under sixteen, children traveling in groups, Native Americans, and passengers
aboard small boats and ferries.

48 A discussion of the "Western Hemisphere Travel Initiative: Proposed Air and Sea
Rule" was posted on the Foreign Affairs Canada website: http://geo.international
.gc.ca/can-am/washington/gov_politics/whti-en.asp (July 24, 2007).

49 Doug Struck, "Canadians Fear Fallout of U.S. Passport Rules," *Washington Post*, January 13, 2007, §A, 16.

50 Hubbard, "Western Hemisphere Travel Initiative." See also the updates on the WHTI,
"Eliminating the Barriers To Cross-Border Tourism Development," Binational Tourism Alliance, http://www.btapartners.com/ (July 16, 2007).

51 Preliminary evidence suggests some justification for the concerns about WHTI's effect on border crossing: the number of Americans visiting Canada dropped by more than 9 percent from 2008 to 2009, a decline hard to disentangle from the impact of the recession on tourism. See Mitch Potter, "U.S. Exempts Canadians from $10 Visitor Fee," http://www.thestar.com (March 10, 2010). See also "Border Barometer," Border Policy Research Institute at Western Washington University and the University of Buffalo Regional Institute (February 2010), http://www.wwu.edu (March 25, 2010).

52 Elaine K. Dezenski, deputy assistant secretary for border and transportation from the U.S. Department of Homeland Security, as quoted in John Mintz, "U.S. Will Tighten Passport Rules: Canada, Mexico Borders to Be Affected by 2008," *Washington Post*, April 6, 2005.

53 Peter Andreas, "A Tale of Two Borders: The U.S.-Mexico and U.S.-Canada Lines after 9-11," University of California, San Diego: Center for U.S.-Mexican Studies (May 15, 2003), 6. http://escholarship.org (March 15, 2010).

54 Connect2Canada/Lien Canada is at http://www.connect2canada.com.

55 That none of the 9/11 terrorists entered via Canada is one of three facts listed under the heading "America's Trusted Security Partner," http://www.connect2canada.com/ (June 25, 2008). On Napolitano's statement and its response see Sheldon Alberts, "Envoy Rebukes U.S. for Linking 9/11 Terrorists to Canada," *National Post (Canada)* April 21, 2009.

56 Information provided by Daniel Abele, academic relations officer, Canadian Embassy, Washington, August 23, 2006.

57 See http://www.connect2canada.com (June 24, 2009).

58 "The Canada-U.S. Border: Free Trade in a Time of Enhanced Security," American Society of International Law, Washington (March 29, 2007), http://geo.international .gc.ca/can-am/washington/ambassador/speeches-en.asp (July 24, 2007); my emphasis.

59 "Prime Minister Harper Outlines Agenda for a Stronger, Safer, Better Canada," Ottawa, February 6, 2007. http://www.pm.gc.ca/eng (July 28, 2007).

60 All quotes from http://www.whitepinespictures.com/border.htm (February 15, 2008).

61 See http://www.cbc.ca/theborder (January 28, 2008). The producer of these shows is the noted Canadian filmmaker and journalist Peter Raymont.

62 "We Will Also Need a Wall between Canada and the United States: Congressman Tancredo in Conversation with Sarwar Kashmeri," http://saknh2008.blogspot.com (January 18, 2008).

63 See Paul Gecelovsky, "Northern Enigma: American Images of Canada," *American Review of Canadian Studies* 37 (winter 2007), 517–35; John Herd Thompson, "Playing by the New Washington Rules: The U.S.-Canadian Relationship, 1994–2003," *American Review of Canadian Studies* 333 (spring 2003), 5–26; and James Laxer, *The Border: Canada, the U.S., and Dispatches from the 49th Parallel* (Toronto: Doubleday, 2003).

64 See also the testimony at a congressional hearing in the fall of 2001 of Senator Byron

Dorgan (Democrat, North Dakota), who decried the porosity of the northern border, as cited in Andreas, "A Tale of Two Borders," 6.

65 Bukowczyk, "The Permeable Border, the Great Lakes Region, and the Canadian American Relationship," 15.

66 Vibha Bhalla, "Detroit and Windsor as Transnational Spaces: A Case Study of Asian Indian Migrants," *Michigan Historical Review* 34 (fall 2008), 99–116 [special issue: "Borderlands"].

CHAPTER FIVE

Greater Southwest North America

A Region of Historical Integration, Disjunction, and Imposition

Carlos G. Vélez-Ibáñez with Dirk Hoerder

I was born *con un pie en cada lado*, that is, born with one foot on either side of the political border between Mexico and the United States.[1] It is by chance that I was not born in Sonora rather than Arizona, and that happenstance is repeated literally today by thousands of others like me. For my generation, being born in either Sonora or Arizona did not really matter too much, because becoming a citizen was a simple matter of where parents chose for children to be born or for themselves to become naturalized. For my father's and mother's generation there was little difference between the two areas: only forty-three years before their birth it had all been Sonora.

Fifty years later new borders of many sorts had been imposed, and I became curious and inquisitive about why it always seemed that people from the south were kept separate from the north. I looked at the fence next to which I was born, and it appeared to have only one side, although identical when viewed from either the south or the north. It seemed that while it separated people, the separation was one-sided: the north trying to keep out the south, whereas from the south there was little or no perception of excluding those from the north.

There are different labels for this region—the Spanish Borderlands, the Southwest North American region, the Greater Mexican Northwest, and even Northern Mesoamerica. We prefer Southwest North America, since it encompasses the southwestern United States of America and northwestern *Mexico*, and the two subregions share an extensive ecology of deserts, mountains, and riverine systems. This region's continuing and developing political ecology and increasingly integrated political economy in its present version has been developing since the middle of the nineteenth century as will be shown.

However, this is not a chapter about "place" as such, but rather an attempt to piece together a mosaic of its cultural history and understand the processes by which human beings with their own life plans and views of the, of their, world moved north into this region and especially into the U.S. Southwest and created a sense of cultural space. A long perspective will deal with the original settlers, the second Hispano/Mexican arrivals, and finally the American *entrada*.

"Cultural Bumping" and the Movements of Populations North

There are a number of cognitive fences that must be negotiated, among the first of which creates a misunderstanding of the region's Mexican population by using a political instead of cultural definition. States provide rights of citizenship but do not necessarily define the material and spiritual cultural systems that people use to survive when facing problems of daily subsistence. The differences between cultural nations are more a matter of how supra-local—in a way distant—states decide who may be "naturalized" (from a prior "unnatural" existence?) and then create a list of acceptable cultural characteristics usually based on myths, language, and ideology. Such norms and normality may have little to do with the way local cultures develop and flourish. Especially when conquest, war, and expansion have decided them, national or imperial prisms will become imposed on others previously present and on those close by but living across a recently drawn borderline. In our case the cultural systems that Mexicans developed are necessary to examine how these men and women organize their lives in social and work-related spheres, what they have to do to earn sufficient income to subsist, and why basic ideas and spiritual views are more important than political frames or even citizenship. It is not that the nation-state has no influence on them, but rather that local versions of culture emerge sometimes in resistance to and sometimes in accommodation of the national prism.

The second fence is the mistaken idea that human populations somehow are culturally pristine. There is no reason to believe that any human population was so isolated that it did not bump into another at one time. The way these processes unfold becomes crucial to understanding the formation of regional and subregional cultural identities and belongings. Sometimes the bumping process is so onerous that it eliminates many of the "bumped" people by a combination of disease, famine, and war. In other instances combinations of repression, accommodation, and integration within specific class groups unfold and reshape the structure of relations within the affected population. At other times even the conqueror changes, and the local versions of a culture become refreshed and enhanced. Whether divided by geography, language, or culture, human populations may become more distinct over time or more similar after bumping into each other.

In this chapter we discuss first the many "Native" peoples' or First Peoples' settling of the region, then the *entrada* of the Spanish, Mexicanized by that time, and finally the most intensive change, the U.S. American *entrada*. The last, on both sides of the border, initiated the formation of an undervalued cultural group, the Mexican residents and their labor, even though these men and women provided the knowledge and training crucial to the economic development of the entire Southwest North American region. Culture and lived identity encompass the ways by which people refer to themselves and to others and by which they define the economic, social, and political relationships that emerge within their groups and between them and their neighbors. One significant identity imposed by the Anglos on Mexicans after the imposition of the border in 1836, 1848, and 1853 is that of being a commodity, with the word "Mexican" becoming a pejorative synonymous with the phrase "cheap labor," thus stripping layers of culture and humanity simultaneously.[2] In a capitalistic economic system, labor, materials, and processes can be bought and sold for a price, and power hierarchies establish price-associated groups to be used and discarded similarly to disposable materials—they become "human material."

After the penetration of American capitalism into the Southwest North American region, not only did Mexicans as a group come to be regarded as cheap labor, but "Indians" were deprived of their ancestral roots and subsistence spaces. Some variations notwithstanding, the history of Anglo-Mexican relations has more often than not been defined by this imposed "commodity identity" and a living space reduced by "barrioization," a process by which people were compressed into segregated Mexican communities within larger Anglo domains. Despite this, Mexican men and women have developed vibrant communities, with continuous cross-border exchanges and relationships.

The following discussion questions the postulated cultural interruption between the peripheries of Mesoamerica and the Southwest North American region, from the pre-Hispanic through the Spanish colonial and Mexican periods to U.S. annexation and conquest. Borders do not necessarily define the historical and cultural mosaic of this region or any other borderland. The people living there are engaged in processes of cultural creation, accommodation, rejection, and acceptance—all occurring simultaneously. The analysis will contextualize ideas so that a holistic emotive vision may emerge rather than a simple nomothetic picture of statistical information, numeral protocols, or inferential enumerations. Complex lives demand of scholars different types of lenses and foci. The region is a polyphonic and polycultural mosaic; this chapter tries to map its multidimensionality of events and processes, ideas and behaviors. A human-centered anthropological approach recognizes the inalienable right of people to earn a living regardless of location and appreciates people's adaptive capabilities, skills, connectivity, and readiness at a moment's notice to seek more agreeable conditions elsewhere for self, household, and their children who will be the future of societies. In this view people with a highly developed aptitude for change and invention have an advantage over those who cling to dysfunctional monocultural or one-way views of (national) culture. For them the boundaries of cultures are more like a permeable membrane—as have been all imaginary political borders constructed through war and treaty in disregard of human lives, practiced cultures, and lived spaces.

Without Borders: The First Peoples' Lives and Visions in the Original Spaces

It is by now accepted knowledge that major parts of the Southwest North American region were well populated at the time of Spanish expansion in the sixteenth century—a period when European empires divided the land mass between themselves and showed little or no regard to the people living there, later shifting them around or discarding them. Archeological evidence and to some degree oral traditions indicate that the First Peoples (or "Indians") were concentrated in urban agricultural pueblos and dispersed in often riverine agricultural settlements (*rancherías*). Uto-Aztecan speakers arrived from the central Mesoamerican region, traversing some 1,500 miles (2,400 km) and carrying maize and squash. They bumped into settled populations, hunters and gatherers, from as early as 300 BCE, and at the beginning of the Common Era further peripheral Mesoamerican groups introduced pottery as well as spiritual, ceremonial, and recreational practices (map 5.1). The complex agricultural societies include the triad of the Hohokam of southern Arizona and Sonora (to use today's place names), the Mogollon of Casas Grandes, Chihuahua, and the mountain Mogollon of southwestern New Mexico, and the Anasazi/Hisatsinom of Chaco Canyon and Mesa Verde, as well as perhaps additional small groups like the Sinagua of the San Francisco Peaks (Flagstaff) region and the Salado of the Salt River region.[3] Along a south-north migration route with many regional variants over time, these peoples carried with them technological hardware and the cultural "funds of knowledge" (Haury) to establish themselves in the aridity of the Sonoran desert region.

According to archeological findings, many of the region's human groups lived in semi-permanent and permanent villages and towns with platform mounds, earth pyramids, irrigation systems, ball courts, and altars. Agricul-

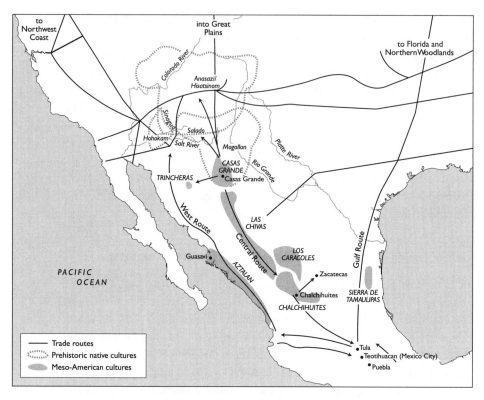

Cultures and trading routes, 350–1350 CE in Mesoamerica and the Greater North American Southwest

tural techniques included floodwater farming, wetland tilling, and canal irrigation. With normal rainfall a surplus was harvested, sufficient to support craft production and long-distance trade between adjoining populations and stretching from and into central Mexico. The agriculturalists developed hybrids of maize adapted to the arid environment and constructed long-distance canal systems. Artifacts, crematory and funerary practices, and the import of the Scarlet Macaw (*Ara macao*), whose feathers were of ceremonial value, as well as of shells from the Pacific and the Baja Golfe de California coasts, indicate long-lasting trading connections. The astronomical rock etchings in Chaco Valley may indicate cultural, spiritual, and perhaps scholarly exchanges. Cosmologies, imported or locally developed, included concepts of an Earth Mother and Sky Father, perhaps the God of Life and Light, Quetzalcoatl, and the God of Death and Darkness, Tezcatlipoca. In and from Mesoamerica the migration of spirituality and its material expressions seems to have occurred step by step from the coastal regions, incorporating sea and wind, to the central plateau of Mexico and onward via Tula to northwestern Mexico and the desert. Trading centers with receiving and distributing functions seem to have developed in Casas Grandes (southern Hohokam) and Chaco Valley (Anasazi/Hisatsinom), as astro-archeological artifacts and analyses indicate. The recipients of these influences were agents of their own in extensive exchange systems, especially from 800 to 1100 CE. Turquoise and finished jewelry, cotton, salt, lac, groundstone tools, and pottery were traded south-north and north-south as well as in many multidirectional micro-regional exchanges. Social hierarchies emerged, and turquoise became the choice mineral of the various elites of the Southwest North American regional centers. A vast and lively interactive sphere or, perhaps, plural interactive systems functioned, expanded, and declined.

There is no doubt that these groups lived in complex social and economic systems and that the Spanish bumped into them in the sixteenth century. The idea that the region was only sparsely settled before the arrival of European-origin populations counters the archeological and demographic data. The Pueblos, Opata, and Piams Altos probably numbered some 220,000 before the Spanish Criollos' expansion. The Opata of northern Sonora, perhaps some 60,000, lived in hierarchically stratified systems of *rancherías*, villages, and towns with public monuments and patterns of ceremonial life when Spanish explorers and missionaries first encountered them. European pathogens advancing before actual contact along the First Peoples' long-distance trading routes decimated these three thriving peoples to perhaps 32,000. Even with this population collapse, the early northward migrants of the second *entrada* still described "kingdoms" and chieftainships with well-populated towns. The later Jesuits, in contrast, describe decayed centers and dispersed agricultural settlements—thus an ahistorical gap was created that became the foundation of the stereotype of an empty physical and cultural space taught to generations in U.S. schools.[4]

In addition to the First Peoples, their sequence of cultures, and the arrival of the *segundos pobladores*, two further developments demand attention. First, many of these original cultures seem to have been deeply affected by an extended drought in the thirteenth century—many vanished around 1250—creating another gap, this one in historical knowledge. Second, in an unrelated migration from the far north (today's Yukon Territory in Canada), the Dene-speaking Navajo and Apache peoples arrived perhaps from as early as 1500 and had formed their societies by the 1700s. As hunting, male raiding, and mobile cultures they traded goods produced by the then existing Pueblo Peoples but also conducted slave raids on them to trade human beings, women and children in particular. Bumping and conflict was an aspect of many First Peoples cultures before the coming of the Euro-Spanish and, in the third *entrada*, the Anglos north-south from Missouri to Santa Fé, New Mexico, and onward east-west to California. Given the ravaging of settled populations by European pathogens, Europeans—with the exception of the very first visitors—would continue to see the region as empty and to be filled with colonizers—an incipient European inundation, as some anthropologists have called it.[5]

North from New Spain:
European Empires and the Second Settlers' Expansion

The second *entrada*, this time of the settlers from New Spain, was more direct, intrusive, and destructive than the first because of the armament of those arriving in quest of imagined cities of gold and subsequently of settlers. Often called "Spanish," most were colony-born *criollos* on whom the Iberian-born *peninsulares* looked down as inferior. The construction of Spanish lineage became one of their identity quests. The northward migration further differentiated them by distance and destination into *Nuevo Méxicanos*, settlers of *Pimería Alta* (Sonora/Arizona), *los Tejanos*, and the missionaries and *pobladores* of *Alta California*. The sequence of northbound moves began with the expedition of Coronado, conquistador and governor of Nueva Galicia. The goal of the advance party in 1539 and the main band of soldiers, 1540–42, was "Cíbola" or the "seven cities of gold"—a mirage in the gold-filtered minds of Europeans. In 1598 Juan de Oñate, with soldier colonists, conquered parts of northern "New Mexico," committing atrocities on the Native Acoma. The region remained Spanish, interrupted by the Pueblo revolts of 1680–96, which were in fact struggles for self-liberation by those seeking to regain control over their own lives. In a North American–European perspective these settlements predated the arrival of the French in Acadia and the St. Lawrence Valley (1600) and of the religious refugees, the Pilgrims and Puritans (1620)—though the latter claimed the status of "Founding Fathers (and mother and children)" and cemented their story by establishing hegemony over historical writing from their "New England" colleges once the United States of America achieved independence in 1776/83. Mexico would achieve its independence in 1821. Until these struggles for independence, the political history of the Americas is an imperial Atlantic history of a jockeying for power among the European major powers.[6]

After the Pueblo revolt of 1680 Nuevo México was resettled from 1693 by further migrants, *Españoles Mexicanos*. This self-designation indicates a classification outside the caste system of established New Spain and a tempering of the arrival of rampaging displaced soldier-sons and other booty-seekers. The newcomers were farmers, skilled artisans, and wage workers in small-scale, intensive agrarian systems of subsistence and exchange. Others were traders, mule drivers, and packers in commerce. With animal husbandry developing, they became the agro-pastoralists who characterized the economy of the region for two centuries. The newcomers after the Pueblo Revolt traded with the Native societies, the Zuñi or A:shiwi in particular, in a coexistence that involved copying agricultural funds of knowledge. They used *genizaros*, hispanized natives from the Pueblos, or uprooted and displaced former slaves and servants in their continuous fighting with warrior Apaches. Church-sanctioned intermarriage and unsanctioned partnerships with Indigenous women provided access to their agricultural expertise and spiritual visions and led to population growth. The emerging society relied on communal economic self-interest, *confianza* (mutual trust), and reciprocal if not friendly relationships. The voluminous southward trading system to Chihuahua also relied on the combined cultural knowledge of couples of trading men and Indigenous women.

In Pimería Alta, the region of the Pima (later southern Arizona), a similar exchange of Euro-Mexican or Mestizo northern Sonorenses as *paisanos* with the Tohono O'odham and Pima established an agro-pastoral economy which needed to defend itself against the western Apache. This *entrada* or second pioneering lasted from 1591 to the early seventeenth century. It involved import of the Jesuit version of ideological Catholicism until the Jesuits were expelled from the Spanish Empire. Missions, then armed presidios, and finally agricultural settlements emerged along the same riverine system that Native Peoples had used for centuries to eke out their subsistence from the harsh and, as regards rainfall, unpredictable environment. The increasing pressure on resources led to a Pima revolt, and the triangle of settled Native agriculturalists, raiding Native groups like the Apache, and intruding Mexican Creole and Mestizo settlers determined the constraints and possibilities of growing sufficient crops (see chapter 11). A military-merchant-bureaucracy class emerged, reinforcing its position through intermarriage among the families and emphasizing a purity of lineage, a "Spanish" genealogy. The scarcity of women, the value of their labor, and the value among established families of their inheritance, as well as the sequence of spousal relations necessitated by death and long absences of men, permitted women a comparatively active role. The early intrusion of Spanish played itself out in and around Tubac (later Arizona), where missionaries settled in 1751 and soon soldier-farmers established a presidio as an outpost of colonizer power. Tucsón, settled in 1776, became the early urban center.[7]

Tejas/Texas—like California—was initially penetrated and settled in response to potential Euro-imperial incursions from the French in the South-

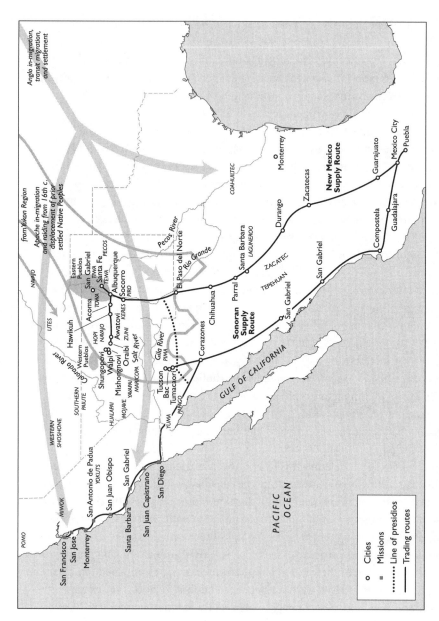

Transitions: New Spain/Mexico—Native Peoples—U.S. Territories

east and the Russians along the Pacific Coast. In Texas the institutional trinity of mission, presidio, and settlement was repeated, and Tlascalan Indians initially served as scouts and auxiliary soldiers on various expeditions from 1688. The new arrivals bumped into sedentary Caddos, who lived in a political structure of three cooperating confederacies. In "international" negotiations the Hasinai, one of the groups, could use the presence of the French to support their independence. But the Spanish, in addition to their faith, carried smallpox. The Caddos, decimated, sent the priests packing. They found unconvincing their explanation of the death as divine punishment. The newcoming settlers were Hispano/Mexicans and, from 1731, Canary Islanders. A ranching, *vecino* economy emerged, totally dependent on Indian labor, and competing with the Franciscans' subsidized mission agriculture using large-scale irrigation. The majority of the settled Native peoples were reduced to involuntary labor; the mobile Comanches remained independent outside raiders. Given the predominance of migration from Northern Mexico, stratification was based on the language of claims—that is, the attempt to "whiten" a family's or individual's social category to gain access to legal, economic, and political privilege. As in all of the northern regions of New Spain and, after 1821, Mexico, stratification along class, caste, and ethnocultural lines became blurred by isolation from the central authority in Mexico City, population admixture, and close economic and physical encounters of all groups. Fictive kinship, *compadrazgo*, crosscut segmentation because of the need for interethnic alliances. The basic cultural and institutional input was from the South, and the bumping process annihilated local cultures.[8]

In Alta California the advance of missions and presidios was meant to counter intrusion from the Russians. Their fishing vessels had moved along the coast from the Aleutians and Russian Alaska, and they had established a small agricultural settlement for purposes of reprovisioning. A more immediate political concern was Indigenous peoples' "rebellions" in reaction to widespread sexual violations of Indigenous women by presidial troops, and a missionary concern about the morality of the Catholic men. Most of the second settlers sent by New Spain's authorities came in domestic units to prevent sexual encounters and violence, to produce needed subsistence items, and to fill the cultural space and visions of the original people with Spanish-cultured ways of life and Catholic dogma. To gain a hold over the Indigenous People, the missionaries reduced them from free lives and mobility to supervised settlement in *reducciones* around the missions. The presidio of San Diego was founded in 1769, the mission of San Gabriel—to become the destination of the trail from Santa Fé—in 1771. In Alta California the missionizing agricultural aspects predominated over military ones, since no Native groups practiced warrior cultures like the Apaches or Comanches further east.[9] Periodic rebellions by local people were put down by superior firepower and brutal punishment so that small communities of Californios, 3,200 by 1821, which were spread out along a five-hundred-mile coastal corridor, lived among a far larger but declining Native population. As in the other three regions, various cooperative and antagonistic relationships between Native Peoples and Hispanos/Mexicanos made Alta California an arena of constant turmoil but also of dynamic change.[10]

The Anglo-American Entrada and the Imposition of Barrioization and Commodity Identity on Mexicans

In the struggles for civil rights of the 1960s Hispanos/Mexicanos in New Mexico asked themselves, "Where are our land grants?" Over a century after annexation in 1848 at the end of the U.S. war with Mexico and the almost forced Gadsden Purchase of the Mesilla Valley five years later, one more challenge began to the Republic's system of property rights under which land, labor power, and cultural practices had been usurped, purchased, annexed, placed in limbo, or destroyed with the connivance of the law courts.[11] A cultural redefinition, due to racial hierarchization and economic impositions, had turned the Hispanos/Mexicanos into an unprivileged class with lesser rights and less access to societal resources, except for the elites. We will discuss the Anglo-American *entrada* in the Southwest North American region as a long process in which the United States availed itself of the instability emerging after Mexican independence, of the penetration of U.S. citizens with capital into the region and far into Mexico (see chapter 15), and of communication advantages. Mexico's north was some 1,500 miles (2,400 km) from the capital and while from 1848 on the annexed territories—Texas included—were even farther from Washington and the commercial and financial hubs of Chicago and St. Louis, the communication routes for mail and trade were faster and safer to travel and the political framework more stable.

The processes of cultural subordination of the Mexican population over time began before annexation. Three developments stand out: the rise of Anglo trapping and commercial activities in the region from St. Louis southward and Santa Fé westward; the combination of the capital-wielding newcomers with elite Hispano/Mexicano families through marriage, partnerships, and alliances; and destructive U.S. merchants' arms sales to Apache, Comanche, and Ute as well as to outlaw U.S. American and Hispano/Mexicano men, which undercut lawful economic activity and social stability. Alliances and marriages were based on liberal Mexican laws which granted citizenship to inmigrating foreign citizens of different social statuses. Just as the migrants from New Spain had viewed the agricultural and urban complexity of Indigenous societies with ease, so the early arriving Anglo men married into Mexican families with ease, acculturated to Mexican religion and customs, and lived everyday lives resembling those of Mexicans—they were *Americanos simpáticos*. However, since incoming *men* married Hispano/Mexicano *women*, contemporary gender hierarchies, different concepts of kin responsibilities, and Anglo acquisitive individualism resulted within a few decades in a shift of property from the dowry of Hispanic brides to their Anglo grooms, though it was the women's cultural capital, knowledge of the Spanish language, familiarity with local customs, and family networks that permitted the strangers to insert their economic activities and northward connections into a functioning, southward-affiliated society.

In the decades preceding the war of 1845–48, the widening of U.S. penetration and expansion matched the diminishing impact of the Spanish version of colonial rule. With ever better access to the Southwest North American region, easy access to Mexican citizenship, and commercial ties to the hubs of the U.S. Northwest and Northeast and thus to the Atlantic economies, American traders, merchants, craftsmen, vagabonds, land seekers, political agents, and southern immigrant families from the slaveholding states began to exert ever greater influence. The extensive kinship alliances between the resident Hispano/Mexicano landowner elites and American traders and merchants made commercial and economic relations increasingly dense. The new networks spun off regional political allegiances distant from a political system nominally controlled by continually changing elites in Mexico City and a state hampered by several European invasions (see chapter 7).

In contrast to the elite intermingling in what became the U.S. Southwest within the broader region, the Hispano/Mexican villagers, rancheros, agro-pastoralists, and wage workers held few pretensions of alliances with Anglos or any expectation of economic advantage. Rather, they were accustomed to confronting the hardships of subsistence survival and the onslaught of Apache, Comanche, and Ute raiding men, whose guns and ammunition were illegally provided by U.S. traders and merchants. The raiding parties, which included some Anglos and Mexicans, took horses and mules and traded them from Texas to Louisiana and from the California missions via Santa Fé to Missouri. This many-cultured illegal economy, which involved slave raiding both on less-well-armed Native groups and on Hispano/Mexican communities, should be considered an important, perhaps major, covert instrument of American expansion and the encroaching capitalist economy.[12]

The U.S. war against Mexico, the conquerors' land policies, the rapid ex-

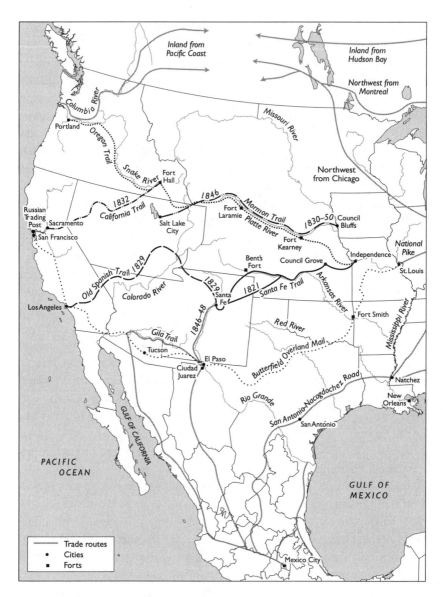

Inland from
Pacific Coast

Inland from
Hudson Bay

Northwest from
Montreal

Columbia River

Missouri River

Portland

Oregon Trail

Snake River

Fort
Hall

Northwest
from Chicago

1832   *California Trail*

1846   *Mormon Trail*

Fort
Laramie   *Platte River*

1830–50   Council
Bluffs

Russian
Trading
Post   Sacramento

San Francisco

Salt Lake
City

Fort
Kearney

National
Pike

Bent's
Fort   Council Grove   Independence

Old Spanish Trail 1829

Colorado River

Los Angeles

1829

1821   Santa
Fe   *Santa Fe Trail*   *Arkansas River*

St. Louis

1846–48

Fort Smith

Gila Trail

Tucson

El Paso

Ciudad
Juarez

Red River

Butterfield Overland Mail

Mississippi River

Natchez

Rio Grande

San Antonio–Nacogdoches Road

New
Orleans

San Antonio

PACIFIC
OCEAN

GULF OF CALIFORNIA

GULF OF
MEXICO

Mexico City

— Trade routes
• Cities
■ Forts

East–West Routes, 1830s–1860s

pansion of a capitalist market, and the impact, especially in Texas and California, of ethnocentric and racialist attitudes compressed and subordinated Hispanos/Mexicanos culturally and politically, except for many of their elites. However, increasingly most changed their attitude toward their new rulers; gone were the days of the *Americanos simpáticos*; instead increasing bitterness took hold. Though most of the wealth, land, and even knowledge of survival for Anglos in the region had come from the labor of Mexican communities, the Hispanos/Mexicanos became "strangers in their own land," in David J. Weber's famous phrase, and apart from the always exceptional elites, were reduced to lives in barrios, confined spaces in an Anglo world. They came to be treated as a commodity to be bought, sold, and periodically expelled.[13]

The development and imposition of the Anglo-Mexicano hierarchy thus may be exemplified by the emergence of a stratified community in Tucson, repeated in different ways in Los Angeles, El Paso, Santa Barbara, San Antonio, and Albuquerque. At the root of the process lay economic changes, the introduction of mining, the construction of infrastructures, large-scale cattle ranching, and other land use. A key shift occurred after the Southern Pacific Railroad in 1870 connected Tucson to markets in the east and brought the inevitable process of making Mexicans' land, resources, and labor part of market forces much beyond local control. In other regions variants of this deep capitalist penetration occurred. Tucson's wealthiest Hispano/Mexicano elite families of 1870 were from the region, twenty-seven who were from Sonora and another half-dozen who had inmigrated from Chihuahua and Sinaloa as well as from Spain and Chile. As merchants most of them traded along the south-north axis. The Mexicano laboring classes, on the other hand, experienced a much larger migratory influx. In 1860 62.6 percent had been born north of the newly established borderline, but in a dramatic shift, by 1880 70.2 percent had been born south of that line in Sonora. Another twenty years later the inmigrants had settled and formed families: 58 percent were born north of the line and 42 percent south of it. By migration and trade the transborder region remained integrated, but by class and culture it became increasingly divided. In 1860 agro-pastoralists accounted for 12 percent of the population; by 1890 they had declined to only 2.4 percent. About 80 percent of the population consisted of blue-collar workers, though by 1900 some of their children had entered white-collar occupations, and this emerging middle class expanded through internal growth and migration from Sonora to Tucson.[14]

Indeed the structure and profit margins of the economy rested on a large reserve of labor for mines, railroad, construction, and ranching. Much of this work was dangerous and poorly paid. Four of every ten Mexicanos worked at dollar-a-day jobs, and 25 percent of the households were headed by widows.

The jobs did not mean that Mexicano men were unskilled but that a segregated labor market assigned them to jobs with poor working conditions, low wages, and high rates of deadly accidents. Even skilled and knowledgeable Mexicanos became a labor-supply commodity paid less than Anglos—the "Mexican rate"—for comparable work. Their neighborhoods, *barrios*, were based on reciprocity, exchange, and need. The low wages are revealed in the poverty of the *barrio* families and the exclusion of their children from equal education. Mental fences imposed by Anglo societies separated the Mexican barrios from access to the Republic's ideals and local jobs. As early as 1860 Anglos—often the children of mixed marriages with the old Mexicano elite—constituted only 20 percent of the population but controlled 87 percent of Tucson's real and personal property, while the 71 percent who were Mexicanos controlled a mere 13 percent. Commodification and reduction from free, mobile citizens to residents of underserviced *barrios* are intricately linked: in the early 1870s Mexican miners in Arizona received from $12 a month to $1 a day, depending on the tasks, while Anglo miners received between $30 and $70 for the same jobs. This dual labor market structure, distinguishing between "Mexican" and (Anglo) "worker's" wages, extended across economic sectors and lasted over time. In the 1920s Mexican women in laundries earned $6 a week, their Anglo sisters-superiors-competitors $16.55. In department stores they were assigned to "basement" sections and earned half as much as Anglo women.

In addition to labor market segregation, cultural subordination exacerbated the sociocultural hierarchies. The educational systems, staffed by often well-meaning but ethnocentric Anglo teachers, taught Mexicano children that the route to educational success and becoming good Americans was to reject Mexican culture; children who went to school in the years before the Second World War still suffered from this regime.[15] In response the Mexicano elites established their own private Catholic schools in the 1870s—a triple-layer, separate-but-unequal schooling system for Anglos, Mexicano elites, and Mexicano working classes. Stereotyping equated Mexicanos with ignorance, laziness, and racial illegitimacy because of the Indian-Spanish admixture.[16] Imposed stereotypes were countered by self-created ones of pure Spanish descent. Still, this stratification was crosscut by a variety of community and regional mechanisms that gave the Mexican community its dynamic character. The maintenance of kinship systems across the U.S.-Mexico border, which would last until the 1950s, provided resources and mobility. The arrival of intellectuals, writers, and revolutionaries from the Sonoran political conflicts of the nineteenth century gave rise to new political leadership and anti-discrimination struggles.

To combat the institutionalized subordination in employment, education, politics, economy, and even recreation, the barrioized and commodified Mexicano families developed household strategies that modified and soothed the harsh impact of discrimination, segregation, and commoditization. The long depression from 1873 to 1896 reduced migration from the south; the population stabilized and, by hard work as well as labor market needs, could accede to some skilled blue-collar and low-ranking white-collar jobs.

However, the beginning of the Mexican Revolution in 1910 sent a million Mexicans fleeing over the mythical border, and Tucson's Mexican population increased by 100 percent within a decade. In 1917 the United States entered the First World War, begun by Europe's empires in 1914, and suddenly labor was needed. A decade after the war's end the Great Depression made workers superfluous. The commodified Hispanos/Mexicanos experienced a form of Americanization of a most peculiar kind, in which populations, to be bought and sold, imported and exported, were sent back across the border. In the United States the attack on Pearl Harbor and the resulting declaration of war increased demand for the labor commodity again—but also for soldiers. As a result, *the* Mexicans—citizens for long—were redesigned as Mexican-Americans.[17]

While U.S. ideologues and many common people ascribed identities to Mexicans—as they did to immigrant groups from Europe and, in the worst form, to "Negroes"—Mexicans continued to migrate to seek better options for their lives and those of their children. From the mid-nineteenth century they moved in small- and large-scale migrations to California's gold fields, the developing cattle ranching and marketing in Texas, the mines of Arizona, the founding of numerous ranches in central and southern Arizona set up under the Homestead Act, and the emerging and intensifying trade and commercial activities in Santa Fé, Albuquerque, and Tucson. Emulating their earlier migrating kin, these nineteenth- and twentieth-century men and women moved throughout the region, border or not, westward, northward, and eastward. The Mexican anthropologist Manuel Gamio in the 1920s documented Mexicans' origins across their native country and their spread across the United States. While the majority stayed in the U.S. states adjoining the border, El Paso's railroad node connected them to the United States as a whole. They were enlisted or attracted by farming, mining, and railroad recruiting agents, or pushed out of Mexico by one-sided development strategies of absentee U.S. investors, the Mexican elite's unwillingness to build a viable modernizing economy, depressions, natural calamities, and political instability as much as by the labor-exploiting stability of the Porfiriato, as well as by displacement during the

Mexican Revolution. This became a further great *entrada* from the south to the north and, often, back again. The U.S. Southwest from Texas to California became bilingual.

The Politics of Survival and Struggle for Cultural Dignity after 1848

In the 1930s in Miami, a copper mining town in Arizona, one Mexican child remembered: "on my first day in school . . . I found out that the people outside Grover Canyon [one of the barrios] were not like us. They looked different, spoke a different language, and they did not like us. It was as if a gigantic fence had been built between us. We were inside the fence looking out, and they in. It was their country, their state, their town, their everything. We, the Mexicans, were the intruders. All the teachers were Americans and not one spoke a word of Spanish. We were in a foreign land when we left our canyon."[18] By 1968 a mere two U.S.-born students of Mexican origin had earned a master's degree in English at the University of Arizona. Some of Tucson's junior high schools still prohibited the use of Spanish on the playgrounds, in the halls, or in the classrooms—though several schools were in the middle of Mexican neighborhoods and the student population was more than 50 percent Mexican.

In a personal and memorable book, Eva Antonia Wilbur-Cruce described the passing of a cooperative civility at the beginning of the twentieth century in rural southern Arizona: "Hispánico" was replaced with "greaser" and "spic." "Mexicans" became "to some an abomination, something to be annihilated from the face of the earth." Anglos became "gringos," "topos," and "basura blanca." Racial hatred became prevalent, "a poison" which forced Hispanicos/Mexicanos into a struggle to survive as human beings, "a poison" which at the same time destroyed the humanity of the Anglos, who reduced their personality to the mere outward marker of skin color.[19] In addition, among the Hispanicos/Mexicanos—as the name indicates—a further racialization blotted out the memory of the Indian contribution in favor of a European-Spanish construction.

Resistance and political action by the Mexican-Americans and immigrant Mexicans may be discussed on two levels: the institutional politics of electoral and governance practices and behaviors or struggles against differential treatment (to use a euphemism) in wages, housing, education, occupational opportunities, public accommodation, and healthcare. We will emphasize the second level over four phases: early cultural rebellions, 1846–1922; unions and labor protests, 1883–1940; benevolent civil societies, 1875–1940; and the "Great Chicano Cultural convulsive transition movement," 1965–75. The last, often referred to as the "Chicano Civil Rights Movement," was in fact much more. It was a movement of extensive proportions with layers that were international, national, regional, and local in scale as well as with gendered and intergenerational layers. The century and a half of struggles began immediately after the U.S. takeover. Many families of the Hispano/Mexicano elites had been favorable to U.S. rule, assuming it to be more lawful and stable than the incessant male-ego driven coups that wracked the Mexican polity. They were disabused of their notion of U.S. adherence to law and of U.S. officers' chivalry when these and their soldiers sexually abused Mexican women and resorted to petty chicanery and large-scale theft of lands, cattle, and rights.[20]

After the annexation and conquest, from California to Texas periodic revolts, wars, border raids, armed and unarmed confrontations, community upheavals, long-term skirmishing, and coordinated rebellions emerged in response to the presence of the military and the economic penetration of large-scale commercial, extractive, and industrial capitalism. Mining and cattle ranching became particularly acerbic arenas of conflict. From California's ephemeral gold rush to the century-long mining for copper and other minerals in Arizona, Mexican miners were discriminated against. In California—which had become foreign soil only one year earlier—the Sonoran miners were attacked and, by the legislature, exploited through a Foreign Miners Tax imposed in 1850. Marauding Texans selling stolen cattle to the miners, drunken explorers (the naturalist J. W. Audubon among them), and the urban political classes saw Mexicans as less than human. Before 1850 some ten thousand Sonorans as well as experienced miners from century-old mining regions of Chihuahua and Zacatecas—and from as far as Peru and Chile—crossed through Los Angeles to the goldfield: a whole district west of San Francisco became known as "Sonora." Violence was heavily ethnicized: 45 percent of Anglos killed by non-Apaches died at the hands of other Anglos, 20 percent were killed by Mexicans; for Mexicans the rate was 80 percent killed by Anglos and 20 percent by Mexicans. Homicidal deaths among Anglos amounted to 13 percent of the population as compared to 5 percent for the Mexicans (figures for 1857 to 1861). In Arizona mistreated miners fought back, destroyed newly placed boundary markers, or walked off the job back to the Mexican section of Sonora, in the first international labor walkouts. In ranching Anglo foremen whipped Mexican cowboys, and one early Anglo pioneer proudly remembered that Mexicans who forgot their place "lasted as long as a snowball in hell." Traditionally Mexican agro-pastoralists concentrated on sheep raising while the immigrant Anglos preferred cattle ranching; long-term range wars erupted along ethno-economic lines.

With the exclusion from politics, a different kind of courage became revered, that of cultural leaders, independent heroes, and social bandits. An example is Joaquín "El Patrio" Murrieta Orozco, who came to California in 1849 or 1850. A social bandit in European class terms (as in the Robin Hood myth), he was also and perhaps more a bona fide cultural hero to Mexicans— a lower-class version of Zorro. Rather than a primitive rebel, he represented a hard-working and innocently wronged (Mexican) population resisting (Anglo) forces of primitive racism. In legends, songs, and documented oral traditions, people passed on the stories of many such heroes, thus undercutting the powerful and the storytelling of their powerful historian gatekeepers, revealed their oppressors' twisted psychological reasoning, and overturned—if only momentarily—Anglo hegemony.[21]

The second period is characterized by large-scale industrially organized developments in mining, construction, railroads, and agriculture as well as ranching. The reopened silver mines around Tubac, Arizona, for example, used skilled and unskilled Mexican labor, men and women, and Spanish-Mexican silver mining technology. The absentee-owner companies, often directed from the U.S. Northeast, developed a system of peonage in which they owned the land and housing in addition to the mines, and forced the workers' families to buy in company stores at extortionate prices. In many communities the companies also owned the schools. Thus Anglos exerted tight control over the standard of living, culture, and teaching of traditions and values. Labor on the *traques* (railway tracks) was dangerous and separated men from their families. Industrial ranching and agriculture, called "factories in the fields," provided jobs at below-subsistence incomes. Such conditions created the basis for work stoppages and protest, and what little change was achieved arose after great struggles, many defeats, and small victories. Mexicans' cultural and social organization provided a platform for mutual support and the development of leadership capabilities. The gendered community structure, workplaces, and U.S. legal system reduced women to auxiliary roles but could not quell their agency. They were at the core of organizing households into material support bases during strikes and struggles for daily survival. In early ranching agriculture Mexican *vaqueros* organized themselves and elected spokesmen, sometimes along consanguineous or fictive kinship ties. From the 1880s Mexican-Americans organized their own labor unions, since most white unions refused to admit them. Organized Anglo-U.S. labor was deeply imbued with racism in many of its branches. Refugee syndicalists, anarchists, and communal organizers from the Porfiriato and after added their capabilities, and women participated actively. A first union of agricultural workers, the Confederación de Uniones Obreras Mexicanas, was established in 1927. Employers reacted by waging a campaign of terrorism and lynchings against organizers and communities, and against legal institutions by refusing rights to Mexicans, whether citizens, immigrants, or temporary migrants. By the early 1940s the National War Labor Board commented that the systemic pattern of discrimination, exploitation, and double standards was "woven into the fabric of the entire community, indeed of the entire Southwest. Unions and employers alike have had . . . a significant part in its creation and continuation." A strike in 1946 led by the radical and integrated International Union of Mine, Mill and Smelter Workers ended the infamous double wage system exactly a century after the U.S. war against Mexico.[22]

Voluntary benevolent associations and a broad range of organized cultural activity paralleled the agrarian and industrial struggles in the century from the end of the Civil War to the civil rights movement. The historical menu is rich in mutual-aid societies (*mutualistas*), protective associations, fraternal lodges, religious associations, women's legal assistance groups, and also women's more informal networking and inter-household or intra-kin groups. Their activities ranged from death benefits and unemployment relief, to rotating credit, to space for community meetings and religious activities, to public and religious events like Cinco de Mayo and saints' days. The "Penitentes" of New Mexico and Colorado, originally a Catholic lay flagellation confraternity, discarded self-inflicted corporal punishment, and women, excluded from the confraternity, formed Auxiliadoras de la Morada, auxiliaries of the local chapters. The Penitentes were instrumental in the Taos Revolt of 1847 against the new U.S. authority and, as registered Republicans, they helped make New Mexico, from the time of statehood, a bilingual state, with training for teachers in both languages, prohibition of school segregation, and provision for free access to public education (Constitution, Article 7-10). The widespread poverty—part of the systemic structure of U.S. political institutions and the capitalist economy—made *mutualistas* an indispensable part of survival strategies in the face of everyday deprivation and discrimination and during the exacerbated conditions of the Great Depression after 1929. The associations' officials established the same sort of dense relations characteristic of the familial thickness of multiple relations, intense interaction, and frequent exchange. These multifaceted and multidimensional associations helped balance the systemic "asymmetries" of U.S. society—a euphemism for racism, discrimination, and inequality.

The Chicano movement, active approximately between 1965 and 1975 and best remembered for its grape boycott and farm workers' strike, and for the names of participants like César Chávez and Gloria Anzaldúa, was in fact a complex cultural, political, social, and psychological movement of protest, rebellion, creation, and determination. It set in motion changes toward cultural pluralism in the nation, the region, and specific states, and within the community between women and men as well as parents and children. This movement of persons, ideas, and action we prefer to call "the great Chicano convulsive transition movement," because it was part of a convulsive worldwide transitional movement of poor and culturally subordinated peoples seeking determined resolutions to their conditions in the light of rising expectations. It was a time of decolonization worldwide, of student rebellions, of African Americans' struggles, and of women's rights — of a new articulation of human rights as once formulated in the Atlantic World's Age of Revolution. For Mexican-Americans in the United States, still "Mexicans in America" in the ideology of die-hard racializers, the struggle had four pillars. First, the traditional quest for land, space, and place was expressed in historical and mythic renditions of the loss of Mexican national territory in 1848 and of family and individual land rights in the war's aftermath. Second, labor conflicts and lack of representation in the fields, orchards, and vineyards of California became part of a vigorous struggle with worldwide support in the grape boycott. Third, cultural and linguistic erosion, the commodification of a whole ethno-culturally defined population, and the forced assimilation and imposition of Anglo-conformity through schools and the mainstream media were questioned and, in the new Chicano literature and arts, subverted. Fourth, the continued exclusion from representative politics and policymaking — constitutional rights notwithstanding — resulted in a questioning of the biased working of the judicial system and a quest for legal redress of discriminatory and racist practices on the job, in schools, in the housing and financial markets, and in public accommodation — in short, in all aspects of daily life.[23]

Having lived through this struggle and participated in it, I wrote this chapter as a rethinking of history and the present that has been shaped by discriminations, struggles, events, and processes. It gained strength from the ideologies that needed to be confronted, from passions and emotions that people in the movement could finally articulate, and it is shaped by the relationships that emerged and the failures that need to be confronted. The south-north theme, the search for cultural space and place, the unmasking of the "Spanish" colonial tradition, and the pointed criticism of racism and ethnocentrism were all given life and born not only in the critique of imposed historical amnesia but also in personal experience and in the whole of the *movimiento*. Human lives are more complex than what traditional historiography based only on written sources of highly literate groups or pretended objectivity can capture. And now this narrative continues with the most recent nativist push, so that populations of Mexican origin can set the historical record in balance and counter the anti-immigrant tendencies of the present day.

Notes

This chapter is based on Carlos G. Vélez-Ibáñez, *Border Visions. Mexican Cultures of the Southwest United States* (Tucson: University of Arizona Press, 1996), chapters 1–3.

1 Carlos G. Vélez-Ibáñez grew up along the border. Dirk Hoerder began his teaching during the civil rights movement and introduced Mexican-American history to American studies in Germany.

2 U.S. historians excluded Mexicans from the memory of the nation until the civil rights struggles of the 1960s and subsequent changes in academia. Vicki L. Ruiz, "Nuestra América: Latino History as United States History," *Journal of American History* 93, no. 3 (2006), 655–72. The few exceptions include Carey McWilliams, Manuel Gamio, and Paul Taylor; for the last two see the Introduction.

3 The naming of these populations remains contested and indicates mobility. "Hohokam" is a Pima word meaning "the people that vanished," people who migrated away for reasons unclear or who in cultural and spatial transformations were the ancestors of present-day Native peoples of the region. "Anasazi," a Navajo term for "ancient people who are not us" or "enemy ancestors," is being replaced by the Hopi, descended from this population, "Hisatsinom," which means "people of long ago."

4 Henry F. Dobyns, *Their Numbers Become Thinned: Native American Population Dynamics in Eastern North America* (Knoxville: University of Tennessee Press, 1983); Emil W. Haury, *The Hohokam: Desert Farmers and Craftsmen* (Tucson: University of Arizona Press, 1976), and Haury, "The Greater American Southwest," *Emil W. Haury's Prehistory of the American Southwest*, ed. J. Jefferson Reid and David E. Doyel (Tucson: University of Arizona Press, 1986), 435–63; Daniel T. Reff, *Disease, Depopulation, and Culture Change in Northwestern New Spain, 1518–1764* (Salt Lake City: University of Utah Press, 1991), 226.

5 The vast archeological and anthropological literature and the results of Native American History are cited in Vélez-Ibáñez, *Border Visions*, chapter 1.

6 Lester D. Langley, *The Americas in the Age of Revolution, 1750–1850* (New Haven: Yale University Press, 1996).

7 See for example Mario Barrera, *Race and Class in the Southwest: A Theory of Racial Inequality* (Notre Dame: University of Notre Dame Press, 1979).

8 See among many studies Arnoldo De Léon, *The Tejano Community, 1836–1900* (Albuquerque: University of New Mexico Press, 1982); Mario T. García, *Desert Immigrants: The Mexicans of El Paso, 1880–1920* (New Haven: Yale University Press, 1981).

9 With the charting of the so-called Old Spanish Trail and its intensive usage from the late 1820s to the 1850s, the raiding of horses, mules, and slaves by warrior Natives and Mexican and U.S. American freebooters emerged but was militarily quelled in the 1860s. Native women were the primary victims of this human trafficking.

10 See for example Antonia I. Castañeda, *Presidarias y Pobladoras: The Journey North and Life in Frontier California* (n.p.: Rosaldo Lecture Series, 1992).

11 George J. Sánchez, *Becoming Mexican American: Ethnicity, Culture, and Identity in Chicano Los Angeles, 1900–1945* (Oxford: Oxford University Press, 1993); Roxanne

Dunbar-Ortiz, *Roots of Resistance: Land Tenure in New Mexico, 1680–1980* (Los Angeles: Chicano Studies Research Center, 1980).

12 Similarly, along the border between the United States and Canada, horse raiding and whiskey smuggling by Americans undermined Native societies and created a hazard for Canadian settlement policies and individual settler families. While many U.S. citizens bought land and blended in as farmers, others noisily celebrated the Fourth of July in Canada as if the three Prairie Provinces were U.S. territory. Dirk Hoerder, *Creating Societies: Immigrant Lives in Canada* (Montreal: McGill-Queen's University Press, 1999), 163–68.

13 David J. Weber, ed., *Foreigners in Their Own Land* (Albuquerque: University of New Mexico Press, 1973).

14 Thomas E. Sheridan, *Los Tucsonenses: The Mexican Community in Tucson, 1854–1941* (Tucson: University of Arizona Press, 1986).

15 See the autobiography of Samuel P. Echeveste, *Grover Canyon: Journey of a Mexican-American from a Small Copper Mining town in Arizona [Miami] to the Reaches of the World* (n.p.: privately printed, 2004).

16 Fredrick B. Pike, *The United States and Latin America: Myths and Stereotypes of Civilization and Nature* (Austin: University of Texas Press, 1992); Deena J. Gonzáles, "La Tules of Image and Reality: Euro-American Attitudes and Legend Formation on a Spanish-Mexican Frontier," *Building with Our Hands: New Directions in Chicano Studies*, ed. Adela de la Torre and Beatriz M. Pesquera (Berkeley: University of California Press, 1993).

17 "The growth of the modern nation-state implied not only the naming of certain peoples as enemies of the nation, but also the expulsion of significant groups for whom the state would or could not assume responsibility." Wars "schooled the new masters of the state apparatus: civilians could become dangerous enemies; fighting could not stop simply because they were there; on the contrary, it was best to eject unwanted or menacing groups when they threatened to weaken the beleaguered nation." "With the First World War, the process accelerated powerfully." Michael R. Marrus, *The Unwanted: European Refugees in the Twentieth Century* (Oxford: Oxford University Press, 1985), quote p. 51.

18 Echeveste, *Grover Canyon*, quote pp. xv–xvi.

19 Eva Antonia Wilbur-Cruce, *A Beautiful, Cruel Country* (Tucson: University of Arizona Press, 1987), esp. 316.

20 Genario Padilla, *My History, Not Yours: The Formation of Mexican American Autobiography* (Madison: University of Wisconsin Press, 1993).

21 The California historian Hubert Howe Bancroft, with all sources and perspectives available to him, wrote White History. See Padilla, *My Heroes*.

22 From among a wide range of studies see Emilio Zamora, *The World of the Mexican Worker in Texas* (College Station: Texas A&M University Press, 1993); Patricia Zavella, *Women's Work and Chicano Families: Cannery Workers of the Santa Clara Valley* (Ithaca: Cornell University Press, 1987); Robert J. Rosenbaum, *Mexicano Resistance in the Southwest: The Sacred Right of Self-Preservation* (Austin: University of Texas

Press, 1981); Carey McWilliams, *North from Mexico: The Spanish-Speaking People of the United States* (New York: Praeger, 1948; repr. 1990), NWLP quote, p. 180; Vicki L. Ruiz, *From Out of the Shadows: Mexican Women in Twentieth-Century America* (New York: Oxford University Press, 1998); Juan Gómez-Quiñones, "First Steps: Chicano Labor Conflict and Organizing 1900–1920," *Aztlán: Chicano Journal of the Social Sciences and the Arts* 3, no. 1 (1973), 13–19; and Gómez-Quiñones, *Chicano Politics: Reality and Promise, 1940–1990* (Albuquerque: University of New Mexico Press, 1993).

23 The first reinsertions of Mexican-American history into the narrative and analysis of the development of the United States subsequent to the struggles for civil rights and the right to historical memory are Rodolfo Acuña, *Occupied America; the Chicano's Struggle toward Liberation* (San Francisco: Canfield, 1972); and Matt S. Meier and Feliciano Ribera, *The Chicanos* (New York: Hill and Wang, 1972; rev. 1993 as *Mexican Americans: American Mexicans*). In the 1980s "culture wars" initiated by conservative and ultra-right fundamentalists attempted to turn the tide back toward a White America Only.

CHAPTER SIX

Independence and Interdependence

Caribbean–North American Migration in the Modern Era

Melanie Shell-Weiss

For residents of the Caribbean migration is a way of life that dates back many centuries. From European settlement to the forced inmigration of African slaves and recruitment of indentured laborers, the nineteenth-century population of the region was almost entirely the result of migration. The legacy of empire—or empires—created a shared culture, language, and history, ultimately shaping realms in which people could move easily to maximize their educational and economic resources. Yet in the early decades of the twentieth century it was modern policymakers, heavily influenced by northern eugenicism, who responded to the economic crises gripping the region by imposing a range of restrictions geared to curtail these international movements (see chapter 3). These measures could not close the doors to migration within the Western Hemisphere. But they did reshape the contours of this movement, shifting the gendered dynamics of Caribbean–North American continental migration and creating new classes of permanent migrants and guest workers.

The Early Twentieth Century, 1891–1930

By the beginning of the twentieth century the number of Caribbean migrants to North America increased dramatically. Between 1820 and 1910 fewer than 250,000 migrants had arrived from the Caribbean (compared to two to four million or more migrants from individual European nations).[1] In the first three decades of the twentieth century, however, close to that number arrived each decade.[2] Where in the post-Emancipation era most of the Caribbean migrants to North America were skilled craftspeople or well-educated professionals, a large number of working-class men and women moved during the early twentieth century.[3] Drawn by the hope of industrial wage work, as well as an abundance of jobs in agriculture and domestic service, more and more men and women began leaving the islands bound for destinations in the United States. Florida remained the most popular destination to 1905, attracting especially large numbers of Bahamians and Cubans. New York was second, followed closely by Massachusetts, drawing migrants from across the Caribbean islands. After 1905 New York—and New York City in particular—replaced all other locales as the most popular destination.[4]

The high concentration of Caribbean migrants in some North American cities and neighborhoods had a significant impact on the political and social fabric of the receiving regions. Although Louisiana was not one of the leading centers for Caribbean migrants, cities like New Orleans boasted a large number of Caribbean residents, many of whom could trace their roots in the city back several generations. This was the case for Homère Plessy, a Haitian American who in 1892 became one of the most prominent figures in American civil rights history when he refused to sit in a blacks-only car on the East Louisiana Railroad. A member of the "Comité des Citoyens," a political group made up of a large number of Haitians as well as African Americans, Plessy intended his action to become part of a test case challenging the rigid white-black racial dichotomy enforced through segregation ordinances across the U.S. South.[5] The case, which was heard before the Supreme Court in 1896, became a landmark in U.S. history, formalizing federal support for "separate but equal" facilities for black and white Americans as well as the "one-drop rule" for delineating racial difference.

In Florida Cuban immigrants challenged prevailing southern norms and had an important influence on international politics. Social clubs, modeled on those to which many Cubans belonged at home, provided cradle-to-grave healthcare, death benefits, and opportunities for recreation, dances, and other activities. Many also had a specifically political aim. As the push by Cubans to end Spain's rule over the island mounted through the late nineteenth century, Ybor City and Tampa became a critical base of revolutionary activities. In 1895 the Cuban independence leader José Martí is said to have given the order for junta leaders living in the United States to invade the island by smuggling a message into Tampa that had been rolled into a cigar. Women like Paulina Pedroso, an Afro-Cuban who had moved to Ybor City from Tampa along with her husband, Ruperto, in the late 1880s, hosted Martí on his visits to Florida; she and her husband were credited with saving him from several would-be assassins.[6] When the United States went to war with Spain in 1898, again the Cuban American community of Tampa and Ybor City was a critical center of support, as well as the major embarkation point for the American military throughout the war.

In Harlem, Caribbean migrants became a critical force in local, national and international politics, art, and culture.[7] Artists and writers like the Jamaican-born Claude McKay and the Guyanese immigrant Eric Waldrond were among the best-known figures of the Harlem Renaissance. Caribbean immigrants lobbied their local congressmen and political representatives to challenge proposed legislation in 1915 that would have barred people of African descent from immigrating and joining American civil rights organizations like the National Association for the Advancement of Colored People.[8] In other cases Caribbean migrants brought their political organizations with them: the Universal Negro Improvement Association, founded by Marcus Garvey in Jamaica in 1914, had its headquarters moved to Harlem when Garvey himself moved there in 1916. By 1920 the organization had more than eleven hundred local chapters in more than forty countries.[9]

The way Caribbean migrants found their way to Harlem mirrored the experience of most newcomers over this period, whether they were leaving the agricultural south for the industrial north or crossing international borders from Europe and elsewhere in the world.[10] Most newcomers relied on family members to aid their passage and find places to live and work. Thus the first points of contact for these newcomers were often centered on fellow countrymen and women. But race, and racism, also played a formative role in shaping the movement of these immigrants, their settlement, and the types of political, social, and cultural ties they built. Because of limits both official and unofficial on where black people could live, Afro-Caribbeans and African Americans often lived in close proximity in American cities. In a neighborhood like Harlem, Afro-Caribbeans were particularly able to shine. West Indians invented the tradition of speaking to crowds on streetcorners as a means of expressing radical political ideas and messages of racial uplift that were not necessarily welcome in more traditional venues.[11] The wide array of national origins, languages, and cultures represented by these immigrants showcased the diversity of the African diaspora in microcosm. This diversity was welcomed in Harlem to a greater extent than in most other places. As one Afro-Caribbean immigrant described it to the black sociologist Ira De A. Reid in the 1930s, in Harlem Caribbean blacks did "not suffer much from the American race prejudice."[12] By the same token, Afro-Caribbeans benefited from the extensive infrastructure built up by African Americans in earlier periods.

Some African Americans resented the preferential treatment that might be afforded to Caribbean blacks by Anglo Americans. The African American writer James Weldon Johnson once described boarding a streetcar in New York with an Afro-Cuban friend. At first the conductor ordered the two men to move to a segregated car. Then he heard them speaking Spanish. "[H]is attitude changed," Johnson wrote. "[H]e punched our tickets and gave them back and treated us just as he did the other passengers in the car."[13] These tensions, as well as differences in status between African Americans and Afro-Caribbeans, have generated a great deal of scholarly debate and inquiry. Together with the resources, political aims, and struggles shared by native and foreign-born blacks, Harlem developed into a special place—one variously described by contemporaries as a "seething melting pot of conflicting nationalities and languages," a "homegrown ethnic amalgam," and a "diversified and complex population."[14]

As in earlier periods, foreign relations also influenced patterns of migration from the Caribbean to North America.[15] The U.S. military occupation of Haiti, which began in 1915 and continued until 1934, inspired renewed waves of emigration from the island. Many of the emigrants settled in Harlem, although some continued north to French-speaking Canadian cities like Montreal. U.S. investment and the federal employment of many West Indian contract laborers and guest workers during construction of the Panama Canal also shaped patterns of migration between the Caribbean islands, to Central America, and inside and outside U.S. borders. The acquisition of Puerto Rico as a U.S. territory in the wake of the Spanish American War and the purchase of the islands of St. Thomas and St. John by the United States from Denmark in 1917 further expanded the borders of the "nation-state" to encompass a greater number of Caribbean residents of many cultural backgrounds and languages.

Social tensions at home, strengthening segregation, and political repression within the United States also pushed other members of the African diaspora abroad. African American soldiers who had been stationed in Europe during the First World War returned to Paris in the immediate postwar period. They were joined by a host of prominent black intellectuals, artists, and activists who found greater opportunities for people of African descent and greater socioeconomic mobility there than at home. As the African American poet Countee Cullen recalled of his own time in Paris in the 1920s, "[I] found across a continent of foam / What was denied my hungry heart at home."[16] Although other African American émigrés had a more mixed experience—finding restrictions abroad every bit as demeaning as those afforded black Americans at home if they were mistaken for black French colonial subjects rather than recognized as Americans—Paris remained a favored home for African Americans throughout the Harlem Renaissance.[17]

For that reason, and because of the city's place as a cultural, intellectual, and political hub for leaders from across the Atlantic world, W. E. B. Du Bois chose Paris as the site of the first Pan-African Congress.[18] Held in 1919, the congress emphasized the importance of decolonizing Africa and the West Indies. It drew fifty-seven delegates from fifteen countries to petition the Versailles Peace Conference, meeting in Paris at that time. Subsequent congresses were held in London, Brussels, Lisbon, and Manchester, convening every two to four years during the interwar period and again in 1945.

Patterns of movement between the Caribbean and the North American mainland also continued relatively unabated, even as the United States moved to restrict international migration to a greater extent than ever before in its history. Between 1917 and 1924 the United States passed a series of restrictions and national origin quotas that virtually shut the door to all but a narrow range of northern Europeans. These built on exclusionary measures aimed at Asian immigrants that had been enacted into law by the federal government in the late nineteenth century. Western Hemisphere nations remained exempt from these quotas. Canada also passed a series of restrictions, starting in 1906 with an act that eliminated free entry and allowed for the deportation of immigrants who were infirm and likely to become public charges. Over the next two decades additional laws barred the entry of enemy aliens, including the Japanese, Germans, and certain groups of East Europeans, as well as of those who were viewed as having a low "probability of becoming assimilated."[19] Prospective African American immigrants were prohibited from entering the country with increasing frequency, and this discouraged many Caribbean residents from migrating as well. But there were important exceptions in labor sectors like mining, steel, agriculture, and domestic service.[20] Rather than cut off the flow of Caribbean immigrants into North America, these laws served to reshape which people came, where they settled, and for how long.

Restriction, Depression, and War, 1931–1962

While Caribbean migrants traveling to North America were either exempt from the national origins quotas or, coming from British possessions like Jamaica, fell under the relatively large quotas given to countries like Great Britain, migration from the Caribbean to the United States fell off sharply by 1930. Many prospective West Indian migrants complained that the U.S., Canadian, and British governments were colluding to keep them out. Jamaicans, for example, reported having numerous problems securing visas from the American consulate in Kingston.[21] Discrimination in local job markets, such as a temporary ban on hiring skilled Bahamian laborers on any public works projects passed by the city of Miami in 1920, discouraged travel by others.[22] After 1930, as the Great Depression deepened, U.S. immigration commissioners began to more rigorously enforce laws prohibiting the entry of anyone likely to become a public charge. Where between 1921 and 1931 roughly 75,000 people had migrated from the Caribbean to the United States, between 1931 and 1940 only 15,500 chose to do so. Increasingly Caribbean migrants also chose to stay for a shorter time, remaining permanent migrants rather than becoming immigrants and seeking to naturalize as U.S. citizens.[23]

With fewer immigrants, however, came a major labor shortage for many North American employers that worsened during the Second World War. Seeking a compromise that would answer employers' need for laborers while satisfying those who worried that renewed waves of international migration would fray the national fabric, the U.S. and Canadian governments instituted a series of guest worker programs. Most of these were focused in agriculture. During the First World War, even as U.S. industrial employers were forced into tremendous labor shortages as a result of war and growing pressure to restrict international migration, agricultural employers were allowed to drive to the Mexican and Canadian borders to contract with foreign workers.

During the Second World War and the immediate postwar period these allowances were formalized and extended. The first major guest worker initiative, the Emergency Labor Importation Program, was launched in 1942. Governments of the United States, Mexico, and the British West Indies agreed to a plan whereby the U.S. government would feed, house, and transport tens of thousands of Mexican and West Indian laborers to work in the United States. Workers were required to enter into no-strike, fixed-term contracts. As such, they were not immigrants but temporary labor migrants, brought in for a time but then required to leave when their services were no longer needed. Rather than end with the war, however, this practice continued. In the two decades following the end of the Second World War, the U.S. government allowed agriculturalists to import close to 4.5 million Mexican and Caribbean "offshore" workers. Similar programs remained in place even with the passage of the McCarran-Walter Act, which placed even more restrictions on permanent immigrants but institutionalized temporary Caribbean farm labor migration.[24] The result, as the historian Cindy Hahamovitch has argued, was a "learned dependence on foreign workers" among big growers that "resulted in the rapid internationalization of the agricultural labor market and the persistence of migrant poverty."[25]

The Cold War also strengthened North American interest in forging stronger economic and political ties across the Western Hemisphere. In the immediate wake of the Second World War the United States launched a program to promote industrial development in its Caribbean territories while meeting its domestic labor shortages in these same job sectors. "Operation Bootstrap" in

Puerto Rico was the largest.[26] Companies engaged in labor-intensive industries like the manufacture of garments and textiles, footwear, electronics, and plastic and metal goods were offered tax exemptions in exchange for establishing operations in Puerto Rico. Thousands of young men and women were also recruited to work on the mainland as farm laborers and as maids. Because they were U.S. citizens, however, employers and government officials could not force them to return to the island at the end of their contracts. Many of them stayed on, transforming the population of cities like New York and Philadelphia.[27]

For migrant workers who entered the United States as part of these programs, what they found was often shocking. Jamaican workers, most of whom were male and of African descent, had a very different experience depending on where they were sent within the United States. In some northern locations workers reported that they were welcomed gladly by local residents and treated well by their employers. Others found themselves expected to bed in miserable, hastily constructed labor camps or to work under exploitative conditions. Yet for the most part conditions were relatively favorable for Jamaican guest workers in the north, where native-born whites viewed them as something of a curiosity rather than a threat. The opposite was true in the South. Fearing that many of the workers would meet violent ends if they did not remain subservient to white employers and abide by the South's rigid racial code, Jamaica's labor adviser Herbert MacDonald demanded that Jamaican workers agree to the "Jim Crow creed" lest they face immediate termination and deportation.[28]

The pull of jobs in the United States and proliferation of guest worker programs, coupled with increasing American ownership of land and industry within the Americas, continued to have a significant impact on the movement of people within the region. Many Caribbean nations were deeply ambivalent about the spread of North American capitalism. This was especially true in Cuba.[29] Although Cuba had been a sovereign nation since the end of the Spanish American War in 1898, North American investment in the island was extensive. Then in 1959 Fidel Castro and his supporters overthrew the existing dictatorial government of General Fulgencio Batista, who had been friendly with the United States, and began implementing a series of first nationalist, then Marxist, policies, including the nationalizing of all property held by religious organizations and foreign interests as well as by upper- and middle-class Cubans. An estimated 215,000 Cubans fled in the early years following the revolution, bound for the United States. The largest number settled in Miami, although enclaves of Cuban exiles also developed in New York, New Jersey, and Illinois.[30]

From 1962 to the Present

The post-1962 period ushered in a host of changes across the region, stimulating sizable renewed immigration and reshaping the political landscape again. In 1962 Jamaica secured independent rule for the first time, as did Trinidad and Tobago. Over the next two decades many other Caribbean societies followed, including Barbados and Guyana in 1966, the Bahamas in 1973, Grenada in 1974, Suriname in 1975, Dominica in 1978, St. Lucia in 1979, St. Vincent and the Grenadines in 1979, Antigua in 1981, Belize in 1981, and St. Kitts and Nevis in 1983. At the same time the civil rights movement to end racial segregation across the United States was also winning many victories, including passage of the Civil Rights Act of 1964, specifically prohibiting discrimination on the basis of race. As a result of this legislation the national origins quotas were declared unconstitutional one year later, reopening the door to the United States to prospective immigrants from around the globe. A similar relaxing of immigration restrictions in Canada, combined with a strong economy, also resulted in a significant increase in international movement. By one estimate the number of people entering Canada from abroad increased threefold between 1962 and 1967 alone. In 1965 immigrants from Asia and the Caribbean made up just 10 percent of the nation's annual immigration totals. By 1969 they made up nearly a quarter.[31]

In the United States, Caribbean immigration also became controversial. While it was civil rights activism that helped bring about an end to the national origins quotas, by the mid-1960s many African American leaders were asking whether equality under the law was enough. Highlighting the rates of unemployment and poverty that in many areas of the country were nearly twice as high for black Americans as for whites, many civil rights activists turned their attention toward pursuing economic equality for all American citizens, emphasizing improved access to educational opportunities and jobs for African Americans.[32] The riots from Washington to Los Angeles in the wake of Dr. Martin Luther King Jr.'s assassination in 1968 only highlighted the poverty gripping America's inner cities.

Border cities like Miami were no exception, even if they did not experience large-scale rioting. Cubans continued to pour into the city whenever Castro would allow them to leave. It was also clear by the mid-1960s that attempts by the U.S. government to structure patterns of Cuban settlement across dispersed locations had failed. Nearly three-fourths of those who were relocated from Miami returned to the city. This movement marked the single largest mass immigration to the United States in more than half a century and the largest in Miami's history.

At first native-born residents welcomed the new arrivals. But as it became increasingly clear that Cubans, who saw themselves as exiles rather than immigrants and therefore intended their stay to be temporary, had no intention of wholeheartedly adopting Anglo-American lifestyles, public sentiment began to shift. As a grand jury report in Dade County noted in 1961: "The Cuban emigration has caused some friction in our community. This is a small price to pay in the overall conflict with a common foe. We must adjust ourselves to the situation and affirmatively seek ways to resolve our mutual problems. We have a right to expect our visitors to obey our laws and conform to our customs and we have a responsibility to lighten the load they have so adequately born."[33] The economic and political successes of Cubans within just a few short years of arriving in the city was equally notable and contradicted what many policymakers had come to assume was required for socioeconomic success. Instead Cubans turned the assimilation model on its head, proving that in Miami it paid to retain one's native tongue, customs, and ties.

Haitians also began arriving in the city in renewed numbers after François Duvalier declared himself president for life in 1964. Through the 1970s and early 1980s a growing number arrived without prior authorization, taking to the sea on small boats. Cubans who were prevented from leaving by Castro's government did the same. Yet the reception afforded to Cubans and Haitians once in U.S. waters or on the U.S. mainland could not have been more different.[34]

Because they had fled a communist country, Cubans were classified as "refugees" rather than "immigrants," which entitled them to federal aid in the form of low-interest loans, job training and placement assistance, and the like—benefits that many impoverished, native-born Americans thought should be made available to them as well. Haitians, who left a country with a dictatorial government that was on friendly terms with the United States, were not afforded the same forms of assistance, regardless of the circumstances surrounding their migration. While Cubans who arrived without prior authorization were granted asylum, Haitians were detained and deported as quickly as possible. Such measures did little to curtail the movement of people, although it did make passage more dangerous. The Bahamas became one interim location for Haitians wishing to reach the United States. Others fled by the thousands across the land border with the Dominican Republic, where they were placed in work camps.

Together these developments transformed a whole host of communities on the frontlines of these migrations. By 1970 Miami had become not only an immigrant city but a minority-majority city, where Latinos and African Americans outnumbered Anglo-Americans.[35] A southern city, Miami had also supported legalized segregation. As a result, many white, native-born residents felt threatened by these transformations and chose to leave Miami, moving north to other cities in Florida and neighboring states.

Meanwhile the migration of Caribbean peoples to various European destinations also increased manifold over this period. Many Jamaicans had served in the British air force during the Second World War, and when not finding jobs after their return to Jamaica, remigrated to Britain and stayed. By 1973 it was estimated that at least 550,000 men and women of Caribbean birth were living in Britain. Nearly 266,000 emigrants had arrived in France from the French-language islands. And by 1988 more than 308,000 Caribbean islanders were living in the Netherlands.[36] Still, North America continued to receive the largest number of Caribbean migrants. According to federal census estimates, close to two million Caribbean-born people were living in the United States by 1990.[37] By the turn of the century Canada became home to another 317,000 Caribbean immigrants as well, with French-speakers concentrating in Montreal. In Toronto the Caribana became the largest ethnic festival in the 1990s, and on such occasions the distinct cultural identities of people from different island states combined into a generic Caribbean one.[38]

Even as nations like the United States worked to more rigidly control the migration of people within the region, financially borders had never been more permeable. In 1983 the United States launched a program called the Caribbean Basin Initiative. The program, which offered a variety of tariff and trade benefits to Central American and Caribbean nations willing to join the program, grew out of a desire on the part of the United States to increase trade and curtail leftist movements that were active within the region. Initially the program was intended to be temporary. In 1990, however, it was made permanent. Ten years later it was expanded further through the Caribbean Basin Trade Partnership Act, which offered particular benefits to garment manufacturers.[39] Among other provisions the act gave apparel and textile products greater access to the American market, suspending duties, quantitative restrictions, and exemptions for most forms of clothing and fabrics produced in the Caribbean.[40]

Those in favor of these programs argued that creating more jobs within Caribbean member nations would also have the effect of curtailing emigration from the region. Critics pointed out that so long as highly mobile foreign capital continues to rely upon inexpensive, semiskilled workers, the programs would both move jobs to people and people to jobs. Yet neither option provides much space for social or economic advancement. As the political scientist Aaron Segal has put it, in this age of globalization, Caribbean nations are "locked into an international political economy with two options: (1) to encourage citizens to emigrate and send back remittances and (2) to stay home and work in low-paying tourism and export processing."[41] In either case it is clear that the present trend is not toward limiting movement within the region; rather, migration continues to be central to life within the Caribbean.

Conclusion

In the present, scholars of Caribbean history and culture emphasize the global nature of Caribbean identities. From music and art to politics and the economy, the international movement of people, ideas, and capital continues to shape life in the Caribbean and its diaspora. Some would argue that migration is one aspect of life that unites Caribbean-born people more than any other. As the Guyanese journalist Ruel Johnson recently observed, "[T]he Caribbean people of today, whose ancestors came from many diasporas, are leaving as one."[42] Those who leave, however, do not relinquish ties to the islands. Family connections, remittances, and various forms of diasporic entrepreneurship continue to be of tremendous importance to those born in this region, even if much of their lives are spent elsewhere in North America or in Europe. In all these ways migration continues to shape Caribbean life and identity as it has for more than three centuries.

Notes

1 U.S. Commission on Immigration, *Statistical Review of Immigration, 1820–1910*, vol. 30 (Washington: U.S. Government Printing Office, 1911), 19–22.
2 Campbell J. Gibson and Emily Lennon, "Historical Census Statistics on the Foreign-Born Population of the United States, 1850–1990" (Washington: U.S. Bureau of the Census, 1999), table 4: Region and Country or Area of Birth of the Foreign-Born Population, with Geographic Detail Shown in Decennial Census Publications of 1930 or Earlier.
3 Winston James, "Caribbean Immigration," *In Motion: The African-American Migration Experience*, ed. Howard Dodson and Sylviane Dioufe (Washington: National Geographic, 2004), 156–69.
4 John C. Walker and Jill Louise Ansheles, "The Role of the Caribbean Migrant in the Harlem Renaissance," *Afro-Americans in New York Life and History*, January 1980; U.S. Bureau of the Census, *Negroes in the United States, 1920–1932*, vol. 2: Population (Washington: U.S. Government Printing Office, 1934), 67–73.
5 Michel S. Laguerre, *Diasporic Citizenship: Haitian Americans in Transnational America* (Boston: Palgrave Macmillan, 1998), 31–74.
6 Nancy Hewitt, *Southern Discomfort: Women's Activism in Tampa, Florida, 1880s–1920s* (Urbana: University of Illinois Press, 2001), 65, 74, 79, 107, 119; Vicki Ruíz and Vir-

ginia Sánchez Korrol, eds., *Latinas in the United States* (Bloomington: Indiana University Press, 2006), 563.

7 On Caribbean immigrants in Harlem over this period see Joyce Moore Turner, *Caribbean Crusaders and the Harlem Renaissance* (Urbana: University of Illinois Press, 2005); Irma Watkins-Owens, *Blood Relations: Caribbean Immigrants and the Harlem Community, 1900–1930* (Bloomington: Indiana University Press, 1996).

8 David J. Hellwig, "Black Leaders and United States Immigration Policy, 1917–1929," *Journal of Negro History* 66, no. 2 (summer 1981), 113.

9 Edmund David Cronon, *Black Moses: The Story of Marcus Garvey and the Universal Negro Improvement Association* (Madison: University of Wisconsin Press, 1969); Mary G. Robinson, *Grassroots Garveyism* (Chapel Hill: University of North Carolina Press, 2007).

10 Philip Kasinitz, *Caribbean New York: Black Immigrants and the Politics of Race* (Ithaca: Cornell University Press, 1992), 19–37.

11 Watkins-Owens, *Blood Relations*, 110.

12 Ira De A. Reid, *The Negro Immigrant: His Background, Characteristics, and Social Adjustment, 1899–1937* (New York: Arno, 1969 [1939]), 204.

13 James Weldon Johnson, *Along This Way* (New York: Viking, 1969), 65.

14 Wallace Thurman and William Jourdan Rapp, "Harlem as Others See It," *Negro World*, April 13, 1929; Doming Romero, typescript in Edward Bruce Papers, box 3, Manuscripts, Archives, and Rare Books Division, Schomburg Center for Research in Black Culture, New York Public Library; William Whyte, ed., *The WPA Guide to New York City* (New York: Random House, 1982 [1939]), 257. All are quoted in Watkins-Owens, *Blood Relations*, 4.

15 Bonham C. Richardson, "Caribbean Migrations, 1838–1985," *The Modern Caribbean*, ed. Franklin W. Knight and Colin Palmer (Chapel Hill: University of North Carolina Press, 1989), 208–12.

16 Michel Fabre, "Paris as a Moment in African American Consciousness," *The Black Columbiad: Defining Moments in African American Literature and Culture*, ed. Werner Sollors and Maria Diedrich (Cambridge: Harvard University Press, 1993), 135.

17 Theresa Leninger-Miller, *New Negro Artists in Paris: African American Painters and Sculptors in the City of Light, 1922–1934* (New Brunswick: Rutgers University Press, 2000), 74, 83.

18 On responses to the conference see H. F. Worley and C. G. Contee, "The Worley Report on the Pan-African Congress of 1919," *Journal of Negro History* 55, no. 2 (April 1970), 140–43.

19 On the history of Canada's immigration policy over this period see Donald Avery, *"Dangerous Foreigners": European Immigrant Workers and Labor Radicalism in Canada, 1896–1932* (Toronto: McClelland and Stewart, 1979); Valerie Knowles, *Strangers at Our Gates: Canadian Immigration and Immigration Policy, 1540–2006*, rev. ed. (Toronto: Dundurn, 2007).

20 For a discussion of these policies see Ninette Kelley and M. J. Trebilcock, *The Making of the Mosaic* (Toronto: University of Toronto Press, 1998), 155–56.

21 Winston James, "The History of Afro-Caribbean Migration to the United States," In Motion: The African American Migration Experience, ed. Schomburg Center for Research in Black Culture, http://www.inmotionaame.org.

22 Melanie Shell-Weiss, *Coming to Miami: A Social History* (Gainesville: University Press of Florida, 2009), 78–79.

23 U.S. Immigration and Naturalization Service, *Statistical Yearbook of the Immigration and Naturalization Service, 1998* (Washington: U.S. Government Printing Office, 2000), table 2, 20–21.

24 On the significance of these policies see David Craig Griffith, *American Guestworkers: Jamaicans and Mexicans in the U.S. Labor Market* (State College: Penn State University Press, 2006); Cindy Hahamovitch, *The Fruits of Their Labor: Atlantic Coast Farmworkers and the Making of Migrant Poverty, 1870–1945* (Chapel Hill: University of North Carolina Press, 1997).

25 Cindy Hahamovitch, "'In America Life Is Given Away': Jamaican Farmworkers and the Making of Agricultural Immigration Policy," *Florida's Working-Class Past: Current Perspectives on Labor, Race, and Gender from Spanish Florida to the New Immigration*, ed. Robert Cassanello and Melanie Shell-Weiss (Gainesville: University Press of Florida, 2009), 198–226. See also Cindy Hahamovitch, "Creating Perfect Immigrants: Guestworkers of the World in Historical Perspective," *Labor History* 44 (February 2003), 69–94.

26 Jorge I. Domínguez, "Latinos and U.S. Foreign Policy," paper no. 06-05, Weatherhead Center for International Policy, Harvard University (May 2006), 17–19.

27 Carmen Teresa Whalen, *From Puerto Rico to Philadelphia: Puerto Rican Workers and Postwar Economies* (Philadelphia: Temple University Press, 2001); Carmen Teresa Whalen and Víctor Vásquez-Hernández, eds., *The Puerto Rican Diaspora: Historical Perspectives* (Philadelphia: Temple University Press, 2005).

28 Hahamovitch, "'In America Life Is Given Away.'"

29 C. A. M. Hennessy, "The Roots of Cuban Nationalism," *International Affairs* 30, no. 3 (July 1963), 345–59; Ramon Eduardo Ruíz, *Cuba: The Making of a Revolution* (New York: W. W. Norton, 1968).

30 Ines M. Miyares and Christopher A. Airriess, *Contemporary Ethnic Geographies in America* (Boston: Rowman and Littlefield, 2006), 127–28.

31 Kelley and Trebilcock, *The Making of the Mosaic*, 347–49.

32 Jeff Diamond, "African American Attitudes towards United States Immigration Policy," *International Migration Review* 32, no. 2 (summer 1998), 451–70; Thomas Wilson, "Americans' Views on Immigration Policy: Testing the Role of Threatened Group Interests," *Sociological Perspectives* 44, no. 4 (2001), 485–501.

33 *Dade County Grand Jury Report* (fall 1961), 12–13, Florida Collection, Miami-Dade Public Library.

34 Alex Stepick, "Haitian Boat People: A Study in the Conflicting Forces Shaping U.S. Immigration Policy," *Law and Contemporary Problems* 45, no. 2 (spring 1982), 163–96.

35 For a detailed discussion of these transformations see Shell-Weiss, *Coming to Miami*, 206–10.

36 Mary Chamberlain, ed., *Caribbean Migration: Globalised Identities* (London: Routledge, 1998), 6.

37 Gibson and Lennon, "Historical Census Statistics on the Foreign-Born Population of the United States, 1850–1990," table 3.

38 Statistics Canada, *2006 Census of Population* (Ottawa: Government of Canada, 2008), table 38.

39 U.S. Trade Representative, "Seventh Report to Congress on the Operation of the Caribbean Basin Economic Recovery Act" (Washington: Office of the Americas, U.S. Trade Representative, December 2007). For an analysis of these measures see Michael Cornell Dypski, "The Caribbean Basin Initiative: An Examination of Structural Dependency, Good Neighbor Relations, and American Investment," *Journal of Transnational Law and Policy* 12, no. 1 (fall 2002), 95–136.

40 Caribbean Basin Trade Partnership Act (2000), section 213(B).

41 Aaron Segal, "The Political Economy of Contemporary Migration," *Globalization and Neoliberalism in the Caribbean Context*, ed. Thomas Klak (Boston: Rowman and Littlefield, 1998), 213.

42 Ruel Johnson, "The Diaspora" (Georgetown, Guyana: UWI-CARICOM, 2009).

CHAPTER SEVEN

Migration to Mexico, Migration in Mexico

A Special Case on the North American Continent

Delia González de Reufels and Dirk Hoerder

While the United States and Canada as well as Brazil and Argentina have been immigration countries and while the Caribbean was repopulated after the genocide or near-genocide of Native Peoples, in New Spain and after 1821 in Mexico, numerous Native or First Peoples provided a rural labor force—once they overcame the European contact-related demographic disaster, a population collapse of about 90 percent in the sixteenth century. Their nineteenth- and twentieth-century descendants formed the urban laboring population. Thus Mexico's migration history differs from that of almost all other societies of the Americas except perhaps for Catholic French-language Quebec.[1]

We discuss the colonial period's Spanish inmigrations and restrictions on entry of non-Catholic Europeans, the importation of African-background people, the migrants from Asia through the Spanish Philippines, and internal migration whether voluntary or involuntary. We also outline the emergence of anti-Spanish and anti-foreigner sentiments from the 1820s to the 1860s, and the inmigration to Texas of Anglo settlers with slaves and of Confederates during the U.S. War of Secession. During the mid-1850s to mid-1870s basic frames for migration emerged: the dispossession and resulting mobilization of Native Peoples and the insertion of a small number of foreign investors, entrepreneurs, and fortune seekers. Porfirio Díaz's dictatorship, 1876–1910, ended internal warfare and attracted foreign capital. Investors sent their personnel to engage in railroad building, mining, and oil extraction. Railroad construction facilitated internal migrations as well as northbound moves to the borderlands and into the United States. We will discuss migrants from Asia who, in circumstances that contrasted with Anglo-American exclusion, arrived in small numbers to the 1930s. We will assess the impact of racist eugenicists, who from around 1900 demanded immigration of Europeans to whiten the mestizo population, as well as of the anti-Chinese movements of the 1930s. The decades from the early Porfiriato to the late 1930s were a time of urbanization and internal migrations. The period of revolutionary warfare, 1910–21, involved mobility of soldiers and dependents and mass flight internally and to migrant communities across the United States border. Labor migrations to the United States brought a new kind of inmigrants, the large number of returnees. At the same time, the southern border with Guatemala remained an integrated border region to the 1920s. Finally we turn to internal migrations to the cities after the Second World War and the emerging *maquiladora* belt along the U.S. border. (See chapter 1 for migration to the United States and chapter 9 for the borderlands.)[2]

We argue that the number of migrants (Span. *inmigrantes*) to Mexico throughout its history was small, but that as investors and entrepreneurs or simply as "Whites" or "U.S. Whites," they had a major impact on both economic development and the emergence of anti-foreigner discourses and diatribes. At the same time both voluntary educational migrants and involuntary political exiles created an image of Mexico in the societies of destination across the Atlantic World. As regards internal migrations, we argue that high inequalities, both economic and ethno-cultural, explain the internal interregional, rural-urban, and interurban migrations.

A brief synopsis will position Mexico's inmigration in the context of the Americas and the Atlantic World. While from 1820 to 1932 the United States received 32.6 million migrants, Argentina 6.5 million, Canada 5.1 million, Brazil 4.4 million, and Cuba 1.4 million, Mexico attracted a mere 270,000, or 0.5 percent of total European overseas migration. Foreigners in Mexico hovered at around 0.5 percent of the population for most of its history, reaching a brief high of just under 1 percent in 1930. In absolute numbers, migrants from Spain and the two neighboring states, Guatemala and the United States, accounted for 12,000 to 14,000 migrants each in 1895; French, British, Germans, and Chinese together accounted for another 10,000. By 1930 Spanish immigrants formed the largest contingent (47,000), followed by Chinese (19,000), Guatemalans (17,000), and U.S. Americans (12,000). From 1950 on U.S. Americans accounted for the largest contingent by far.[3] These data indicate the importance of transborder migrations between neighboring states—of which the Guatemalans as workers or refugees rather than investors have received little notice in scholarship.[4] The borders, politically drawn by distant national governments between 1823 and 1842 in the south and in 1836, 1848, and 1853 in the north, would be constructed socially over a century and, from 1924, be guarded by a new, armed U.S. Border Patrol.

In discussing internal migration and emigration, we outline the dispossession of Native and Mestizo families of their land since the Liberal reforms of the 1850s and the consequences by the late nineteenth century for increased mobility across larger distances within Mexico, and finally northward to the United States. The south-north railroads built by U.S. capital would facilitate this mobility. The southern border region, in contrast, for long remained a region of intense but local migrations.

Migrations to and in New Spain

The movements of people to New Spain were neither spontaneous nor free. By 1503 the Spanish Crown had installed the "Casa de la Contratación" in Seville to watch over American trade and to monitor and channel migrations to and from Spanish America. Keeping away unwanted persons, such as criminals, vagrants, Jews, heretics, and gypsies was one of its most important tasks. Foreigners were also excluded from immigration, yet they boarded ships clandestinely.[5] Exceptions were only made for non-Spanish members of religious orders, soldiers, and servants of distinguished Spaniards.

Legal immigration to Spanish America and Mexico was bureaucratically cumbersome and costly: it included moving to Seville, where future immigrants had to appear personally before the Casa and wait until all the paperwork was finished. Controls were strict and thorough, as immigrants had to prove that they were descended from an unbroken lineage of Catholics and had never been prosecuted by the Inquisition. Thus Spanish colonization of Mexico is an example of strict migration rules and population policies of a metropolis; it also shows that overseas migrations were linked with the movements of people within Spain, and on a larger scale within Europe. Because trans-European labor migration included Iberia, migration to New Spain tended to retain the patterns of these earlier population movements, rendering circular migration typical during the early years.

In the beginning New Spain attracted many Spaniards already living in the Caribbean through secondary migrations. Soon migrants from the peninsula started to arrive directly, again mostly unskilled young men, military men, and adventurers. The married among them left their wives and children in Spain because they sought neither a religious haven nor land to cultivate, but only wealth. This pattern would change after the creation of the viceroyalty in 1535, especially between 1540 and 1560, when settlers, in particular artisans and professional men as well as an increasing number of women and children from Andalusia, Castile, Extremadura, and New Castile, started to arrive in larger numbers. Their networks would last over centuries, enabling chain migrations. By 1570 about 63,000 "whites" were thought to be living in Mexico, but figures are uncertain because of a lack of censuses and a growing number of illegal immigrants. From 1580, when Spain and Portugal formed one kingdom, many Portuguese arrived, but they were banned after 1640. Gallegos and Basques migrated as well, and inhabitants of the Canary Islands were recruited in the eighteenth century for the frontier garrison at what was to become San Antonio, Texas.

Private letters from the sixteenth and seventeenth centuries provide a rare glimpse of the migrants' life and their reasons for migration. As poverty had motivated most of them to leave Spain—"that miserable land," as one Juan Fernández, writing from Mexico City called it—the letters frequently offered an opportunity to boast about new wealth and how individual migrants ate more meat in a week than all the inhabitants of their home village taken together.[6] Some complained about loneliness and illnesses, and even though they might have sought a privileged life they had to work hard.[7] The Spaniards who wrote or, if illiterate, dictated letters to public scribes showed little compassion for the indigenous population, which they considered inferior. Few Spaniards married indigenous women. Andrés García, however, commented in 1571 that his wife had saved his life and insisted that "here you do not lose your honor" by marrying an Indian,[8] thus proving that the question of status was always on the migrants' minds. Most never married but had children with Indian women who were their concubines or servants, while male Indians, even members of the indigenous nobility, only rarely formed unions with Spanish women.

The conquest of Peru and news of its richness had a direct effect on migrations, but New Spain reclaimed its importance when the mines in Taxco and Zacatecas were discovered. For decades Indians constituted most of the mine labor force, and their brutal exploitation resulted in a further dramatic loss of indigenous population shortly after the demographic collapse at the time of first contact. The surviving Indian population endured forced migrations and resettlement in Indian villages and on *encomiendas*, always performing heavy labor and struggling with hitherto unknown diseases. The Indian population reached its lowest point in 1625–50.

As the Spaniards moved into northern Mexico they had to adjust to the so-called frontera, where European (i.e. Spanish) civilization ended and the zone of daily contact between immigrants and baptized, non-baptized, and non-integrated indigenous peoples began. Here Spaniards depended more on negotiations with Indians but also on the use of violence. Punitive missions to "pacify" the North served to abduct and enslave Indians. Missionaries, especially the Jesuits, pushed northward all the way to Baja California and Arizona.

When in 1767 the Order was expelled from all Spanish kingdoms, New Spain was notably affected: 678 Jesuits had to depart, leaving many parishes unattended and some schools deserted even though the Franciscans sought to replace them. Bourbon reforms, which had aimed at increasing colonial profit and reducing the power and the wealth of the church, brought an important influx of non-Spanish migrants: Swiss, French, and Walloon soldiers.

But Mexican society was not only about Indians and Europeans, it also was about *chinos* and Africans. *Chinos*, the name by which slaves from the Philippines were known, were proof of the close relation between the viceroyalty and Spanish Asia, which included exchange of goods and the regular transfer of Mexican silver.[9] The first Africans to arrive came in 1519 from Cuba as slaves, fighting during conquests with their masters. Free men of mixed racial ancestry were also among the so-called black conquistadors.[10] The number of Africans increased after 1535 as domestic slaves were imported, and grew again at the end of the sixteenth century. By then house slaves or African domestic servants marked social prestige, so much so that members of the indigenous nobility like Pedro de San Miguel and his wife from Tepeaca aspired in 1557 to own a female slave.[11] Soon high demand for workers determined the policy of substituting Indians by Africans, now forcibly migrated directly from Africa, in all the economically relevant sectors (mines, sugar mills, workshops). The governors who argued that too many slaves would "plunge the land into confusion" received little attention:[12] during the century of conquest African immigration became quantitatively larger than white immigration. The final ban on Indian slavery in 1543 made the following century the century of the greatest forced African migration, just as Mexico was in the full process of development. From the eighteenth century demand for slaves declined. After reorganization of the slave trade and the creation of the royal companies the importation of Africans practically ended, and in December 1817 it was abolished altogether. Approximately 200,000 Africans had been brought to New Spain between 1519 and 1817. But by the time of independence only a few slaves were left. Humboldt traveled through Mexico and reported the existence of about 10,000 slaves (6,000 Africans, 4,000 mulattoes). They would be counted as part of the "castas" who in 1810 included 1,338,700 people, while the Indians with 3,676,300 constituted the largest group, and Spaniards and Spanish Americans, or *criollos*, together accounted for 1,098,000 inhabitants of New Spain.[13] By the end of the colonial period immigration from Spain and other parts of Spanish America had reached an all-time low. The political convulsions in Europe and other parts of the Spanish Empire had an immediate effect on Mexico.

Migrations and Attitudes to Immigrants and Foreigners, 1820s to 1860s

After more than a decade of warfare against Spanish-sent troops and fervent Mexican-born royalists as well as a prolonged civil war, Mexico achieved its independence in 1821.[14] In the five decades after this so-called conservative revolution Mexico faced five foreign invasions. When the new Creole government promoted a decree to expel the Spanish-born in 1827, Conservatives supported a short, quixotic, and unsuccessful Spanish invasion in 1829. As a result some 25,000 Spaniards, also called *peninsulares* or pejoratively *gachupines*, fled. Many were merchants who took their money and businesses with them and thus caused economic dislocation—and, unintendedly, provided opportunities for European entrepreneurial migrants of other nationalities.[15] In 1837 Britain and France mounted a brief military intervention to collect debts. Thirdly, "Yankee" immigrants, invited by the federal government to settle and vitalize the state of Texas, brought their slaves and resisted the resulting government-mandated second abolition of slavery in 1829. These roughly thirty thousand newcomers, who outnumbered the resident nine thousand or so Spanish-speaking Mexican citizens, turned to invasion and seceded in 1836. The United States annexed Texas in 1845.[16]

The dismembering of the state by the U.S. aggression in 1846–48 and the loss of control over finances to foreign powers and private U.S. financiers (because of an internally volatile system of rule) added to the anti-foreigner sentiments that had been a constituent element of the conflict between *criollos and peninsulares*, pitting Mexican-born *Americanos* against Spanish-born immigrants. At the end of the war, along with the vast territories, the United States annexed an estimated 50,000 Mexicans and perhaps 100,000 "Indians," who under Mexican law had been citizens. Only some 3,000 Euro-Mexicans responded to a call to repatriate,[17] mostly taking residence in the thinly settled northern states that the Mexican government had decided to populate, thus converting the aftermath of war into a new colonization scheme.[18] Anti-Yankee feelings added themselves to the anti-Spanish.

The fifth invasion occurred when the France of Napoleon III developed its new imperial pretensions; the royalist French "grand dessin" resembled the U.S. Republic's "Manifest Destiny." Having occupied Saigon in Indochina in 1859 and pushing plans for a canal across Nicaragua, it resumed the hostility of 1837 and used a Mexican moratorium on debt payments as a cue in 1862 to lead a European invasion that lasted to 1867. Maximilian, a Habsburg scion installed by Napoleon III as Mexican emperor, brought among others European musicians and artists to the country. Further anti-European feeling added itself to the existing grievances.

The eighteenth-century immigrant Spaniard's claim to superiority was emulated by immigrant Europeans and, from mid-century, by U.S. entrepreneurs and investors. A well-founded xenophobia was the result, from which only the southern rural transborder migrants from Guatemala were excepted, as described later.

Both anti-invader warfare and the intermittent coups and armed struggles in the decades between 1821 and 1876 dislocated families and hindered urban economic developments and even the rural cultivation of sufficient food supplies. It also gave rise to mobile and lawless groups of uprooted civilians and straggling soldiers. Internal displacement rather than goal-directed mobility was high, and as it expanded from southern and central to northern states, it became generalized over the whole territory.

A further war, the U.S. War of Secession in 1861–65, added to the inmigrations. Monterrey on the Pacific and the ports of the Gulf of Mexico, especially Brownsville/Matamoros, became centers of Confederate cotton trading, which permitted the accumulation of capital and subsequent industrialization. In the aftermath of this war, during the French invasion, Conservatives invited Confederate expatriates as technical personnel and settlers. Emigrant engineers worked as surveyors for Mexican railroad lines, settlers founded a few agricultural colonies, and other expatriates sought opportunities, but Union troops closed the Rio Grande border in 1866—or attempted to do so—to end the exodus.

The beginnings of two other migratory movements for which Mexico is known—the political exile of Mexicans and the inmigration of European artists—also date from this period and were to last for a century. The endless internal struggles between those in power and insurgents and, once the latter had seized power, the next insurgents, forced defeated politicians, generals, and other local warring chieftains ("warlords") to seek exile, most often in the United States, Cuba, which remained a Spanish colony to 1898, or Europe. In the United States arms for further struggles could be bought, and the Union Army supplied arms to President Juárez to fight the French invaders. Given the U.S. government's lack of interest in Mexican politicking, exiles could form political parties and foment further rebellions. After 1867 many of the royalist-minded Conservatives, who had hoped for an immigrant king from Europe's nobility and thus supported the French-sent Austrian Maximilian, had to go into exile: New York, Havana, and European cities like Paris became their destinations.

Simultaneously European artists and intellectuals migrated to Mexico, attracted by landscape, adventure, perhaps male gun and horse cultures, and especially urban lifestyle and governmental positions. This exchange of members of the elites, many of whom returned to Europe as circular migrants, remained small in number but was influential for both culture and politics. Immigrant and Mexican-born painters created the conventions for how to depict Mexico's landscapes; the first directors of the Academy of Fine Arts were European, a necessity from the Europhile Creoles' point of view. Mexican artists, in turn, went to Europe, especially Italy, to study. Mexico was both part of the Atlantic World and a special case.

Thus during these decades four ethno-cultural groups of inmigrants may be discerned: the traditional Spanish; recent arrivals from the United States, especially Texas; Guatemalans along the southern border; and commercial and other entrepreneurs, or "trade conquistadors,"[19] from France, Germany, and Great Britain.[20] Xenophobia existed alongside xenophilia: the Creole elites had long looked upon Spain as a source of backwardness while other European metropoles were their cultural frame of reference and the example they sought to emulate.[21] The elites, in particular the landed segment, generally disdained commercial and financial activities, and thus the Mexican state and the elite as a class were dependent on economic inmigrants bringing capital, expertise, and connections in international trade. On the whole, in the decades after independence immigration was hampered by political instability, frequently changing legal provisions, and discrimination against non-Catholics. However, the quasi-constitutional Laws of 1836 defined the rights of Mexicans and foreigners.

Establishing the Frame: The Liberal Decades, 1855–1876

In a second, overlapping period from the mid-1850s to the mid-1870s the Liberal government's dispossession of Native villages and Mestizo tenant peasants, as well as the middle class's hostility to commercial and financial activities, deeply inscribed migration-inducing landlessness and a deficit in urban economic growth on the socioeconomic frame of the society. Ever more internal migration and inmigration of foreigners with capital and commercial connections resulted.

La Reforma, from 1855 to 1861, was intended to liberalize economic life from the corporatist fetters associated with Spanish rule but not from the economic power of the landowning elite. Britain, France, and Germany were considered examples. Only about one-sixth of Mexico's territory is agriculturally usable, and ownership of these lands was concentrated in the hands of Spanish-origin Creoles, who in colonial times had been excluded from high offices and thus established themselves as quasi-nobility. In addition, 48 percent of the land had come into possession of the church through bequests and donations. This pattern vastly differed from that prevailing in immigrant-attracting countries like Argentina, Brazil, the United States, and Canada.[22] The Ley Lerdo of 1856 (and Article 27 of the Constitution of 1857) left private ownership intact but was intended to deprive the Catholic Church of its vast landholdings (unless in active use for spiritual purposes). However, it also deprived *corporaciones civiles*, Native Peoples' communities, of their common land, *ejidos*. The minister responsible, Miguel Lerdo de Tejada, expected a wave of European immigrants to buy and settle the disentailed lands. Since no immigration tradition existed and since potential migrants could easily reach the North American or Argentine Plains, only a few thousand came. Most of the land went to Mexican speculators and landowning families—some close to the Liberal Party. In 1863 the *Ley de baldíos*, Law of Unoccupied Lands, dictated by Juárez, gave foreigners yet again easier access to the confiscated territories. But the Liberal Party's ideology of establishing a thrifty, hardworking, and reliable white-skinned middle class of yeomen farmers remained a chimera. Nevertheless this law had its sequels in 1883 and 1894, creating instruments for privatizing more public lands.

The countryside was severely undercapitalized. Without banks and the former lending capacity of the church, the extent of alienation of Mestizo and First Peoples' rural families from their land was dramatic. Before *La Reforma*, the peasantry still held 25 percent of the country's arable land, but after half a century of Liberals' and President Díaz's rule, only 2 percent of the arable land was still held in common by peasant communities (1910). In other words, 96.7 percent of rural farming families owned no land. By depriving people of their economic basis, including their daily subsistence, successive governments mobilized rural Indian and mestizo families for vast, poverty-driven migrations—internally to jobs in export-oriented large-scale agriculture and to the cities, and externally northbound to the United States.

Rural-urban migrations had a tradition that dated back to colonial times. In 1811 one-third of the residents of Mexico City were inmigrants; 43 percent of the women living in the city were migrants, thus continuing patterns established since the seventeenth century, when Indian women sought employment as servants or washed laundry and sold food. The ratio was similar in Guadalajara in 1822: the majority of the inmigrating women came from neighboring Indian villages, and only one-sixth of the migrants came from beyond the borders of the state of Jalisco.[23] Most internal migration was short-distance and remained within the boundaries of a particular state during the first three-quarters of the nineteenth century. In fact Mexico's industrialization, which had begun in the 1820s and 1830s with the textile industry and thus resembled developments in other parts of the Atlantic World, had centered on populous, labor-providing regions before expanding to sites to which workers had to migrate over increasing distances.

In the towns and cities, where craftsmen and shopkeepers were well represented, no substantial middle class developed. The Mexican elite's aversion to commerce and banking left a gap in the scale of socioeconomic activities into which foreigners could and did insert themselves. To expand the role of the Mexican middle class, President Juárez charged Gabino Barreda, an educational migrant who had studied in France with Auguste Comte, to develop institutions for change; one result was the establishment of the National Preparatory School to train the nation's elite children for entry into university. In some respects Mexico's development resembled that of east central and eastern Europe, where rural serfs were bound to nobles and no indigenous urban middle classes could develop. Invited by rulers, migrants from neighboring realms, mainly Jews and Germans, became "inserted middle classes." In Mexico entrepreneurs were lacking, urban craftsmen were available as skilled labor, and unskilled laborers could be drawn from among the dispossessed rural families. From the 1830s U.S. "trade conquistadors," replacing the expelled Spanish and the French, British, German, and—subsequently again—Spanish, expanded into industry, mining, and large-scale cash-crop agriculture and seized control of these sectors. By 1850 British investors held most privately owned mines.

These and U.S. investors formed "unassimilated expatriate communities," according to Jürgen Buchenau. Most did not intend to become permanent immigrants. In sequential migrations men with capital and a business would call on younger male relatives to join or replace them. Self-segregated, they shunned private social contacts, came for temporary sojourns only, and—the Spanish inmigrants excepted—avoided intermarriage by delaying family formation until after return to their society of origin. Their "otherness" was reinforced by linguistic conventions: unlike English but somewhat like German, the Spanish language resists hyphenated designations, like "French-Mexicans," to signify acculturation processes. Thus the Mexican *criollos*, sometimes calling themselves *Americanos* (in distinction to the *peninsulares*), faced *extranjeros*, among whom the Yankees formed a special group.

From mid-century some European businessmen and technicians installed themselves permanently, learning Spanish and bringing in their families. Some acculturated; others sent children back to the culture of origin for their education. Foreigners had to nationalize to achieve full citizenship and all the rights this encompassed. Their children and grandchildren would be Mexican, as *ius solis* applied. During the nineteenth century the status and rights of foreigners were defined by the specific *leyes de extranjeros*, and it would not be until 1908 that Mexican law established mechanisms for the selection of immigrants. The inmigrating capitalists imported personnel and left only low-paying jobs to Mexicans—setting a pattern that U.S. investors would exacerbate. European labor migrants would not choose Mexico as a destination, since they would have to compete with an oversupply of underpaid native-born workers. The "inserted," hardly ever amounting to more than 0.5 percent of the population, were "quantitatively insignificant" but "had an enormous impact in qualitative terms."[24] Mexico's economy was part of an Atlantic World characterized by "trade and investor diasporas," to use and expand Curtin's term. With the intensification of transpacific connections, their family networks might encompass three or four continents.[25] The Liberals' policies prepared Mexico for the penetration of foreign capital and created an impoverished, mobile labor force. President Juárez's engagement of Barreda created an important precedent for the following Mexican government of Díaz, which would rely strongly on foreign experts and French-educated politicians.

Pro-Foreigner Policies and the Beginning of Labor Outmigration, 1876–1910

President Díaz's regime, the Porfiriato, lasted from 1876 until 1910 and was built on Liberalist foundations. It amended the pro-foreign middle-class policies to give preferential treatment for powerful Yankee investors, who usually remained absentee multinational capitalists. Even before acceding to power Díaz had established alliances with U.S. capital (see chapter 15). Immigration, temporary inmigration, internal migration, and emigration were influenced by the economic stagnation of the so-called Long Depression from the 1870s to the mid-1890s—but also by the stability of the regime that ended the destructive internal wars and coups of pretenders for power.

Immigration remained low: the census data (beginning in 1895), though not always exact, are nevertheless an indicator of demographic development. They list 58,180 foreigners for 1900, 116,530 for 1910, 108,080 for 1921, and 140,590 for 1930. At the beginning European and U.S. citizens came in roughly equal numbers; by 1930 the ratio had shifted only slightly, to 5:6. Central Americans first appeared in the national census in 1895, Cubans in 1900; by 1900 migrants from Arabia were also listed, and a new pattern, transpacific migration, intensified. Chinese and then Japanese reached Mexico in the mid-1870s: from a few thousand before 1900 their number grew to 20,195 (1910) and 29,030 (1930). Mexico kept its door open to Asians when the United States and Canada decided on exclusion in the 1880s, ignoring deliberately the diplomatic tensions this created. Only in the 1930s would state politicians react violently to these foreign "others" whose presence challenged so many Mexican racial assumptions.

The first Chinese came after the end of their indentures in Cuba and in Latin American countries; others came in reaction to U.S. exclusion in 1882, often with intention to continue to the United States across the land border (see chapter 14). From the 1880s Chinese seized opportunities in Mexico and in Sonora in particular. They inserted themselves into small business, preferably in new mining towns and railroad settlements to avoid competition with established Mexican merchants. Their pattern of settlement followed the expansion of U.S. investments, and a few wholesale merchants established themselves in Guaymas and Hermosillo. In Baja California the Chinese formed a petite bourgeoisie. These traders' role expanded during the Revolution, when they were regarded as neutral. By 1910 Chinese resided in all but one of the Mexican states, but except for Sonora, numbers remained small. There "the sons of Confucius," as they were sometimes called, in the 1920s came to be viewed as degenerate and as creating a "Chinese problem"; a racist campaign drove them from small commerce. During the Great Depression this movement was backed by state authorities; the governor supported anti-Chinese violence and prohibited marriages between Mexicans and Chinese. As a result some migrated to the United States, where they had business connections; others migrated internally to more hospitable states.[26] The Japanese who had first arrived in Mexico in 1891 and 1892 did not fare much better, even though numbers first remained small and hostilities were unusual. Between 1901 and 1907 numbers rose when approximately eight to ten thousand Japanese were brought to Mexico to work the northern mines, especially in Coahuila. Most of them decided to return to their places of origin, some moved to the United States. By then poor working conditions, low wages, racism, and the open hostility of Mexicans, who labeled them "chinos," would drive them out of the country. Of the mere 2,623 Japanese listed in the census of 1910, many left for good during the early years of the Revolution.[27]

U.S. financiers, in control of Mexico's national debt, received concessions to build the country's railroad and transportation system in lieu of payment. The connection from the Gulf port of Veracruz to Mexico City was completed in the 1870s, and the first northward line from the capital reached the U.S. border in the mid-1880s. In El Paso it connected to four major U.S. lines north-, east-, and westward. By the end of the 1880s the capital was also connected to Piedras Negras and Nuevo Laredo on the border to Texas. In contrast to the south-north lines, the first trans-isthmus line began to operate only in 1894. From 400 miles (640 km) of track in 1877 the rail network expanded to 12,000 miles (19,000 km) in 1910. Railroad building required labor; those mobilized moved along the lines—in Spanglish *traque*, from English "track" rather than the *ferrocarril*—and crossed the northern border effortlessly. In the United States the exclusion of Chinese in 1882 and of Japanese in 1907 had created a demand for Mexican laborers. Some Mexicans brought their families; others returned home for regular visits. While Mexican governmental policies had produced a landless proletariat, U.S. capital facilitated its mobility. The railroads also brought mass-produced U.S. goods to Mexico's urban markets and Mexican-factory-produced goods to the hinterlands—thus dislocating local artisans who, with their families, would join the migrations.

After 1895, at the beginning of a new upward economic cycle, railroad building, the commercialization of agriculture, and oil exploration led to rapid growth, and the policies of the mid-1880s advantaged foreigners even further. Foreign railroad and mining interests and new surveying and land development companies acquired vast tracts of land. Soon more than one-fifth of Mexico's total surface was foreign owned. The outsiders, often in collusion with Mexican businessmen, used political connections and legal expertise to deprive villagers of their best lands (i.e. of whatever was left after decades of loss). Once again anti-foreigner sentiment and a sense of nationalism was fueled; official xenophilia was mirrored in popular xenophobia.[28] The U.S. and British investors in cooperation with Mexico's elite capitalized on the Liberals' and the Porfiriato's policies, which had created the landless proletarians-in-the-making, many of whom would have to migrate to the United States in the absence of a viable *national* labor market.

Factories, mines, and oil extraction, established with foreign capital, equipment, and know-how, were staffed with technical personnel sent in by the absentee investors, while no proletarian migrants from Europe chose Mexico. Thus a new "labor aristocracy" of white over brown occupied the best jobs even when Mexican skilled personnel was available—trained local artisans and craftsmen had to accept inferior jobs. The racist and exploitative working conditions once again added to anti-foreigner sentiment. However, labor unions and mutualist societies had come into being after 1867, influenced by the Paris Commune of 1871, and took up socialist, syndicalist, and anarchist ideas partly mediated through migrating radicals from Europe. The so-called U.S. international unions and craft brotherhoods, on the other hand, pursued a racialized, white-over-brown, or U.S.-American-over-Mexican, strategy. Since U.S. American and Mexican groups worked on both sides of the border, racialization was a transborder issue.

Ever more internally migrating men and women moved farther than to the next city and in increasing numbers crossed state borders. Job opportunities, in particular since the 1890s, drew large numbers of campesinos, especially to Mexico City. Women, constituting more than half of the migrants between 1895 and 1910, increased their participation in wage labor. Family structures changed, and single women as heads of households became part of urban society. Popular Catholicism changed when migrants left traditions behind. Out-migration from the villages also changed gender roles for women in the villages: they had to work in the fields or seek jobs in neighboring villages. While internal migration grew fast, northward transborder migrations remained low to the end of the Porfiriato, though they expanded from railroad workers to other economic sectors. Railroad workers spread across the United States with their free passes, and small communities sprang up in northern U.S. cities. But most migrants concentrated in the borderlands from Los Angeles via Arizona to Texas (see chapters 1 and 9).

Mexico's Southern Border and the Region's Transborder Labor Markets

Different from the northern border region was the southern border between Mexico and Guatemala, disputed for decades and firmly and officially established along the Suchiate River and across the Sierra Madre only in 1882. The region's rural population, mobile agricultural laborers included, lived in long-established family networks and economic relations that were thus formally severed. In the following decades border crossings continued as part of everyday lives, and ascribed national belonging of "Mexicano" or "Guatemalteco" mattered little. But in 1926 Mexico's "New Law of Migration" imposed onerous fees and complex personal identity papers on *inmigrantes*. By the 1930s both governments began to increase control: the Guatemalan one to extract labor from local Native Peoples for the often foreign-owned plantations; the Mexican one to restrict land ownership and new land grants under Cárdenas's reforms to Mexican citizens. Thus local and inmigrant Mexicans might benefit from Mexican citizenship on their side of the border while Guatemalans—especially indigenous people—might suffer from Guatemalan citizenship. Trading and migration, which had been integral to the whole region and had prompted people to settle on both sides of the border regardless of ethno-cultural or state-imposed belonging, was interrupted. While local *campesinos* might own land on one side of the border but customarily sell their produce on the other side—in a functioning local economy—that practice was further disrupted by the imposition of vagrancy laws on transborder commuters in the 1930s. Chinese inmigrants began to occupy this niche of small local trade. Thus governmental regulation reduced the possibility of mobile and resident local peoples to determine their belonging and nationality according to their own interests and disrupted their ways of gaining daily sustenance in the process.

The political border notwithstanding, powerful economic interest demanded mobile labor, and migrations were encouraged by *finca* owners and the transborder economy of coffee plantations, which involved forced labor under the *enganche* system. Workers mixed across cultural affinities or were forced to do so as an indebted plantation labor force. During the Great Depression coffee prices collapsed and high unemployment mobilized workers. Guatemalans fled the authoritarian regime of President Jorge Ubico, 1931–44. During his regime the United Fruit Company, based in the United States, established itself as the largest plantation owner in Guatemala, shifting production to bananas. With the U.S. Central Intelligence Agency it supported the coup of Carlos Castillo Armas in 1954, whose dictatorship set in motion the northbound refugee migrations that added to the labor migrations. At first limited to crossing the border into Mexico and relying on existing networks, the persecution and oppression of Indigenous peoples led to the emergence of large refugee camps that existed over decades. From these Canada admitted some migrants as refugees—they could move openly and legally. In contrast, the U.S. government remained reluctant to accept those displaced by its own Cold War policies from the 1950s to the 1980s. This large-scale generation of refugees, which came to be compounded by other Central (and subsequently South) American dictatorships, set in motion the northbound migrations that are, together with the problems of the Central American economies, at the origins of the transmigrant networks and routes (see chapter 17).

Social Movements, Race Thought, and Migration to 1942

Several social movements struggled to change the position of the rural populations, the emerging working classes, and women. Their success or failure would influence options for and patterns of migration. *Agrarismo*, the movement to improve the lot of the peasant masses, Natives included, had but little impact. The women's movement, in contrast, was successful in improving their position, at least in urban contexts. Some women migrants returning from the United States brought new views of gender roles; others clung to Mexican customs in Anglo society. As regards the labor movement, at the beginning of the twentieth century major strikes involved some cooperation of internally migrant Mexican and internationally migrant U.S. workers. In general, and given both the labor regime and the slow expansion of the labor market compared to population growth and rural outmigration, ever more rural and working-class men chose exit to the north over voice and struggle in Mexico.

Selectivity of migrants depended on exclusion and inclusion in a deeply divided Mexican society—with Indians marginalized and racialized. This issue, meant to be resolved, was in fact acerbated when under Díaz the *Cien-*

tíficos—influential scholars, political advisers, and ministers—advocated a "scientific" and "rational" approach to government. Their policies, social Darwinist in their outlook, resulted in support for both foreign investors and the indigenous metropolitan bourgeoisie. Education, exile, or at least mental roots in Europe imbued them with an admiration for models of French culture and British economics, which they Mexicanized from a nationalist intent. They considered the non-education of Indians a major obstacle to the nation's development, picking up on the old tradition that had always considered "the Indian" an obstacle to national progress. Some, pursuing eugenicist paradigms, advocated European immigration to "whiten" the population. Others demanded education for common people. However, the doyen of the group, Justo Sierra, as minister of education was unable to have the necessary funding appropriated, nor did he respect Native culture and languages. The "Indian problem," as it had long ago been envisioned, was to be solved by interbreeding, by biologically eradicating and "mestizoizing" Native Peoples. The "Indian problem" was in fact a problem of Euro-Mexican racism.

The Mexican Revolution brought an important change in perspective. The juxtaposition of an allegedly inferior internal Native population and a self-styled superior Anglo neighbor in the north induced José Vasconcelos,[29] first minister of the Secretaría de Educación Pública, to conceptualize a unique Mexican identity based on the people's global migratory background. His *La raza cósmica* (1925) envisioned a "fifth race" of European, Asian, African, and American background synthesizing and hybridizing cultures and genes. This Mestizo race concept countered Yankee claims of racial purity and race-based domination. In practice the concept, which did justice to immigration and *mestizaje*, excluded Native Peoples and African Mexicans. Rather than include living Natives, Vasconcelos referred to the complex pre-contact Mexica cultures whose temples, at the time of his writing, archeologists were excavating and reconstructing. The northern, self-described pure-blooded Yankees were in fact also a mestizo population, as has been emphasized by scholars in recent decades.[30]

Intellectual ferment, economic development, and Díaz's gerontocratic regime led to revolution in 1910. At this time "foreign investors, including some of the leading companies of the United States and Europe, controlled 130 of Mexico's 170 largest business concerns, of which the Mexican National Railways was the largest," as John Hart has noted.[31] The massive, often involuntary mobilization of men for the many armies of different factions in the years to 1921 assumed the geographic mobility of women, who in the absence of a commissary corps and cantinas, traveled with the troops as *soldaderas*. Of the total population, 15.1 million by 1910, hundreds of thousands had to flee and moved to the United States as refugees or proactively as labor migrants. Many returned; net immigration is estimated at 200,000. Thus in addition to the immigration of foreigners, circular migration to the United States and repatriation of migrants from the United States under programs of Mexico's federal government in the 1920s and 1930s resulted in many return migrants. After some acculturation to the Anglo society, they shaped their communities of origin by becoming migrant innovators.

Mexican society from the 1920s was the destination of exiles: from the turmoil of the Russian Revolution; from Stalinism, Trotsky most prominently; and from the Spanish Civil War after the fascist forces under Franco won. Among the latter group of exiles were those historians who would found the important Colegio de México. In the 1930s a large number of refugees came from fascist Germany, many Jews included;[32] French and Italians also found asylum. Mexican laws had been modified to provide legal spaces for those affected by European fascism and for those who had survived the Second World War. They were, in the words of the German immigrant Gustav Regler, "those who had been saved, those who had failed, those who were looking for something, those who had given up."[33] In the 1950s U.S. intellectuals fleeing the McCarthyite persecutions of the Cold War would arrive.[34] Thus for a century and a half Mexico sent insurgents, politicians, and intellectuals into exile while granting asylum to the politically and racially persecuted of many cultures of the Atlantic World and other areas. Soon Lebanese fleeing the civil war, beginning in 1975, arrived and became a vital part of Mexican society, especially in the capital.[35]

After the Revolution a first program was to improve the situation of the rural population; land distribution was to provide an economic basis. This was successful in that at the end of Cárdenas's administration (1934–40)—almost a century after the Liberalist dispossession—50 percent of the arable land was again in the hands of small owners and in that some *ejido* common holdings were reinstituted. Some emigrants remigrated from the United States to take up land. Internal migration until the 1920s had involved teachers and priests moving to the countryside; from the mid-1920s a migration to the cities for educational purposes reversed the direction. A government-mandated Mexicanizing of the railroad labor force and nationalization of the oil industry improved working conditions. However, at the same time the population continued to expand, and the upper classes of the highly stratified Mexican society still did not invest in the economy to a degree that sufficient jobs would be created. Therefore while the reforms implicitly reduced the need for temporary or permanent labor migrations, population growth, class hierarchies, and the economic framework remained countervailing forces.

Immigration, high by Mexican standards in the 1920s, hardly declined during the Depression. But its composition changed. In the established economy options for investor migrants had declined. Farmers from the United States came with capital to settle real estate acquired by the U.S. surveying and land companies. Like that of the earlier merchants, the foreign technicians' diasporas slowly integrated. The Depression decade brought in many voluntary returnees from the United States, encouraged by a repatriation program of the Mexican government, but also through massive deportations under the auspices of the U.S. government. At a time of economic crisis, Mexican society faced the inmigrations and labor market needs of about half a million returnees.

The Mexican migration laws of 1926 and 1930 for the first time included restrictions and stipulated more control of foreigners, aiming at protecting the interest of the Mexican people and the national economy. The General Law of the Population of 1936, the first law of this name, prohibited indefinitely the immigration of workers and imposed fines on enterprises that did not obey. The tone of these laws clearly is that of postrevolutionary Mexico and its new nationalism, but they also mirror new economic grievances.

Emigration and return migration assumed new proportions in 1942, when the U.S. and the Mexican governments negotiated a treaty guaranteeing a supply of workers or "braceros" to the U.S. economy during the Second World War. The new patterns established the basis for migration to the present. It resembles in some respects the transatlantic migrations before 1914, when about one of ten migrants had been in the United States before and could act as guides to those who traveled the route for the first time. Many of the so-called immigrants, whether of European or Mexican origin, came and continue to come temporarily. Around 1900 one-third of the migrants returned to Europe; they came as "guestworkers" or "braceros," to use these problematic terms, because borders were open and permitted transnational family life through multiple moves.

Trends since the 1950s and Transmigration

Total immigration to Mexico, according to the census data, grew from 140,600 in 1930 to 223,500 in 1960, and after a decline in 1970 to 340,800 in 1990. Given population growth, this did not mean any increase in the percentage of foreigners in the total population. From 1941 to 1982 the "economic miracle" of new import substitution industries improved the urban labor market for internal migrants. After the Second World War young women, especially of indigenous cultures, migrated to the capital and other cities in search of employment as domestics for the expanding middle classes. Family and social networks expanded in scope and intensity, and gender roles were further modified. The Mexican capital continued to grow, a development that reached a climax in the years between 1965 and 1970, when the city was the destination of 47.8 percent of all interior migrations in Mexico. Only recently this trend seems to have been reversed, possibly owing to massive environmental problems in the capital.[36]

The emergence of right-wing dictatorships in many Latin American countries, often supported by the U.S. government or U.S. corporations, changed inmigration to Mexico, which became a haven for Chileans after 1973, for example. Ever more refugees crossed the country on a trek northward hoping to enter the United States—usually without documents. Some of these transmigrants stayed in Mexico for cultural reasons or lack of funds. Refugee communities emerged, connected to other segments of refugee diasporas, and remained connected to the communities back home (see chapters 16 and 17). The rightwing Guatemalan regime supported by the United Fruit Company brought changes in migration at Mexico's southern border, while the traditional cross-border seasonal labor migrations into Chiapas and Tabasco became refugee migration without hope for return. Some continued to the United States or Canada. The multiplicity of transmigrants' routes through Mexico at the beginning of the twenty-first century reflects the many routes that European migrants of a hundred years before had taken to the port cities, and "runners" exploited migrants in port cities, though no large-scale gangs developed (see chapter 18). States were still in control, though they kept their borders open for both exit and entry.

As of 2010 some 10 percent of Mexico's population lived in the United States, and the Mexican presidency had been won partly by appealing to voters north of the Río Grande. Immigrants in Mexico, on the other hand, amount to a mere 0.4 percent of the population. In contrast to the national tradition of the nineteenth century, present-day Mexico claims in the fourth article of its Constitution the "pluricultural composition" of the nation, whose foundations are recognized as indigenous. The awareness of the diversity of Mexico's cultural roots has grown. Burgeoning migration studies in Mexico give a full picture of the movement of people to, from, and within Mexico as part of a continent-wide migration framework.

Notes

1 In Quebec the church's opposition to industrialization and urbanization resulted in high rates of emigration to New England from the 1840s, and development of an

internal middle class was hampered both by Anglo immigration and the church's rural-centered ideology.

2 A survey and a bibliography of immigration are provided by Moisés Gonzáles Navarro, *Los extranjeros en México y los mexicanos en el extranjero, 1821–1970*, 3 vols. (Mexico City: Colegio de México, 1993–94), and Dolores Pla, Guadelupe Zárate, Mónica Palma, Jorge Gómez, Rosario Cardiel, and Delia Salazar, *Extranjeros en México (1821–1990): Bibliografía* (Mexico City: INAH, 1994).

3 Data from Jose C. Moya, *Cousins and Strangers: Spanish Immigrants in Buenos Aires, 1850–1930* (Berkeley: University of California Press, 1997), 46, and Jürgen Buchenau, *Tools of Progress: A German Merchant Family in Mexico City, 1865–present* (Albuquerque: University of New Mexico Press, 2004), 14.

4 On Mexico's southern border the United Provinces of Central America, 1823–38, had not included Chiapas, which after considerable politicking was annexed by Mexico in 1842, incorporating a sizable population that considered itself Guatemalan. The borderline cut through an ethnically integrated region. Cross-border migrations extend to the present.

5 The classic studies are Richard Konetzke, "La legislación sobre immigración de extranjeros a América durante la época colonial," *Revista Internacional de Sociología* 3 (1945), 269–99; and Charles F. Nunn, *Foreign Immigrants in Early Bourbon Mexico, 1700–1760* (Cambridge: Cambridge University Press, 1979).

6 Juan Fernández Sigurilla to Juan García Corbero, December 13, 1589, in *Cartas privadas de emigrantes a Indias, 1540–1616*, ed. Enrique Otte (Mexico City: Fondo de Cultura Económica, 1993), 117; for the diet see Hernán Sánchez to his brother, San Martín, New Spain, November 7, 1569, 218 f.

7 Enrique Otte, "Die europäischen Siedler und die Probleme der Neuen Welt," *Jahrbuch für Geschichte Lateinamerikas / Anuario de historia de América Latina* 6 (1969), 1–40.

8 Andrés García to his nephew in Colmenar Viejo, Spain, Mexico City, November 10, 1571, in Otte, *Cartas privadas*, 60–61.

9 María Fernanda García de los Arcos, "Las relaciones de Filipinas con el centro del virreinato," *México en el mundo hispánico*, ed. Oscar Mazín Gómez, vol. 1 (Zamora: Colegio de Michoacán, 2000), 51–67.

10 Peter Gerhard, "A Black Conquistador in Mexico," *Hispanic American Historical Review* 58, no. 3 (1978), 451–59.

11 Norma Angélica Castillo, "Mujeres negras y afromestizas en Nueva España," *Historia de la mujeres en España y América Latina*, ed. Isabel Morant, vol. 2 (Madrid: Átedra, 2006), 583–609, quote p. 593.

12 Luis de Velasco to the Spanish king, 1553, quoted in Gonzalo Aguirre Beltrán, "The Slave Trade in Mexico," *Hispanic American Historical Review* 24 (1944), 412–31, quote p. 413.

13 Census "Estado de la población del reino de Nueva Espana en 1810" as reprinted in 1859.

14 The "Bourbon Reforms," mandated from Spain, attempted to center the colony more on Europe and had accorded a privileged position to migrants from Spain. A

reform decree of 1804 ordered all funds of the Catholic Church in New Spain to be turned over to the cash-starved Crown. Since no banks existed the church had functioned as moneylender, and the colony's credit system collapsed, wreaking havoc in the economy. The indigenous Creole bourgeoisie thus turned to political independence as a remedy.

15 Harold D. Sims, *The Expulsion of Mexico's Spaniards, 1821–1836* (Pittsburgh: University of Pittsburgh Press, 1990); Clara F. Lida, "Los españoles en México: Población, cultura y sociedad," *Simbiosis de Culturas. Los inmigrantes y su cultura en México*, ed. Guillermo Bonfil Batalla (Mexico City: Fondo de Cultura Económica, 1993), 425–54; and Luz María Martínez Montiel and Araceli Reynoso Medina, "Inmigración europea y asiática, siglos XIX y XX," 245–424, *Simbiosis de culturas: Los inmigrantes y su cultura en México*, ed. Guillermo Bonfil Batalla (Mexico City: Fondo de Cultura Económica, 1993).

16 Since the Anglo migrants to Texas were mostly Protestant, an anti-Protestant feeling was part of this particular anti-foreigner stance.

17 Richard Griswold del Castillo, *The Treaty of Guadalupe Hidalgo: A Legacy of Conflict* (Norman: University of Oklahoma Press, 1990), 63–64.

18 Delia González de Reufels, *Siedler und Filibuster in Sonora* (Cologne: Boehlau, 2003).

19 Walther L. Bernecker, *Die Handelskonquistadoren: Europäische Interessen und mexikanischer Staat im 19. Jahrhundert* (Wiesbaden: Steiner, 1988).

20 In Spanish California, Russians had settled and established a small agricultural colony to provision ships coming from Vladivostok via Alaska (Russian to 1867) for fishing or sealing along the coast.

21 Jürgen Buchenau, "Small Numbers, Great Impact: Mexico and Its Immigrants," *Journal of American Ethnic History* 20, no. 3 (2001), 23–49, esp. 25–27.

22 Walter Nugent, *Crossings: The Great Transatlantic Migrations, 1870–1914* (Bloomington: Indiana University Press, 1992).

23 No other statistics exist for the period before the establishment of a national census in 1895. John M. Hart, "Mexican Revolution: Causes," and Robert McCaa, "Migration: Internal," in *Encyclopedia of Mexico: History, Society, and Culture*, ed. Michael S. Werner and Robert M. Salkin (Chicago: Fitzroy Dearborn, 1997), 2:847–50, 886–90.

24 Buchenau, "Small Numbers, Great Impact," quote p. 23, and Buchenau, *Tools of Progress*.

25 Philip D. Curtin, *Cross-Cultural Trade in World History* (Cambridge: Cambridge University Press, 1984).

26 Gerardo Reñique, "Región, raza y nación en el antichinismo sonorense: Cultura regional y mestizaje en el México posrevolucionario," *Seis expulsiones y un adiós*, ed. Aarón Grageda Bustamante (Mexico City: Plaza y Valdés, 2003), 231–89; Charles Cumberland, "The Sonoran Chinese and the Mexican Revolution," *Hispanic American History Review* 40, no. 2 (1960), 191–211; H. H. Dubs, "The Chinese in Mexico City in 1635," *Far Eastern Quarterly* 1 (1942), 387–89; Evelyn Hu-Dehart, "Coolies, Shopkeepers, Pioneers: The Chinese of Mexico and Peru (1849–1930)," *Amerasia Journal* 15, no. 2 (1989), 91–116.

27 Frédéric Johansson, "El peligro amarillo en México: La obsesión norteamericana frente a la inmigración japonesa en México a principios del siglo XX," *Un continente en movimiento: Migraciones en América Latina*, ed. Ingrid Wehr (Madrid: Vervuert, 2006), 411–20.

28 John M. Hart, *Empire and Revolution: The Americans in Mexico since the Civil War* (Berkeley: University of California Press, 2002).

29 Vasconcelos had experienced both Mexican and U.S. American culture when attending school in Texas while living close to the border and when abroad as an exile from Díaz's administration.

30 Gary B. Nash, "The Hidden History of Mestizo America," *Journal of American History* 83, no. 3 (December 1995), 941–64.

31 Hart, *Empire and Revolution*, 850.

32 Corinne Krause, *The Jews in Mexico: A History with Special Emphasis on the Period from 1857 to 1930* (Pittsburgh: University of Pittsburgh, 1970).

33 Gustav Regler, *Verwunschenes Land Mexiko* (Munich: List, 1954), 11.

34 Diana Anhalt, *A Gathering of Fugitives: American Political Expatriates in Mexico, 1948–1965* (Santa Maria, Calif.: Archer, 2001); Rebecca M. Schreiber, *Cold War Exiles in Mexico: U.S. Dissidents and the Culture of Critical Resistance* (Minneapolis: University of Minnesota Press, 2008).

35 Theresa Alfaro-Velcamp, *So Far from Allah, So Close to Mexico: Middle Eastern Immigrants in Modern Mexico* (Austin: University of Texas Press, 2007).

36 Haydea Izazola and Catherine Marquette, "Emigración de la ciudad de México Estrategia de sobrevivencia frente al deterioro ambiental," *Hacia la demografía del siglo XXI*, ed. Raúl Benítez Zenteno et al. (Mexico City: IISUNAM-SOMEDE, 1999), 113–35.

CHAPTER EIGHT

The Construction of Borders

Building North American Nations,
Building a Continental Perimeter, 1890s–1920s

Angelika E. Sauer

By the early twentieth century North America's three continental nations developed as modern states, embracing their citizens in a "network of identification and classification" and drawing strict lines of demarcation between members of the community and aliens.[1] State-to-state cooperation enforced the distinctions of mutually exclusive bodies of citizens, and modern states built the administrative infrastructure to enforce their physical and social borders, as defined by the legislative process. The construction of borders has never just addressed concerns of the physical security of the homeland. The three state-building projects in early-twentieth-century North America coincided with transnational and national discussions about health, morality, and race mixing. These discourses competed for attention with debates about the distribution of the economic benefits of the nation and its relationship with the outside world, embodied in the "foreignness" of other people. This concept of foreignness assumed sharper contours through statutory exclusions and government control of immigration.

Statutory exclusions served several purposes. Publicly advertised in pamphlets widely distributed abroad, they were a deterrent to various categories of people, warning that they would likely not pass muster and might as well stay home. More obviously, exclusions protected the resident population from perceived threats. A study of the identification and definition of threats provides insights into the production and reproduction of the nation, its institutions of control, and its social hierarchies of race, gender, and class.[2] Finally, statutory exclusions have a disciplinary effect: after undergoing the public spectacle of examination, immigrants were placed in the social hierarchy and initiated into the demands of industrial citizenship, with its tedious routines, unquestioning obedience, and lack of autonomy.[3] The content of exclusionary legislation can thus be divided into economic and public safety categories as well as more metaphorical categories that delineated fitness for civic, moral, and industrial citizenship—often expressed as racialized exclusions. All of these had gendered meaning and informed each other.

The State Takes Charge

The authority to exclude and select became centralized in the national governments of all three North American countries. It was the newly formed Canadian Confederation that pioneered the move toward federal responsibility in regulating immigration. Although Canada's first Immigration Act, passed in 1869, reconfirmed the joint responsibility of federal and provincial governments for immigration, an amendment in 1872 gave the Governor-in-Council the authority to issue proclamations prohibiting the landing of any criminal or any other "vicious class" of immigrants.[4] In the United States the federal government continued to operate in partnership, and sometimes in conflict, with individual states. The Page Act (1875) and Immigration Act (1882) foreshadowed federal control over establishing and eventually enforcing regulations. In 1892 the Supreme Court supported centralization when it ruled that control over immigration was a matter of foreign relations and national sovereignty.[5] Congress passed its first set of statutory exclusions in the Immigration Acts of 1891, 1903, and 1907; Canada followed with amendments in 1906 and 1910 to the Immigration Act of 1869; Mexico passed its first Ley de Inmigración in 1908.[6]

As national governments took charge of immigrants, they had to create a control apparatus to implement and enforce a growing set of policies and regulations. The administrative histories of immigration in the three North American countries show a roughly parallel transformation from a free-market ideal to a control-oriented, gatekeeping approach.[7] Washington created a Bureau of Immigration in the Treasury Department in 1891 and transferred it to the Department of Commerce and Labor in 1903. The bureau was expanded to include naturalization in 1906 and transferred to the Department of Labor in 1913. Canada's Immigration Branch was part of the Department of Agriculture from 1867 to 1892, when it was placed in the Department of the Interior; it became a separate Department of Immigration and Colonization in 1917. Porfirian Mexico located its immigration bureau in the Ministerio de Fomento, seeing it as part of commercial development; however, after the turn of the century *fomento* officials began to discuss the legal distinction between

a colonist—either a foreign-born one or a Mexican with capital who was cultivating the land—and an immigrant who had no capital but came to work for
wages. Increasingly discussions about immigration addressed its perceived
threatening aspects, such as the importation of diseases and foreign habits
and customs. Before the Mexican Revolution the Department of the Interior
took charge of immigration, a role that it retained in the 1920s.[8]

These administrative histories also tell a story of what could be called a
thickening and extension of the border in both space and time. The border became a process within which a migrant, encoded in a network of identification
and qualification papers, passed a succession of qualifying entry points over
a long period. In the United States the Page Law (1875) and the Chinese Exclusion Act (1882) were early signposts of several of these developments; they relied on federal officials abroad for enforcement and attached a growing paper
trail, including photographs and questionnaires, to the migrant. The certifica-
tion or permit papers for limited groups, issued by federal officials overseas,
eventually evolved into a general requirement for a state-issued document of
legitimate mobility, the passport. As regulation imposed more conditions on
entry, pertinent examinations and certifications were also transferred abroad,
to the point of departure. Efforts to keep the perceived migrant threat at arm's
length culminated in the introduction of visa requirements by the 1920s.[9]
Henceforth immigration flows could be regulated by stationing visa-granting
officers in select geographical regions.

Implementing an ever-increasing regulatory system outside the boundaries of the sovereign territory required the cooperation of both foreign governments and private businesses. Transportation companies had to be bul-
lied and cajoled into acting as the enforcers of government regulations. The
deterrent of steep fines and the promise of good business drove steamship
lines to develop prescreening procedures, keep proper records, and share information with government officials. Foreign governments were somewhat
less pliable, since they had fewer incentives to cooperate with North American governments. As the power of the modern state was projected externally,
it was also felt internally as immigrants were identified and controlled after arrival. Neither Canada nor the United States as yet followed the European trend
toward internal passports or registration papers to monitor and police alien
residents. In 1886 Porfirian Mexico too abolished an old requirement for foreigners to register and did not reinstate another requirement until the 1920s.[10]
However, there were other ways to target immigrants. Deportation drastically
changed after the turn of the century from a simple tool to correct a mistake
made at the entry point to a long-term instrument to control and discipline
immigrant behavior for years after entry.[11] If deportations were an instrument

of social control, thus extending the border inward for newcomers, the threat of detection and removal also helped to define the social reality of the new "illegal immigrant." The illegal alien became a category in the U.S. Immigration Act (1891) as a person "who entered in violation of the law" and as such could be deported for an ever-expanding period. The Canadian Immigration Act of 1910 specified violations of the law as entering outside a port of entry, eluding examination, and entering through misrepresentation or stealth. Canadian law held out fines, arrest, detention, and deportation for these violations. Mexican immigration law in 1926 simply declared that a person who entered illegally was not an immigrant. Illegality and potential removal were inevitable concomitants of restrictive immigration laws, as every excludable class caused new enforcement problems. Wherever there were borders, it turned out, there would be border transgressions. This became obvious from the moment the U.S. Congress suspended the admission of Chinese laborers for a decade, starting in 1882.

Border Transgressions and Border Diplomacy

The Chinese Exclusion Act undoubtedly helped change the nature of continental North America.[12] In one of many, typically unintended consequences that often follow immigration restrictions, Chinese exclusion advanced the construction of the American-Canadian and American-Mexican borders as physical, legal, and social realities, while the enforcement of American exclusion laws contributed to discrepancies between the two borders. Chinese exclusion introduced the tools, rhetoric, and ideology of gatekeeping into U.S. immigration history, but as Yukari Takai demonstrates, people's determination to circumvent restrictions, and the lucrative business opportunities that arose from the demand for illicit entries, diverted the American state's attention from the coastal ports of entry to the open "back doors" into U.S. territory. Chinese exclusion laws initiated the transformation of two abstract lines across the continental map into modernizing and hardening international land borders. Furthermore, migration to and within North America became an issue of bilateral diplomacy and of American pressure on its continental neighbors.

When the U.S. Congress was debating exclusion, the United States had about 105,000 Chinese residents, Canada had slightly more than 4,000, and Mexico a few hundred. After three decades of increasingly restrictive policies following 1882, the Chinese population in the continental United States had dropped to well below 100,000, while in Canada it had risen to 28,000 and in Mexico to 13,000. Soon after the new rules were implemented, U.S. newspapers began to comment on human trafficking in the Pacific Northwest, the

Southwest, Texas, and the Great Lakes region.[13] In response the U.S. public and elected officials clamored for America's neighbors to adopt U.S. exclusionary policies on Chinese immigration. Twice, in 1888 and 1890, Congress demanded negotiations with Mexico and Canada, either to implement a continental ban on Chinese immigration or to commit to preventing the illegal entry of Chinese laborers from their territories into the United States.[14] The State Department was not happy with this ham-handed public diplomacy, although there was common ground on the issue.[15] However, in Canada and Mexico the political context and the economic situation were vastly different from conditions in the United States. Excluding Chinese laborers was neither feasible nor desirable, and bilateral negotiations quickly moved into less public arenas. The Canadian Pacific Railway (CPR) signed an agreement with the U.S. commissioner general of immigration in 1903 providing that any Chinese landing in Canada en route to the United States would be transported under guard to one of four designated land ports of entry, where they would undergo full inspection. This provision necessitated the funding of border stations, against the accepted Congressional wisdom of the 1890s that it would be "practically impossible to place sufficient numbers of inspectors on the [Canadian] border" to prevent the entry of those who took the "circuitous route" through Canada.[16] By tackling only Chinese entries in 1903 and channeling them through a limited number of land border crossings, the Immigration Service was able to demonstrate the feasibility to lawmakers of a gated land border. Consequently more land border inspection points followed, complete with buildings and staff.

The southern land border was not far behind; U.S. border officials hinted strongly at a need for more resources to secure it as well. The U.S. Immigration Service attempted to pursue the same strategy used at the northern border, seeking a similar agreement in 1907. Unfortunately, calm enforcement diplomacy at the Mexican-American border had been preceded by more than a decade of enforcement transgressions by U.S. officials in their war on smugglers and "contraband." Both American customs officials and later immigration inspectors frequently crossed the border to apprehend not only smugglers but Chinese whom they suspected of planning to cross the border. Increasingly, Mexican authorities judged these violations of sovereignty as "unconstitutional" and "undignified." Eventually the Mexican government instructed the local authorities to "prevent any foreigner, whatever his position, from carrying out official acts in Mexican territory."[17] The bitterness resulting from these transgressions surely contributed to the failure to reach an arrangement. Although the Mexican government gave a nod to U.S. concerns by incorporating in its immigration law of 1908 a clause for the special health inspection of groups of more than ten laborers, Chinese migrants continued to arrive in Mexico and move northward. U.S. authorities resorted to more policing of the border on the American side, initiating a lasting trend.

Exclusion, Inclusion, Selection, and Discipline

While the most overt acts of exclusion started with a racial category, early immigration regulation generally responded to the perceived imperatives of public safety and to economic rationales. One of the first exclusions in federal U.S. and Canadian immigration regulation was the economic category of destitute migrants. Late-nineteenth-century fears constructed a psychological profile of poverty, inscribing it on the immigrant's mind as a permanent trait that was passed on to children and led to a cycle of dependence and delinquency.[18] The migration of British charity cases, including orphaned children and juveniles, vexed North America throughout the first half of the 1880s. President Chester A. Arthur complained in December 1883 that impoverished Britons continued to arrive in droves, including large numbers who came across the border from Canada.[19] The lasting legacy of the concern in the 1880s with destitute immigrants was the exclusion of people "likely to become public charges" (known as LPC) because of their background, health, age, or marital status. The United States began federal enforcement of the LPC clause in 1891; Canada followed in 1906, including "professional beggars and vagrants" in the category. In 1908, after an influx of Syrian and Turkish peddlers and dry-goods traders into Veracruz, Mexico barred public charges and beggars along with those unable to work because of health or age.[20] By the early twentieth century an immigrant to continental North America, by definition, had to be a person who could take care of him- or herself.

The question of what constituted a desirable wage laborer also predominated in early economic categories of regulation. The relationship between capital and foreign labor generated complicated negotiations involving employers, unions, labor recruiters, and governments. In 1885 Congress passed the Foran Act, prohibiting the importation of foreigners contracted to perform labor, but this law proved difficult to enforce from the beginning. New York State's immigration commissioner, Charles Tinkor, complained in 1888 that immigrants rejected in Castle Garden for being contract laborers would simply land in Halifax, Nova Scotia, and cross the land border. Up to fifty thousand European immigrants allegedly entered by way of Canada in the second half of 1890 alone. After federalization of enforcement in 1891, an agreement in 1894 between the U.S. Treasury and Canadian transportation companies attempted to ameliorate the problem by allowing U.S. inspectors to examine

U.S.-bound passengers on CPR vessels and trains.[21] The influential American Federation of Labor, under Samuel Gompers, insisted that the Foran Act be strictly enforced against all workers coming from Canada, not just transmigrants. This angered Canadian members of American-based international unions who were refused entry into the United States throughout the later 1890s. Partially in retaliation for the curtailment of Canadian workers' freedom of movement in the North American labor market, the nationalist wing of the Canadian Trade and Labor Congress lobbied the Liberal Laurier government to pass similar legislation.[22] The Alien Labour Act in 1897 made it illegal to assist in the importation of contract labor. Still, complaints continued that Canadian companies were importing strikebreakers, including large numbers from the United States.[23]

Instead of better protection of native-born workers against foreign competition, what emerged was a new transnational system that recruited, coached, and guided foreign laborers into any of the three countries with a labor demand.[24] The transnational entrepreneur who became known in the United States as the "padrone" acted as a broker between workers in underdeveloped areas and employers in North American industries.[25] The padrone system distributed Mexican, Italian, Syrian, and Greek workers to remote mines and railroad tracks throughout the continent. Legislation attempting to put a stop to the importation of contracted laborers did not suit the employers in remote locations who needed a docile, mobile, and temporary labor force. In fact the CPR circumvented the Canadian Alien Labour Act by hiring a padrone in Montreal, Antonio Cordasco, to provide Italians for its seasonal track work in western Canada. At the U.S.-Mexican border, padroni such as Roman Gonzales also benefited by channeling Mexican peons through El Paso into railway construction in the American Southwest. When caught in the border inspection process as excludable under the Foran Act, Mexican workers would simply wander "a few miles off our examining station and [cross] the border by foot" somewhere else.[26] The Mexican government, unlike Canada's, did not come up with a contract labor act of its own. The need of the mostly foreign-owned companies for experienced workers created a very different context for the nexus between labor-market and immigration policies.

While economic rationales dominated early efforts to define borders as both porous and sturdy, the modern state used the category of public safety exclusions to demonstrate the very raison d'être of borders and state institutions of control. Attempts to control the entry of "vicious classes" or to authorize the removal of anyone who might threaten public safety and national security preceded many other border-building activities. The decades after 1880 saw what was perhaps the first American terrorism scare focusing on anarchists, culminating in the assassination of President McKinley in September 1901. The Immigration Act of 1903 added to the list of excludable classes anarchists or persons who believed in or advocated the overthrow of the government or the assassination of public officials.[27] The Canadian government refrained from barring anarchists and subversives but added a clause to the Immigration Act in 1910 that allowed the reporting and potential deportation of those advocating the violent overthrow of British, dominion, and foreign governments. Mexico also added anarchists to the list in 1908. With an industrial workforce of 750,000 by 1910 and increasingly violent strikes, Mexican elites may have been afraid of foreign radical instigators, ironically Americans for the most part.[28] More likely the category was geared toward foreign investors and American regulations, and rooted in Mexico's wish to avoid being accused of functioning as a backdoor for anarchists.[29]

Both economic and security categories reveal national differences in the definitions of priorities, but it is obvious that once the United States had identified a threat, Mexico and Canada could not ignore it. But who or what constituted a threat, and what was the nature of it? Medical criteria most clearly demonstrate the difficulty of drawing any distinction between real and imagined threats. Medical inspection (as opposed to earlier quarantine regulations) became a tool for selecting and rejecting prospective immigrants at the port of entry, with disease becoming a powerful metaphor for the undesirable or unfit alien.[30] The U.S. Immigration Act of 1891 introduced the procedure of individual medical inspection by government officials. The first condition to make it on to a growing list of excludable medical conditions in 1897 was trachoma, an eye disease. It represented a disease imported by immigrant groups from China, Eastern Europe, and the Middle East; because of its threat of blindness, trachoma also represented future dependency and marked an immigrant as unfit for the industrial economy.[31] By 1903 a rudimentary classification listed trachoma and tuberculosis as excludable contagious diseases, and favus, leprosy, syphilis, and gonorrhea as loathsome diseases. After the Immigration Act of 1907 mental defects were added, along with conditions that categorized the sufferer as LPC, ranging from hernia and heart disease to varicose veins, old age, and pregnancy.

Once medical inspection was in place on Ellis Island and other ports of entry, the biggest concern was that steamship companies would attempt to subvert regulations by taking diseased immigrants to Canadian ports, where they could take a train across the land border. American newspapers cried foul. In 1902, a U.S. official complained that "a very large number of people from Europe who are either diseased or likely to become public charges" were being channeled into the United States via Canada; the Canadian border, according to another medical official, was a bad "leak in the health dam." In up-state New York another official griped that there was little point in spending so much money on Ellis Island when a wide-open door was so close.[32] The Canadian government, which was conducting an active immigrant recruitment campaign, was initially not interested in implementing medical examinations. Officials of the U.S. Immigration Service and the U.S. Public Health and Marine Hospital Service had to look for a different ally. In 1901 they renegotiated and extended the so-called Canadian Agreement of 1894 to permit American medical officers and immigration officials to examine passengers arriving in Canada en route to the United States. The new likelihood of Canada getting stuck with American medical rejects induced the Canadian government to put its own medical regulations in place.[33] In August 1902 the Canadian Cabinet passed an Order-in-Council prohibiting the landing in Canada of immigrants suffering from loathsome, dangerous, or infectious diseases; this was incorporated into the Canadian Immigration Act, which also prohibited the entry of epileptics, mentally afflicted and insane immigrants, and those with physical defects such as deafness, blindness, or infirmity. The openly stated Canadian focus, beyond reconciling American and Canadian procedures, was utilitarian selection rather than discipline or exclusion.

Overall one can observe a convergence of medical control philosophy on both sides of the Canadian-American border. The American medical rejection rate of immigrants crossing the border from Canada dropped to less than one-quarter of a percent of all arrivals by 1911.[34] The U.S. immigration control identified the Mexican border as a trouble spot of a different order, another back-door through which "diseased, criminal and other classes of immigrants who have failed to get through the regular ports" were pouring into the southern United States.[35] Much of this early medical concern was not directed at fellow North Americans but at immigrants from Europe and Asia, including the Middle East. Between 1903 and 1906 American authorities negotiated with the Mexican government to produce an agreement similar to the Canadian arrangement, which would allow American officials to inspect transoceanic immigrants bound for the United States on Mexican trains or in Mexican ports, but they made little progress.[36] Instead the Mexican government developed its own health inspections. Effective March 1909 the new immigration law prohibited the landing of immigrants with chronic or infectious diseases, epileptics, elderly people without family, and others unable to work because of physical or mental defects. The regulations were to be enforced in ports and at land crossings.[37] Despite the obvious similarities, which suggest that the most important prompts were taken from American legislation, American officials never trusted Mexican medical inspection. As Amy Fairchild concludes, the

United States "never regarded the Mexican medical inspection as remotely comparable to that conducted by Canadian officials. Its own officers remained the primary defenders of the nation."[38]

With the Mexican Revolution another medical border issue arose that helped transform the character of the U.S.-Mexican border into a much harsher line of demarcation. The revolution and its resulting social chaos produced outbreaks of epidemic diseases. The ability of numerous Mexican laborers to cross the border daily—virtually unimpeded and unexamined, especially into Texas—was seen as posing a great public health risk. Accordingly a vaccination, disinfection, and cleansing regimen was introduced at the Mexican border in 1917. If daily border crossers were cleansed and made fit for cohabitation, they were also slowly transformed into immigrants by exposing them to medical inspections. After 1917 officers looked for medical conditions that symbolized to them social chaos and lack of control, such as syphilis in single men and pregnancy in single women.

Gendered Borders

The control of male and female sexuality at the border points to another dimension of nation building. Syphilis, which was on the excludable U.S. and Canadian lists early on, was defined in enforcement procedures as a masculine disease. Before diagnostic testing methods were developed, any attempt to identify syphilis on the immigrant body targeted unmarried males. During the turbulence of the First World War and the Mexican Revolution, syphilis was more explicitly linked with soldiers; uncontrolled male sexuality was seen as a threat to the nation's military prowess.[39] Similar fears of the undermining of American manhood lay behind excluding those guilty of crimes of moral turpitude in 1891, including bigamy, rape, and sodomy; and classifying persons "with abnormal sexual instincts" as excludable imbeciles in 1917; or more specifically, ruling homosexuals to be of "psychopathic personality."[40] At the farthest end of the spectrum was the male prostitute. Possibly one of "the most bestial refinements of depravity" and "the most accursed business ever devised by man," male prostitution, which tied a young male companion to an older man, was considered by the U.S. Immigration Commission (set up in 1907 and chaired by Senator William Dillingham) as an example of the "vilest practices brought here from continental Europe." The commission concluded that old world depravity, just like the lax and tolerant European attitude toward it, should be kept at bay by U.S. officials.[41]

With such a strong emphasis in U.S. discussions on the importation of sexual immorality, women at the border fell into one of three categories, all constructed on the basis of an assessment of their economic and moral value as viewed through the lens of race and sexuality: the prostitute, the vulnerable, unaccompanied woman, and the wife and mother. Femininity and female sexuality were produced and reproduced in the entry process, linking fears about the permeability of any border to gendered concepts of risk and vulnerability.

The emphasis on prostitution as a threat to the nation had already found early expression in the Page Act (1875). Throughout the last third of the nineteenth century American efforts to externalize prostitution focused on the racialized Asian woman. Linking sexual behavior to race made female immorality visible to the man guarding the border against threats to American values, cultural forms, and institutions.[42] Early debates about immigrants and prostitution in the 1870s portrayed Chinese women as both victims of slave-like conditions and an active threat to America's urban male youth, hinting at the hidden dangers of interracial sexual encounters.[43] This two-pronged focus on those who enslaved women for sexual work, along with the foreign prostitute as an imported threat to public morality, remained a constant in subsequent controls of immigration. Congress incorporated a statutory exclusion of prostitutes and procurers into the Immigration Act of 1903. Attention shifted to European immigrant women and their participation in the sex trade, both willingly and as "unfortunate or degraded victims."[44] This statutory exclusion did not produce convincing results. In fact, the numbers of immigrant prostitutes detected and barred from entering the United States were consistently low: one historian has calculated an annual mean of 131 for the years from 1892 to 1920.[45] The size of the actual problem had no relation to the public hysteria surrounding the issue of imported immorality and the so-called white slave trade in the early 1900s.

Once again it was the land borders that caused American officials the biggest headaches. The "backdoor" argument made in discussions about Chinese laborers, contract workers, and medical exclusions reappeared. There was an unsubstantiated assumption that smuggling and trafficking of prostitutes occurred across the land borders. The Dillingham Commission reported that procurers worked in Canadian ports, enticing newly arrived immigrant women. How did immigrant prostitutes end up in the United States despite American exclusion laws? "Of late, many come through Canada."[46] Again the emphasis was on transoceanic migrants, not Canadian or Mexican women. In the usual mix of gamblers and prostitutes in Texas-Mexico border towns such as El Paso, French and Eastern European Jewish women made an appearance.[47] Mexican women, however, were not specifically targeted with exclusion on the basis of prostitution. Mexican sex workers were not regarded as "white slaves" but as part of the regular cross-border commerce and not an immigration issue.[48] Luckily for American enforcement, both Canada and Mexico became easy allies in the fight against sex trafficking. Canada incorporated prostitutes and procurers into its list of prohibited classes in 1906; Mexico followed in 1908. This pleased at least one American commentator, who concluded that "theoretically both Canadian and Mexican inspections were similar to our own, and there was ground for hope that the ancient and troublesome smuggling of undesirable aliens from contiguous territory would at least cease."[49] As long as the emphasis was on the commerce of sex trafficking, not on the immoral woman, a North American moral perimeter could be built.

A different approach prevailed in all three countries regarding unaccompanied women at the border. American immigration control suspected the single woman at the border of actual or potential immorality—a threat to the American family—and rejected her on that ground. Rather than use a clause in U.S. immigration law that excluded women who came to the United States for "immoral purposes" (besides outright prostitution), immigration officials employed the "likely to become a public charge" clause, against women more often than men.[50] Detailed explanations for the gendering of LPC differ. Some historians focus on the construction of female economic vulnerability outside the family wage economy. They suggest that poverty was treated by American immigration officials as "a gendered disease," and that a female body was an indicator of future poverty.[51] Others more forcefully argue that moral judgments prevailed over economic concerns, invalidating women's real economic skills.[52] A single woman who was pregnant, or who admitted to sexual relations outside marriage, was the most likely to be rejected as LPC or in an undesirable class.[53] It was in these different ways that U.S. immigration regulations erected a moral border based on marriage and domesticity, a border that seemed particularly difficult for single women to penetrate.

Neither Mexico nor Canada fully followed this example. Mexico did not conceive of single female immigrants as a problem, because the vast majority of its immigrants were single men or family groups. Later, when the composition of immigration had changed in the 1920s, women under the age of twenty-five traveling without a legal guardian were added to the prohibited classes. Mexico's strongest nod to patriarchy followed in a regulation in 1932 requiring any unaccompanied woman at the border to prove that she was a widow or a no-fault divorcée, or that she had her husband's or parents' permission to travel.[54] Conversely, American officials were often more lenient in allowing entry to Mexican single women, even with children, than they were with European women. Unaccompanied Mexican women crossed the moral border as temporary and mobile workers, not as immigrants.[55]

The Canadian government and employers placed high economic and social value on some single women immigrants. The morally selective and protective functions, picking worthy candidates for migration and guarding their respectability, were left to women's organizations.[56] Thus ninety thousand British single women came to Canada in the decade before the Great War, along with eight thousand Scandinavian and fifteen thousand Central and Eastern European domestics.[57] On the other hand, a program in 1911 to import one hundred French-speaking Catholic Caribbean domestics for Quebec homes was discontinued amid unsubstantiated allegations that the women were morally unfit.[58] By 1920 the Canadian government took over the responsibility for selecting and receiving single women by creating a Women's Division in the new Department of Immigration, which was to look after all female arrivals.[59] Like their Mexican counterparts, increasingly Canadian single women also crossed the land border, as did French Canadians. Unlike Mexican women, however, a majority of Canadian women who entered the United States as clerical workers, professionals, students, blue-collar workers, and domestic servants stayed.[60] Not all Canadian women necessarily did find better opportunities in the U.S. labor market, but when they did have to apply for private relief, they were treated not like immigrants but like the domestic poor.[61]

Literacy was the final metaphorical category of selection and exclusion. Linking ethnicity, race, and gender, the debates about introducing a literacy test made it clear that immigrant wives and mothers could be made to seem just as threatening as their husbands.[62] Thus the first extended congressional debate about adding illiterates to the list of excluded classes in 1896–97 focused on the threat to American families posed by categories of immigrants who had too many children and did not raise them properly. The focus later shifted, and the final, successful attempt to introduce a literacy test in 1917 exempted wives from the educational criteria, instead aiming at stopping the flood of unskilled male workers from southern and eastern Europe. The literacy test and the spirit of exclusion that it represented had a ripple effect. As in the United States, Canadian employers in industry and mining had long resisted a literacy test. Yet the U.S. immigration legislation of 1917 changed the balance of the argument. In 1919 Canadian politicians noted that Canada's standards of immigration needed to be as exacting as those of her southern neighbor, and an educational test was necessary to prevent the hordes of illiterates rejected by the United States from "descending" on Canada.[63] Seven years later, in 1926, Mexico also enacted its first statutory prohibition of the entry of illiterates, in an act that generally marked the turning-point in Mexico's liberal immigration policy. By the 1920s literacy had become the latest weapon in the arsenal of regulatory mechanisms that defined nations and the continent.

Three Nations and a Continent

Throughout the early decades of enforcing immigration restrictions, there was an unspoken acknowledgment of a fundamental difference between an alien (i.e. a transoceanic migrant) who was presumed to be an immigrant-settler and a continental North American who was a natural byproduct of borderlands commerce and continental economic integration. By the early twentieth century North America developed a continental labor market that increasingly kept immigrants at bay and relied on a redistribution of its own human resources. Asymmetrical connections of the three North American economies in trade and investment patterns were reflected in migration patterns; all factors suggested profound interdependencies.

By 1910 there were 20,000 American-born residents in Mexico, and more than 200,000 Mexican-born residents in the United States. Between 1900 and 1914 over 500,000 (about two-thirds of them native-born Americans) moved from the United States to Canada; by 1911 Canada had over 300,000 American-born residents. During the first decade of the twentieth century 180,000 Canadians headed southward, joining the 1.18 million Canadian-born already living in the United States (see chapter 2). According to one estimate about 1,000 Canadians lived and worked in Mexico.[64] North Americans seemed to circulate with a remarkable degree of freedom during a time when legal and physical borders became a growing reality in the migration projects of transoceanic migrants. Throughout this chapter we have seen the growth of land borders as a second line of defense used by American immigration authorities against the undetected, illegal entry of excluded immigrants from Europe and Asia. In the mid-1890s the wide-open Canadian border, and a decade later the Mexican border, were defined as problems *not* because they allowed freedom of movement for North Americans but because they enabled unwanted *overseas* aliens to enter U.S. territory. Calls for the inspection of aliens, not Canadians, led to the establishment of designated points of entry along the Canadian-American border after 1900. Only starting in 1906 did Canadian-born border crossers have to fill out a form that left a permanent record of their arrival in the United States.[65] Along the Mexican border as well, Asians, Middle Easterners, and certain types of Europeans, not Mexicans, were the principal concern of border officials. While the immigration service began to record entries and inspect aliens at the southern border in 1903, Mexicans were exempt. Entries at the land border were not tallied until 1908.[66] The two land borders were built in a way that restricted and facilitated entry at the same time. The tension between division and connection, between bordered lands and borderlands, defined the character of the North American continent.

The building of borders in and around North America created new legal, physical, and social realities. Much of the border-building impulse came from the United States, but Canada and Mexico, both involved in their processes of state building, began to establish their own control apparatuses. North Americans themselves did not yet consider each other as aliens in the same sense. The construction of the "immigrant" to continental North America as a legal category, social phenomenon, and political issue was an early-twentieth-century development and directly articulated the construction of modern borders. The twentieth-century transoceanic migrant would have to navigate an international system of states, while migration itself increasingly became an issue of international cooperation and conflict. In the first decade of the century continental North Americans enjoyed a brief respite from these developments. The Mexican Revolution and the Great War in Europe soon rearranged the variables of North American immigration patterns, but they were based on a firmly established foundation. The contradictions, limitations, and challenges of building three states on one continent were as obvious then as they are today.

Notes

1 John Torpey, *The Invention of the Passport: Surveillance, Citizenship and the State* (Cambridge: Cambridge University Press, 2000).

2 Eithne Luibhéid, *Entry Denied: Controlling Sexuality at the Border* (Minneapolis: University of Minnesota Press, 2002).

3 Amy L. Fairchild, *Science at the Borders: Immigrant Medical Inspection and the Shaping of the Modern Industrial Labor Force* (Baltimore: Johns Hopkins University Press, 2003).

4 Ninette Kelley and Michael Trebilcock, *The Making of the Mosaic: A History of Canadian Immigration Policy* (Toronto: University of Toronto Press, 1998).

5 Roger Daniels, *Guarding the Golden Door: American Immigration Policy and Immigrants since 1882* (New York: Hill and Wang, 2004), 27–29. Aristide R. Zolberg, *A Nation by Design: Immigration Policy in the Fashioning of America* (Cambridge: Harvard University Press, 2008), 225.

6 Moisés González Navarro, *Los extranjeros en México y los mexicanos en el extranjero*, vol. 3 (Mexico City: Colegio de México, 1993), 29–30.

7 Erika Lee, *At America's Gates: Chinese Immigration during the Exclusion Era, 1882–1943* (Chapel Hill: University of North Carolina Press, 2003).

8 Silke Nagel, *Ausländer in Mexico: Die 'Kolonien' der deutschen und US-amerikanischen Einwanderer in der mexikanischen Hauptstadt, 1890–1942* (Frankfurt am Main: Vervuert, 2005), 108–16.

9 Zolberg, *A Nation by Design*, 264–67.

10 Jonathan C. Brown, "Foreign and Native-Born Workers in Porfirian Mexico," *American Historical Review* 98, no. 3 (June 1993), 792.

11 Mae Ngai, *Impossible Subjects: Illegal Aliens and the Making of Modern America* (Princeton: Princeton University Press, 2004).

12 This brief discussion, unless noted otherwise, is based on Erika Lee, "Enforcing the Borders: Chinese Exclusion along the U.S. Borders with Canada and Mexico, 1882–1924," *Journal of American History* 89, no. 1 (2002), 54–86; and Patrick Ettinger, "'We Sometimes Wonder What They Will Spring on Us Next': Immigrants and Border Enforcement in the American West, 1882–1930," *Western Historical Quarterly* 37 (summer 2006), 159–81. See also chapter 14 in this volume.

13 Lawrence D. T. Hansen, "The Chinese Six Companies of San Francisco and the Smuggling of Chinese Immigrants across the U.S.-Mexican Border, 1882–1930," *Journal of the Southwest* 48, no. 1 (spring 2006), 37–61; William H. Siener, "Through the Back Door: Evading the Chinese Exclusion Act along the Niagara Frontier, 1900 to 1924," *Journal of American Ethnic History* 27, no. 4 (summer 2008), 71–99.

14 Kennett Cott, "Mexican Diplomacy and the Chinese Issue, 1876–1910," *Hispanic American Historical Review* 67, no. 1 (1987), 63–85, esp. 73; Ettinger, "'We Sometimes Wonder What They Will Spring on Us Next,'" 170.

15 W. Peter Ward, *White Canada Forever: Popular Attitudes and Public Policy toward Orientals in British Columbia* (Montreal: McGill-Queen's University Press, 1978); Evelyn Hu-DeHart, "Racism and Anti-Chinese Persecution in Sonora, Mexico 1876–1932," *Amerasian Journal* 9, no. 2 (1982), 1–27.

16 E. P. Hutchinson, *Legislative History of American Immigration Policy, 1798–1965* (Philadelphia: University of Pennsylvania Press, 1981), 115; Bruno Ramirez, *Crossing the 49th Parallel: Migration from Canada to the United States, 1900–1930* (Ithaca: Cornell University Press, 2001), 42.

17 Cott, "Mexican Diplomacy and the Chinese Issue," 77–78.

18 Ian Dowbiggin, *Keeping America Sane: Psychiatry and Eugenics in the United States and Canada, 1880–1940* (Ithaca: Cornell University Press, 1997).

19 Hutchinson, *Legislative History of American Immigration Policy*, 85. Kelley and Trebilcock, *The Making of the Mosaic*, 88–89.

20 Theresa Alfaro-Velcamp, *So Far from Allah, So Close to Mexico: Middle Eastern Immigrants in Modern Mexico* (Austin: University of Texas Press, 2007), 31–43.

21 Hutchinson, *Legislative History of American Immigration Policy*, 87–88, 97, 100–101.

22 David Goutor, *Guarding the Gates: The Canadian Labour Movement and Immigration, 1872–1934* (Vancouver: UBC Press, 2007), 112–13, 122.

23 Donald Avery, *Reluctant Host: Canada's Response to Immigrant Workers, 1896–1994* (Toronto: McClelland and Stewart, 1995), 35.

24 Gunther Peck, *Reinventing Free Labor: Padrones and Immigrant Workers in the North American West, 1880–1930* (Cambridge: Cambridge University Press, 2000), 93; Mark Reisler, *By the Sweat of Their Brow: Mexican Immigrant Labor in the United States, 1900–1940* (Westport: Greenwood, 1976), 8–11.

25 Robert F. Harney, "The Padrone System and Sojourners in the Canadian North,

1885–1920," *Immigration in Canada: Historical Perspectives*, ed. Gerald Tulchinsky (Toronto: Copp, Clark, Longman, 1994), 249–64. See also Peck, *Reinventing Free Labor*, 21.

26 Peck, *Reinventing Free Labor*, 102–3.

27 Hutchinson, *Legislative History of American Immigration Policy*, 423.

28 Nagel, *Ausländer in Mexico*, 116–17; John M. Hart, *Anarchism and the Mexican Working Class, 1860–1931* (Austin: University of Texas Press, 1978).

29 Samuel Truett, *Fugitive Landscapes: The Forgotten History of the U.S.-Mexico Borderlands* (New Haven: Yale University Press, 2006), esp. chapter 6.

30 Barbara Lüthi, *Invading Bodies: Medizin und Immigration in den USA 1880–1920* (Frankfurt am Main: Campus, 2009).

31 Fairchild, *Science at the Borders*, 30–37. Much of this discussion is based on Fairchild's excellent study.

32 Fairchild, *Science at the Borders*, 144–45, 147 n. 101.

33 Barbara Roberts, "Doctors and Deports: The Role of the Medical Profession in Canadian Deportation, 1900–20," *Canadian Ethnic Studies* 18, no. 3 (1986), 17–36; and Alan Sears, "Immigration Controls as Social Policy: The Case of Canadian Medical Inspection, 1900–1920," *Studies in Political Economy* 33 (autumn 1990), 91–112.

34 Fairchild, *Science at the Borders*, 146.

35 Quoted in Alexandra Minna Stern, "Buildings, Boundaries and Blood: Medicalization and Nation-Building on the U.S.-Mexico Border, 1910–1930," *Hispanic American Historical Review* 79, no. 1 (February 1999), 41–81, esp. 64.

36 Alfaro-Velcamp, *So Far from Allah, So Close to Mexico*, 39–43.

37 Nagel, *Ausländer in Mexico*, 117.

38 Fairchild, *Science at the Borders*, 152.

39 Fairchild, *Science at the Borders*, 175; Stern, "Buildings, Boundaries and Blood," 66–67.

40 Luibhéid, *Entry Denied*, 9, 15, 77.

41 U.S. Immigration Commission, Report, vol. 37, part 2, *Importation and Harboring of Women for Immoral Purposes* (Washington: U.S. Government Printing Office, 1910), 85–86.

42 Martha Gardner, *The Qualities of a Citizen: Women, Immigration, and Citizenship, 1870–1965* (Princeton: Princeton University Press, 2005), 50; Luibhéid, *Entry Denied*, chapter 2.

43 Karen J. Leong, "A Distinct and Antagonistic Race: Constructions of Chinese Manhood in the Exclusionist Debates, 1869–78," *American Dreaming, Global Realities: Rethinking U.S. Immigration History*, ed. Donna R. Gabaccia and Vicki L. Ruiz (Urbana: University of Illinois Press, 2006), 141–57, esp. 147–49.

44 Gardner, *The Qualities of a Citizen*, 66–71; U.S. Immigration Commission, Report, vol. 37, part 2, 54.

45 Deirdre M. Moloney, "Women, Sexual Morality, and Economic Dependency in Early U.S. Deportation Policy," *Journal of Women's History* 18, no. 2 (summer 2006), 95–122, esp. 98.

46 U.S. Immigration Commission, Report, vol. 37, part 2, 67–69.

47 Moloney, "Women in Early U.S. Deportation Policy," 104–5.

48 Gardner, *The Qualities of a Citizen*, 66.

49 Prescott F. Hall, "The Recent History of Immigration and Immigration Restriction," *Journal of Political Economy* 21, no. 8 (October 1913), 735–51, esp. 737.

50 Moloney, "Women in Early U.S. Deportation Policy," 98.

51 Gardner, *The Qualities of a Citizen*, 90, 94.

52 Moloney, "Women in Early U.S. Deportation Policy," 97, 113.

53 Luibhéid, *Entry Denied*, 6; Moloney, "Women in Early U.S. Deportation Policy," 99; Gardner, *The Qualities of a Citizen*, 82–83.

54 Nagel, *Ausländer in Mexico*, 125, 130.

55 Gardner, *The Qualities of a Citizen*, 89, 102–3.

56 Lisa Chilton, *Agents of Empire: British Female Migration to Canada and Australia, 1860s–1930* (Toronto: University of Toronto Press, 2007).

57 Marilyn Barber, *Immigrant Domestic Servants in Canada* (Ottawa: Canadian Historical Association, 1991), 2.

58 Agnes Calliste, "Race, Gender and Canadian Immigration Policy: Blacks from the Caribbean, 1900–1932," *Journal of Canadian Studies* 28, no. 4 (winter 1993–94), 131–48, esp. 141–42.

59 Rebecca Mancuso, "Work 'Only a Woman Can Do': The Women's Division of the Canadian Department of Immigration and Colonization, 1920–1937," *American Review of Canadian Studies* 35, no. 4 (December 2005), 593–620.

60 Ramirez, *Crossing the 49th Parallel*.

61 Nora Faires, "Poor Women, Proximate Border: Migrants from Ontario to Detroit in the Late Nineteenth Century," *Journal of American Ethnic History* 20, no. 3 (spring 2001), 88–109.

62 Jeanne Petit, "Breeders, Workers, and Mothers: Gender and the Congressional Literacy Test Debate, 1896–1897," *Journal of the Gilded Age and Progressive Era* 3, no. 1 (January 2004), 35–58.

63 Lorna McLean, "'To Become Part of Us': Ethnicity, Race, Literacy and the Canadian Immigration Act of 1919," *Canadian Ethnic Studies* 36, no. 2 (2004), 1–28.

64 J. C. M. Ogelsby, *Gringos from the Far North: Essays in the History of Canadian–Latin American Relations, 1866–1968* (Toronto: Macmillan, 1976); Christopher Armstrong and H. V. Nelles, "A Curious Capital Flow: Canadian Investment in Mexico, 1902–1910," *Business History Review* 58, no. 2 (summer 1984), 178–203.

65 Marian L. Smith, "By Way of Canada: U.S. Records of Immigration across the U.S.-Canadian Border, 1895–1954," *Prologue* 32, no. 3 (fall 2000), http://www.archives .gov/publications/prologue/2000/fall/us-canada-immigration-records-1.html.

66 Lee, *At America's Gates*, 172. Reisler, *By the Sweat of their Brow*, 12–13.

CHAPTER NINE

The United States–Mexican Border as Material and Cultural Barrier

Omar S. Valerio-Jiménez

The reconfiguration of national borders in the nineteenth century forced American Indians, Mexicans, and Anglo-Americans to confront new material and cultural barriers. By 1800 European colonial powers and indigenous nations had forged borderlands of intercultural mixing and exchange. These borderlands would become "bordered lands" in 1848 when the U.S.-Mexican War fixed the boundaries between the United States and Mexico.[1] Indigenous nations witnessed their homelands divided, their movements restricted, and their hunting grounds reduced in size by the new international boundary. Both federal governments sought to control the movement of goods and people across their shared boundary, but neither had the resources to monitor or completely stem this flow. Throughout the twentieth century the border gradually became more restrictive as both federal governments increased enforcement. Each nation promoted cross-border trade and stronger economic interdependence while seeking to control population movements. By the first decade of the twenty-first century this boundary line and its borderland had become increasingly contested as both governments attempt to impose control while ignoring the needs of local residents. Yet the divide remains permeable to material and cultural forces insistent on crossing.

Indigenous Peoples and the Making of the Border in the Nineteenth Century

European expansion in the seventeenth and eighteenth centuries disrupted indigenous societies, forcing Indian nations to migrate, others to resist, and many to adapt to colonial powers. The Spanish forcibly incorporated some Indians (such as the Pueblos) through missions, while others (like the Apaches and Utes) remained apart and became frequently provoked by violent raids for indigenous slaves. The Comanches traded Indian captives for horses with Spanish colonists, horses for manufactured items with American colonists, and bison products for guns with French traders. Through a combination of gift giving and military force, Spanish settlements established tenuous alliances with several indigenous nations (such as the Pimas, Navajos, and Kiowas).[2] These tentative agreements fell apart in the early nineteenth century as Mexico's struggle for independence from Spain redirected military and financial resources away from the northern frontier. Simultaneously Anglo-American expansion decreased indigenous nations' hunting grounds and agricultural regions, and also pushed some groups into conflict with others and with Mexican communities. Persistent Indian attacks further weakened the Mexican presence, devastated its northern settlements, and compromised its ability to ward off American expansion during the U.S.-Mexican War (1846–48).[3]

Indigenous nations adapted to the changing international boundary by attacking American and Mexican settlements and fleeing across the newly erected border to escape reprisals. Mexicans unleashed a war of extermination against Comanches and Lipan Apaches that paralleled American campaigns against the Kiowas and Comanches. As the raids persisted, the Mexican and American governments blamed each other for harboring Indians and purchasing their stolen livestock. By the end of the nineteenth century the region's indigenous populations had plummeted after suffering years of government campaigns and forced relocations.[4] Indigenous people had lost increasing territories to Mexican and American governments intent on establishing fixed national boundaries during the nineteenth century (see chapter 5).

The new international boundary led to the formation of a Mexican border culture, most pronounced in regions where the new boundary divided Mexican communities that had previously lived on both sides of the Rio Grande. After the river became the international divide, new towns emerged opposite the older settlements; in some cases the new settlements (El Paso opposite Ciudad Juárez) were on the American side, while in others (Nuevo Laredo across from Laredo) they sprouted on the Mexican side. Along the western part of the boundary twin cities and Mexican border culture developed later (Tijuana became paired with San Diego, and Nogales, Sonora, with Nogales, Arizona, in the 1880s).[5] These sets of twin cities were initially economically dependent on one another and on binational trade. Their population was mostly ethnically Mexican with some Anglo-Americans and European immigrants, residents sharing family and friends on both sides. Political and linguistic differences gradually distinguished American border residents from their Mexican counterparts. In business, politics, and social life Spanish and English became increasingly intermixed, although Spanish remained the lingua franca of the border. Mexican and American border towns fostered bicultural influences by celebrating national holidays jointly. Border residents frequently crossed the river to partake in cultural events, pay social visits, engage in commerce, and attend religious services. Daily migrations across the Rio Grande of workers, merchants, and shoppers helped residents absorb cultural influences from both nations. Complicating this shared culture were antagonisms and suspicions between Anglo-Americans and Mexicans resulting from years of military campaigns over territory.[6]

Mid-nineteenth-century political turmoil fomented conflict along the border and cast a long shadow over race relations across the annexed territories. After Texas gained independence (1836) Anglo-Texan vigilantes and squatters began a systematic campaign against Mexican Texans that forced many to abandon their lands in central Texas and move southward toward the border. Adding to the tensions were the incursions of opposing armies and filibusters. Tensions culminated in the U.S.-Mexican War (1846–48) when the U.S. Army invaded Mexico's territory.[7] American volunteers and the Texas Rangers terrorized Mexico's population, stole property, and desecrated Catholic churches. Although guaranteed equal citizenship rights by the Treaty of Guadalupe Hidalgo (which ended the war), Mexican Americans in the annexed territories could not obtain civil rights and equal representation. In addition to losing land through legal and illegal means, they witnessed some of their cultural practices, such as attending popular dances and bathing in rivers, legally restricted. Anglo-Americans pointed to Mexican Americans' maintenance of Mexican cultural traditions as evidence of disloyalty to the United States. Residents of Coahulia, Nuevo León, and Tamaulipas grew resentful of Anglo-Texans' involvement in armed campaigns to destabilize their state governments, foment a rebellion, and establish another separatist republic with friendlier trade policies than Mexico offered.[8] Tensions were further inflamed when criminals (from either side) fled across the river to escape prosecution. Municipal officials in Mexico (where slavery had been abolished with independence) grew frustrated by American slave catchers who entered the country illegally and attempted to recapture runaway slaves. While African American slaves fled southward, a much greater number of laborers from Mexico headed northward. These migrants crossed the river to obtain higher wages, but also to flee their debts. Through their escape beyond legal jurisdiction, slaves and indebted workers dismantled labor controls along a wide swath of the U.S.-Mexico border and created a culture of free labor.[9]

Several indigenous nations have crossed and recrossed the international boundary to escape persecution and maintain their culture. The Kumeyaay along the California–Baja California border and the Tohono O'odham of the Arizona-Sonora region have witnessed their homelands divided by the international boundary. American expansion in the eighteenth and nineteenth centuries drove the Kickapoo from their original Great Lakes homelands to Texas. In response to constant violence from Texans, groups of Kickapoo migrated to Oklahoma and others crossed into Coahuila in the mid-nineteenth century. To avoid the U.S. Civil War, some Kickapoo from Kansas and Missouri crossed into Mexico, where Seminoles and African Americans joined them. Mexico provided sanctuary and land grants to Kickapoo who fought alongside and within its army to repel Comanche and Mescalero raids. Subsequent migrations occurred from Mexico into Oklahoma and back as the U.S. military pursued the Kickapoo into Mexico in an effort to remove them from the border region. In Mexico the Yaquis of Sonora experienced a similar process of persecution as they attempted to remain an autonomous indigenous nation. After years of successfully resisting the Mexican military's war of extermination, some were forcibly removed to southern Mexico to labor on Yucatan plantations, while others crossed into Arizona. Additional exoduses occurred in the early twentieth century as Yaquis joined fellow sojourners as farm laborers and miners in Arizona while others settled among the Tohono O'odham. The Yaqui, unlike the Tohono O'odham, failed to obtain official recognition as American Indians from the U.S. government, making them ineligible for land or federal aid. Like the Kickapoos, the Yaquis escaped government persecution by repeatedly fleeing across the border as they attempted to maintain cultural ties among scattered groups separated by the international boundary.[10] For still other indigenous groups the borderland was the site for careful negotiations in which they sought to adapt their way of life to the changed political and demographic circumstances they faced. The Pima, for example, expanded the market for their agricultural produce to the traders, miners, and settlers who migrated to their homeland in the Gila River Valley of Arizona during the mid-nineteenth century (see chapter 11 in this volume).

International Trade and Foreign Investment

By the early nineteenth century international commerce had become a significant part of Mexico's northern economy. Merchants in Paso del Norte (renamed Ciudad Juárez in 1888) fostered commerce as part of the Santa Fe–Chihuahua Trail (approximately five hundred miles in length). Matamoros, near the Rio Grande's mouth, became a conduit for smuggling into Mexico before becoming an official port in 1823. From then until 1848 American and European merchants dominated Mexico's northeastern trade. Merchants imported foreign-manufactured items and exported specie and livestock products from Mexico's northeast. The cross-border trade inverted the longstanding economic arrangement by which merchants in Mexico's center supplied the nation's periphery; subsequently traders along Mexico's northern periphery would increasingly supply the nation's north and north central regions.[11] After the U.S.-Mexican War merchants shifted their operations to American border cities like Brownsville (opposite Matamoros) and El Paso (opposite Paso del Norte). The American towns flourished while their Mexican counterparts languished, in part because of the nations' differing trade laws. Mexico imposed import tariffs and taxed the transportation of foreign goods within the country, while the United States established relatively low tariffs and did not tax internal trade. This disparity led to a sharp differential in prices for clothing and food, which cost up to four times more in Mexican than American border towns. The higher cost of goods in Mexico and higher wages in the United States attracted male and female laborers north. Between 1848 and 1873 at least 2,812 indebted workers (accompanied by 2,572 family members) left Coahuila and Nuevo León for Texas; women labored as domestic servants, cooks, and laundresses, men as ranch hands, teamsters, and railroad workers.[12]

National economic and political developments would subsequently influence the distribution of the local border population. To combat the disparity in the cost of living, the states of Tamaulipas and Chihuahua established a free-trade zone in the late 1850s to exempt imports from tariffs along the border. This incentive drew merchants back to Mexico, triggering a population decline in American border towns. During the American Civil War the population of Mexican border towns increased further when American merchants sought refuge there. The free-trade zone fueled the smuggling of American imports into Mexico's interior, and European manufactures into the United States. Because they avoided tariffs, the foreign-made contraband items were priced lower than domestic goods in Mexico (and similarly in the United States), prompting merchants in each nation's interior to complain about the unfair advantage that the free-trade zone gave to border traders. Despite protests from merchants in central Mexico and the loss of tax revenues from the tariff exemptions, the federal government extended the free-trade zone across the nation's entire northern border in 1885. American traders and government officials continued to complain about the free-trade zone's damaging economic impact on the U.S. border communities until 1905, when Mexico repealed the zone's exemptions. The arrival of railroads in the late nineteenth century ushered in another reconfiguration of trade and population as American border towns became the dominant commercial centers.[13]

While the international boundary facilitated legal trade, it also led to a rise in smuggling. Outside the free-trade zone Mexico's import tariffs created an opening for smugglers to profit from contraband. Smuggled imports included tobacco, textiles, and liquor, while silver specie was the main smuggled export. Merchants in Monterrey capitalized on smuggling to convert the city into a trade capital that quickly surpassed Matamoros and Saltillo in population and commerce.[14] Cattle theft flourished in the postwar years because thieves crossed the river to escape prosecution and sell their bounty. While American and Mexican investigative committees reached the predictable conclusion that residents and officials in the other nation harbored thieves, their reports tacitly acknowledged each nation's inability to control the movement of goods and people across their shared boundary. During the Civil War the border's strategic importance grew as the Confederacy shipped cotton to European markets through Matamoros (the only port to escape the Union blockade). The Union and Confederacy recruited Mexican nationals and Mexican Americans as soldiers, and also courted Mexican political parties and military leaders for their support.[15]

Mining attracted Americans south, spurring the development of new communities along Mexico's northwestern border, fostering its economic integration with the United States, and creating an international and multiethnic labor force there. Beginning in the 1850s the discovery of silver and gold deposits spurred several mining booms further west in Baja California. Attracted by the possibility of bonanzas, American miners, merchants, and filibusters flocked to the region. After witnessing several American filibustering efforts in Baja California and Sonora (including that of the infamous William Walker), the Mexican government unsuccessfully attempted to restrict the entrance of foreigners across its northwestern border. Meanwhile the mining booms transformed Tijuana, San Diego, and other border communities from sleepy outposts to vibrant towns.[16]

In the 1880s changes in Mexican laws paved the way for massive foreign investment in mining concerns (see chapter 15). Silver, gold, lead, and copper deposits made Sonora and Chihuahua the most productive mineral regions in Mexico. Railroad development in the late nineteenth century further tied the nation's extractive industries to the U.S. economy. With financing from American investors, the Mexican Central Railroad Company linked Mexico City with El Paso, while the Mexican National Railroad Company, financed by French and English capitalists, connected Mexico City with Monterrey (the northeastern trade capital) and Laredo, Texas. American railways connected U.S. border towns to Midwestern markets, continuing from there to Canada and the U.S. Northeast. These trade connections demonstrated the increasing continental economic integration and pervasive influence of American capital by the late nineteenth century. Mexico's northern region also benefited from inexpensive labor and proximity to American smelters. Among the workers were Yaqui and Opata Indians, who labored seasonally to supplement subsistence agriculture. Chinese immigrants also entered Arizona and Sonora in the 1870s to work in railroad construction, hotel service, and trade. Some Chinese remained in Mexico to work as farmers, as ranchers, and in skilled trades, while others used Mexico as a corridor to the United States, crossing the border illegally after the Chinese Exclusion Act of 1882 (see chapter 14). Further adding to the diversity of northern Mexico, in the 1880s some American Mormons journeyed south after polygamy was outlawed in the United States.[17]

The ascendancy of the Mexican dictator Porfirio Díaz in 1876 substantially strengthened U.S.-Mexico economic integration and facilitated foreign ownership and the export of raw materials. Díaz welcomed foreign capital to promote the nation's development of mining, railroads, and export agriculture. The Porfiriato (Díaz's period of rule, 1876–1911) opened the border to external capital and spurred foreign ownership of many of the nation's industries. By 1911 American and European capitalists exercised a majority ownership of mining and railroad operations (U.S. companies owned 80 percent of Mexican railroad stock in 1902); they also controlled several million acres of northern Mexico's land. The American Daniel Guggenheim owned various mines and smelters, including the nation's largest privately owned enterprise. By creating a railroad network connecting northern Mexico to American rail lines, Díaz's administration cemented the economic interdependence of both nations. The railroads increased the border region's importance by facilitating transportation of its agriculture and minerals to distant American markets. Yet this interconnectedness did not yield an equal relationship, because Mexico (like Canada) developed an economy dependent on American core capital and markets. Land values, populations, and manufacturing along Mexico's northern boundary increased, but the nation's economy remained firmly in foreign hands. Although Mexico's annual economic growth rate held steady at 8 percent, only a few Mexicans benefited from the nation's modernization.[18] Land consolidation begat landless peasants, while mechanization forced artisans and skilled workers to find new employment. The railroads accelerated the process of step-migration, as the unemployed moved from small rural areas to larger urban ones, before arriving at Mexican border towns and eventually crossing into American border towns.

Railroad construction in Mexico and the United States coincided with the explosive growth of the American Southwest's agricultural industry. The concurrent spread of irrigation increased the land usable for commercial agriculture, and the development of the refrigerated railcar allowed produce to reach distant markets. American employers increasingly turned to Mexican immigrants (who traveled by railroad) to harvest crops. Labor agents traveled into Mexico to recruit workers for agriculture, mining, and railroad construction. Subsequently banned from recruiting within Mexico by a U.S. immigration act passed in 1917, contractors waited for immigrants at the border to redirect them to openings across the country. Labor recruiters, who were paid a commission by employers and a transportation fee by laborers, continued to operate a booming business until the 1920s (see chapter 8).[19] Beginning in 1910 and continuing for almost a decade, the turmoil of the Mexican Revolution (which deposed Díaz) pushed Mexicans into the United States. Between 1900 and 1930 an estimated 10 percent of Mexico's population moved across the border. The number of immigrants increased rapidly—while 50,000 Mexicans immigrated in the 1890s, approximately 119,000 immigrated during the first decade of the twentieth century; in the following decade at least 206,000 Mexicans immigrated legally, while many others arrived as undocumented immigrants or refugees. The American economic boom during the First World War further increased the demand for laborers. By 1920 the Mexican-born population in the United States numbered approximately 478,000 (see chapter 1).[20]

Consequences of Immigration

The massive early-twentieth-century population movement had significant cultural impacts on the United States. Drawn by social networks and familiar cultural practices, most Mexican immigrants settled in longstanding Mexican-American communities. Their arrival increased the number of Spanish-speakers in each community, customers of stores catering to Mexicans, and readership of Spanish-language newspapers. Mexican music and other forms of popular culture were reinvigorated, as were ethnic restaurants, cultural celebrations, and Spanish-language churches. Accompanying the immigrant workers were union organizers and political activists, supporters of Mexican anarchists and revolutionary leaders, including the brothers Enrique and Ricardo Flores Magón, who published an exile newspaper and led an anarcho-syndicalist movement from San Antonio, El Paso, and St. Louis. The political upheaval in Mexico also inspired an armed insurrection in southern Texas, where longstanding Mexican-American residents underwent a loss of property and political influence with the arrival of numerous Midwestern farmers. The rebellion, which began with the irredentist Plan de San Diego proposal (named after a small town near Corpus Christi, Texas), called for a multiethnic alliance of Mexican Americans, African Americans, Japanese Americans, and American Indians to reclaim Mexico's lands lost to the United States. From 1915 to 1916 rebels attacked law enforcement personnel, burned bridges, and sabotaged railway lines. The Texas Rangers and vigilantes retaliated with lynchings and mass shootings, targeting Mexican Americans. As a result ethnic relations deteriorated while Anglo-Texans increasingly suspected Mexican Americans of disloyalty. Cross-border raids by rebels and U.S. military personnel threatened to ignite a war with Mexico until American military forces suppressed the rebellion in 1916.[21]

The large wave of Mexican newcomers intensified an already heated debate in the United States about immigration. Most labor unions opposed further immigration, blaming new arrivals for depressing wages and working as strikebreakers. Influenced by the nativism directed at southern and eastern Europeans, restrictionists charged that Mexicans were racially and culturally inferior, so that their continued admission would degrade American society and create a race problem worse than in the American South. In contrast, spokesmen from the agriculture, railroad, and mining industries argued that Mexicans were needed to work in jobs that few Americans would fill because of low wages and harsh working conditions. Characterizing Mexicans as indolent, lazy, and docile, employers argued that these "backward" traits made them ideal workers. They attempted to reassure opponents by arguing that Mexicans were temporary workers who would not settle permanently but preferred to return to Mexico. Even among Mexican Americans reaction to the migrant influx was mixed. Although commonalities in culture and ancestry tied recent arrivals to long-term residents, internal schisms created tensions and hostility. The divisions emerged from economic competition over housing and jobs. In addition, cultural differences pitted Mexican Americans accustomed to American culture and social freedoms against Mexican immigrants with distinct regional traditions and social mores. Some Mexican Americans sought to distance themselves from recent arrivals to avoid the stigma placed on immigrants, frequently characterized as poor and uneducated peasants. These arguments would recur throughout and beyond the twentieth century as the United States struggled to control immigration while demand for low-wage labor continued unabated.[22]

The borderlands became sites of instability and contestation, especially in periods of political crisis. During the Mexican Revolution arms, troops, and refugees flowed across the border. Mexico's northern states figured significantly in the conflict, because several revolutionary leaders hailed from border states, which provided financial support and access to safety in the

United States. American border towns, San Antonio, and Los Angeles meanwhile served as bases from which political adherents of Francisco Madero and the Flores Magón brothers launched armed attacks against Mexico's government and captured Mexican border towns. Allying with American socialist and anarchist labor unions, the Flores Magón brothers directed workers' strikes in Mexico and armed incursions into Baja California. Military confrontations sparked refugee movements to American border towns, which became overburdened as immigrants crowded into unsanitary and decrepit housing. In northern Sonora, Mexican revolutionaries encouraged civilians to flee to Arizona border towns for safety; Arizonan law enforcement approved the border-crossing practice but remained on alert for incursions into U.S. territory. After the U.S. government recognized a political rival's government, Francisco "Pancho" Villa killed American engineers in Chihuahua and attacked Columbus, New Mexico. In response General John J. Pershing and six thousand troops crossed into Mexico in an unsuccessful attempt to capture Villa. After vigilantes attacked Mexican Americans, officials in El Paso narrowly avoided a riot by imposing martial law. Cross-border raids fueled the deployment of federal troops and Texas Rangers to El Paso. Contemporary American postcards and films prominently highlighted the violence of the Mexican Revolution and depicted lawless Mexican border towns. After Pershing's unsuccessful expedition several American films appeared focusing on the U.S. militarization along the border. Mexico's military conflict was nourished by U.S. arms sales that funneled weapons into Mexico ($270,832 worth in 1911 and $1.3 million in 1915). From the boundary between California and Baja California to those between Sonora and Arizona and between Texas and Chihuahua, battles between Mexican government troops and rebels exploded and heightened tensions.[23]

Meanwhile Mexican immigrants became an indispensable labor force for many industries in the American Southwest. The migration often occurred in family groups, but occasionally single men or women made the journey north. Women joined men as agricultural workers and often harvested crops with children in tow. Other women worked as cooks in labor camps, ran boardinghouses, or took in laundry and sewing work. Migrants journeyed to labor in Midwestern agriculture, railroad, and meatpacking industries. Women also worked alongside men in the sugar-beet harvests and packinghouses, while men made inroads into the auto and steel industries. Whether they participated in the formal or informal economy, women were essential for sustaining immigrant families, often working "double days" by completing household labor after a full day of paid work.[24] The relative proximity of Mexico allowed immigrants to participate in circular migration whereby they journeyed back and forth for several months or years. This circular migration explained the arrival of approximately 628,000 temporary workers between 1910 and 1920. With a few exceptions most Mexican immigrants could easily cross into the United States until 1917. In that year an immigration law imposed a literacy test and head tax on all immigrants, temporarily decreasing the entry of Mexican immigrants until American employers pressured the federal government for an exemption. The immigration debates eventually led to the quota laws of 1921 and 1924. Employers' dependence on this low-wage labor motivated growers to successfully lobby the U.S. Congress to exempt Mexicans and other Latin Americans from the quotas.[25] Still, restrictionists could take comfort in a renewed federal concern with Mexican immigration when the Border Patrol was established in 1924.

Mexican border cities had attracted tourists by the early twentieth century, but the advent of Prohibition in the United States (with the Volstead Act of 1919) saw a boom in tourism, as Americans made regular visits south of the border to satiate their thirst for liquor and gambling. During Prohibition many American owners of casinos and nightclubs moved their operations to Mexican border cities. The proximity to a large customer base led to the establishment of numerous casinos, cabarets, and nightclubs in Mexican border cities during the 1920s. The vice industry that flourished during Prohibition expanded the shady commerce of border cities like Tijuana and Mexicali that had established red-light districts replete with brothels and opium dens in the preceding decade. These zoned districts offered visitors a crosscultural mix of American jazz, Chinese food, and Mexican games of chance in buildings that blended Mexican, Moorish, and Baroque architecture. Owned by Mexican and American entrepreneurs, the tourist attractions included racetracks for horses and dogs, bullfight arenas, and venues hosting cockfights. Mexican chambers of commerce advertised in American newspapers and magazines to promote tourism. Attracted by the red-light districts, conference business in American border cities grew. Prostitution flourished during Prohibition from the constant flow of American customers across the border. The border's vice industry became a prominent story in American films featuring gangsters smuggling alcohol and drugs; subsequently Hollywood produced films about the smuggling of Mexicans and Chinese across the border. Among the tourists were wealthy visitors, including celebrities and movie stars from California, who ventured south to enjoy hot spring baths, a golf course, a casino, and a private airport offered at Agua Caliente, a luxury hotel in Tijuana that was a joint Mexican and American venture.[26]

The increase in vice tourism financed several municipal projects in Mexico, including transportation improvements and public works. These infrastructure projects were especially critical to meet the demand of a population increase that pushed Tijuana from 1,028 residents in 1921 to 8,384 by 1930, and Ciudad Juárez from 10,621 in 1910 to 40,000 in 1930. Private investors established racetracks, liquor distilleries, and breweries to meet the foreign customer demand. In turn municipal governments added new international bridges, improved water and sewage systems, and paved main thoroughfares. The region's infrastructure development halted when Prohibition ended and vice tourism subsided. Mexican border cities struggled with this era's legacy: an enduring bad reputation from a surge in crime as the drug, alcohol, and gambling businesses led to murders, robberies, and frequent gun battles among bootlegging rings. Even now Mexicans continue their struggle to change the border cities' vice-ridden image and to put forward a more realistic portrait of Mexico's national culture.[27]

With the onset of the Great Depression nativism in the United States increased, and the flow of people across the border reversed. As the nation's economy deteriorated, various local and federal agencies began targeting Mexicans for deportation. In December 1930 Secretary of Labor William N. Doak argued for reducing unemployment by deporting foreigners to free up jobs for citizens. In 1931 he ordered agents of the Immigration Bureau (under the Department of Labor) to identify and deport all undocumented immigrants, beginning with striking workers.[28] This was the federal government's first involvement in the mass expulsion of immigrants. Encouraged by the federal government's actions, state and county agencies eager to avoid providing relief aid sought to persuade Mexicans to leave for other regions. In Los Angeles police raided parks to round up unemployed Mexicans, who were jailed and then forced to work on public works projects. Instead of providing wages, officials gave immigrants bus or train tickets to Mexico. Likewise, city and state relief agencies informed Mexicans that their aid would end and also offered tickets.[29]

Harassment and intimidation induced many immigrants to "voluntarily" repatriate, as did increasing job competition. Fearing increasing discrimination against its citizens and wanting to reverse years of labor drain, Mexico's consulates began helping Mexican nationals return home by facilitating paperwork and paying for their passage. Providing additional motivation was the Mexican government's belief that immigrants had acquired valuable skills as machinists, welders, and factory workers, as well as the acquisition of labor discipline that Mexico believed was necessary for its industrialization.[30] From 1929 to 1937 between 350,000 and one million people returned to Mexico through deportation and repatriation; included in this figure were Mexican Americans (mostly American-born children) who accompanied their Mexican-born families.[31] Portraying Mexicans and Mexican Americans as "foreigners" and "aliens" rendered them vulnerable to expulsion. Scholars continue to disagree on the federal government's role in deportation, and on the number of returnees resulting from "voluntary" repatriations and forced deportations.

The Bracero Program and Undocumented Immigration

After the reverse migration of Mexicans in the 1930s immigration rebounded with the entry of the United States into the Second World War. The war created labor shortages when Americans left civilian jobs to join the military. The shortages hit the agriculture industry severely, as rural workers migrated to cities for better-paying and more stable jobs. Mexican women found employment in the defense industry and various war-related occupations in the West and Midwest.[32] Agriculture expanded rapidly during the 1940s, because the war reduced American farmers' competition from Europe. The American Southwest became critical, surpassing the Midwest as the nation's main agricultural producer. In response the Mexican and American governments established the Bracero Program in 1942.

The bracero guest-worker program facilitated the employment of male Mexican workers throughout the American West. Although both national governments had a responsibility to ensure that employers and workers fulfilled their obligations, contracts were difficult to enforce. Abuse was common, especially in Texas. Between 1942 and 1947 approximately 250,000 braceros worked in the agricultural and railroad industries. The United States and Mexico formalized a new agreement (Public Law 78) to extend the Bracero Program in 1951 (during the Korean War) and continuously renewed it until 1964. Employers argued in favor of the program because they claimed to need temporary workers even in periods without labor shortages. American agribusiness benefited mightily from the guest-worker arrangement because it obtained workers for arduous, low-wage jobs. The Mexican government sought to continue the program because the braceros contributed to its social security system, and their remittances boosted its economy. Under increasing criticism from religious organizations, labor unions, and Mexican American groups, the U.S. government ended the Bracero Program in 1964. Overall the program employed approximately 4.8 million Mexicans in twenty-two years, often with workers who agreed to multiple contracts over the course of several years. Most braceros found employment in border states (three-quarters of the total worked in California and Texas), but some obtained jobs in the Midwest and the Pacific Northwest (see chapter 1).[33]

The Bracero Program's longevity spurred an increase in undocumented immigration. During the program's operation the Border Patrol caught approximately five million people attempting to enter the United States illegally. Many who were not detected found employment as undocumented laborers. Some were former guest workers who had fulfilled their contracts, returned to Mexico, and then entered the United States illegally to work in the same region where they had previously been employed. Using social networks of friends and family that they had established while working as braceros, these undocumented laborers easily found housing and employment opportunities.[34]

Demographic and economic pressures in Mexico fueled the migration north. Although the Mexican economy had expanded in the 1940s and 1950s, its benefits had been distributed unevenly; the wealthy had made considerable gains, but the working poor's wages had not kept pace with inflation. The nation's industrialization had been accompanied by massive population growth, from 16 million in 1934 to 32 million in 1958. The nation's increasingly urban population fed an internal migration attracted to higher wages in its northern states. The northern states' industries had expanded to supply increased wartime demands for exports and to replace the decrease in American imports (which the United States directed to its war effort). Nuevo León's explosive industrial development made Monterrey second in the nation in manufacturing (after Mexico City). The federal government invested heavily in the border states' agricultural infrastructure, converting it into the nation's most technologically advanced and export-oriented region. Nevertheless, the region lacked enough jobs to absorb the population boom. The proximity of the United States and the lure of higher wages proved too tempting for unemployed workers, who often crossed the international boundary illegally.

By hiring undocumented immigrants, some American employers avoided the Bracero Program's stipulations to pay a minimum wage, provide adequate housing, and respect a work contract—stipulations widely flouted but sporadically enforced. The rise in unauthorized entries reflected the Border Patrol's apprehensions, which soared from 182,000 in 1947 to over 850,000 in 1953. The Cold War's xenophobia, coupled with a rise in anti-immigration sentiment, provided the political motivation for a federal crackdown against Mexican migrants called Operation Wetback, a quasi-military campaign begun in the American Southwest in 1954 by the Immigration and Naturalization Service (INS). The campaign spread across the nation and led to the capture and deportation of over one million undocumented Mexicans over several months. Latino civil rights groups, some of which had disagreed over immigration, began to unite in their opposition to the deportations. While the INS dragnets punished illegal immigrants, they also split up families, disrupted Mexican-American communities, and increased ethnic tensions.[35]

Beginning in the Second World War, Mexico and the United States invested heavily in their border states and created a robust regional economy with strong binational integration. Wartime cooperation strengthened their economic integration as the output of Mexico's extractive industries (e.g. copper and lead) was funneled to armament manufacturers in the American Southwest. The rise in mineral exports necessitated improvements in transportation in Mexico's north. The building of new roads and the modernization of railroads created better access between Mexico's interior and American markets. The transportation improvements facilitated overland trade and boosted tourism as the number of Americans crossing surged from 8 million in 1940 to 39 million by 1960. Sales to tourists rose from 15 percent of all Mexican exports of goods and services in 1940 to 27 percent in 1960. The United States rewarded Mexico's wartime cooperation by providing technological innovations and expertise to improve its agricultural industry. Both federal governments supported water projects; by 1960 the amount of irrigated land had more than doubled since the Great Depression. Moreover, bilateral cooperation fueled a surge in trade throughout border cities, from 1 million tons of goods in 1930 to 3.3 million in 1960.[36]

The wartime economic trends accelerated in the following decades to facilitate international trade and more closely tie the Mexican and American economies. In the postwar years the border region's economy shifted from mining and agriculture to manufacturing, technology, and services. The amount of irrigated land continued rising, but so did land consolidation. Agribusiness concerns replaced family farms, and operations grew increasingly mechanized throughout the region. Mexican border states accounted for a larger share of the nation's agriculture, fishery, forestry, and livestock. In the United States 20 percent of all farm products originated in the four border states, with California alone boasting 13 percent of national production. However, fewer border residents worked in the agricultural industry because of technological innovations and the rise of other industries. While the region remained an important source of metals and minerals, the region's economy increasingly depended on manufacturing after 1960.

The expansion of the defense and technology industries in the United States saw a corresponding increase in manufacturing and assembly plants in Mexico. The Mexican government's adoption of the Border Industrialization Program in 1965 helped redirect the economy toward *maquiladoras* (assembly plant operations), which attracted American and Asian corporations. The program permitted companies to import raw materials and components duty-free to use in the manufacture of electronic and textile products that were exported to the United States. The proximity to the U.S. market and the availability of a low-wage workforce (mostly nonunionized) provided additional motivation. The number of maquiladoras mushroomed after the mid-1970s; 80 percent were situated in the border states, although they expanded into Mexico's interior after 1972. Laborers assembled electronics, clothing, and furniture that accounted for 17 percent of U.S. imports in 1987. By 1996 the number of maquiladoras in Mexican border cities had grown to 2,200, employing some 700,000 workers. Assembly-plant employment (which paid wages 25 percent higher than in other regions of Mexico) fueled migration to the border cities. The maquiladoras employed a majority female workforce, which indirectly contributed to an increase in male emigration as men sought jobs in the United States.[37]

By the late twentieth century a transborder consumer market had developed that pulled Mexicans north for manufactured items and Americans south for entertainment and health services. The northern states' strong demand for American manufactured goods motivated Mexico to attempt to redirect Mexicans' consumer spending from American to Mexican border cities. By permitting Mexican border merchants to import American-made products duty-free, a law in 1971 attempted to promote retail sales and keep consumer spending within Mexico. The program achieved mixed success: Sales of imports increased, but it discouraged the manufacture of similar products in Mexico and ultimately sparked even more demand for American goods. This consumption surged as Mexican assembly-plant workers spent as much as 40 percent of their wages in American border cities. These preferences led to a continuous flow of consumer money from Mexico into the United States for the purchase of appliances, clothing, and groceries. The peso devaluations that began in the mid-1970s accomplished what legislation could not by curbing Mexicans' spending. Retail sales in American border cities fell precipitously after currency devaluations throughout the 1980s. In turn, the dollar's increasing purchasing power encouraged Americans to visit Mexican border cities to obtain medical and dental care. As health costs soared, more Americans crossed the border to obtain medical services and inexpensive pharmaceuticals (often without a prescription). Entertainment and tourism brought additional American dollars into Mexico. In particular, Mexican border nightclubs with lower drinking ages continue to attract American teenagers. A flood of college students during spring break generates seasonal revenues for beach resorts along the Gulf and Pacific coasts. Moreover, the economy of Baja California has received infusions of dollars from occasional American movie productions and from real estate purchases by retirees.[38]

The Twenty-first-Century Border

The growth of the drug trade and the rise of anti-immigrant sentiment during the last two decades of the twentieth century contributed to the increasing militarization of the border. Americans' appetite for illegal drugs fueled the expansion of Latin American trafficking networks and the concentration of Mexican distribution rings. Smuggling drugs across the U.S.-Mexican border delivered approximately $13.8 million in sales per year. This lucrative trade has unleashed a rash of violence among smugglers and government forces, and among competing traffickers, that has left more than eleven thousand dead since 2006. While the U.S. government criticizes Mexico for losing control to drug cartels, the Mexican government has called on the United States to stop the flow of American-sold weapons that feed the violence. The United States has beefed up border security by employing sophisticated surveillance equipment, deploying National Guard units, and constructing new physical barriers. Funding for the Border Patrol increased from $200 million in the 1980s to $1.6 billion in 2006, and the number of agents from 2,500 to over 12,000 during the same period. Mexico has deployed more than 45,000 soldiers to battle the drug cartels throughout the nation, especially to border cities like Tijuana, Ciudad Juárez, and Matamoros, where the soldiers supplant local police. The targeted infusion of officers and surveillance equipment has transformed the U.S.-Mexico border into the world's most militarized boundary between two peaceful nations (see chapter 17).[39]

In the 1990s the Border Patrol launched several operations to add agents near major crossing routes in urban areas. The increased patrols in the San Diego, Nogales, and El Paso areas resulted in the shift of smuggling routes to more remote desert regions and expanded the business for *coyotes* (human smugglers), who facilitated an estimated 90 percent of the one to two million annual unauthorized entries.[40] Along the perilous desert routes undocumented border crossers died as they ran out of food and water, suffered extreme temperatures, or became lost in mountain and desert passageways. Tragedies mounted when smugglers of human traffic crashed overloaded vans while engaging in high-speed attempts to escape Border Patrol pursuits. The number of recorded border-crossing deaths of migrants increased from 241 in 1999 to 472 in 2005, most occurring in the Arizona desert region near Tucson. In response to the border crossers' plight, several humanitarian groups began placing water tanks along migrant routes and deploying patrols that offered food and medical assistance.[41]

The construction of a "border wall" has become one of the most polarizing issues in recent years. In 2006 the U.S. Congress passed the "Secure Fence

Act," authorizing the construction of approximately seven hundred miles of additional sections of a double-layered border wall and the extension of a "virtual fence" of advanced surveillance equipment along other parts of the international boundary. While some residents welcomed the wall, others argued against it, citing the likely decline of tourism, change in daily border life, and affront to binational relations. The planned barrier met with vigorous opposition from local residents and from environmental and immigrant rights advocates. Opponents argued that the border wall would not stop unauthorized entry but merely divert immigrants to the thirteen hundred miles of the boundary that were left unfenced. To hasten construction the Department of Homeland Security obtained over thirty-seven waivers to cultural and environmental protection laws.[42] In Arizona the wall cut across land owned by the Tohono O'odham Nation, which opposed the construction because the barrier would make it more difficult for tribal members to visit relatives and other Tohono O'odham in Mexico. Along the Texas border (which accounts for some 1,254 miles of the 2,000-mile divide), property owners filed lawsuits to prevent the construction of the wall on their property, and local mayors complained about wall levees that would need to be removed during hurricanes. Bending to public pressure, the government accommodated some requests, such as the one from the University of Texas, Brownsville, which successfully argued against construction of the fence across its campus. Nevertheless, the wall's construction resulted in floods in southern Arizona, the destruction of sixty-nine graves of the Tohono O'odham, and the severing of wildlife corridors that threaten to decrease the number of pronghorn antelopes, ocelots, jaguars, and other endangered species.[43]

The U.S.-Mexico border continues to pose challenges for both nations. The significance of the border is apparent in its attention from the press, politicians, and the public. For many immigrants it has replaced Ellis Island as the unofficial port of entry. These new arrivals have contributed to reinforcing cultural traditions in Mexican-American communities and expanding them to regions without a previously significant Latino population. Mexican music, food, and traditions have spread beyond the Southwest borderlands to unlikely outposts in Alaska and Iowa.[44] Since the passage of the North American Free Trade Agreement (NAFTA), the United States has remained Mexico's first trading partner and its most significant foreign cultural influence (to the consternation of some Mexicans). Both governments have exerted more control over their shared boundary, but residents have also persisted in undermining restrictions. The United States continues to pressure the Mexican government to control its northern border if it wishes to obtain future American government aid and assistance. The fortified "border wall" seems like a relic of bygone eras, when nondemocratic regimes attempted to keep people from crossing international boundaries. Yet it has not stopped drug smugglers and undocumented immigrants, who have dug tunnels and used ramps to bypass the structure, or taken to transporting contraband by air and sea.[45] The border wall has succeeded in poisoning binational relations and confirming to borderland residents that distant central governments continue to misunderstand the region's needs. Fewer immigrants are making the journey north because of the declining American economy, but the increased security has also kept undocumented workers in the United States longer as circular migration becomes more difficult.[46] As in the nineteenth century, the U.S. demand for contraband goods and inexpensive labor persists. Moreover, American politicians and a segment of the public remain wary of immigrants who might become permanent U.S. residents and eventually press for full citizenship rights.

Notes

1 Jeremy Adelman and Stephen Aron, "From Borderlands to Borders: Empires, Nation-States, and the Peoples in Between in North American History," *American Historical Review* 104, no. 3 (June 1999), 814–41.

2 James F. Brooks, *Captives and Cousins: Slavery, Kinship, and Community in the Southwest Borderlands* (Chapel Hill: University of North Carolina Press, 2001); Pekka Hamalainen, "The Western Comanche Trade Center: Rethinking the Plains Indian Trade System," *Western Historical Quarterly* 29, no. 4 (winter 1998), 485–513.

3 Brian DeLay, *War of a Thousand Deserts: Indian Raids and the U.S.-Mexican War* (New Haven: Yale University Press, 2008); Pekka Hamalainen, *The Comanche Empire* (New Haven: Yale University Press, 2008).

4 Oscar J. Martínez, *Troublesome Border* (Tucson: University of Arizona Press, 1988), 53–71.

5 Daniel D. Arreola, *Tejano South Texas: A Mexican American Cultural Province* (Austin: University of Texas Press, 2002), 1–22; Roberto R. Alvarez Jr., *Familia: Migration and Adaptation in Baja and Alta California, 1800–1975* (Berkeley: University of California Press, 1987), 36–45.

6 Daniel D. Arreola and James R. Curtis, *The Mexican Border Cities: Landscape Anatomy and Place Personality* (Tucson: University of Arizona Press, 1993), 13–41; Omar Valerio-Jiménez, *Rio Grande Crossings: Identity and Nation in the Tamaulipas-Texas Borderlands* (Durham: Duke University Press, forthcoming), chapter 4.

7 Raúl A. Ramos, *Beyond the Alamo: Forging Mexican Ethnicity in San Antonio, 1821–1861* (Chapel Hill: University of North Carolina Press, 2008).

8 Juan Mora-Torres, *The Making of the Mexican Border* (Austin: University of Texas Press, 2001), 40, 46; Martínez, *Troublesome Border*, 40.

9 Mora-Torres, *The Making of the Mexican Border*, 23–28; Valerio-Jiménez, *Rio Grande Crossings*, chapter 5.

10 Evelyn Hu-DeHart, *Yaqui Resistance and Survival: The Struggle for Land and Autonomy, 1821–1920* (Madison: University of Wisconsin Press, 1984), 56–117, 155–56; Martínez, *Troublesome Border*, 71–76; Eric V. Meeks, *Border Citizens: The Making of Indians, Mexicans, and Anglos in Arizona* (Austin: University of Texas Press, 2007), 71–97; Paul Ganster and David E. Lorey, *The U.S.-Mexican Border into the Twenty-first Century* (Lanham, Md.: Rowman and Littlefield, 2008), 53–54.

11 Mora-Torres, *The Making of the Mexican Border*, 30–31.

12 Mario Cerutti and Miguel A. González Quirroga, *El norte de México y Texas, 1848–1880: Comercio, capitals, y trabajadores en una economía de frontera* (San Juan Mixcoac, México: Instituto Mora, 1999), 115–81; Mora-Torres, *The Making of the Mexican Border*, 27–28, 31–32; Oscar J. Martínez, *Border Boom Town: Ciudad Juárez since 1848* (Austin: University of Texas Press, 1978), 12–15.

13 Martínez, *Troublesome Border*, 14–15, 112.

14 Mora-Torres, *The Making of the Mexican Border*, 33.

15 Jerry D. Thompson, *Civil War and Revolution on the Rio Grande Frontier: A Narrative and Photographic History* (Austin: Texas State Historical Association, 2004).

16 Lawrence D. Taylor, "The Mining Boom in Baja California from 1850 to 1890 and the Emergence of Tijuana as a Border Community," *On the Border: Society and Culture between the United States and Mexico*, ed. Andrew G. Wood (Lanham, Md.: SR, 2004), 1–17; Martínez, *Troublesome Border*, 38–46.

17 Taylor, "The Mining Boom in Baja California," 18–21; Paul Ganster and David E. Lorey, *The U.S.-Mexican Border into the Twenty-first Century* (Lanham, Md.: Rowland and Littlefield, 2008), 35–39; Grace Peña Delgado, "At Exclusion's Gate: Changing Categories of Race and Class among Chinese *Fronterizos*, 1882–1904," *Continental Crossroads: Remapping U.S.-Mexico Borderlands History*, ed. Samuel Truett and Elliott Young (Durham: Duke University Press, 2004), 183–207; Samuel Truett, *Fugitive Landscapes: The Forgotten History of the U.S.-Mexican Borderlands* (New Haven: Yale University Press, 2006), 83–130; John J. Bukowczyk, "Migration, Transportation, Capital, and the State in the Great Lakes Basin, 1815–1890," *Permeable Border: The Great Lakes Basin as Transnational Region, 1650–1990*, by John J. Bukowczyk, Nora Faires, David R. Smith, and Randy William Widdis (Pittsburgh: University of Pittsburgh Press, 2005), 29–77.

18 Bukowczyk, "Migration, Transportation, Capital, and the State," 50–74; Ganster and Lorey, *U.S.-Mexican Border*, 35–41.

19 David G. Gutiérrez, *Walls and Mirrors: Mexican Americans, Mexican Immigrants and the Politics of Ethnicity* (Berkeley: University of California Press, 1995), 40–45; Ganster and Lorey, *U.S.-Mexican Border*, 67–68.

20 Gutiérrez, *Walls and Mirrors*, 45; Ganster and Lorey, *U.S.-Mexican Border*, 66.

21 Benjamin Heber Johnson, *Revolution in Texas: How a Forgotten Rebellion and Its Bloody Suppression Turned Mexicans into Americans* (New Haven: Yale University Press, 2003), 38–143; Ganster and Lorey, *U.S.-Mexican Border*, 62–66.

22 Gutiérrez, *Walls and Mirrors*, 46–65.

23 Ganster and Lorey, *U.S.-Mexican Border*, 60–63; Mario T. García, *Desert Immigrants:*

The Mexicans of El Paso, 1880–1920 (New Haven: Yale University Press, 1981), 175–77, 186–96; Claire Fox, *The Fence and the River: Culture and Politics at the U.S.-Mexico Border* (Minneapolis: University of Minnesota Press, 1999), 70–81; Dominique Brégent-Heald, "Projecting the In-Between: Cinematic Representations of Borderlands and Borders in North America, 1908–1940," *Bridging National Borders in North America: Transnational and Comparative Histories,* ed. Benjamin H. Johnson and Andrew R. Graybill (Durham: Duke University Press, 2010), 261–63; Martínez, *Border Boom Town,* 38, 42–46; Milo Kearney and Anthony Knopp, *Border Cuates: A History of the U.S.-Mexican Twin Cities* (Austin: Eakin, 1995), 153–57; Truett, *Fugitive Landscapes,* 166–67.

24 Vicki Ruiz, *From Out of the Shadows: Mexican Women in Twentieth-Century America* (New York: Oxford University Press, 1998), 3–25; Dionicio Nodín Valdés, *Barrios Norteños: St. Paul and Midwestern Mexican Communities in the Twentieth Century* (Austin: University of Texas Press, 2000), 52–56; Zaragosa Vargas, *Proletarians of the North: A History of Mexican Industrial Workers in Detroit and the Midwest, 1917–1933* (Berkeley: University of California Press, 1993), 24–53.

25 George J. Sánchez, *Becoming Mexican American: Ethnicity, Culture, and Identity in Chicano Los Angeles, 1900–1945* (New York: Oxford University Press, 1993), 38–41; Ganster and Lorey, *U.S.-Mexican Border,* 67–71.

26 Arreola and Curtis, *Mexican Border Cities,* 96–117; Eric M. Schantz, "All Night at the Owl: The Social and Political Relations of Mexicali's Red-Light District, 1909–1925" *On the Border,* ed. Wood, 91–143; Brégent-Heald, "Projecting the In-Between," 266–67.

27 Schantz, "All Night at the Owl," 91–143; Kearney and Knopp, *Border Cuates,* 198–202.

28 Abraham Hoffman, *Unwanted Mexican Americans in the Great Depression* (Tucson: University of Arizona Press, 1974), 39.

29 Camille Guerin-Gonzales, *Mexican Workers and American Dreams: Immigration, Repatriation, and California Farm Labor, 1900–1939* (New Brunswick: Rutgers University Press, 1996), 77–94; Francisco E. Balderrama, *In Defense of La Raza: The Los Angeles Mexican Consulate and the Mexican Community, 1929 to 1936* (Tucson: University of Arizona Press, 1982), 1–13.

30 Sánchez, *Becoming Mexican American,* 209–26.

31 Varying estimates for the total number of people repatriated (350,000 to 1 million) result from different figures kept by the U.S. and Mexican governments, the use of unequal time periods to calculate the total, and disparities in the official estimates (approximately 500,000), which did not include Mexicans who had left the United States on their own. Francisco Balderrama and Raymond Rodríguez, *Decade of Betrayal: Mexican Repatriation in the 1930s* (Albuquerque: University of New Mexico Press, 1995; rev. 2006), 149–51, 336; Hoffman, *Unwanted Mexican Americans,* 126–27; Gutiérrez, *Walls and Mirrors,* 72; Guerin-Gonzales, *Mexican Workers and American Dreams,* 94, 111.

32 Richard A. Santillán, "Rosita the Riveter: Midwest Mexican American Women during

World War II," *Perspectives in Mexican American Studies* 2 (1989), 115–47; Ruiz, *From Out of the Shadows*, 82–84.

33 Gutiérrez, *Walls and Mirrors*, 182; García y Griego, "The Importation of Mexican Contract Laborers to the United States, 1942–1964," *Between Two Worlds: Mexican Immigrants in the United States*, ed. David Gutiérrez (Wilmington, Del: Scholarly Resources, 1996), 45–85; Zaragosa Vargas, *Labor Rights Are Civil Rights: Mexican Workers in Twentieth-Century America* (Princeton: Princeton University Press, 2005), 204–5, 277–80.

34 García y Griego, "Importation of Mexican Contract Laborers," 71.

35 Ganster and Lorey, *U.S.-Mexican Border*, 81–84; Peter Andreas, *Border Games: Policing the U.S.-Mexico Divide* (Ithaca: Cornell University Press, 2000), 33–34; Gutiérrez, *Walls and Mirrors*, 163–68.

36 Ganster and Lorey, *U.S.-Mexican Border*, 78–87.

37 Ibid., 89–113.

38 Ramon Eduardo Ruíz, *On the Rim of Mexico: Encounters of the Rich and Poor* (Boulder: Westview, 1998), 229–31; Lawrence A. Herzog, *Where North Meets South: Cities, Space, and Politics on the U.S.-Mexico Border* (Austin: Center for Mexican American Studies, 1990), 146–48.

39 Marc Lacey and Ginger Thompson, "Obama's Next Foreign Crisis Could Be Next Door," *New York Times*, March 25, 2009; David Crary, "Drug War Also Raging on the 'Other Border,'" Associated Press, June 27, 2009; Ganster and Lorey, *U.S.-Mexican Border*, 176; Patrik Jonsson, "US Guns in Mexico: Will New Data Help Change Law?," *Christian Science Monitor*, June 18, 2009; Ken Ellingwood and Tracy Wilkinson, "Calderon's Drug Offensive Stirs 'Wasp Nest,'" *Los Angeles Times*, July 14, 2009; Douglas Massey, "The Wall That Keeps Illegal Workers In," *New York Times*, April 4, 2006.

40 Andreas, *Border Games*, 85–100.

41 "Illegal Immigration: Border-Crossing Deaths Have Doubled since 1995; Border Patrol's Efforts to Prevent Deaths Have Not Been Fully Evaluated," United States Government Accountability Office, August 2006, GAO-06-770, 9, http://www.gao.gov (August 2, 2009).

42 Jonathan Weisman, "With Senate Vote, Congress Passes Border Fence Bill," *Washington Post*, September 30, 2006; Nicole Gaouette, "To Fence Border, Fed Will Skirt Environmental Laws," *Los Angeles Times*, April 1, 2008; Randal C. Archibold, "28-Mile Virtual Fence Is Rising along the Border," *New York Times*, June 26, 2007.

43 Ralph Blumental, "Some Texans Fear Border Fence Will Sever Routine of Daily Life," *New York Times*, June 20, 2007; Diana Washington Valdez, "Lawmakers: Border Fence Has Drawbacks," *El Paso Times*, July 25, 2009; Tim Vanderpool, "A Tribe's Tale of Three Identities," *Christian Science Monitor*, April 30, 2003; Weisman, "With Senate Vote, Congress Passes Border Fence Bill"; Cary Cardwell, "Ocelots Are Collateral Damage," *Salon*, September 13, 2007; Nicole Gaouette, "Feds Compromise with Locals on Border Fence," *Los Angeles Times*, February 8, 2008; Katherine Mangan, "Texas University Resolves Dispute with Federal Government," *Chronicle of Higher*

Education, August 1, 2008; Scott Kraft, "Border Drug War Is Too Close for Comfort," *Los Angeles Times*, February 19, 2009.

44 Dennis Nodín Valdés, *Al Norte: Agricultural Workers in the Great Lakes Region, 1917–1970* (Austin: University of Texas Press, 1991); Erasmo Gamboa, *Mexican Labor and World War II: Braceros in the Pacific Northwest, 1942–1947* (Austin: University of Texas Press, 1990), 5–21; David G. Gutiérrez, "Globalization, Labor Migration, and the Demographic Revolution: Ethnic Mexicans in the Late Twentieth Century," *The Columbia History of Latinos in the United States since 1960*, ed. David G. Gutiérrez (New York: Columbia University Press, 2004), 68; Balderrama and Rodríguez, *Decade of Betrayal*, 8.

45 Solomon Moore, "Border Proves No Obstacle for Mexican Cartels," *New York Times*, February 2, 2009; Randal C. Archibold, "As U.S. Tightens Mexico Border, Smugglers Are Taking to the Sea," *New York Times*, July 18, 2009.

46 Richard Marosi, "Arrests Drop as Border Traffic Slows," *Los Angeles Times*, March 8, 2009; N. C. Aizenman, "Despite Economy, Illegal Immigrants Unlikely to Leave U.S." *Washington Post*, January 14, 2009; Julia Preston, "Mexican Data Say Migration to U.S. Has Plummeted," *New York Times*, May 15, 2009; Sacha Feinman, "A New Danger Awaits in the Desert," *Los Angeles Times*, July 19, 2009.

PART THREE

Complicating Narratives

CHAPTER TEN

Migration and the Seasonal Round

An Odawa Family's Story

Susan E. Gray

In this chapter I tell a migration story spanning more than a thousand miles and nearly three hundred years. Because my approach is unabashedly biographical—the history by generations of a single Indigenous family—I do not pretend to offer a macro-analytical model of Native North American migration. Instead, within a specific, dynamic historical context I consider the problem of the relationship between Native patterns of migration and conceptions of space. This problem has been fraught with controversy for ethnohistorians, at least since the publication of Calvin Martin's contentious *Keepers of the Game* in 1978, because it speaks directly to the effect on Indigenous lifeways of the encounter with Europeans and neo-Europeans, to use Alfred W. Crosby's term for colonists and their descendants.[1] Patterns of migration and conceptions of space are complexly interconnected, representing two different, but related, kinds of mobility.

By migration I refer here to linear mobility—a Native group's relocation of its base of operations, or homeland. The history of North American Indigenous peoples is a history of countless relocations, many of them predating 1492. In this chapter I focus on the linear migrations that formed part of one Odawa family's encounter with Europeans and neo-Europeans. Warfare and direct state pressure run like bloody threads through this story, but more indirect dealings with colonizers also resulted in migration. By conception of space I refer to territorial mobility in the form of a seasonal round, a Native group's systematic exploitation of natural resources at certain places within a given area—a homeland—at certain times of the year. Like other Indigenous peoples of the northern and eastern United States and Canada, the

Odawas pursued their seasonal round in family groups, traveling year after year to sites for planting, fishing, and gathering. Hunting, another mainstay of the round, occurred in well-defined family territories. The seasonal round therefore united livelihood with social organization in a single conception of space.[2] But fundamental as it was to their way of life, the round was not the sole conception of space on which the Odawas relied. Like other Indigenous peoples, their homeland was, and remains today, freighted with cosmological and moral significance. This latter dimension of Native spatiality lies outside the scope of this chapter.[3]

The multigenerational history of an Odawa (Ottawa) family of the Upper Great Lakes reveals the linkages between linear and territorial mobility. The Odawas are related by culture, language, and kinship to their northern Ojibwe (Chippewa) and southern Potawatomi neighbors, the nations considering themselves the Three Fires of a single people known as the Anishnaabeg. Historical connections between the Odawas and the far more numerous Ojibwes have been particularly close. Nevertheless, the history of the two groups is not identical, so I will restrict my use of the term *Anishnaabeg* accordingly. I will refer to the Odawa family whose history will unfold here as the Waukazoos, for such is the surname of many of their descendants today. The linkages between linear and territorial mobility illuminated by Waukazoo family history make that history preeminently a borderlands story, shaped in stages by the larger geopolitical history of North America: from the beginning of the fur trade and imperial competition and warfare between France and England in the seventeenth century to the ouster of France from North America a century later; from the renewal of imperial competition and warfare between Great Britain and the United States to the War of 1812 and the political defeat of Great Lakes Indians; and from the development of American and Canadian policies for managing Native populations through the Era of Assimilation in the United States in the late nineteenth and early twentieth centuries.[4]

Let us begin not at the beginning but in the middle. In the mid-1790s the Odawa adoptive mother of an adolescent white captive named John Tanner, who later wrote of his adventures in a memoir, decided to leave her home near the Straits of Mackinac and travel to the Red River Country near present-day Winnipeg. Her decision reflected geopolitical concerns shared with other members of the bands residing at Wawgawnakezee, or L'Arbre Croche (Crooked Tree), the heart of the northern Odawa homeland, along the eastern shore of Lake Michigan just south of the straits. For much of the eighteenth century Odawas, whose name means "trader," had served as middlemen in the fur trade of the Upper Great Lakes. From Michilimackinac at the straits they had managed the exchange of peltries for trade goods and gifts, between

Ojibwes to the north and west and European officials and traders. Odawas also played a vital role in provisioning the post with corn, fish, and fruit. They had retained their commanding geopolitical position despite the defeat of their French allies during the Seven Years' War and the British takeover of Michilimackinac and the fur trade after 1763.[5]

By the 1790s, however, the Odawas' position was by no means as secure as it had once been. After the American Revolution all Native peoples of the Great Lakes region watched in dismay as American settlers, backed by military force, advanced into the Ohio Country to the south, and they looked to their British allies for assistance in halting the incursion. For their part, British officials in a newly formed Canada sought to maintain the Indian alliance as a buffer against the threat of American invasion without actually risking war with the aggressive young republic. To this end the British refused to come to the aid of Native warriors in the Battle of Fallen Timbers in northwestern Ohio in 1794, resulting in an Indian defeat that paved the way for the cession of much of the Ohio Country to the Americans in the Treaty of Greenville in 1795. That same year the British agreed in Jay's Treaty finally to abandon their posts, including Michilimackinac, in the Northwest Territory, a region ceded to the United States in the Peace of Paris (1783). Plans for the development of Upper Canada (Ontario) as a commercial, agrarian colony reinforced the British geopolitical decision to shift the focus of the fur trade north and west of Lake Superior, leaving the territory south of the straits open to American exploitation.[6] These events left the Odawas struggling to reconfigure their own geopolitics.

It was not the first time that the Odawas' encounter with Europeans had resulted in migration. The earliest written accounts of these people, the work of French officials and Catholic missionaries, dating from the early seventeenth century, place the Odawas on Manitoulin Island and the Bruce Peninsula on the eastern shore of Lake Huron. Manitoulin remains the homeland of Odawas today. Anishnaabe tradition says that the people of the Three Fires migrated to the Great Lakes from the east coast of North America long before the arrival of Europeans on the continent.[7] From their homeland beside Lake Huron the Odawas pursued a seasonal round that distinguished them both from their more sedentary and agricultural Huron and Potawatomi neighbors to the south and from the hunter-gatherer Ojibwes to the north. Living in a climate with at least 144 frost-free days a year, the Odawas could raise corn and other crops. Horticulture in combination with hunting, gathering, maple sugar making, and fishing were the mainstays of their seasonal round.

Within a few years of the first European reports of Odawa life, however, the Indians had fled their homeland for Chequamegon Bay at the western end of Lake Superior. There they sought refuge among the Ojibwes from the Iroquois, whose rampage throughout the Great Lakes region in the second half of the seventeenth century formed part of the violent contest between French and English imperial interests in North America. At Chequamegon Bay a multiethnic village emerged as an Odawa trading center and sanctuary for Odawa, Huron, and other Native refugees. The village also became a staging ground for a multifront war waged by the Anishnaabeg against the Iroquois for control of the upper lake country. In the last years of the seventeenth century the campaign culminated in a series of major battles in present-day southern Ontario that permanently broke Iroquois military power. Thereafter the Odawas gradually returned south and east and formed two major settlements on the eastern shore of Lake Michigan—one in the Grand River Valley around present-day Grand Rapids, Michigan, and the other at Wawgawnakezee, or L'Arbre Croche, to the north. At the straits they also asserted control of the fur trade, provisioning the fort at Michilimackinac and serving as middlemen between their Ojibwe kinsmen and the French. These arrangements remained stable until the late eighteenth century, when geopolitical circumstances again prompted the migration of some Odawas, including John Tanner's adoptive mother and a man named Waukazoo.[8]

Waukazoo may have had more reason than other Odawas to make the trek to the Red River Country. According to his nephew Andrew J. Blackbird, Wakauzoo's "remote ancestors" were captured by an Odawa war party traveling west "toward the Rocky Mountains," an episode that doubtless dates from the late seventeenth century, when some Odawas were living among the Ojibwes at the western end of Lake Superior. In part because of the displacements of Indians further east, the Ojibwes were themselves engaged in a contest for territory with Dakota peoples that would in the eighteenth century encourage the latter to forsake the woodlands for the pursuit of buffalo on the plains. Waukazoo's captive ancestors were known among the Odawas as the "Undergrounds" for "making holes large enough for dwelling purposes."[9] This detail suggests that the Undergrounds were the people identified by William Warren in his *History of the Ojibwe People* as Gi-aucth-in-in-e-wug ("men of the olden times"), according to the Ojibwes, and as Gros Ventres, according to the French. Until driven out by the Dakotas, the Gros Ventres lived in the region of the headwaters of the Mississippi. On relocating to the eastern shore of the upper Missouri River, the Gros Ventres and their neighbors the Arikaras found themselves subject to raiding by Ojibwes, among others. The Gros Ventres then crossed the Missouri and established new villages, where they were later decimated by smallpox.[10] Warren's description suggests that the "men of the olden time" may have been Hidatsas, one of three peoples—along with the Arikaras and the Mandans—living in earthen lodges near the banks of the upper

Missouri River by the beginning of the seventeenth century. Before reaching the Missouri they may have lived as far east and north as northern Minnesota and southern Manitoba. A distinct, sedentary people not to be confused with the nomadic Gros Ventres of the Plains (Atsina), the Hidatsas were sometimes known as Gros Ventres of the Missouri.

Whoever the captive Undergrounds were, they were adopted by Odawas, and they became Blackbird's ancestors, founding a line of distinguished hereditary war chiefs. Thus, as he contemplated his journey to the Red River Country, Waukazoo may have recalled family stories that took Anishnaabe raiding parties from the lake country to the plains. According to Blackbird, Waukazoo and his brother Mackadepenessy (black hawk), Blackbird's father, "stayed about twenty years in the country of Manitoba . . . among other tribes and white fur traders," long enough for an adult John Tanner to encounter them again on the eve of the War of 1812.[11] Waukazoo's abilities as a leader impressed Tanner, as did the prowess as a hunter of the headman's son, Oge-mainne (chief man, later Joseph Waukazoo). Tanner also remembered the day when Mackadepenessy, "an Ottawwaw of Waw-gun-uk-ke-zie, or L'Arbre Croche . . . arrived from Lake Huron to call us all home from the country."[12] By Lake Huron Tanner probably referred to Drummond Island, where the British had established a new garrison after abandoning Michilimackinac in 1796, and where Assiginac, a brother of Waukazoo and Mackadepenessy, was then living. Tanner witnessed Mackadepenessy recruiting warriors for Assigi-nac's war party, which during the War of 1812 would fight Americans along the Wabash River in Indiana, along the Niagara Peninsula in New York, and with Tecumseh at Moraviantown in Ontario.[13]

Some members of the Waukazoo family undoubtedly returned to the Red River Country after the Treaty of Ghent and the arrival of the American Fur Company at Mackinac in 1815. Waukazoo himself died in Manitoba after the war, according to Blackbird. Blackbird's father, however, and cousin Oge-mainne were based at Wawgawnakezee in the 1820s, Mackadepenessy being one of the headmen who had committed themselves to adjusting Odawa lifeways to the new American geopolitical reality. Founding a new village at Weekwitonsing (Harbor Springs) in 1829, Mackadepenessy and other members of the Waukazoo family embraced Catholicism and other elements of "civilization," including schooling for their children and a more sedentary lifestyle entailing an expanded role for agriculture in their economy. In addition, to compensate for their declining role in the fur trade, they increased commodification of other elements in the round, maximizing their production of maple sugar, devoting more time to gathering berries and fishing, and marketing their products through Mackinac.

These adjustments were scarcely in place before the federal government compelled the Odawas to sell their lands. In the Treaty of Washington (1836), Odawas and Ojibwes ceded the western half of the Lower Peninsula of Michigan north of the Grand River and the eastern half of the Upper Peninsula east of the Chocolate River. As negotiated, the treaty set aside large permanent reserves for the Indians throughout the cession, a provision that the U.S. Senate rejected in favor of temporary reserves in anticipation of the Indians' eventual removal from Michigan. Although not a removal treaty per se, the Treaty of Washington threatened removal, making the Anishnaabeg's continued residence in Michigan after five years contingent on federal approval. When the treaty commissioner, Henry Rowe Schoolcraft, met with the Odawa and Ojibwe signatories on Mackinac Island in July 1836 to obtain their approval for the changes, he found his most persuasive argument in article 13 of the treaty, which granted the Indians the right to hunt and the "usual privileges of occupancy, until the land is required for settlement." Schoolcraft contended that the Anishnaabeg could "indefinitely" range throughout much of the ceded area in accordance with the seasonal round because so much of the land lay far north of American settlements.[14]

A "second-class chief" (a headman not yet as influential as older men), Ogemainne heard Schoolcraft make his case for article 13 as grounds for accepting the Senate's changes to the treaty. Skeptical that the use-rights provision would provide the refuge for the Anishnaabeg that Schoolcraft claimed, he pressed the acting superintendent of Indian affairs about the disposition of the annual treaty-annuity moneys also promised by the treaty. Schoolcraft agreed that the moneys could be used to buy land.

Ogemainne's subsequent behavior shows that he viewed the benefits of land ownership in two ways. He understood first that real property was a marker of "civilization," one that would give him and his people a claim to citizenship and make it much more difficult for the federal government to remove them from Michigan. He also saw land ownership as a means of perpetuating the seasonal round by creating a permanent base from which the Indians could exercise their use rights under article 13.

Ogemainne was not alone among the Odawas in his thinking about land ownership. Nor was he alone in his belief that buying land required the assistance of sympathetic whites. In the late 1830s, therefore, Ogemainne allied himself and his band with a Congregational minister, the Reverend George N. Smith, and a local benevolent society, the Michigan Society to Benefit the Indians. With their help the Odawas bought land at the mouth of the Black River, near present-day Holland, Michigan, and founded Old Wing Mission, one of three missions established within a few years after the Treaty of Washington on the basis of Protestant denominational sponsorship as provided by treaty, and land purchased by the Indians with treaty annuity money. Because the as yet unsurveyed cession was not open for purchase, the missions were all south of the Grand River.[15]

Ogemainne's choice of land for a mission had a logic beyond federal dictate. The Black River region was his customary winter hunting ground. From the perspective of George Smith and other white supporters of the mission, purchase of land would enable the Odawas to give up the seasonal round in favor of plow agriculture, a sine qua non of "civilization." Instead Smith continually found his attempts to preach and teach disrupted by the seasonal round, as the Indians left the mission to hunt, fish, gather cranberries, and make maple sugar, and to market these commodities in Chicago and elsewhere. They engaged in some farming, but their refusal to live on their land during the summer severely limited this endeavor and was a perpetual bone of contention between them and Smith. Ironically, the Odawas may have done more farming than Smith would concede because of the geography of the round: Ogemainne and his family spent their summers at Weekwitonsing.

Ogemainne died at Old Wing in 1845. Three years later his brother Pendunwan (scabbard in English translation, Christian baptized name Peter Wakauzoo) and George Smith cooperated to move the mission north, selling the mission lands to Reformed Dutch settlers who now surrounded Old Wing. In the north the Odawas bought more land on the tip of the Leelanau Peninsula, north and west of present-day Traverse City. This second refuge from white encroachment would not last much longer than the first.

By 1855 the peninsula was overrun by white lumbermen and settlers and awash in alcohol. That same year the federal government finally settled the question of removal left unresolved for nearly two decades by making a new treaty with the Odawa and Ojibwe parties to the 1836 treaty that dissolved tribal affiliations and allotted land within designated townships. Six of these townships were on the northern end of the Leelanau, home to a number of Odawa and Ojibwe bands, only some of whom were associated with Old Wing and a second Protestant mission at Omena. The process by which federal agents recorded Indian selections of land and unclaimed parcels for purchase by white lumbermen and settlers proved every bit as fraudulent as the implementation of allotment under the far better known Dawes Act of 1887. Over time Indians lost much of their property in land on the Leelanau and elsewhere in the cession.[16]

Competition from white settlers made it increasingly difficult for Native people throughout the Traverse region, including at Wawgawnakezee, to rely for their subsistence on the seasonal round of hunting, fishing, maple sugar making, horticulture, and gathering, although they continued to find markets for their sugar, berries, fish, and to a limited extent furs. Some of the further adjustments that the Anishnaabeg made to the round in the second half of the nineteenth century can be seen in the economic practices of Ogemainne's nephew, Payson Wolfe, who was also the son-in-law of George N. Smith. To support his family Wolfe expanded the seasonal round to include part-time agricultural work for his father-in-law, behavior that reflected as well his obligations as an Odawa man to his wife's parents. He also shot and barreled passenger pigeons for the restaurant market in Chicago and traded horses between Chicago and northern Michigan.[17] Other Indians in the Traverse region followed similar pursuits, such as cutting and selling the timber from their allotments and working as wage laborers in the nascent fruit and tourist industries. Seasonal activities took many outside the region—to the Upper Peninsula to logging camps and lumber mills and, after the beginning of the twentieth century, to the auto industry in Detroit.[18] It is difficult to specify the spatial dimensions of this stage in the history of the round with any precision, because of the constant movement in and around a homeland that increasingly lacked a land base. Until the reassertion of treaty rights and drive for tribal recognition in the late twentieth century, Indians in northern Michigan were an absent presence, largely ignored by whites, but enduring all the same.

Yet there have been witnesses to Native cultural adaptability and persistence, as revealed in patterns of mobility over time. Stella M. Champney was the mixed-race daughter of Payson Wolfe and great-granddaughter of Waukazoo, and her career as a newspaperwoman exemplifies what Philip Deloria has called "Indians in unexpected places," the engagement of Native peoples with modernity in the Era of Assimilation. In the late 1920s and early 1930s Champney went on the road and on the water for the *Detroit News*, traveling extensively throughout the Upper Great Lakes region and then journeying to northern Ontario, the prairie provinces, and finally the Yukon Territory and Alaska. In her stories she retraced the stages in the encounter between Native Peoples and colonizers, much as I have outlined them here over the generations of her family. Retracing Waukazoo's route, Champney followed the fur trade from Michilimackinac to Manitoba. As her travels took her further north and west, she sought out still-active fur trade posts, drawing comparisons between the present and earlier stages of the encounter. Champney alternated her stories from the road for the *Detroit News* with Anishnaabe tales about the trickster Nana'b'oozoo that she set with geographical precision in the Traverse region. How significant these stories were for her personally may be gauged by her use of family names—her grandfather Miengun (wolf), her grandmother Kinnequay, and her uncle Pendunwan—as fictitious datelines. Through her stories of her travels and of Nana'b'oozoo, in other words, she presented her own version of the two kinds of mobility—migration and the seasonal round—that I proposed at the outset of this chapter. Through the record of her own travels she recapitulated her family's history of movement outward across the continent and loyalty to a homeland. Through the trickster tales she placed herself and her family squarely within Odawa cultural tradition. In so doing she created both a usable past for herself as an urban mixed-race woman and demonstrated to white readers the connection between an Indigenous past and a living present.

Notes

1 Calvin Martin, *Keepers of the Game: Indian-Animal Relationships and the Fur Trade* (Berkeley: University of California Press, 1978); Shepard Krech III, *Indians, Animals, and the Fur Trade: A Critique of "Keepers of the Game"* (Athens: University of Georgia Press, 1981); Shepard Krech III, *The Ecological Indian: Myth and History* (New York: W. W. Norton, 1999); Alfred W. Crosby, *Ecological Imperialism: The Biological Expansion of Europe* (New York: Cambridge University Press, 2004).

2 Frank G. Speck, "The Family Hunting Band as the Basis of Algonkian Social Organization," *American Anthropologist*, new series 17, no. 2 (April–June 1915), 289–305; Frank G. Speck and Loren C. Eisley, "Significance of Hunting Territory Systems of the Algonkian in Social Theory," *American Anthropologist*, new series 41, no. 2 (April–June 1939), 269–80; John M. Cooper, "Land Tenure among the Indians of Eastern and Northern North America," *Pennsylvania Archeologist* 8 (1938), 55–59; John M. Cooper, "Is the Algonquian Family Hunting Ground System Pre-Columbian?," *American Anthropologist*, new series 41, no. 1 (January–March 1939), 66–90.

3 On Anishnaabe cosmology see Basil Johnston, *The Manitous: The Spiritual World of the Ojibway* (St. Paul: Minnesota Historical Society Press, 2001); Theresa S. Smith, *Island of the Anishnabeg: Thunderers and Water Monsters in the Traditional Ojibwe Life-World* (Moscow: University of Idaho Press, 1995). On the moral significance of places in Indigenous landscapes see Keith Basso, *Wisdom Sits in Places: Landscape and Language among the Western Apache* (Albuquerque: University of New Mexico Press, 1996).

4 The major sources of Odawa history are James M. McClurken, "'We Wish to Be Civilized': Ottawa-American Political Contests on the Michigan Frontier" (Ph.D. diss., Michigan State University, 1987); James M. McClurken, *Gah-Baeh-Jhagwah-Buk the Way It Happened: A Visual Culture History of the Little Traverse Bay Bands of Odawa* (East Lansing: Michigan State University Museum, 1991); James M. McClurken, "Ottawa," *People of the Three Fires: The Ottawa, Potawatomi, and Ojibway of Michigan*, by James A. Clifton, James McClurken, and George Cornell (Grand Rapids: Michigan Indian Press, Grand Rapids Inter-Tribal Council, 1986), 1–38; Charles E. Cleland, *Rites of Conquest: The History and Culture of Michigan's Native Americans* (Ann

Arbor: University of Michigan Press, 1992); Helen Hornbeck Tanner, ed., *Atlas of Great Lakes Indian History* (Norman: University of Oklahoma Press, 1987). Older but still useful is W. Vernon Kinietz, *The Indians of the Western Great Lakes, 1615–1750* (Ann Arbor: University of Michigan Press, 1965), 226–307.

5 John Tanner, *The Falcon: A Narrative of the Captivity and Adventures of John Tanner during Thirty Years Residence among the Indians in the Interior of North America* (New York: Penguin, 1994 [1830]), 19. The classic account of this period in the history of the upper lakes is Richard White, *The Middle Ground: Indians, Empires, and Republics in the Great Lakes Region, 1650–1815* (New York: Cambridge University Press, 1991).

6 On the British theater of operations in the Great Lakes region between the American Revolution and the War of 1812 see Alan Taylor, *The Divided Ground: Indians, Settlers, and the Northern Borderlands of the American Revolution* (New York: Alfred A. Knopf, 2006). On the expansion of the fur trade north and west of Lake Superior see Donald G. Creighton, *The Empire of the St. Lawrence* (Toronto: Macmillan, 1956), 87–204.

7 William W. Warren, *History of the Ojibway People* (St. Paul: Minnesota Historical Society Press, 1984 [1885]), 43–44.

8 A good general account of seventeenth-century Great Lakes geopolitics is Colin G. Calloway, *One Vast Winter Count: The Native American West before Lewis and Clark* (Lincoln: University of Nebraska Press, 2003), 213–64. On the military defeat of the Iroquois by the Anishnabeg see Leroy V. Eid, "The Ojibwa-Iroquois War: The War the Five Nations Did Not Win," *Ethnohistory* 26, no. 4 (autumn 1979), 297–324; and Peter Schmalz, "The Role of the Ojibwa in the Conquest of Southern Ontario, 1650–1751," *Ontario History* 76 (1984), 326–52.

9 Andrew J. Blackbird, *History of the Ottawa and Chippewa Indians of Michigan: A Grammar of Their Language and Personal and Family History of the Author* (Ypsilanti: Ypsilantian Job Printing House, 1887; repr. Charleston, S.C.: Nabu, 2010), 93. Harold Hickerson, *The Chippewa and Their Neighbors: A Study in Ethnohistory* (Prospect Heights, Ill.: Waveland, 1998); Andrew C. Isenberg, *The Destruction of the Bison: An Environmental History, 1750–1920* (New York: Cambridge University Press, 2001).

10 Warren, *History of the Ojibway People*, 178–79.

11 Blackbird, *History of the Ottawa and Chippewa Indians of Michigan*, 27.

12 Tanner, *The Falcon*, 158, 162.

13 McClurken, *Gah-Baeh-Jhagwuh-Buk*, 5.

14 "Treaty with the Ottawa, Etc.," *Indian Treaties, 1778–1883*, ed. Charles J. Kappler (New York: Interland, 1972), 450–56; Henry Rowe Schoolcraft to Lewis Cass, July 18, 1836, Michigan Superintendent of Indian Affairs, NARA, RG 75, M1, roll 37.

15 Isaac McCoy, *History of the Baptist Indian Missions* (1840; repr. New York: Johnson Reprint, 1970), 494–97; Charles A. Weissert, "The Indians of Barry County and the Work of Leonard Slater, the Missionary," *Michigan History Magazine* 16, no. 3 (summer 1932), 321–33; Etta Smith Wilson, "Life and Work of the Late Rev. George N. Smith, a Pioneer Missionary," *Michigan Pioneer and Historical Collections* 30 (1905), 190–212. The best primary accounts of Old Wing Mission are the journal (1842–45)

and memoranda books (1838–48) of George N. Smith in the Michigan Historical Collections, Bentley Historical Library, University of Michigan, Ann Arbor. These and other documents related to the mission have been transcribed and published in Robert P. Swierenga and William Van Appledorn, eds., *Old Wing Mission: Cultural Interchange as Chronicled by George and Arvilla Smith in their Work with Chief Wakazoo's Ottawa Band on the West Michigan Frontier*, Historical Series of the Reformed Church in America in Cooperation with the Van Raalte Institute, no. 58 (Grand Rapids: Eerdmans, 2008).

16 McClurken, "'We Wish to Be Civilized,'" 272–85, 321–23; Richard White, "Ethnohistorical Report on the Grand Traverse Ottawas, Prepared for the Grand Traverse Tribe of Ottawa and Chippewa Indians (unpublished paper, n.d.); Cleland, *Rites of Conquest*, 234–63; William James Gribb, "The Grand Traverse Band's Land Base: A Cultural Historical Study of Land Transfer in Michigan" (Ph.D. diss., Michigan State University, 1982).

17 On Payson Wolfe's seasonal round see George N. Smith Memoranda Books, 1849–79 (Washington: Library of Congress), January 10, 1853; July 28, 1854; June 29, 1855; July 19, 1855; January 23, 1856; September 18, 1859. On his wage labor see August 26, 1854; August 15–17, 1859; August 7–8, 10, 15–16, 1860; May 16–17, July 25, August 5–6, 8–9, 12–16, 1861; July 23–31, August 2, 7, 18–19, 23, September 5, 1862. On his participation in Chicago markets see Etta S. Wilson, "Personal Recollections of the Passenger Pigeon," *Auk* 51 (April 1934), 157–68.

18 Bradley J. Gills, "The Anishnabeg and the Landscape of Assimilation" (Ph.D. diss., Arizona State University, 2008), 142–320; Edmund Danziger, *Survival and Regeneration: Detroit's American Indian Community* (Detroit: Wayne State University Press, 1991).

CHAPTER ELEVEN

Market Interactions in a Borderland Setting

A Case Study of the Gila River Pima of Arizona, 1846–1862

Dan Killoren

The colonizing of indigenous people is often described in terms that highlight its exploitative and marginalizing effects. Though doing so paints a true picture in many settings and circumstances, a closer examination of the colonial process reveals that indigenous peoples have made significant contributions toward facilitating settlement of their territories. For the Pima and Maricopa Indians living in the middle Gila River Valley during the mid-nineteenth century, new commercial markets for their agricultural surpluses resulted from the migration of miners, traders, and soldiers through their homeland. Not unlike many indigenous groups, the Gila Pima had cultural and economic structures that proved highly adaptable to the changes resulting from the shifting colonial boundaries that intersected their settlements. The Gila Pima demonstrated proficiency not only in negotiating commercial exchanges but also in leveraging their economic and geographic position to influence the power dynamics between government officials and Natives. The process by which the Gila Pima integrated their communities into the new economic and political environment created by the interventions of the United States in 1845–48 and 1853 demonstrates how indigenous groups used the market to retain communal agency in the face of rapid change.

The case of the Gila Pima raises the question of whether colonial Spanish, Mexican, and U.S. institutions could have taken shape in their historic form or configuration if not for the assistance of indigenous groups that provided much-needed supplies, local knowledge, and active participation in military campaigns with the United States against their mutual enemy, the Apaches. Many of the same dynamics that shaped Pima society before colonization continued to influence the form of capitalist development that occurred in the region around the mid-century. The Gila Pima proved adept at seizing the opportunities created by new markets and new economic systems, largely because of their experience in trading with other Native and colonial groups. Identifying the continuity in certain elements of Gila Pima society is therefore critical not only to analyzing Native societal and economic adaptation but also to understanding how colonial systems take root in a new territory.

This chapter details the economic and political interactions between the Gila Pima and Euro-American migrants during the initial period of contact and exchange in the mid-nineteenth century. A number of stages are apparent in these interactions. A limited barter trade characterized the initial relationship between the Gila Pima and travelers through the region. As trade increased as a result of the U.S. presence, the Gila Pima modified their productive activities and commercial behaviors to leverage their position as a primary source of food supplies in the region. Military protection provided the necessary conditions for settlers and traders to establish more consistent transportation and exchange networks that connected the Gila Pima communities to larger markets. It took just two decades for the market conditions in the region to change more than in the entire century prior to U.S. colonization. The Gila Pima retained a central role in the economic development of the region by adapting both their productive activities and their political alliances in the changing colonial landscape.

The Structure of Gila Pima Society

The composition of Native settlements along the middle Gila River Valley in the nineteenth century is itself a product of numerous migrations that brought together the Akimel O'odham (Pima) and Piipaash (Maricopa) people into contiguous settlements. Pima Indians occupied the middle Gila River well before the first Spanish contact in the late seventeenth century. During the late eighteenth century and the early nineteenth intertribal warfare caused the Maricopa to move from their homes along the Lower Colorado River to an area near the confluence of the Gila and Salt rivers. By the 1820s the Maricopa shifted their area of settlement further east to a location just west of the Pima villages. The previously separate clusters of Maricopa and Pima settlement were unified into contiguous communities by the mid-nineteenth century, occupying a twelve- to fifteen-mile stretch along the Gila River. The migratory patterns of the Maricopa reflect the high degree of mobility that characterized most Native societies in the region.[1]

Gila Pima society was organized around an integrated subsistence strategy dictated by the conditions of their natural environment. The availability of water was the single greatest determinant of livelihood. The middle Gila River Valley is in the northern portion of the Sonoran Desert, a region characterized by extreme aridity. It receives less than ten inches of precipitation per year on average, nearly half of which falls during July, August, and September. The geographic and ecological orientation of the region is north to south, encompassing a portion of central and southern Arizona and the northern states of Mexico. The landscape consists of long, flat plains covered by the greatest variety of native vegetation found in any desert in North America. Steep mountain ranges interrupt the flat land and river valleys lined with dense alluvial vegetation cut across the desert. Most of the rivers in the Sonoran region are ephemeral, with flows that fluctuate significantly during wet periods of the year. Despite its aridity the ecosystem inhabited by the Pimas was biologically rich and afforded many subsistence opportunities, including the cultivation of crops, harvesting of wild vegetation, fishing, and hunting.[2]

Contrary to most conceptions of so-called sedentary agricultural communities, the Gila Pima settlements were highly mobile, expanding and contracting in response to a variety of forces, including population, subsistence methods, and the threat of outside attack. The structure and organization of Gila Pima society proved critical in allowing them to expand their agricultural production in response to a growing market.[3] The annual subsistence cycle of the Gila Pima included the cultivation of two seasonal crops, one in late March or early April and the second in August. Corn, wheat, beans, squash, watermelon, pumpkin, and other crops were grown, in addition to cotton of high quality, which the Pima used to make clothing. Produce grown in family gardens was supplemented by harvesting a diverse array of Native plants, including mesquite beans, saguaro fruits, cholla blooms, and wild greens. Hunting and fishing provided an additional source of food to a diet that was divided almost equally between agricultural produce and wild sources of sustenance. Thus the subsistence cycle of the Gila Pima was closely aligned with the natural environment, but it was also the result of cultivating the land through irrigation.[4]

Irrigation is essential for any extensive agriculture in the Sonoran Desert, and documentary sources indicate that the Gila Pima began practicing irrigated farming by 1744. Archaeological evidence shows the use of irrigation along the middle Gila River as early as AD 700 by the Huhugam (Hohokam). Canals were communal property, and residents shared responsibility for construction and maintenance. Land was divided into small family plots known as *rancherias*, which were organized into districts that lined the banks of the Gila River. Each district comprised several family plots, a portion of the irrigation system, and a community meeting place. Districts were sophisticated organizational units delineated by their own roads, communication networks, language structures, and political hierarchies. Close linkages were maintained between the districts, largely for purposes of defense from Apache raiding. Word of an attack spread rapidly through the districts by way of posted lookouts. The requirements of mutual defense and agricultural production shaped the organization of the Gila Pima communities.[5]

The constant threat of Apache raiding impeded Spanish colonization of the northern regions of New Spain, and as a result the Gila Pima never came under direct colonization. The ability to maintain the viability of their settlements despite the threat of outside attack made their communities physically isolated. However, the Gila Pima did adopt elements of Spanish society, the most significant being the introduction of wheat into their agricultural cycle. It is not known when the Gila Pima started growing wheat; its cultivation is documented as early as 1744. Wheat filled a niche in the Pima subsistence cycle because it was harvested in the summer months, when wild sources of sustenance were less prevalent. By the late eighteenth century it was a major part of the Pima agricultural cycle.[6]

The Role of Wheat in the Market Economy of the Gila Pima

The production of wheat had a significant impact on Gila Pima society by stimulating regional trade and migration. During harvest time the Tohono O'odham traveled from their settlements in northern Mexico to the Gila Pima villages as seasonal laborers. There are indications that this labor migration was in progress even before Spanish colonization, but its growth was due in large part to the increased cultivation of wheat. The practice was so common that the Gila Pima devoted a portion of their wheat fields (known as a *tiigi*) to feed the Tohono O'odham when they arrived for the harvest, as they were often malnourished from their journey.[7] The Tohono O'odham worked at harvesting and threshed the wheat in exchange for a portion of the total harvest. The harvesting in May and June coincided with the period of greatest scarcity for the Tohono O'odham, who relied more heavily on wild sources of sustenance owing to the scarcity of water in their desert settlements. The availability of a seasonal labor force allowed the Gila Pima to increase wheat production above the levels that their own community could traditionally sustain.[8]

The Tohono O'odham were intermediaries in the regional trade between Native groups and colonial officials. The networks they established were based on centuries of intergroup relationships and provided the basis for the diffusion of crops and manufactured goods. The Tohono O'odham's northernmost settlements were connected to the Yuman-speaking settlements along the Colorado River, and the southern settlements engaged in a similar process of exchange during harvest periods along the Altar River Valley in northern Mexico. Castetter and Bell write, based on their field studies in the late 1930s: "At these places they traded numerous articles and labored in return for food, in historic times chiefly wheat, but formerly maize and beans, as well as cotton."[9] The seasonal migration of the Tohono O'odham was the foundation for the exchange of agricultural products as well as manufactured goods, and it provided the Gila Pima a link to Mexican and Spanish settlements. The production of agricultural surpluses allowed the Gila Pima to develop trade practices that continued after the United States acquired the region.[10]

Beginnings of United States Intervention

The initial period of U.S. intervention began in 1846, when soldiers participating in military reconnaissance first encountered the Pima settlements. The memoirs and accounts left by members of these expeditions provide important details about the Gila Pima and their reaction to visitors. Many of the military observations noted the productive capacity of the Pima settlements, along with the eagerness of the Gila Pima to both engage in trade and render assistance to those in need. The Gila Pima understood the political and economic implications of rendering assistance to military personnel and travelers. From the earliest interactions they used their agricultural bounty to position their settlements as an important production center and a strategic asset for the interests of the United States. The cycle of contact and exchange between the Gila Pima and various migrant groups during this period continued well into the next decade, when more established transportation networks and a heightened military presence allowed for increased commercial activity.

Two U.S. military reconnaissance missions, carried out through the northern states of Mexico in 1846, passed through the Gila settlements. The U.S. military's exploration served a dual purpose: to collect geographical information that could facilitate future settlement of the region, and to provide information for future military operations against Mexico. The first mission to reach the Gila Pima settlements was led by Stephen Watts Kearny, who commanded the "Army of the West." President Polk ordered Kearny to proceed to California in August 1846 after he had captured the Mexican town of Santa Fe. The Army of the West passed through the Pima settlements in November 1846, making them the first group of U.S. soldiers to come into contact with the Gila Pima.[11]

William H. Emory, a member of the Topographical Corps and an experienced explorer, was the official recorder for the mission. On November 10,

1846, he recorded his first encounter: "The [Gila Pima] town was nine miles distant, yet, in three hours, our camp was filled with Pimos [*sic*] loaded with corn, beans, honey and zandia (water melons). A brisk trade was at once opened."[12] The Gila Pima demonstrated an eagerness to trade with the travelers, and a few days later the soldiers "procured a sufficiency of corn, wheat and beans from the Pimos [*sic*]."[13] This initial trade established a precedent that continued in subsequent years, as the U.S. military presence in the region increased. In recognition of the favorable reception that the Gila Pima offered the expedition, General Kearny provided the Pima chief Juan Antonio Llunas with a letter "directing all United States troops that might pass in his rear to respect his excellency, his people, and their property."[14] Kearny's assurances proved important for the Gila Pima in asserting their economic utility and territorial autonomy in subsequent interactions with representatives of the United States.

Leaving Santa Fe a month after Kearny's expedition and taking an alternative route to the Gila Pima villages was the Mormon Battalion under the command of Philip St. George Cooke. They arrived at the Gila Pima settlements along the Southern Route by way of Tucson, where they drove out the Mexican soldiers stationed there. Arriving in December 1846, the Mormon Battalion immediately engaged in similar trade with the Pima. Cooke noted: "The camp is full of the Indians, and a great many have some eatables, including watermelons to trade; and they seem only to want clothing or cotton cloth and beads."[15] He continued: "The Indians brought to camp lots of corn, beans, meal and pumpkins to trade for clothes, buttons, beans, needles and thread, money they refused, saying it was no good and no use to them."[16] The early pattern of Pima trade with Euro-Americans followed along much the same lines as the barter system that the Pima engaged in with their indigenous and Mexican neighbors. The refusal of the Pima to accept money shows that a commercial market with fixed prices had not been formed.

Increased Migration and Settlement

The discovery of gold in 1848 at Sutter's Mill stimulated a westward migration of Euro-Americans to the mining regions of California. The location of the Gila Pima villages along a major westward route provided ample opportunities for contact with migrants. In their interactions with soldiers, traders, and travelers, the Gila Pima displayed a commercial prowess, along with a political astuteness about the impact that shifting national boundaries could have on the protection of their rights. No exact figures exist on how many migrants passed through the Gila Pima settlements, but a conservative estimate places the total in the tens of thousands during the middle decades of the nineteenth century.

Travelers followed one of two trails through New Mexico and Arizona, most using the Southern Route by way of Tucson and some the Gila Trail along the Gila River through Arizona, which had been the Kearny expedition's route. Most migrants, lacking sufficient knowledge of the territory, relied on the written reports of military reconnaissance missions or popular accounts to guide their journey. Newspapers in the eastern United States catered to these westward travelers, such as the *New York Tribune*, which in December 1848 called the overland route via Santa Fe and the Gila River the best route to California.[17]

Most of the migrants were unprepared for the extreme conditions of the Sonoran Desert. Little water and animal feed was available along the ninety-mile stretch of road between the Tucson and the Pima villages. As a result, many travelers were in desperate need of supplies by the time they arrived at the Gila River. The precarious condition of these travelers might have motivated the Pima to demand more in return for their produce. The account of John Durivage, a reporter for the *New Orleans Daily Picayune*, who came by way of the Southern Route in June 1849, attests to this: "They brought corn, pinole, beans and little bread into camp for sale, and the greatest trade was soon driven. Their prices were enormously high, a shirt being demanded for a very small quantity of any of the articles mentioned."[18] Other accounts provide a different perspective. C. C. Cox, who visited the Pima settlements shortly after Durivage in September 1849, wrote: "The Indians seem to have no established price for their produce, but were reasonable in their charges, and any kind of clothes or ornaments is a better currency with them than gold or silver."[19] Rather than exaggerate the value of their goods, it is likely that the Pima based their trade on the supply of surplus produce and their immediate need for the items that travelers were willing to trade. Before the establishment of fixed prices and the use of currency, commerce with the Gila Pima was carried on without a high level of consistency.

The combination of two forces, increased migration and shifting territorial boundaries, complicated the political and economic position of the Gila Pima within the region. With the signing of the Treaty of Guadalupe Hidalgo in 1848, Mexico ceded much of its northern territory to the United States. In 1849 the international boundary was established along the Gila River, again positioning the Pima villages strategically between two nations. On August 4, 1854, Congress authorized the Gadsden Purchase, which moved the U.S.-Mexico boundary from the Gila River to its present location further south. Part of the motivation behind the U.S. acquisition was to use the emigrant roads as a possible route for a Pacific railroad line.[20] Between January and March 1854

John G. Parke carried out a reconnaissance mission along the thirty-second parallel from the Pima villages to the Rio Grande. Further survey expeditions in 1856 were made to determine the best route for an overland road to California. In that year the United States sent four companies of soldiers to Tucson to take formal possession of the lands acquired in the Gadsden Purchase.

Several important developments in 1857 and 1858 influenced the commercial and political fortunes of the Gila Pima. During this period U.S. military and government officials debated with more frequency the issue of protecting Gila Pima lands. Sylvester Mowry, a soldier and mining promoter, wrote in his report to the commissioner of Indian affairs in 1857: "The Pima and Maricopa Indians should be allowed to retain their present locations. They are in all respects reservations, and have the advantage of being their homes by title of law and preference."[21] Earlier that year the U.S. Congress had authorized the postmaster general to establish a contract for the transport of mail to California. The contract was awarded to John Butterfield in June 1857, who preferred the southern route to San Diego by way of El Paso. The route positioned the Pima villages as an important rest stop for wagons and stagecoaches on the section between Tucson and Fort Yuma. The first stagecoach arrived at the Pima villages in October 1858, and from that point the Gila Pima became an essential part of the supply network for this important transportation route.[22]

In February 1859 Mowry addressed the American Geographical and Statistical Society in New York: "Much as we value our superior government, no measures have been taken to continue our friendly relations with the Pimos [*sic*]; and to our shame be it said, it is only to the forbearance of these Indians that we owe the safety of the life of a single American citizen in Central or Western Arizona, or the carriage of the mails overland to the Pacific."[23] Only a few weeks later, on February 28, 1859, President James Buchanan signed the Indian Appropriations Act, which included a provision for establishing a reservation for the Gila Pima. Congress also appropriated $10,000 for the purpose of "making suitable presents to the Pimas and Maricopas, in acknowledgment of their loyalty to this government and the many kindness heretofore rendered by them to our citizens." In 1859 Mowry was put in charge of distributing the supplies from the appropriation, which included axes, shovels, plow, and knives in addition to a variety of other tools.[24] The difficulty in carrying heavy objects along the transportation routes in the region made such implements very costly. Mowry's delivery of agricultural tools added greatly to the productive capacity of the Gila Pima, expanding on the already established practices of irrigation and canal construction. The U.S. government made these gifts for the express purpose of increasing the production capacity of the Gila Pima and fostering their friendly relationship with the U.S. military.

Soon after the inception of mail service, agents and traders started to act as middlemen between the Gila Pima and potential buyers of their grain. Their involvement had the effect of stimulating greater agricultural production by the Pima. However, the Gila Pima were no longer completely in control of who purchased their crops. Shortly after the passage of the Indian Appropriations Act in 1859 the Bureau of Indian Affairs appointed Silas St. John as special Indian agent to the Pima and Maricopa. The extent to which political and economic priorities intertwined with the Gila Pima is evident from the selection of St. John, a paid employee of the Butterfield Overland Mail Company. In his report to the commissioner of Indian affairs, St. John puts the total wheat sold to Butterfield in 1859 at 300,000 pounds. This precipitous increase in output was partially facilitated by the donation of agricultural implements. The Butterfield Company became a major purchaser of Pima produce, as indicated by the figures given by J. R. Brown. "In 1858, the first year of the Overland Mail Line, the surplus crop of wheat was 100,000 pounds, which was purchased by the Company . . . In 1859 . . . they sold 250,000 pounds of wheat and . . . [i]n 1860 they sold 400,000 pounds of wheat—all the Mail Company could purchase."[25]

With the beginning of the Civil War in 1861, the U.S. military became a more sustained presence in the Southwest, mainly for the purpose of protecting the overland mail line. The heightened military occupation increased the demand for the supplies produced by the Gila Pima. Before, the military had procured most of its supplies from either Fort Leavenworth or San Francisco, but the high costs of overland and sea transportation made supplies acquired locally an attractive proposition. The Civil War had a significant impact for the troops in the region. In December 1861 General James H. Carleton, commander of the California Column of the Union Army, ordered the establishment of a sub-depot at the Pima villages. As part of his order Carleton requested that ten thousand yards of *manta* (Spanish for cloth) be brought along to acquire wheat for the soldiers stationed at the Pima settlements. In February 1862 Sherrod Hunter, commander of the region's Confederate troops, moved his troops to the Pima villages and captured Ammi White, a trader who had constructed a flour mill in the community a year earlier, along with a small unit of Union soldiers. Hunter's men destroyed portions of White's mill and returned to the Pima fifteen hundred sacks of wheat purchased previously by White. The Confederate company left the Pima villages shortly after, and in April new Union troops under Colonel Joseph R. West reached the Gila Pima and began making preparations for the subdepot ordered by Carleton. The Pima traded back to the soldiers the flour from White's mill that had been given them by Hunter's troops.[26]

In May 1862 Colonel West detailed the trouble he had had in acquiring wheat from the Pima: "I have as yet only succeeded in eking out daily a supply of forage for the command. I can neither get any stock of forage in advance, nor have the Indians yet produced their flour in any but trifling quantities."[27] West was having difficulty acquiring supplies because the ten thousand yards of manta ordered by Carleton had not yet arrived. Based on previous experiences in trading with the military, the Pima were savvy about withholding their produce until payment in cloth could be made. West commented: "A brief observation of these people and their habits shows me that they are disinclined to sell their produce or any other property unless the article offered in exchange is such as they habitually at the moment need."[28] The extent of the trade is clear from West's next letter, in which he noted that the Pima had already provided wheat on credit for a total obligation of three thousand yards of manta. The Pima's price of flour, at one-half pound of wheat for every yard of manta, meant that they had supplied approximately 13,500 pounds of wheat. When the requested supplies of manta did arrive in mid-May, West reported that 30,000 pounds of wheat had been taken in, but he warned that "there is no guarantee how long the flow of grain will continue, as there are no means of ascertaining how much they have in reserve."[29] This statement demonstrates that the Pima had developed strategies for controlling the market for their products through the use of credit. West's comments also show the extent to which the U.S. military relied on the Gila Pima to supply their activities in the region. In total, the Pima sold the army 1,000,000 pounds of wheat in 1862 and 600,000 pounds the following year.[30] The creation of a commercial market had clearly become the basis for the relationship between the Gila Pima and the federal government.

Conclusion

In analyzing the effects of colonization on Native societies it is important to recognize elements of change and continuity. Existing systems and lifeways influenced the indigenous responses to colonial agents, and these responses in turn influenced the formation of colonial institutions. The case of the Gila Pima demonstrates the extent to which the United States relied on indigenous resources and production to facilitate the settlement and development of a region. The U.S. government's response to the Gila Pima was shaped by perceptions of utility and productivity, with the Pima seen as industrious, useful Indians in the minds of the colonizers, in opposition to the Apache, who were portrayed as hostile savages. Despite their contribution to early settlement, the Gila Pima saw their land and water rights subverted by later settlers along the Gila River in the 1870s. The government failed to adequately protect the natural resources that the Pima required to cultivate their reservation. The increased settlement, which the Pima supported through their agricultural production and trade, ultimately contributed to the loss of their ability to continue their livelihood.

Native societies and people are often portrayed as victims of the market forces instituted by colonial agents. This perspective diminishes the capacity of most indigenous societies before colonization to establish and maintain commercial networks that relied on complex relationships between producers, laborers, and traders. Rather than victims of the market, Native societies in most cases were victims of colonial institutions, which imposed new political and legal structures over the land and other natural resources that supported colonial interests at the expense of existing patterns of production and exchange. The initial period of contact between the Gila Pima and Spanish, Mexican, and U.S. interests shows a high level of cooperation and even interdependence. These relationships were the basis for how the Gila Pima negotiated the effects of colonization on their community.

Notes

1 Leslie Spier, *Yuman Tribes of the Gila River* (New York: Cooper Square, 1970), 5, 11, 37–38; Frederick Webb Hodge, ed., *Handbook of American Indians North of Mexico*, part 2 (Washington: U.S. Government Printing Office, 1910), 252.

2 Robert C. West, *Sonora: Its Geographical Personality* (Austin: University of Texas Press, 1993), 1–13; Amadeo M. Rea, *At the Desert's Green Edge: An Ethnobotany of the Gila River Pima* (Tucson: University of Arizona Press, 1997), 56–61; Edward F. Castetter and Willis H. Bell, *Pima and Papago Indian Agriculture* (Albuquerque: University of New Mexico Press, 1942), 12–18.

3 Rea, *At the Desert's Green Edge*, 43; Steadman Upham, "Aspects of Gila Pima Acculturation," *Alicia: The History of a Piman Homestead*, ed. Glen Rice, Steadman Upham, and Linda Nicholas, *Arizona Archaeologist* 16 (1983), 45.

4 Rea, *At the Desert's Green Edge*, 42–46; Joseph C. Winter, "Cultural Modifications of the Gila Pima: A.D. 1697–A.D. 1846," *Ethnohistory* 20 (winter 1973), 67–77.

5 Michael R. Waters and John C. Ravesloot, "Landscape Change and the Cultural Evolution of the Hohokam along the Middle Gila River and Other River Valleys in South-Central Arizona," *American Antiquity* 66, no. 2 (April 2001), 285–99; J. Andrew Darling, John C. Ravesloot, and Michael R. Waters, "Village Drift and Riverine Settlement: Modeling Akimel O'odham Land Use," *American Anthropologist* 106 (2004), 282–95.

6 Daniel S. Matson, trans., *Before Rebellion: Letters and Reports of Jacobo Sedelmayr, S.J.* (Tucson: Arizona Historical Society, 1996), 5; William Doelle, "The Adoption of

Wheat by the Gila Pima: A Study of Agricultural Change," unpublished manuscript, Arizona State Museum; Rea, *At the Desert's Green Edge*, 336–43.

7 *Tiigi* is derived from the Spanish word *tequio*, meaning tax or charge.

8 David DeJong, "'None Excel Them in Virtue and Honesty': Ecclesiastical and Military Descriptions of the Gila River Pima," *American Indian Quarterly* 29, nos. 1–2 (winter–spring 2005), 24–55; Winter, "Cultural Modifications," 71; Russell, *Pima Indians*, 93.

9 Castetter and Bell, *Pima and Papago Indian Agriculture*, 46.

10 Spier, *Yuman Tribes*, 102.

11 William H. Goetzmann, *Army Exploration in the American West, 1803–1863* (New Haven: Yale University Press, 1959), 111, 127–28.

12 William Emory, *Lieutenant Emory Reports: A Reprint of Lieutenant W. H. Emory's Notes of a Military Reconnaissance*, introduction and notes by Ross Calvin (Albuquerque: University of New Mexico Press, 1951), 131. Emory's original report was published in 1848.

13 Ibid, 134.

14 Ibid.

15 Philip St. George Cooke, *Exploring Southwestern Trails, 1846–1854: The Journal of Philip St. George Cooke, the Journal of William Henry Chase Whiting and the Diaries of François Xavier Aubry* (Glendale, Calif.: Clark, 1938).

16 Ibid.

17 Ralph Bieber, "The Southwestern Trails to California in 1849," *Mississippi Valley Historical Review* 12, no. 3 (December 1925), 342–75; James E. Turner, "The Pima and Maricopa Villages: Oasis at a Cultural Crossroads, 1846–1873," *Journal of Arizona History* 93, no. 4 (winter 1998), 353; Patricia A. Etter, *To California on the Southern Route, 1849: A History and Annotated Bibliography* (Spokane: Arthur H. Clark, 1998), 35.

18 John E. Durivage, "Through Mexico to California . . . ," *Southern Trails to California in 1849*, ed. Ralph P. Bieber (Glendale, Calif.: Arthur H. Clarke, 1937), 217–21.

19 Mabelle Eppard Martin, ed., "From Texas to California in 1849: Diary of C.C. Cox," *Southwestern Historical Quarterly* 29 (October 1925), 128–46.

20 W. Turrentine Jackson and William H. Goetzmann, *Wagon Roads West: A Study of Federal Road Surveys and Construction in the Trans-Mississippi West, 1846–1869* (Lincoln: University of Nebraska Press, 1979), 22.

21 Sylvester Mowry, *Report to the Commissioner of Indian Affairs for 1857* (Washington: U.S. Government Printing Office, 1858).

22 Walter B. Lang, *The First Overland Mail: Butterfield Trail St. Louis to San Francisco, 1858–1861* (New York: Octavo, 1940), 14–17.

23 Sylvester Mowry, *Arizona and Sonora: The Geography, History and Resources of the Silver Region of North America* (New York: Harper and Brothers, 1864), 30.

24 Sylvester Mowry, *Report to the Commissioner of Indians Affairs for 1859* (Washington: U.S. Government Printing Office, 1860), 354.

25 J. Ross Browne, *Adventures in Apache Country: A Tour through Arizona and Sonora*

with Notes on the Silver Regions of Nevada (New York: Harper and Brothers Publishers, 1869), 110.

26 Darlis A. Miller, *Soldiers and Settlers: Military Supply in the Southwest, 1861–1885* (Albuquerque: University of New Mexico Press, 1989), 13–15; Andrew E. Masich, *The Civil War in Arizona: The Story of the California Volunteers, 1861–1865* (Norman: University of Oklahoma Press, 2006), 38; Douglas C. McChristian, *Fort Bowie, Arizona: Combat Post of the Southwest, 1858–1894* (Norman: University of Oklahoma Press, 2006), 44.

27 Joseph R. West to Benjamin C. Culter, 4 May 1862, in *The War of the Rebellion: A Compilation of the Official Records of the Union and Confederate Armies* (Washington: U.S. Government Printing Office, 1902), 1050.

28 West to Cutler, 5 May 1862, *Official Records*, 1052.

29 West to Cutler, 13 May 1862, *Official Records*, 1070–71.

30 Browne, *Adventures*, 111.

CHAPTER TWELVE

Paying Attention to Moving Americans

Migration Knowledge in the Age of Internal Migration, 1930s–1970s

James N. Gregory

Two mass-market books reached bookstores in late 1972 and early 1973: *A Nation of Strangers* by Vance Packard, a journalist and pop sociologist, and *The Moving American* by George Pierson, a historian at Yale. Both called attention to what the authors considered very high rates of geographic mobility, echoing a pattern of journalistic and academic literature that for several decades had focused on internal migration, relocations of Americans across state lines and from farms to cities to suburbs. Packard, a chronicler of social trends, considered mobility a phenomenon that Americans needed to watch and worry about, as the title's reference to "strangers" indicates. Using terms like "restless" and "uprooted," he argued that geographic mobility had the potential to harm communities, families, and personalities and to produce loneliness, disorientation, and social fragmentation.[1] The historian Pierson celebrated the mobility of Americans, emphasized its continuity over time, and argued that it was part of "the American character." Ocean- and mountain-crossing pioneers had built his America, and to him geographic mobility showed a spirit of yearning, ambition, and self-reinvention that boded well for the nation's future.[2]

Reflecting two different disciplinary traditions—sociology and social dislocation, history and American character—these books capped a long period of public and academic interest in moving Americans. To read them is to revisit a time when internal migration competed with cross-border immigration for headlines and when multiple institutions of knowledge production and knowledge circulation focused on the problem of mobility. The period from the 1930s to the 1970s was the golden age of migration research, when public funds and public interest fueled studies by sociologists, demographers, economists, and historians; and when journalists, novelists, and mass entertainment industries spread scholarship's results beyond campus walls. The interface between scholars and publics at that time is worthy of our consideration. Migration scholars today—at a moment when more people around the world are in motion and living outside natal countries than at perhaps any time in human history—seem less capable of influencing broad publics than in the age of internal migration.

This chapter explores the rhythms of migration studies. It traces the shifts that have occurred in the relationship between producers of migration research and the institutions of communication that can give added social and political significance to this research. It will also discuss the relationship between two of the disciplines that produce migration studies. Historians and social scientists have not only differed in methods and findings but also interacted on different terms with the popular media. Analyzing the differences can help us think about what might be done to widen the channels of public access for current studies. Doing so is important, because migration knowledge is itself significant in the social systems that condition and respond to migration. When it circulates widely, migration research helps set the terms for migration decisions, migration receptions, migration politics, and also migrant identity formation.[3]

The Age of Internal Migration

Migration was once front-page news. In nearly every mass medium, from newspapers to magazines, to radio and television, to film and fiction, even popular music, the topic of moving Americans captivated the public. The fiction is perhaps best remembered today. Novels like *The Grapes of Wrath, Native Son, Invisible Man, Go Tell It on a Mountain, The Dollmaker,* and *On the Road* remind us of a time when migration was treated as a complex social and personal issue and when mobility was thought to be emblematic of some central part of the American experience.[4] The patterns of popularity show up in the *Readers' Guide to Periodical Literature,* which has been indexing magazine articles since the 1890s.

Figure 12.1 shows the number of articles indexed in five-year intervals under two subject headings: U.S. immigration/emigration and internal migration.[5] Notice the fluctuating interest in immigration versus internal migration, which follows reasonably closely changes in American immigration laws and migration patterns. There were few articles about internal migration until the debates over immigration were resolved with the passage of the Immigration Restriction Act of 1924. The little hump of articles on internal mi-

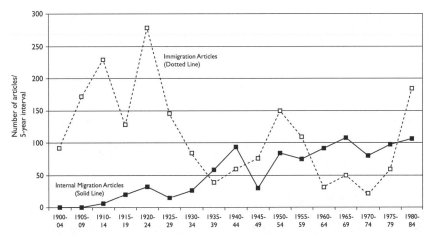

Figure 12.1 Popular magazines: Immigration and internal migration articles indexed by *Readers' Guide*, 1900–1984

gration articles during the First World War and early 1920s is largely about black migration out of the South. But as the doors shut and the volume of immigration from Europe and Asia plummeted, popular magazines shifted their focus. In the 1930s domestic mobility became an important subject, with the number of articles exceeding immigration articles during the ten years of 1935 to 1944. With the end of the Second World War a surge of articles about war refugees, braceros, and the McCarran Act temporarily renewed interest in border-crossing migrants, although attention to internal migration also remained strong and became dominant again in the 1960s and 1970s. The graph confirms that the half-century from the 1930s through the 1970s was when internal migration held the public's attention.

The same period was also the heyday of internal migration studies for social scientists. Figure 12.2 displays the number of articles published in thirty-seven sociology journals catalogued by the *JSTOR* Consortium. They are divided between articles that appear to be about immigration or emigration and those focused on internal geographic mobility.[6]

Figure 12.3 expresses these data as a percentage of all articles in these journals. It should be emphasized that this database is far from complete. It includes only a selection of sociology journals. Another indication of the volume of internal migration research by sociologists, economists, and demographers is found in the bibliography *Rural-Urban Migration Research* (1974), which lists 1,232 articles and books on the subject, most of them published between 1955 and 1973.[7]

Historians were equally committed to internal migration studies. Figure

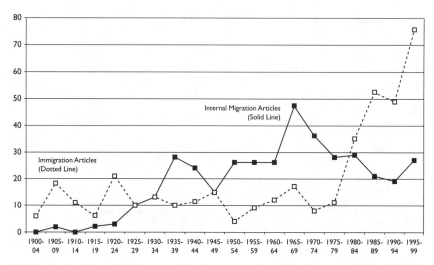

Figure 12.2 Sociology journals: Immigration versus internal migration articles, 1900–1999

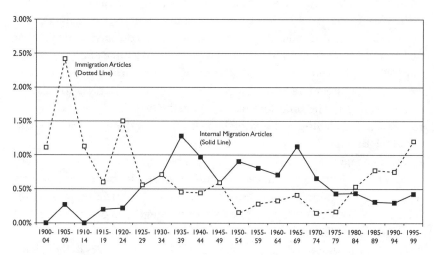

Figure 12.3 Sociology journals: Immigration and internal migration articles as percentage of all articles, 1900–1999

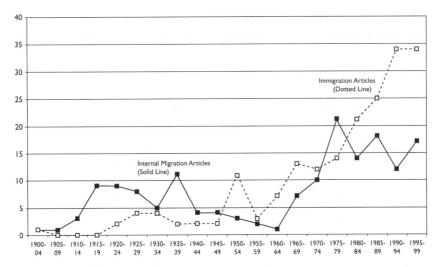

Figure 12.4 History journals: Immigration and internal migration articles, 1900–1999

12.4 is based on thirty-four history journals catalogued by *JSTOR*. The numbers are less reliable than in the field of sociology, because historians often use creative and idiosyncratic titles that interfere with keyword searches. Thus I may have missed articles that would be counted as being about internal migration. I wonder in particular about the small number of articles on domestic mobility themes indicated in figure 12.4 for the period 1940–64, because it conflicts with the impression given by the *Harvard Guide to American History*, 1954 and 1974 editions. Also noteworthy is that the graph shows a surge of historical writing about immigration starting in the 1950s, well ahead of the sociologists, who do not warm to that subject until the 1980s.[8]

Migration Research

Let us begin by briefly examining the different kinds of research undertaken by social scientists and historians, before turning to the interactions between the mass media and academic migration research that helped keep the issue before the public. Migration studies had been a concern of researchers since the late nineteenth century, forming part of the emerging fields of demography and sociology. For American academics much of the work done before the 1930s centered on immigration from Europe and Asia and two forms of internal migration: migration from farms to cities; and tramping, or casual labor migration. The former reflected concerns about country life and rural depopulation and the well-funded field of rural sociology, the latter an ancient fascination with tramps and fears of the menace that they posed to stable society. Carleton Parker's *The Casual Laborer and Other Essays* (1919) and Nels Anderson's *The Hobo: The Sociology of the Homeless Man* (1923) were the most famous of this generation of mobility studies.[9]

Migration research exploded in resources and significance during the Great Depression, helped by public anxiety about transients looking for jobs and relief assistance. Federal agencies—notably the Department of Agriculture, Federal Emergency Relief Administration, and Works Progress Administration—funded scores of studies focusing on transient families, migratory farm workers, the Dust Bowl exodus, and other examples of poverty-induced labor migration. But scholars also seized the opportunity to think more broadly about patterns of interstate mobility and to find data and methods that improved understandings of who moved, when, where, and why. C. Warren Thornwaite's study *Internal Migration in the United States* (1934) and the follow-up *Migration and Economic Opportunity* (1936), with Carter Goodrich as lead author, marked the emergence of full-blown, massively funded research on national patterns of mobility. Based on work by huge teams of researchers who gathered data from public and private sources across the country, they also developed new statistical measures and new forms of presentation, including maps with dots and maps with arrows. Another team, led by Dorothy Swaine Thomas for the Social Science Research Council, expanded the search for data and improved methods.[10]

All of this set the stage for changes in government data collection: first with a revised questionnaire for the 1940 census, featuring a set of questions about where people had lived five years earlier, then with the development of Current Population Surveys starting in 1941. The culminating publication of this drive to improve data and map contemporary and historical migration patterns may have been *Population Distribution and Economic Growth: United States, 1870–1950* (1957–64), a three-volume compendium funded by the Rockefeller Foundation and produced by a team led by Simon Kuznets and Dorothy Swaine Thomas.[11]

Another research direction focused on the social and personal dimension of migration. This work was grounded in theories of dislocation and assimilation that sociologists at the University of Chicago had developed to explain the adjustment trajectories of immigrants from eastern and southern Europe. Starting in the 1920s and continuing through the next four decades, sociologists would in effect draw together the figure of the immigrant and the figure of the internal migrant, applying Robert Park's concept of the "marginal man" caught between two cultures, and the broader theory of sequential adjustment that became known as "race-relations" theory. It is important to clarify that Chicago race-relations theory was fundamentally a theory of migration. Especially in its early formulations, race and ethnicity were less significant than the transition from peasant community to complex urban environment. The peasant, whether from Poland or America, whether Jewish, black, or Anglo-American Protestant, was understood to experience a traumatic set of challenges in the city that would take place in group contexts and follow a predictable set of stages, from conflict and social disorganization to social reorganization and eventual assimilation.[12] In hundreds of urban adjustment studies that centered on black migrants, Appalachian and other southern whites, and also on northern whites who moved from farm to city, social scientists from the 1930s to the 1970s understood domestic migration as a dislocating experience not much different from immigration across borders and national cultures. Using the concept of "uprooting" and looking for symptoms of trauma, they collected evidence of "maladjustment" and evaluated potentials for eventual assimilation.[13]

Historians were also writing about moving Americans, but in different ways. For much of the period they did not even use the same terminology—rarely mentioning "migrants" until the 1960s, writing about pioneers and settlers instead. The one subgenre of historical literature that did use the term "migration" shows just how much the disciplines were at variance. When historians before 1960 used the label "the Great Migration" in the titles of books and articles, they rarely referred to African Americans leaving the South. Their Great Migrations involved English people coming to America in the seventeenth and eighteenth centuries or their descendents moving west on the Overland Trail.[14]

The differing terminology reflected other disjunctures between the disciplines. Anglo Americans were the usual migrants of interest to historians throughout much of this period. Although Carl Wittke had added other Europeans to the field of immigration history with *We Who Built America* in 1939, followed by Marcus Lee Hansen's *The Atlantic Migration* (1940) and Oscar Handlin's *Boston's Immigrants* (1941), and although Carter G. Woodson and the *Journal of Negro History* had initiated a subgenre of writing by black scholars about black migration even earlier, neither of these enterprises registered strongly with mainstream historians until the 1950s. The historical profession remained riveted to the migration dramas of the distant past, the sagas of movement across space that connected to issues of American foundations and American expansion. Explorers, settlers, and colonizers who moved across the Atlantic in the seventeenth and eighteenth centuries; and frontiersmen, gold rushers, land rushers, farm builders, town builders, and other westward-moving (mostly Anglo-American) pioneers of the nineteenth century—these were the moving Americans most interesting to the historical profession until late in the age of internal migration.

Yet the questions that historians asked were broader than those of social scientists. The historians' project was usually grounded in the frontier theory of the turn-of-the-century historian Frederick Jackson Turner. Turner's thesis emphasized a particular kind of space—the frontier—as a zone of continuous migration and community building. The existence of a frontier shaped American political development, sustaining opportunity, individualism, and democracy throughout the first century of the nation's history. For historians writing about early American migration, settlement became the chief analytic concern, and it had several dimensions. As settlers, migrants were understood to have not only a personal stake in relocation but also a community-building and society-building stake. Historians in effect followed their migrants further than sociologists did, connecting geographic movement to historical outcomes in a way that the social sciences would not do.

The Turnerian agenda also meant that historians mostly employed a different tone and valuation scheme. The migrants appearing in historical research endured hardship transitions and came out of the experience not traumatized, as the sociologists worried, but reinvented. They were less apt to be understood as victims of migration experiences and more likely to be masters of their own fate. As historians told it, migration in earlier centuries had been an empowering experience, key to the making of America.

Journalism and Mass Circulation

Scholars nowadays understand that the production of an idea or text is separate from its circulation and impact, that if a great theory remains unread it is probably not very great at all in its own time, or at least that there are differences between ideas that circulate widely and those that do not. Journalism, popular fiction, and the entertainment media are key mechanisms of circulation; they are capable of spreading ideas both to broad audiences and to influential elites and also are often responsible for translating complex ideas into new forms, changing them in the process. Journalism (broadly defined) and academic research have long been paired in this way. Some of the founding scholars in the fields of sociology, political science, and economics worked as newspapermen, a prime example being Robert Park, the leader of the University of Chicago's famous Sociology Department. Park had earlier spent eleven years as a newspaper reporter and editor and, as Rolf Lindner argues, his Chicago brand of sociology developed a set of methods and orientations that reflected a commitment to "urban reportage."[15]

It was a two-way relationship. Journalists monitored key areas of social science, harvesting compelling stories and issues. They in turn flagged some of the issues in ways that set agendas for researchers. A good example is the circulation that began with Paul Taylor, the labor economist at Berkeley who discovered and named the Dust Bowl migration. His article in *Survey Graphic*, "Again the Covered Wagon" (1935), noted the movement into California of thousands of "drought refugees" looking for work in the cotton fields of San Joaquin Valley.[16] Magazines and newspapers jumped on the story, attracted by and replicating Taylor's dramatically contrasting metaphors: refugee and covered-wagon pioneer. That in turn opened the door for dozens of research projects, including a massive one by the Bureau of Agricultural Economics that surveyed the children of recent migrants in thousands of schools in California. Congress got into the act, establishing the Tolan Committee in 1939 to investigate "the Interstate Migration of Destitute Citizens," accompanied by more funding, more studies, more journalism, and one extraordinary novel that worked the tension between refugee and covered wagon into one of the classics of American literature. The road to *The Grapes of Wrath* had begun with Paul Taylor and gone back and forth between the linked worlds of social science, history, and journalism.

While journalists in the 1930s and early 1940s had interacted readily with social scientists studying the poverty migrations of the Depression and the defense migrations of the war years, it was not until the 1950s that other aspects of social-science-based migration research began to move out of the academy and into journalism and popular discussion. Before then migration was almost always journalistically framed as a social problem, linked either to poverty, the decline of farming, or challenging impacts on cities. In the 1950s and 1960s the new demographic data helped fuel a surge of popular interest in the high rates of mobility among all sorts of Americans and in the social and psychological implications of relocation. We can see the subject shift in figure 12.5, which shows the changing distribution of articles catalogued under three subcategories of migration in the *Readers' Guide*: (1) black migration, (2) migrant labor, and (3) the more general categories of "mobility," including the subject terms "moving" and "internal migration." Notice that not until the 1950s did the general "mobility" categories become important. Much of what was written in the 1930s and 1940s was indexed under the label "migrant labor" and included articles on Okies, farm workers, other itinerant workers, and the defense migrants of the Second World War.

The ups and downs of "black migration" articles are revealing. Initially

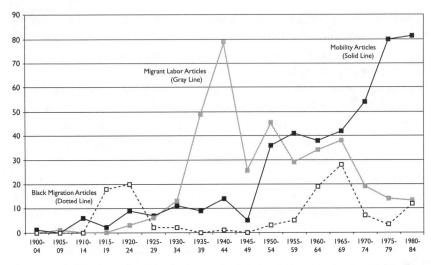

Figure 12.5 Subthemes of articles on internal migration indexed by *Readers' Guide*, 1900–1984

dominating magazine publishing about internal migration during the First World War and the early 1920s, this subject heading almost disappears between the 1930s and the late 1950s. This does not mean that journalists had stopped writing about black migrants, but it does indicate a different way of writing and indexing that reflects the influence of sociological thinking.[17] Sociological research in the 1930s and 1940s deemphasized race, particularly in connection with migration. African Americans were understood to be experiencing a transition from peasantry, as were white farm-to-city migrants. This perspective seems to have influenced journalism. Instead of writing directly about the second Great Migration that began during the Second World War and had such powerful effects on cities across the North and West, magazines usually folded black migrants into stories about "defense migrants," covering white migrants as well, often in ways that deemphasized racial differences. Typical headlines in the 1940s include "Whither the Migrants" (*Newsweek*), "Strangers in Town" (*Survey*), and "Rolling Tide of War Migrants" (*New York Times Magazine*). It was not until the late 1950s, as civil rights struggles heated up, that stories on black migration returned to the magazine headlines. Here are some from 1958, the last two prompted by a short-lived segregationist proposal to deport blacks who demanded civil rights: "Race Problem Moves North" (*U.S. News and World Report*), "Far Flowing Negro Tide" (*Newsweek*), "Senator Russell Wants Negroes to Move" (*U.S. News and World Report*), and "Tickets for Negroes?" (*Newsweek*).

A new category of postwar journalism may be discerned from the headlines of other articles from 1958, indexed under the generic headings of "mobility," "moving," and "internal migration":

— Americans on the Move to New Jobs, New Places (*Life*)
— 40 Million on the Move (*American Home*)
— Don't Move Until You Read This (*Good Housekeeping*)
— If You Have to Move (*House and Garden*)
— Child in a New Neighborhood (*New York Times Magazine*)
— New Family in Town (*McCall's*).

This second batch of articles reveals a new fascination with demographic numbers that in the postwar years were widely reported in the news media and convinced Americans that their society has become highly and uniquely mobile. Second, they reveal an interest in the mobility of "ordinary" white families and their movement from cities to suburbs and from east to west. Third, and most important, they reveal the dimension that sustained much of the popular attention to migration throughout the middle twentieth century: a fascination with its psychological implications.

The Dislocated American

Migration studies attracted media attention in part because of perceived social problems, in part because of exciting new data, but also in part because of a set of exciting ideas—theories that were captivating in their logic and implications. Among these ideas were the social adjustment and social dislocation theories mentioned earlier, which were part of a larger fascination with the insights of social psychology. In *The Romance of American Psychology* Ellen Herman explores how in the decades following the Second World War, psychological theory and psychological experts "carved out a progressively larger sphere of social influence" that extended through many academic disciplines and policy arenas, and that fundamentally reshaped discourse and culture, seeping "into virtually every facet of existence."[18] For educated Americans of the postwar generation, social psychology offered an entrancing theory of the self and society—an under-the-hood glimpse into the social mechanisms that supposedly structured personal development and into the psychological mechanisms that supposedly structured social problems. Fascination with the insights of social psychology animated any number of public debates and media crusades in the postwar period, including campaigns against racism, bigotry, and the "authoritarian personality." Migration was one of the arenas where these debates and crusades were played out, and an important one, as journalists and novelists joined sociologists and psychologists in understanding migration as a disorienting process that produced stressful adjustments at a personal and social level.

Social and psychological adjustment theories had been crossing over into migration journalism and popular literature for some time by the 1940s, showing up in the way subjects were framed and in the circulation of key terms like "uprooted," "social disorganization," and "marginal man." The popularizers often misunderstood the theory and used it selectively and in ways that bothered the experts, and much of what they were borrowing and translating was considered out of date by social scientists. It is best to think of the process not as a close translation of ideas but as a mediation that transformed ideas even as it gave them much wider circulation and potentially great potency. This circulation and mediation can be seen in many of the migration novels of the day, including such classics as Richard Wright's *Native Son*, in which the author tried to incorporate migration theory of the Chicago sociologists. His main character, Bigger Thomas, is a migrant disoriented by the transition from rural community to bewildering big city, and doubly marginalized because of his race. Ralph Ellison's *Invisible Man* also takes key constructs from migration and marginalization theory and may have even owed its title to Park's well-traveled concept of the marginal man. Other borrowings are evident in *Go Tell It on a Mountain* by James Baldwin and *The Dollmaker* (1954), Harriett Arnow's novel about a white Appalachian family struggling and failing in Detroit.[19]

These books were part of a broader system of popularization that included journalism and entertainment media. We may not recognize the finer points of academic theory in the proliferation of comedic films, television situation comedies, and popular songs that focused on dislocated Americans in the era of internal migration, many of which used the old trope of the rube in the city to achieve their laughs. But it is no coincidence that some of the most popular entertainment productions of the time featured migrants and their adjustment travails—from *Amos 'n' Andy* on radio in the 1930s, through *The Beverly Hillbillies*, the most popular television show of the 1960s, to country music's endless songs about wanderers and homesickness. What animated all of this was a concern with dislocation, uprooting, and being out of place that had been elevated out of academic publishing and into public discourse. The moving American was the dislocated American, engaging in a complicated personal transition. This was the kernel of the social theory that artists, journalists, and even television producers seized upon in the great age of migration writing. Bigger Thomas was out of place. The Joads were out of place. *The*

Real McCoys and *The Beverly Hillbillies* were out of place. And all of this out-of-placeness was thought to be of great consequence.[20]

Vance Packard brought the dislocated American conversation to a point of culminating clarity when he published *A Nation of Strangers* in 1972. Throughout his career Packard profited from the interaction between academia and journalism. The most famous of the tribe of journalists who read, reinterpreted, and popularized the work of social scientists, Packard was emblematic of the way ideas moved across the academic barrier. His biographer Daniel Horowitz details the tensions in the relationship. As he cranked out a sequence of bestselling books of social criticism starting with *The Hidden Persuaders* (1957), Packard faced harsh reviews from academics who accused him of sensationalizing, oversimplifying, and otherwise misusing research and who resented his ability to reach audiences far larger than their own.[21] Packard's books fed the popular fascination with social psychology even as he plundered select bits of academic research. Whether he was writing about the anxious middle class (*The Status Seekers*), the culture of affluence and corporate planned obsolescence (*The Waste Makers*), or threats to privacy and individuality posed by government and corporate surveillance (*The Naked Society*), his books climbed the bestseller lists by identifying disturbing trends and issues in contemporary life and delivering a mix of sharp criticism and what readers took to be up-to-date research.

In 1968 Packard turned his attention to recent reports and data on internal migration, especially the statistic that close to forty million Americans, 19 percent of the population, changed residence each year. Four years later *A Nation of Strangers* appeared with the fanfare that usually greeted his books and immediately made the nonfiction bestseller list of the *New York Times*, reaching the number six spot and remaining in the top ten for eight weeks.[22] The book focused on what Packard took to be historically high rates of mobility while working with notions of the dislocated American that he culled selectively from social adjustment and mental health studies. Packard's argument was that excess mobility, often in service to corporations that casually shift jobs and people from place to place, disrupts lives and communities, creating a rootless and disoriented people, a nation of strangers.

While friendly articles in the *Ladies' Home Journal* and some other popular venues helped to promote the book, sociologists hammered *A Nation of Strangers* and its author.[23] The *American Journal of Sociology* invited three scholars to evaluate the book in a special symposium. Amos Hawley, Claude Fischer, and Brian Berry were unanimous in dismissing its conclusions, its research, and especially its core logic, pointing out that there was no reason to believe that rates of mobility were higher than they had been in the past, nor that "because we are mobile . . . we are a 'nation of strangers.'" In voicing these criticisms they implicitly distanced themselves from the body of scholarly literature that Packard and other journalists had been highlighting. He had borrowed his thesis of the dislocated American from decades of sociological research, albeit while taking it out of context, twisting some of its meanings, and milking its alarmist potentials—all of which were standard consequences of the commingling of journalism and social science.[24]

George Pierson's *The Moving American* achieved nowhere near the sales of Packard's book but suffered the same sort of criticism at the hands of academic reviewers, who found it underresearched, inconsistent in argument, and out of date. Pierson, the Yale historian, had been working on this book for years, probably decades. *The Moving American*, clearly intended for a general audience, is written in a breezy style and consists of discrete essays that do not readily cohere, some of them barely revised versions of articles that Pierson had been publishing since the early 1940s. He shares Packard's view that excess mobility can be dangerous. But the Turnerian American dominates as he moves back into history, showing the migrant as a pioneer, a builder, the quintessential American. Rowland Berthoff and William Gottesman were harsh in their reviews, ridiculing Pierson's attempt to fashion a new theory of migration (which he called the "M-factor") based on principles introduced by the demographers E. G. Ravenstein and Everett Lee. The reviewers were equally impatient with his research, noting that he ignored the work of social historians who for more than a decade had been revising understandings of eighteenth- and nineteenth-century mobility and community patterns and who no longer embraced the overly psychologized and monolithic concept of "American character."[25]

Both books stand as end-of-an-era markers, highlighting and summarizing perspectives that were still circulating outside the academy but were no longer fashionable inside. They also mark the end of a relationship that enabled some of the research to reach a broader public, helping a generation of Americans to see mobility as a subject of interest and of some importance.

Losing Public Attention

Since the 1970s public awareness of moving Americans has faded. News media and other popular venues have been less eager than before to circulate information about mobility. We no longer see magazine stories like those that ran in 1958 about moving day, strangers in town, or millions of Americans changing residence or leaving cities. In part this reflects changes in migration patterns. Americans have become less mobile since the early 1970s. Each year from 1948, when the Census Bureau began its Current Population Survey, until 1970, roughly 19 percent of Americans would report a change of residence in the previous twelve months. Rates then began a slow decline, falling to an average of 17 percent moving per year in the 1980s, 16 percent in the 1990s, and 14 percent since 2000, dropping to 11.9 percent in the recession year of 2008.[26]

While domestic mobility has slowed, journalists have refocused their attention on the dramatically increased volume of cross-border immigration. The Immigration Reform Act of 1965 was almost ten years old before magazines began to catch on. The "boat people," refugees from Vietnam, Cuba, and Haiti, were often in the headlines in the 1970s, but concern about illegal immigration and curiosity about the new demography of immigration, largely from Asian and Latin American countries, soon followed. A set of headlines from *U.S. News and World Report* suggests the scope of magazine coverage in the 1970s:

— Now a Growing Surge of Immigrants from Asia (1973)
— How Millions of Illegal Aliens Sneak into U.S. (1974)
— Rising Tide of Immigrants to U.S. (1975)
— Latest Wave of Immigrants Brings New Problems to U.S. (1976)
— U.S. Opens Its Doors to the Floating Refugees" (1977)
— Still a Land of Refuge (1979)
— Now It's Haiti's Boat People Coming in a Flood (1979).

Then in the 1980s media attention soared. *Readers' Guide Retrospective* identifies almost as many magazine articles on immigration in the first three years of the 1980s (131) as had been printed in the two previous decades combined (160).[27]

Journalists did continue to write about certain internal migration sequences, especially those involving rearrangements of political power and race. The Sunbelt migration became a story in the late 1970s and gained importance through the 1980s and early 1990s, as the South reversed its historic role as a population-sending region and started to pull millions of jobs and people out of the Northeast and Midwest. Gentrification migrations also earned headlines in the same period, as whites moved back into the big cities, raising property values, transforming urban spaces, and changing balances of power within the urban electorate. There was some attention to the movement of black families, focusing both on their relocation from central cities into the suburbs and also on the return migration of African Americans to the South, which journalists highlighted as one of the ironic effects of the Sunbelt surge.[28]

But there have been noticeable differences in the tone as well as the volume of internal migration journalism since the mid-1970s. Population movements within the United States are reported without much sense of urgency, mostly as curious phenomena that readers may find interesting. When significance attaches to these demographic changes, it is primarily on the level of politics and the economy. The Sunbelt shift is taken to be important for the regions that were losing and gaining jobs, people, and voting power. What has been missing is the tense personal and social dimension that animated journalism during the age of internal migration. The issues of adjustment are no longer at the center or often even part of the story. The moving American is no longer the dislocated American. Moving is now taken to be only mildly interesting on both a personal and social level. People move. So what?

The "so what" in earlier decades had come from sociological and psychological theory, and its absence from current journalism reveals an important shift in American intellectual life. The passing of the age of big sociological theory and particularly social psychology theory has registered in American journalism since the 1970s. It has changed the way Americans understand migration and much more. Academics now work either with smaller theories that lack the power to interest journalists or are so complex and unwieldy (as with poststructuralism of various kinds) that reporters ignore them. Social science research still finds its way into newspapers and magazines, but journalists seem more interested in new data than in the analysis that scholars develop. Especially since the 1980s, it seems that social research finds fewer outlets in the popular media and that the walls between academic knowledge and public knowledge have grown thicker.[29]

Does it matter that migration research no long seems to circulate and that important geographic mobility patterns remain unacknowledged in major media, and thus are much less visible to broader publics than they would have been thirty or forty years ago? It certainly matters to those who do migration research and to funding agencies. But it also has consequences for moving Americans and for all Americans.

Immigration politics have almost certainly been affected by the new isolation of academic research. Journalists have paid scant attention to the studies of new immigrants produced by sociologists, demographers, and anthropologists. Newspapers will occasionally quote economists who debate whether immigration produces economic growth or drains public resources, but anything more complex is ignored. This includes work like Douglass Massey's well-documented finding that militarized borders have an unintended consequence, turning temporary illegal immigrants into permanent illegal immigrants who are afraid to go home because they will not be able to return.

Despite the obvious relevance to current policy debates, the mass media have failed to expose and explore this and other research.[30]

On the other hand, the lowered lighting that now accompanies some migrations may have positive consequences. Many of the newer patterns of internal migration would have attracted journalistic attention, and with it heightened controversy, a generation ago. The black families who have been moving steadily out of central cities and into what had been largely white neighborhoods; the Latino families moving into what had been black neighborhoods as well as white neighborhoods; the gay and lesbian redistributions—all of these fundamental rearrangements of cities and suburbs have been taking place without the kind of media attention that in the mid-twentieth century might have ramped up anxieties.

The media spotlight is dimmer now; journalists are writing less about domestic migration, and this means that most Americans are thinking less about who is moving and what moving means. The mobility itself continues, at rates that are still high in comparison with those in many other societies. In most years close to forty million Americans change residences, moving short distances or long distances, sometimes radically shifting personal contexts, sometimes rearranging neighborhoods or larger communities where they settle. That we are no longer paying attention to internal migration does not alter the basic patterns of movement and settlement, but it does change some of the meanings and interactions.

Notes

1 Vance Packard, *A Nation of Strangers* (New York: McKay, 1972). On Packard see Daniel Horowitz, *Vance Packard and American Social Criticism* (Chapel Hill: University of North Carolina Press, 1994).

2 George W. Pierson, *The Moving American* (New York: Alfred A. Knopf, 1973).

3 See for more detail James N. Gregory, *The Southern Diaspora: How the Great Migrations of Black and White Southerners Transformed America* (Chapel Hill: University of North Carolina Press, 2005); Alex Morrow, "Studying the 'Problem' of Migrant Labor: Social Science, Transient Workers, and the Depression," unpublished paper, Pacific Coast Branch American Historical Association meeting, August 28, 2006; Carol H. Weiss and Eleanor Singer, *Reporting of Social Science in the National Media* (New York: Russell Sage, 1988); Alice O'Connor, *Poverty Knowledge: Social Science, Social Policy, and the Poor in Twentieth-Century America* (Princeton: Princeton University Press, 2001).

4 Farah Jasmine Griffin, *"Who Set You Flowin'": The African-American Migration Narrative* (New York: Oxford University Press, 1995); Lawrence R. Rodgers, *Canaan Bound: The African-American Great Migration Novel* (Urbana: University of Illinois

Press, 1997); Erin Royston Battat, "Literature, Social Science, and the Development of American Migration Narratives in the Depression Era," *Literature Compass* 4, no. 3 (2007), 539–51.

5 Compiled from *H. W. Wilson Databases: Readers' Guide Retrospective* (April 28, 2006). The internal migration category is a combination of the following subject headings: "Migration, internal," "migrant labor," "blacks/migration," "moving," "social mobility." I edited the results, eliminating scholarly journals and articles that did not appear to be related to geographic mobility in the United States. The database ends in 1982. To maintain the five-year interval I have extrapolated the period 1980–84.

6 While the *Readers' Guide* indexes articles by subject headings, I am relying on keywords that appear in titles or abstracts in the *JSTOR Archive*: versions of "immigrant," "emigrant," "immigration," "emigration," "migrant," "migration," "mobility," "adjustment," "migratory," "floating," "resettlement." I have edited the output, sometimes moving items from the immigration to internal migration or vice versa after reading the abstract.

7 Daniel O. Price and Melanie M. Sikes, *Rural-Urban Migration Research in the United States: An Annotated Bibliography and Synthesis* (Washington: National Institute of Child Health and Human Development, 1974).

8 *JSTOR* catalogues 158 history journals. I included only those that focus substantially on U.S. history. Some important journals are not part of *JSTOR*, including the *Journal of American Ethnic History*, which began in 1975, and *Journal of Social History*, which began in 1967. Keywords used were the same as above, with the addition of variants of "settler" and "pioneer."

9 Examining this literature are Frank Tobias Higbie, *Indispensable Outcasts: Hobo Workers and Community in the American Midwest, 1880–1930* (Urbana: University of Illinois Press, 2003); Morrow, "Studying the 'Problem' of Migrant Labor"; Kenneth Kusmer, *Down and Out on the Road: The Homeless in American History* (New York: Oxford University Press, 2002).

10 Jennifer Platt, *A History of Sociological Research Methods in America, 1920–1960* (New York: Cambridge University Press, 1996), 142–54; Dorothy Swaine Thomas, *Research Memorandum on Migration Differentials* (New York: Social Science Research Council, 1938).

11 *Population Redistribution and Economic Growth: United States, 1870–1950*, prepared under the direction of Simon Kuznets and Dorothy Swaine Thomas (Philadelphia: American Philosophical Society, 1957–64); Platt, *A History of Sociological Research Methods in America*, 150–58; Margo J. Anderson, *The American Census: A Social History* (New Haven: Yale University Press, 1988).

12 Seminal works include W. I. Thomas and Florian Znaniecki, *The Polish Peasant in Europe and America* (New York: Alfred A. Knopf, 1927); and Robert Ezra Park, "Human Migration and the Marginal Man," *Race and Culture* (Glencoe, Ill.: Free Press, 1950). On the influence see Fred H. Matthews, *Quest for an American Sociology: Robert Park and the Chicago School* (Montreal: McGill-Queens University Press, 1977).

13 More than two hundred urban adjustment studies are listed in Price and Sikes, *Rural-Urban Migration Research*.

14 Examples from WorldCat (OCLC): Nellis Maynard Crouse, *Causes of the Great Migration* (1932); Edwin Clarence Guillet, *The Great Migration: The Atlantic Crossing by Sailing-Ship since 1770* (1937); Edmond S. Morgan, "Provisions for the Great Migration," *New England Quarterly*, March 1939; Philip Parrish II, *The Great Migration: 1842* (1943); Allen French, *Charles I and the Puritan Upheaval: A Study of the Causes of the Great Migration* (1955). The only book in WorldCat to use the label in reference to African Americans before 1960 is William Morgan Markoe, *A Great Migration* (1924). Black journalists like Markoe began using the term in the 1920s. By the 1940s it was appearing in the social science literature in reference to African American migration.

15 Rolf Lindner, *The Reportage of Urban Culture: Robert Park and the Chicago School*, trans. Adrian Morris (New York: Cambridge University Press, 1996).

16 See also James N. Gregory, *American Exodus: The Dust Bowl Migration and Okie Culture in California* (New York: Oxford University Press, 1989), 80–113.

17 Gregory, *The Southern Diaspora*, 59–79.

18 Ellen Herman, *The Romance of American Psychology: Political Culture in the Age of Experts* (Berkeley: University of California Press, 1995), 2–3.

19 Carla Cappetti, *Writing Chicago: Modernism, Ethnography, and the Novel* (New York: Columbia University Press, 1993).

20 For more detail on comedic representations of hillbillies and black southerners see Gregory, *The Southern Diaspora*, 54–79; Anthony Hawkins, *Hillbilly: A Cultural History of an American Icon* (New York: Oxford University Press, 2004).

21 Horowitz, *Vance Packard*, esp. 185–95.

22 Adult *New York Times* bestseller lists for 1972, Hawes Publications, http://www.hawes.com (July 24, 2009).

23 "A Nation of Strangers," *Ladies' Home Journal*, September 1972, 104.

24 *American Journal of Sociology* 79 (July 1973), 165–75.

25 Rowland Berthoff review: *Journal of American History* 60 (December 1973), 767–68; William Gottesman review: *American Historical Review* 79, no. 1 (1974), 213–14.

26 "Current Population Survey: Annual Geographical Mobility Rates, by Type of Movement, 1947–2008," U.S. Bureau of the Census, http://www.census.gov (August 8, 2009). On historic migration rates see Larry E. Long, *Migration and Residential Mobility in the United States* (New York: Russell Sage, 1988).

27 Compiled from *H. W. Wilson Databases: Readers' Guide Retrospective* (April 28, 2006).

28 I have tracked these subjects in the annual editions of *Readers' Guide to Periodical Literature*.

29 Weiss and Singer, *Reporting of Social Science in the National Media*, 175–207, did not find major changes in the volume of news reporting of social science research between 1970 and 1982. Other reports stress declining policy access without looking at journalism: David L. Featherman and Maris A. Vinovskis, eds., *Social Science and*

Policy-making: A Search for Relevance in the Twentieth Century (Ann Arbor: University of Michigan Press, 2001); Charles E. Lindblom and David K. Cohen, *Usable Knowledge: Social Science and Social Problem Solving* (New Haven: Yale University Press, 1979); Andrew Rich, *Think Tanks, Public Policy, and the Politics of Expertise* (New York: Cambridge University Press, 2004).

30 Massey has reported this study in numerous publications, most comprehensively in an anthology edited with Jorge Durand, *Crossing the Border: Research from the Mexican Migration Project* (New York: Russell Sage, 2004).

CHAPTER THIRTEEN

The Black Experience in Canada Revisited

Sarah-Jane (Saje) Mathieu

Blacks are a constitutive population in Canada, having been there from the earliest European contact. The first blacks in New France, as present-day Quebec and Nova Scotia were then known, were interpreters and negotiators for French and Portuguese colonists. These same European settlers introduced indentured and enslaved Africans to New France, an important historical fact often overlooked by Canadian historians. In truth, slavery played a critical role in black people's decisions to either flee Canada or, once England abolished the institution in 1833, to turn to British North America as a haven from American enslavement. Consequently, as of the eighteenth century, urgent need for political asylum consistently drove black migration to or from Canada, especially with each new outbreak of war between Britain and the United States. The number of African Americans looking to Canada for shelter dramatically increased by the nineteenth century with the rise of Jim Crow, the legal and social exercise of white supremacy often violently reinforced.[1]

Ethnic cleansing, banishment, and lynching forced millions of African Americans out of the South, with many heading to Mexico, the Caribbean, Africa, and Canada. Their arrival inspired interesting—and at times disconcerting—debates in Canada about the desirability of a black citizenry, with many white Canadians calling for the exclusion of all African-descended migrants. Regardless of some white Canadians' objections, blacks continued pouring into the Dominion of Canada. As of the 1850s black migrants came as entrepreneurs, explorers, entertainers, laborers, farmers, transportation workers, and students. In other words, whether from the Caribbean, the United States, Europe, or Africa, black migrants mirrored the aspirations and resolve of all other migrants desperate to eke out new lives in Canada. Blacks too were driven by wanderlust, a wish for self-rule, and the desire to play an important role in their new nation. Accordingly, their experiences reflect the full range of triumphs and tragedies of immigrant life.

Whatever their ultimate aspirations, once in Canada blacks faced the reality that many white Canadians often held conflicting stances about their belonging. For instance, white colonists called for more Africans, but only if they came as slaves. In Nova Scotia the arrival of black Loyalists and Jamaican Maroons was celebrated as relief from chronic labor shortages, but once those blacks stood up to white officials, the clamor for the extradition of black people back to Africa reached a fever pitch. So long as blacks came to Canada as domestics, porters, and entertainers, they had a place, but when those same migrants banded together as unionized workers and civil rights activists, Jim Crow reared its head in ever more aspects of Canadian life.

In the end, shaping and defining the black experience in Canada has always been at the heart of the challenge for African Canadians. Too often, whites in Canada vacillated between giving wide berth to blacks' exercise of freedom, only to quickly curtail those freedoms by citing blacks' lack of fitness for citizenship. From the seventeenth to the nineteenth centuries the mixed status of blacks—in some cases as slaves, free persons, war veterans, prisoners of war, or political asylum seekers—formed the core of the problem. Throughout the twentieth century Canada's black population increasingly demanded full citizenship rights and attacked practices like de facto segregation that undermined their sense of belonging. To be sure, continued black immigration complicated the meaning of black citizenship in Canada, particularly after the 1960s. By the century's close foreign-born blacks dramatically outnumbered Canadian ones, forcing a redefinition of blackness and revitalizing debates about race, place, and meaningful citizenship in twenty-first-century Canada.

From First Contact to Rebellion

New France colonists embraced slavery and repeatedly besought King Francis I for more traffic in African chattel and stronger legal defense of slaveholders' rights. Thus under both French and British rule, from 1534 to 1833, slavery held the force of law in present-day Canada. Yet despite three centuries of slaveholding tradition, most Canadians would unflinchingly insist that slavery never existed in their country.[2] Too many Canadian historians either ignore the topic of slavery or minimize its import to early settlers, stressing that slaves were either few in number or that they were spared the horrors of southern or West Indian exploitation. Whatever the rigors of everyday life for bondsmen, the fact remains that as chattel, even those in Canada were not free and were legally precluded from the most basic human rights. Whether in Kingston, Savannah, or Montreal, they could not marry, control the value of their labor, nor safeguard their children from abuse. Thus throughout North America enslaved black people remained painfully and dangerously victim to white whim. Against that background the national amnesia that absolves Canadians from their hand in North American slavery has very important implications for how we imagine a people's belonging, citizenship, and commitment to their nation.

Priests and profiteers were the earliest slavers in Canada. Clergymen, bureaucrats, and traders introduced Africans to New France for the singular purpose of serving as slaves. Unlike the Panis, First Nation People, who were mostly enslaved for fur trading and transportation, blacks worked as domestics and farmers, though at times the two groups toiled alongside each other. But if some Panis could escape back to their homes, Africans could not, aggravating their dislocation and despair, even when working and living conditions were less taxing than West Indian or American alternatives.[3] Slavery became more firmly entrenched into law and practice in 1689, when Louis XIV endorsed the rapid development of both New France and the sale of slaves. The burgeoning economy, not as reliant on large agricultural pools of labor as the American colonies, never heavily depended on black slaves.[4] Those who could afford them profited from enslaved black workers in industries like fur trading, fishing, mining, logging, and farming.[5]

Just like their brethren along the Atlantic seaboard, blacks in Canada found creative ways of resisting enslavement. Rumor spread quickly among slaves that in some cases the promise of manumission in word carried as much weight as in deed. They tested the theory by leaving their slavers at a rate that alarmed colonial bureaucrats, who then pleaded with France for stronger *Code Noir* regulations, and got them by 1724.[6] Thus if early settlers practiced a haphazard commitment to slavery, by the eighteenth century they, like American and West Indian colonists, clamored for firmer slave laws by pointing to an intensification of the institution throughout North America.[7]

Most blacks in Canada called Montreal home until the American Revolutionary War of 1776. Faced with diminishing recruits and the possibility of defeat at the hands of rebels, desperate British commanders turned to enslaved African Americans. In the summer of 1775 the royal governor of Virginia issued a proclamation freeing any slave or indentured laborer who took up arms for the British. In Virginia alone an estimated two thousand African Americans responded to the governor's call to arms, ignoring slavers' death threats and making perfectly clear the cost they were willing to bear for freedom. Before long neighboring colonies appealed to their African American denizens, with

Sir Henry Clinton of New York issuing the Phillipsburg Proclamation in 1779, promising land, manumission, and protection to all blacks who crossed over to British lines.[8] As many as five thousand Black Loyalists—some free, others not—made their way to Canada, while others headed for the Caribbean, England, and other parts of Europe. The historians James Walker and Amani Whitfield have produced rich studies of black Loyalist communities, especially those in Nova Scotia, where 50 percent of war-driven migrants settled between 1783 and 1785.[9] Their arrival changed the status of blacks in Canada from a predominantly urban servant class based in Quebec and Montreal to a population who inhabited all points of Canada and worked in a broader range of pursuits, including farming.

African American émigrés established expatriate communities along the Canadian-American border from the Atlantic coast to Lake Huron and faced the same daily privations of farming life as other immigrants. Frustrated by British officials unwilling to deliver on their promise of land and provisions, black Loyalists did their best to coax crops from effectively barren lands. Further complicating matters, once in Canada black Loyalists often lived alongside white Loyalists, who had taken issue with American independence, not slavery itself. The arrival of Loyalist slave owners breathed new life—and institutional know-how—into Canada's flailing slave system. In Nova Scotia alone white Loyalists brought some two thousand black slaves with them and quickly put them to work clearing and planting their new lands. Accordingly, Upper Canada (present Ontario), Lower Canada (present Quebec), and the Maritimes saw the influx of pro-slavery white American Loyalists at the same time and into the same regions where formerly enslaved black Loyalists began testing the full range of their freedom.[10]

The Emancipation Era

The question of freedom, belonging, and citizenship for black migrants weighed heavily on Canadian minds by the late eighteenth century. While some white Canadians held slaves, especially in the Maritimes, by the 1790s slavery's legal and moral legitimacy was being questioned. To be clear, British North America came late to the region's debate over slavery. As of the 1770s New York, Massachusetts, Vermont, and Rhode Island had already adopted measures to limit or ban the trade in enslaved Africans.[11] White slaveholders in British North America increasingly worried that their days of profiting from the exploitation of unwaged labor were limited. Their fears proved well founded when courts in the 1790s began reversing or at least finding null and void the terms of the Treaty of Paris (1763) guaranteeing slavery in Canada.

Progress in the courts notwithstanding, by the 1790s many blacks in Canada tired of their tenuous station. Tensions were also rising between whites and blacks in densely populated counties in the Atlantic provinces, and even between many blacks themselves. By the time back-to-Africa plans surfaced in 1791, many blacks in Canada felt that they had nothing to lose by chasing their fortunes back across the Atlantic. For example, in 1792 the Englishman Thomas Clarkson, a devout abolitionist and Christian, persuaded approximately twelve hundred black Maritimers to emigrate to his West African colonist experiment in Sierra Leone. African Canadian settlers faced great hardships during their early days in Africa: recalcitrant cases of fever, lack of farming tools, uncleared lands, rampant corruption, and persistent food shortages—matched only by the problem of rotting food supplies—made life in Sierra Leone all the more grueling. Within six months nearly 60 percent of settlers in Freetown were either dead or dying.[12]

Soon after the departure of the émigrés for Sierra Leone, the Maritimes saw the influx of Maroons, rebels ousted from Jamaica and sent to a cold climate as a particularly harsh punishment for their political insurgency. They arrived in the summer of 1796 in time to fill the labor lacuna created by the departure of black migrants for Sierra Leone. Local British managers immediately put Maroons to work building the famed Citadel in Halifax, the city's fortress. What started as a relatively smooth transition for both Maroons and white Nova Scotians quickly soured. Complaints from Maroons and the superintendents sent to monitor them escalated through 1799, when talk of relocation to Sierra Leone surfaced again as a solution to the difficulties that blacks faced in fitting in. Whether Maroons wished for it or not, British administrators plotted their emigration in the summer of 1799, with the goal of removing all Maroons to West Africa. After paying their passage and equipping them with clothing and a few months of provisions, they left the Maroons to their own devices to prosper or perish in Sierra Leone. More than 90 percent of Jamaican Maroons in Nova Scotia were forced out of Canada in August 1800, their displacement driven by British political and economic expediency.[13]

Throughout their time in the Maritimes the British vacillated between treating the Maroons like free people and treating them like prisoners of war. The mixed management of blacks in Canada, partly free and largely not, was the product of a society in flux over the status of its black denizens. In the Atlantic provinces, where during the early nineteenth century blacks could be free persons, indentured, enslaved, or prisoners of war, the confusion becomes clear. The courts' piecemeal dismantling of slavery as of the 1790s did little to assuage local tensions or clarify the real status of blacks in Canada. The end of slavery in 1833, however, did radically transform blacks' standing.

Indifference more than wholesale disdain for slavery brought about the institution's end in British North America. That Canada bordered American free states further weakened slavery's footing: slaves could and regularly did escape in any number of directions south and west, voicing in the process the greatest condemnation of Canadian slavery.[14]

With slavery ended in British North America after 1834, Canada increasingly became home to a different type of black migrant: the fugitive slave, or Freedom Seeker. The distinction is important because before the 1830s blacks in Canada were either slaves, indentured workers, or war veterans (of 1776 and 1812). Veterans, whether black Loyalists, Maroons, or the Refugees of 1812, had earned their freedom through war service and thus were distinguished from other black migrants. For one thing, if necessary they were prepared to defend their interests by force.

Robin Winks posits that the rise in Canadian antagonism toward blacks during the nineteenth century directly coincides with the arrival of African Americans between about 1810 and the 1860s.[15] No longer chattel or symbols confirming their owners' wealth, blacks in Canada after emancipation increasingly became emblems of destitution, charges in need of guidance and council on the proper exercise of citizenship. Written off as childlike and unruly, African Americans who had successfully escaped to Canada were subjected to a tug of war between well-meaning if at times infantilizing abolitionists and those black Canadians determined not to see their experiment in free living unseated.

Of the two thousand refugees who came to Canada by 1814, more than 55 percent settled in the Atlantic provinces, with most boarding British ships in Georgia, North Carolina, Virginia, Maryland, and Louisiana.[16] New to the climate and the type of farming practices needed, the migrants of 1812 struggled under more setbacks than most could bear. Illness, especially smallpox, and death took many before their full taste of freedom. Others staked their claims with administrators appointed to care for them, not fully realizing that this aid would soon run out. By 1816 the lieutenant governor of Nova Scotia, Earl Dalhousie, for whom Halifax's prominent university is named, concluded that "little hope can be entertained of settling these people so as to provide for their families and wants. . . . Slaves by habit & education, no longer working under the dread of the lash, their idea of freedom is Idleness and they are altogether incapable of Industry."[17] Before long white Nova Scotians resuscitated calls for exile to Sierra Leone, the region's knee-jerk response to blacks who did not seamlessly fold into society.

African American refugees migrated from a variety of regions and plantation economies. They also came to Canada with a range of agricultural skills, but fewer artisanal crafts than their predecessors. Their labor was surely needed in the Maritimes, but less urgently than when the Maroons had arrived a generation earlier. Moreover, the migrants of 1812 were concentrated in Nova Scotia, while earlier black Loyalists had fanned out from Windsor to Cape Breton. Those who farmed fought crushing seasons and infestations. Even those white administrators less hostile to the refugees threw up their hands by 1815 and joined the chorus for extradition to Sierra Leone.[18]

Unlike earlier settlers who went to Sierra Leone, refugees were suspicious, believing among other things that they would simply be sold back into slavery either in the American South or worse, in the West Indies. That they would rather stay in Nova Scotia and starve to death, which many did, speaks volumes to the violence wrought on one's soul by slavery. That resolve also makes evident that these migrants, like the tens of thousands of Freedom Seekers who came during the mid-century, believed so strongly in their freedom that they were prepared to die for it. Refugees who refused to leave for Africa were most often labeled public charges and a tax on white Nova Scotians' purses and patience, perpetuating the notion that African-descended people were undesirable as would-be citizens. In other words, indifference to blacks under slavery turned to deep-seated racialized resentment by the 1830s, when newly freed African Canadians also in need of support during the transition from slavery were added to the numbers of refugees needing help.[19] Because refugees did not spread throughout the Atlantic region and because of their failed farming efforts, by the mid-nineteenth century they lived almost exclusively in Halifax and became ever more reliant on smaller employment options and shrinking alms. Accordingly, patterns of segregated housing and population distribution became entrenched in the region.[20]

Just as Maritimers struggled with what to do about their newly free black population, Upper and Lower Canada faced the same question, though there the blacks arriving were overwhelmingly Freedom Seekers from the United States. Scores of free African Americans headed for Canada during the antebellum era, worried that even northern free states like Ohio and New York could revert to slavery. Since the traffic in slaves from Africa had been cut off by 1807, at least legally, the price of slaves soared, as did the kidnapping of free blacks for sale south of the Mason-Dixon line. Fearing for their freedom and their lives, free African Americans—mostly artisans and other professionals—sold what they could and took shelter in Windsor, London, Toronto, Montreal, and Halifax, forming a highly politicized black expatriate community along the Canadian-American border. They formed Canada's abolitionist vanguard, working with whites who also opposed slavery. They quickly established a black press, *Voice of the Fugitive* and the *Provincial Freeman*, which gave voice to their abolitionist mission. The pages of Canada's early black press, as evidenced by the newspapers' very names, chronicled the lives of African Americans who made their way to Canada before the American Civil War.

Whatever their ultimate fate once there, enslaved African Americans braved harsh terrain, unforgiving weather, and death to reach Canada. To their aid came the Underground Railroad, a clandestine network of abolitionists, both black and white, determined to funnel as many African Americans as possible out of slavery. Escape favored the most healthy, young, resourceful, and steadfast, while geographic location also played a hand in who could even chart a path to freedom. The distance between Memphis and Montreal was obviously greater than from Baltimore to Quebec. Neither physical nor legal obstacles, however, could deaden the resolve to be free, and Canada's black press celebrated each successful escape into Canaan, as British North America came to be known among African Americans. The seductive myth of Canada as the Promised Land, publicized in the black and abolitionist press, conveniently coincided with emancipation, sweeping aside Canada's own legacy as a slave society from which just decades earlier enslaved blacks had sought sanctuary to New England and other northern American states.

Escape took on a fresh urgency for African Americans, particularly after passage of the Fugitive Slave Act of 1850. Whereas African Canadians on the run from their slavers in the eighteenth century operated largely on their own, during the nineteenth century African American Freedom Seekers had abolitionists working in their defense. Canadians refused to return Freedom Seekers to the United States, citing not only a healthy disdain for slavery but also a very real fear for runaway slaves' lives. That argument, frequently stressed in government and court records, most notably in the case of John Anderson in 1860, formed the legal foundation for Canada's twentieth-century refusal to extradite those charged in cases involving the death penalty.

The number of Freedom Seekers who came to Canada in mid-century is not clear, though estimates place them at up to forty thousand in Quebec and Ontario alone, certainly the largest rush of black political asylum seekers ever seen in the region.[21] While most folded easily into city life, others established all-black townships along Lake Ontario as racial utopian experiments.[22] These black townships predated by several decades those later seen in the Georgia Sea Islands, Tennessee, Arkansas, and Oklahoma. In all cases these black settlements were fueled by the same visions, which Americans called Reconstruction ideals but which in fact had taken shape earlier on Canadian soil: land ownership, suffrage, education, free religion, black enterprise and control of the economy, and freedom from white gaze. In Chatham, for example, Freedom Seekers found blacks who ran their own government and circulated their free thoughts in a black press that they owned. Likewise, they operated their own schools and managed their own black-owned businesses.[23]

Once Americans' tempers cooled in 1865, many of the African Americans who had sought political sanctuary in Canada returned to the United States. Some historians insist that all but a few of these black migrants returned by the 1870s. In reality many felt the inescapable pull of family drawing them back into what too often proved still dangerous territory for free-minded blacks. Like Mary Ann Shadd Cary, owner and editor of *Provincial Freeman*, who shuttled between the mid-Atlantic and Ontario, a large number of African Americans bounced between the border regions of Canada and the United States, leading lives on both sides of the international boundary.[24] From the 1870s on they increasingly led lives that defied borders, coming to Canada for work, to chase their fortunes in the West, for family, for travel, and for political shelter as the need arose. They did so, moreover, despite mounting racial tension during the twentieth century and without regard for Canada's hostile stance toward black immigrants.

Race in Post-emancipation Canada

Canadian historians contend that blacks left Canada en masse by the 1870s, setting off a nearly eighty-year period of virtually no inward migration. In actuality African Americans and West Indians migrated to Canada at consistent rates throughout this period, despite various measures to keep them out. The collapse of Reconstruction in 1877 and the institutionalization of Jim Crow by the 1890s made clear for many southern African Americans that conditions in the United States would worsen before they improved. When in 1896 Canada launched its western homesteading program, giving 160 acres of free land to would-be farmers, many African Americans sold their holdings and hopped a train for Winnipeg and points west. Blacks were not new to the Canadian West, however; as early as the 1850s a group of black Californians had set sail for British Columbia and established small but vibrant communities in Vancouver and Victoria.[25]

Blacks who migrated west at the beginning of the twentieth century did so largely to farm and established agrarian communities throughout Manitoba, Saskatchewan, and Alberta. Though the official number of African Americans coming between 1896 and 1914 would not exceed fifteen hundred, white Canadians, particularly those in the West, panicked over what one newspaper in Alberta proclaimed were "Negroes Swarming the West."[26] White Canadians warned of all kinds of calamities, including the rape of white women and the advent of lynchings to halt alleged assaults, should black migration go un-

checked. Indeed the Department of Immigration resolved that Canada be preserved as the "last white man's land."[27] The solutions advanced in the Canadian press included sequestering those blacks already in the country; the
mass deportation of African-descended people; the imposition of head taxes
on black migrants; or an outright ban on black immigration. Prime Minister
Wilfrid Laurier opted for the last, banning black immigration in 1911. Though
the edict was short lived, its central principle survived until the 1960s, so that
most black migrants trying to enter Canada ran headlong into border guards
determined to complicate or discourage their passage.[28]

In spite of federal resistance, black migrants came to Canada, in large part
because the Canadian Pacific Railway sought them out for their profitable
sleeping car service. The largest employer of blacks in Canada by the time of
the Great War, the railway industry came to define twentieth-century black
life. Within steps of any railway station in Canada's major cities were thriving
black communities. Indeed 60 percent of blacks in Canada lived in cities by
1921, with Quebec (80 percent) and Manitoba (88 percent) the provinces with
the highest percentages of urban blacks. Within only two decades Montreal's
black population grew by 49 percent, Winnipeg's swelled by 96 percent.[29] Just
as American cities like Philadelphia, Cleveland, Chicago, and Detroit saw a
dramatic increase in their black populations thanks to the Great Migration,
Canada registered a new wave of migrants as African Americans poured into
every major Canadian city looking for work and safe harbor from Jim Crow.[30]
Still, at mid-century Canada's black population remained quite small, never
exceeding twenty thousand, and young, with more than half under the age of
twenty-five in 1931.

The arrival of blacks from the United States and the Caribbean unnerved
many white Canadians, who after the First World War called for more separation of the races. White Canadians and their government insisted that blacks
were ill-suited for Canada's cold weather, making them "climatically unsuit-
able" for citizenship, ignoring that African Canadians had already been in the
country for three centuries.[31] In a letter to W. E. B. Du Bois publicized in the
Crisis, bureaucrats from the Canadian Department of Immigration emphasized "that it is not the policy at present of the Government to encourage the
settlement of coloured people in Canada, as it is believed that the climate and
other conditions of this country are not . . . congenial to coloured people."[32]
Because they were highly urbanized, blacks came to embody Canadians' anxieties about the city's corrupting influences—in this case drugs, alcohol, sex,
and jazz.[33]

During the interwar years Canada moved ever closer to the de facto segregation exercised in most of the American North and West. Where Canadi-

ans had flirted with segregation before the First World War, especially in the Maritimes, after the war "white-only" signs adorned many storefront windows across Canada. Blacks who wished to see a movie, play, or concert were cordoned off in separate seating sections, whose names, likes "crow's nest" or "monkey cage," made clear segregation's dehumanizing mission. In Nova Scotia and Ontario black children sometimes attended segregated schools. Meanwhile shops in Montreal and Toronto refused black applicants for employment. Throughout the first half of the twentieth century white railroaders threatened strikes unless black sleeping car porters were Jim Crowed into separate contracts. In Halifax orphanages segregated white and black children and made sure that Jim Crow ruled over the dead too by keeping cemeteries racially divided.[34]

Race, Rights, and Reform in the Postwar Era

Black Canadians spent the interwar years much like everyone else: enjoying the good times and bracing themselves during tough ones. The Great Depression hit blacks especially hard because most worked in a single industry—transportation for men, domestic work for women—and were excluded from other lucrative options.[35] The Second World War resuscitated hope that with military service abroad, blacks could gain full citizenship rights. African Canadian veterans returned more committed than ever to advancing civil rights and working transnationally to do so. That renewed approach to dismantling Jim Crow was witnessed in the Supreme Court case of *Christie v. York* (1940), the radicalized tenure of African Canadian newspapers like the *Clarion*, and civil rights actions like the lunch counter sit-ins in Ontario in 1949.[36] Throughout the 1950s blacks in Canada exchanged ideas and strategies with African Americans mounting an assault on Jim Crow and Antilleans casting off imperial rule. In other words, freedom and human rights movements swept up blacks from Alberta to Alabama and Antigua. While Americans defined their reforms as a civil rights movement, Canadians—white and black—marshaled the language of human rights when dismantling discriminatory practices in housing, education, labor, immigration, and leisure. The *Bill of Rights* (1960) and the *Immigration Act* (1967) set new terms for Canadian citizenship and forced open the country's borders to populations previously dismissed as undesirable: Asians, Latin Americans, and African-descended people.

Immigration typified the black experience in Canada during the second half of the twentieth century. While African Americans trained their attention on freedom movements and confronting the Vietnam War, blacks in Canada approached immigration reform with a fresh urgency after the 1950s, especially once decolonization gained speed across the British Empire. Black migration during the 1960s and 1970s reached numbers never before seen in Canada and produced important shifts in the makeup and definition of blackness in the latter half of the twentieth century. Until the 1960s blacks in Canada had been largely born there, but by the 1980s most Canadians imagined blacks as people from an exotic elsewhere; whitewashing blacks from Canadian history helped fuel this popular perception. Indeed, the definition of blackness changed after the 1980s: whereas during the 1930s 80 percent of blacks in Canada were Canadian-born, by 1981 85 percent of blacks were foreign-born. Most white Canadians erroneously interpreted that transformation as meaning that black people were altogether new to the country. Never larger than 1 percent of the total population before the 1980s, the black population in Canada doubled within a very short time, almost singularly because of immigration. Between 1951 and 1961 Canada's black population grew by 56 percent, and between 1981 and 2001 it nearly tripled once again, from 239,500 to 662,200.[37]

Between the 1960s and the 1980s Jamaicans became Canada's largest black ethnic group, accounting for 30 to 40 percent of all black immigrants; during the 1970s and 1980s Haitians made up the second-largest black ethnic group, though they almost exclusively settled in French-speaking Quebec. During the closing decades of the twentieth century more Africans arrived, especially Somalis and Ethiopians, infusing a linguistic, cultural, and religious diversity into Canada's black citizenry. Whereas before 1961 African migrants accounted for only 1 percent of blacks in Canada, that figure rose to 48 percent between 1991 and 2001.[38] In all cases children accounted for an important portion of this migration, approximately 30 percent in 2001, making blacks in Canada a younger population than the population as a whole, of which 19 percent were children.

That so many blacks in Canada are below the age of twenty-five is demographically very important, especially since various trends indicate that some black constituencies, as in the United States, show early signs of distress. According to the Canadian census (2001) 46 percent of black children under the age of fifteen lived with only one parent, usually their mother, compared to 18 percent of other Canadian children. Given that women, particularly black ones, consistently earn less than their white counterparts, the likelihood that black children grow up in poverty is decidedly increased. In fact the 2001 census confirmed that 44 percent of black children lived in low-income households, compared to 19 percent of other Canadian children. Where black children grow up greatly informs their social mobility as well. With 47 percent of

African Canadians residing in Toronto, Canada's most expensive city, limited funds stretch even less far.[39] The gap in social standing is alarming considering that during the mid-twentieth century blacks in Canada had made steady strides toward the middle class, with many early migrants heading to university for professional degrees. Their children, however, have had less success in maintaining their middle-class footing. At the beginning of the twenty-first century blacks in Canada still pointed to discrimination in housing and employment as their most urgent concerns, making clear that blacks' quest for full citizenship rights remains a work in progress.

Conclusion

Throughout their four centuries in Canada—whether as slaves, indentured workers, war veterans, Freedom Seekers, farmers, political asylum seekers, or immigrants—blacks in Canada have been on an indefatigable pursuit of full citizenship rights and a sense of belonging. That quest has sparked important debates about the desirability and fitness of African-descended people as citizens. Without a doubt white Canadians have always been more comfortable with the idea of a black servant class; yet when blacks turned to Canada with clearly defined political expectations, many white Canadians voiced ever-mounting reservations. More often than not they pointed to blacks as a problem population, either unable to assimilate the principles of democracy and citizenship or portending social blight. This proved true with black Loyalists demanding that British administrators deliver on their promises of freedom, land, and provisions. When sleeping car porters rallied around their union, and when African Canadians mobilized in defense of their rights, many white Canadians threw the weight of their support behind upholding de facto segregation in housing, employment, immigration legislation, education, and leisure. Nevertheless African Canadians joined forces with African Americans fighting violations of their civil rights and Antilleans shaking off centuries of imperial rule, delivering in the process an assault on white supremacy that spread across North America after the Second World War. By the 1960s blacks in Canada recorded real advancements, most importantly with an immigration act that lifted barriers to black migrants and forced a broader societal discussion about black belonging and citizenship.

For those migrants who began pouring into Canada from the Caribbean and Africa in the 1970s, a new round of challenges raises questions about how they too will fare in the twenty-first century. Given that a significant segment of the black population suffers from social and economic marginalization, the implications for the nation are both urgent and alarming. The twenty-first century will require a new rhetoric to bridge black populations that are often as multicultural and diverse as the country they call home.

Notes

1 I will use "African American" when referring to blacks born in the United States, and "African Canadian" for all blacks in Canada. "African" refers to people born on the continent, though they may be living in North America. Although Jim Crow is an American sociopolitical ideology, we witness its international application during the twentieth century.

2 Robin Winks, *Blacks in Canada: A History*, 2nd ed. (Montreal: McGill-Queen's University Press, 1997), ix–xv.

3 Marcel Trudel, *Dictionnaire des esclaves et de leurs propriétaires au Canada français* (Ville La Salle, Quebec: Hurtubise HMH, 1994).

4 Winks, *Blacks in Canada*, 16–18.

5 Ibid., 5.

6 The Treaty of Paris (1763) clarified the terms of slavery: Panis and blacks could be sold and held by colonists. The Imperial Act of 1790 expanded the institution further still by allowing immigrants to bring their chattel into New France duty free.

7 Winks, *Blacks in Canada*, 6–17.

8 Ira Berlin, *Many Thousands Gone: The First Two Centuries of Slavery in North America* (Cambridge: Harvard University Press, 2000), 295–305.

9 James Walker, *The Black Loyalists: The Search for a Promised Land in Nova Scotia and Sierra Leone, 1783–1870*, 2nd ed. (Toronto: University of Toronto Press, 1992); and Harvey Amani Whitfied, *Blacks on the Border: The Black Refugees in British North America, 1815–1860* (Montpelier: University of Vermont Press, 2006). After 1793, at least in Upper Canada, slave children became free at the age of twenty-five and their children, if born to an enslaved person under the age of twenty-five, were born free and could not be enslaved.

10 Walker, *Black Loyalists*; Winks, *Blacks in Canada*, 24–60.

11 Vermont, the first state to abolish slavery, did so in 1777.

12 Winks, *Blacks in Canada*, 70–80.

13 Ibid., 78–95. Children made up about 40 percent of the approximately 550 Jamaican Maroons banished to Sierra Leone.

14 Ibid., 252–56.

15 Ibid., 114–30.

16 Ibid., 114–41; Whitfied, *Blacks on the Border*, 43–62; George and Willene Hendrick, *Black Refugees in Canada: Accounts of Escape during the Era of Slavery* (Jefferson, N.C.: McFarland, 2010).

17 Winks, *Blacks in Canada*, 122. Dalhousie later served as governor general of British North America from 1820 to 1828.

18 Ibid., 122–34.

19 Ibid., 132–40.

20 Ibid., 39–40.

21 Daniel G. Hill, *The Freedom Seekers: Blacks in Early Canada* (Agincourt, Ont.: Book Society of Canada, 1981).

22 Winks, *Blacks in Canada*, 164; Benjamin Drew, ed., *Refugees from Slavery: Autobiographies of Fugitive Slaves in Canada* (Mineola, N.Y.: Dover, 2004); Samuel G. Howe, *The Refugees from Slavery in Canada West: Report to Freedmen's Inquiry Commission* (Manchester, N.H.: Ayer, 1969).

23 Winks, *Blacks in Canada*, 144–52.

24 Jane Rhodes, *Mary Ann Shadd Cary: The Black Press and Protest in the Nineteenth Century* (Bloomington: Indiana University Press, 1999); Whitfield, *Blacks on the Border*.

25 Crawford Kilian, *Go Do Some Great Things: The Black Pioneers of British Columbia*, 2nd ed. (Burnaby, B.C.: Commodore, 2008).

26 *Lethbridge Herald*, March 22, 1911.

27 Adam Shortt and Arthur Doughty, eds., *Canada and Its Provinces: A History of the Canadian People and Their Institutions by One Hundred Associates*, vol. 1, *Immigration by Races*, by William D. Scott (Toronto: Publisher's Association of Canada, 1914), 531.

28 Sarah-Jane Mathieu, *North of the Color Line: Migration and Black Resistance in Canada, 1870–1955* (Chapel Hill: University of North Carolina Press, 2010); Constance Backhouse, *Colour-Coded: A Legal History of Racism in Canada, 1900–1950*; Valerie Knowles, *Strangers at Our Gates: Canadian Immigration Policy, 1540–1997* (Toronto: Dundurn, 1997), 89–91.

29 *Census of Canada, 1911*, 370–71; *Census of Canada, 1921*, 722–36.

30 Steven Hahn, *A Nation under Our Feet: Black Political Struggles in the Rural South from Slavery to the Great Migration* (Cambridge: Harvard University Press, 2005), 465–71; Thomas Sugrue, *The Origins of the Urban Crisis: Race and Inequality in Postwar Detroit* (Princeton: Princeton University Press, 2005), 3–14.

31 According to the census of 1901, 63 percent of blacks in western Canada lived in the Yukon, no doubt drawn there years earlier by the Gold Rush. *Census of Canada 1901*, 392–405, 446–47.

32 F. C. Blair to W. E. B. Du Bois, 4–7 March 1911, Immigration Branch Records, RG76 v. 192, Library and Archives Canada.

33 Ida C. Greaves, *National Problems in Canada: The Negro in Canada* (Orillia, Ont.: Packet-Times, 1929), 70–74; Emily F. Murphy, *The Black Candle: Canada's First Book on Drug Abuse* (Toronto: Thomas Allen, 1922).

34 James Walker, *'Race,' Rights and the Law in the Supreme Court of Canada: Historical Case Studies* (Waterloo: Wilfrid Laurier University Press, 1998), 122–34; Sarah-Jane Mathieu, *North of the Color Line*.

35 Canadian railway companies began importing black railroaders as of the 1880s; see Immigration Branch Records, RG76-I-A-1, Library and Archives Canada. Immigration Branch records also indicate that the first program to import Caribbean domestic workers to Canada began in 1913, though it would gain greater appeal by the

1950s. Also see Winks, *Blacks in Canada*, 439–42; and Christiane Harzig, "The Movement of 100 Girls: 1950s Immigration Policy and the Market for Domestic Labour," *Zeitschrift für Kanada Studien* 36 (1999), 131–46.

36 Winks, *Blacks in Canada*, 432, 405–10; Backhouse, *Colour-Coded*, 254–55; Ross Lambertson, "The Dresden Story: Racism, Human Rights, and the Jewish Labour Committee of Canada," *Labour / Le travail* 47 (spring 2001), 43–82.

37 Anne Milan and Kelly Tan, *Blacks in Canada: A Long History*, Statistics Canada Catalogue 11-008, spring 2004, 3.

38 *Spotlight: Black Population*, Statistics Canada, http://www.statcan.gc.ca.

39 Milan and Tan, *Blacks in Canada*, 5–6.

CHAPTER FOURTEEN

Circumnavigating Controls

Transborder Migration of Asian-Origin Migrants
during the Period of Exclusion

Yukari Takai

On the morning of July 25, 1907, the British-owned steamship *Kumeric* arrived
at Vancouver from Honolulu carrying 1,177 Japanese—the largest number that
had been brought to this port from Hawai'i. Because their numbers far exceeded the capacity of Japanese boarding houses in Vancouver, eight hundred
were reported to have moved along the Frazer River to be camped at Steveston.
Local dailies in Vancouver and Victoria depicted the landing of the *Kumeric* as
the arrival of "the little brown men" who covered "the deck of the big steamer
... like a swarm of ants."[1]

At about the same time Charlie Sam in El Paso operated an illegal opium
and Chinese smuggling business along the southwestern border. Known as the
"mayor of Chinatown," Sam acted as a go-between for officials in El Paso and
local Chinese, for whom, whenever one was arrested, he would arrange bail.
U.S. Immigration officers would tease Sam about the Chinese he smuggled
north of the border each week, and Sam—a respectable, extremely friendly,
and sociable man who spoke impeccable English—would smile broadly.[2]

This chapter sheds light on the history of tens of thousands of Asian
laborers, farmers, lumber camp workers, fishermen, merchants, and students,
as well as a smaller number of wives and prostitutes, who traveled across the
Pacific to Canada, the United States, and Mexico, and then crossed the land
borders northward or southward during the so-called Exclusion Era from the
1880s to 1930s. Asian land-border migration occurred at a critical time, when
the formerly porous borders were gradually and selectively being closed on the
basis of the race, citizenship, class, and gender of those trying to cross. With
a series of laws and regulations, the three North American states, along with

some of the migrants' home governments, sought control of the hitherto little regulated travel of foreigners considered undesirable.

The enhanced state control notwithstanding, Asian men and women continued to move across the increasingly guarded land borders with or without help from third parties like Charlie Sam and transpacific transporters. The seemingly uncontrollable Asian cross-border and transpacific migration exacerbated racism, xenophobia, and fear of the "yellow peril" among white residents and immigration authorities on the Pacific Coast, far more deeply than much larger movements of "dark," "swarthy," or "olive" people from southern and eastern Europe and the Middle East.[3] Such frustration in turn propelled the North American governments to tighten border surveillance and enforcement.

This chapter discusses how Asian transborder migration shaped North American concepts of borders more powerfully than those from European or Eastern Mediterranean cultures. Asian migrants' mobility across the Pacific and North America's land borders reveals how class, race, and gender affected the construction of racially exclusionary legal regimes and their articulation. It also shows how migrants, state regulators, and the hitherto understudied third parties of migration—transpacific steamship companies and labor contractors, ethnic merchants, and smugglers—allied, fought, or negotiated with one another to enforce or circumvent immigration inspection and border control. U.S. authorities were concerned with transatlantic migrants who arrived in Canada, especially in Montreal, and for various reasons crossed the border southward to the United States, while some Italians arriving in New York traveled in the opposite direction, northbound to Montreal. Concern about this mass movement in the northeastern part of this continent (see chapter 2) may have influenced efforts to control the far fewer Asian border crossers on the opposite end of the continent.

Drawing on selected writings in English, Spanish, and Japanese, this chapter addresses some of the central issues regarding Chinese, Japanese, and to a lesser extent East Indian migrations across the two North American land borders. These sources illuminate the interconnected and complementary history of migration across the Pacific and North American borders and the consolidation of continental national borders during the Exclusion Era.

The Canadian-U.S. Border:
Ethnic Merchants, Contractors, and Migrant Laborers

The porous international boundary in the Pacific Northwest permitted Chinese, Japanese, and East Indians to explore opportunities on both sides of the border in search of jobs, better wages, more consistent hours, and non-monetary rights and privileges. Asian workers and merchants had been crossing the northern border well before exclusionary legislation.[4] This migration peaked at the very time when the governments of the United States, Canada, and later Mexico came to monitor and control border crossings from the 1890s to the 1920s.[5]

Kornel Chang has observed that thousands of Chinese laborers from railroad construction sites and mining camps throughout Washington, Oregon, and California left the United States to work for the Canadian Pacific Railroad (CPR) in the 1880s. The CPR relied almost exclusively on Chinese labor, as did all railroad companies in the North American West. Between 1881 and 1885, when the line was completed, the CPR Chinese labor contractor Yip Sang supervised close to seven thousand Chinese workers. Japanese laborers were also transient workers. Because salmon fishing paid "the best money," as many as seven hundred Japanese migrated between the United States and Canada to fish on the Fraser River during the season. East Indians, the largest number of whom were lumber workers in the Pacific Northwest, also moved back and forth across the border from sawmills in Bellingham, Washington, to those in British Columbia, "selling their labor to the highest bidders."[6]

Like the over eleven hundred passengers on board the *Kumeric*, many Japanese migrant workers who arrived in Vancouver or Victoria did not come directly from Japan. Of the over eight thousand Japanese who landed in Canada in 1907, only one-fifth traveled directly from Japan, whereas more than one-third came from Hawaiʻi. Moreover, 45 percent holding passports to the United States—issued by the Japanese government in agreement with the U.S. government—crossed the southern border immediately upon arrival.[7] An estimated 40,000 to 57,000 Hawaiʻian Japanese, composed mostly of sugar plantation laborers, remigrated to the continental United States during the decade from 1898 to 1908. By passing through British Columbia they circumvented the restrictive regulations placed on their mobility by the U.S. immigration authorities (1907) and President Roosevelt's executive order (1908), until this route was closed by Canada's Continuous Journey Clause (1908).

Ethnic merchants and labor contractors, often the same people, played a central role in mobilizing the labor of overseas nationals. Just as they traded goods across the international boundaries, these merchants of human labor shipped people from Asia and Hawaiʻi to logging camps in British Columbia and Washington, coal mines in Idaho, salmon canneries in British Columbia and Alaska, and agricultural fields along the Pacific coast and inland. In 1905 and 1906 Yamaoka Ototake, the head of the Oriental Trading Co. (Tôyô Bôeki Gaisha), based in Seattle, imported two thousand Japanese laborers from Hawai'i.[8] After the Executive Order of 1907 barring Japanese migration from Hawai'i to the mainland, the Oriental Trading Co. and its competitors rerouted their transpacific passengers through British Columbia, swelling the number of arrivals in Victoria and Vancouver.

Labor contractors like Yamaoka took advantage of the fact that Hawai'ian Japanese resided beyond the jurisdiction of the Meiji government and thus fell outside the restrictions that severely limited its citizens and subjects from traveling abroad.[9] The annexation of Hawai'i to the United States in 1898 also facilitated the movement of Japanese plantation workers from the Pacific islands to the mainland.[10] In addition to financial gain, ethnic merchant-contractors, such as Yip Sang in Vancouver and his collaborators and competitors in Seattle and elsewhere, gained power and prestige from their capacity to arrange and exploit the labor and mobility of their co-ethnics in ways similar to Greek, Italian, and Mexican labor contractors, or *padroni*.[11] Yip Sang, a native of Guangdong who was one of the most affluent merchants in Vancouver in 1907, had arrived in San Francisco in 1864. Having worked in the Yukon and Vancouver and then returned to China, he returned to Vancouver in 1888, where he opened his own business of importing and exporting Chinese goods and contracting migrant workers. He recruited and transported Chinese laborers for the CPR's construction sites, logging camps, and mining pits throughout British Columbia. He sold foodstuffs and provisions on credit and deducted fees for finding jobs, transportation, and accommodations, and the cost of provisions, from workers' paychecks, amassing a significant fortune.

While ethnic contractors had enormous power in determining the destinations, jobs, and living and working conditions of their co-ethnics, Asian laborers did organize in opposition to the companies, labor contractors, and employers in the North American West.[12] However, their exclusion from the national polity and from working-class unions did make the task more difficult. More commonly, Asian workers resisted coercive and unfair labor practices with their own feet. In September 1907 a crew of Japanese laborers deserted an isolated railroad construction camp north of the boundary between Washington and British Columbia for higher wages at the salmon canneries south of the border.

The violation of workers' rights around non-monetary issues could also fuel tensions. When a foreman of a cannery stopped a Chinese worker from taking a salmon home, sixteen other Chinese immediately walked out. The foreman had broken the unspoken rule that allowed cannery workers to take salmon whenever they wanted. Asian laborers were aware of the time-sensitive value of their labor for the region's extractive industries of hop farming, salmon canning, and fisheries. This helped them leverage their mobility when labor demand was high during the harvest season.

Building the Northern Border: Race Mattered

Beginning in the 1880s the legal and administrative apparatuses in the United States and Canada converged and sometimes conformed to one another, for the purpose of narrowing and ultimately closing to Asian migrants the hitherto loosely controlled U.S.-Canadian border. The passage of the U.S. Chinese Exclusion Act in 1882, after the restrictive Page Law of 1875, began the demise of the labor-contracting empire orchestrated by entrepreneurs like Chin Gee Hee and others.[13] Canada did not exclude the Chinese, but its Immigration Act of 1885 levied an arrival fee, later called a head tax, of $50 on every Chinese arrival. The amount was raised to $100 in 1900 and $500 in 1903.[14] The reaffirmation of U.S. labor contract laws in 1903 crystallized the de facto exclusion of Japanese laborers. After the Gentlemen's Agreement between the United States and Japan in 1907–8, Canada and Japan signed the Hayashi-Lemieux Agreement in 1908. That same year President Theodore Roosevelt issued Executive Order 589, which barred foreign contract laborers (especially Japanese) from entering the United States from Canada, Mexico, and insular possessions like Hawai'i. Canada echoed this executive order in 1908 by adopting a similar regulation, a Continuous Journey Order-in-Council, which required all immigrants to travel directly from their country of birth to their Canadian destination.[15]

Additional obstacles for Asians included a ban on contract labor and the "Likely to Become a Public Charge" (LPC) clause, which forced Chinese, Japanese, and South Asian migrants to demonstrate their ability to earn a living in the United States, while they also had to avoid suggesting that they were entering the country with a contract in hand. Far fewer women went to North America as laborers, but under the LPC provision they were even more constricted, because unaccompanied female migrants, especially those of color, were suspected of prostitution.[16] The Continuous Journey Clause, initially targeted at Japanese, also blocked immigration from East India, because there were no direct steamship lines between the subcontinent and Canada. The incident of *Komagata Maru* in April 1914 is a sober reminder of the power of the nation-state: authorities refused the landing of 376 East Indians, mostly Sikh laborers, in Vancouver. Chartered by Gurdit Singh, a wealthy businessman from Hong Kong, the steamer—with British subjects as passengers—departed Hong Kong for Vancouver, where anti-Asian racial tension had led to violent riots as late as September 1907. The vessel collected additional passen-

gers at Shanghai, Moji, and Yokohama. The provincial newspaper, totally un-
informed about Sikh religion, called the arrival a "Hindu Invasion," although
in fact there was only a handful of Hindus on board. On July 23, 1914, after
two months of detention on board the ship and denied food and water, the
steamer was forced to leave for Calcutta.[17]

The U.S. Immigration Act of 1924 completed the shift toward barring the
entry of Asian migrants and restricting immigration from southern and eastern Europe. A parallel shift in Canadian policy had taken place in 1923, when
an Order-in-Council (P.C. 182) excluded "any immigrants of any Asiatic race,"
except agriculturalists, farm laborers, female domestic servants, and the wife
and children of legal immigrants. In practice these seemingly diverse exemptions hardly affected the exclusionary measures, as the Chinese Immigration
Act, passed in the same year, terminated Chinese immigration. The exceptions
were negated for the Japanese when their government agreed to reduce radically, from 400 to 150, the quota assigned by the Canada-Japan Gentlemen's
Agreement in 1908. In 1930 the Dominion government passed an Order-in-
Council (P.C. 2115) that reinstated the ban on any Asiatic immigrant, except
the wives and minor children of Canadian citizens. The order also removed the
earlier exceptions for farmers, farm laborers, and domestics.[18]

What explains the emerging link between U.S. and Canadian policies?
In her study of Chinese immigration during the Exclusion Era (1882–1943),
Erika Lee argues that the American goal of preventing Chinese illegal land
border migration coaxed the Canadian government to adopt laws and regulations that closely reflected U.S. ideology and practices.[19] The U.S. government and immigration authorities were initially unsuccessful at having their
demands heard by their Canadian counterparts when they negotiated what
came to be known as the Canadian Agreement of 1894. It assigned U.S. inspectors to Canadian seaports and inland points beyond the territorial boundaries
of the United States. These officers were to conduct examinations of all passengers bound for the United States. Ultimately, Lee asserts, a shared antagonism toward Chinese immigrants and the historically amicable relationship
between the two countries helped the United States to persuade Canada to cooperate in the closer inspection and enforcement of the northern border. This
diplomatic approach of pressure and inducement contrasted sharply with the
antagonism and violence that characterized U.S. enforcement of the Mexican
border.

In her more recent work Lee expands and further substantiates her claim of
the transnational nature of anti-Asian racism. She examines how the synchro-
nized discourses of "yellow peril" and the anti-Asian legal structure developed
throughout North and South America as well as the Caribbean and the Pacific.

Further, she emphasizes the centrality of the United States in this "symbiotic development"[20] of anti-Asian discourse and an anti-Asian legal regime.

Stimulating and provoking as Lee's contentions may be, they have also raised criticisms and questions. Kornel Chan argues that Lee's analysis of U.S. border enforcement is overly simplistic, considering the disjointed efforts that characterized the national polities in the Pacific Northwest. Instead he emphasizes the agency and resistance of Chinese immigrants, whose cross-border mobility "challenged and thwarted the politics of border diplomacy." The national border was the site of "everyday contests between local groups and interests over space and mobility."[21]

Yet another perspective complements the familiar interpretive framework that casts the land border migration of Asian migrants as a polarized battle between them and state regulators. One such example is my recent analysis of the practice of transshipment that U.S. and Japanese transporters engaged in to circumvent the state regulations designed to curb their passengers' mobility.[22] One of the strongest voices of discontent about border enforcement came from the transpacific steamship companies, notably the U.S. lines. They fought vehemently against some of their own federal government's legal barriers, which squeezed their business interests. Companies such as Dodwell and Co. perceived the Canadian Agreement of 1894 as detrimental to their business of carrying passengers directly to the United States, while favoring the Canadian Pacific Railway's steamer connection. Together with the increasingly restrictive laws and regulations discussed earlier, the sense of unfairness and the allegedly shrinking market share of the U.S. lines propelled them to file dummy manifests that listed Canada as the final destination of Japanese passengers disembarking in Vancouver or Victoria, although many were actually bound for the United States. Once the passengers cleared immigration examinations by Canadian officers, they boarded ship again for the last leg of their voyage to their destination in the United States. Successful transshipment depended partly on the false testimony of the passengers before the U.S. Board of Special Inquiry at Canadian ports. More importantly, the steamship companies were at the forefront in circumventing the U.S. immigration laws in these cases; the migrants were following directions given to them rather than acting on their own.

Moving the debate further inland, one may ask how political and economic conditions of a specific region or country countered or fortified the anti-Asiatic discourse in the legal framework of the nation-state. Evelyn Hu-Dehart has revealed in her work on Mexico and Peru from 1849 through the 1930s the extent to which socioeconomic profiles of Chinese expatriates in these countries affected the vigor of anti-Chinese campaigns.[23] Lee's macro-regional examination is less concerned with the differences created by each locality or country than with the connections and links between the national polities. Further questions arise. What dynamics did local labor markets, social practices, and cultural contacts in each local, regional, and national political economy create? In what ways did these dynamics distinguish the contours of anti-Asian racism and the legal regime in the Americas and the Pacific region?

Illegal Entry into the United States from Canada

If the exclusionary laws and regulations resulted in curbing the mobility of Asian laborers across North America and, by extension, the power of their labor contractors, the legislative and administrative apparatuses of the two North American states were also contested by the Chinese, Japanese, and East Indian migrants themselves. Reactions and interactions among migrants, states, and various middlemen were part of a larger system, as the nation-states shored up their monopoly on human mobility across the Pacific and the continent in the late nineteenth century, throughout the twentieth century, and to this day. James Cameron illustrates in depth one of the most intense smuggling rackets, led by Fred Yoshy (Saburo Yoshiye)—an interpreter for the Japanese Consulate in Victoria and a founder of the Nippon Supply Company—and Canadian immigration authorities in British Columbia during the interwar years. Clearly Yoshy was not the only interpreter who occupied and exploited borderlands, nor were his practices unique along the northern border. As Patrick Ettinger observed at the border between El Paso and Ciudad Juarez, many interpreters, Chinese, U.S., or Mexican, figured in periodic charges of corruption.[24]

The struggle between the states and Asian migrants along the border took many forms. The use of counterfeit passports was one well-known practice. Japanese and South Asian migrants in Washington State sold their passports to recent arrivals in British Columbia who wanted to cross the border to the south. Some would also swim in the ocean, cross rivers, and climb over hills in every possible attempt to reach their destination in the United States. Others would trick immigration officers. Still others would choose to cross the border between Blaine and the Cascade Mountains, where thick forests along the international border hampered detection.[25]

Cross-border migrants also relied on smugglers and "guides" who orchestrated the entry of their human merchandise into the United States from Canada, where Chinese entries were taxed but not excluded, admission of Japanese laborers was regulated but not banned, and East Indians, as members of the British Empire, were unwelcome but at least officially allowed free passage provided that they arrived on a continuous journey from their own country. Smuggling along the border was a lucrative business that generated fees from $100 to $1,000 per person. Ethnic labor contractors were key. The Japanese labor agent Sengoku T. stated that he took "300 Japanese across the border at Blaine" and "placed them at work in the state of Idaho in the building of the Great Northern Railway." Amerindians also played significant roles. With their detailed knowledge of local geography, they navigated Chinese and Japanese from British Columbia to Washington for as little as $3.[26] Together with other agents of migration, including boardinghouse operators and shopkeepers in Vancouver, Victoria, Seattle, and San Francisco, these guides and smugglers—ethnic, U.S., and Canadian (as well as Mexican)—formed an illicit border-breaching network.

In the course of the early 1900s the massive increase of the Canadian head tax made crossing the border increasingly prohibitive for Chinese migrants, who subsequently sought entry into the United States. In 1906 the U.S. commissioner general reported a sharp decline in Chinese smuggling through Canada as he declared his office had "the Canada-border situation well in hand." What the commissioner general failed to mention was that the improvement of border enforcement along the northern border nurtured old and new problems.[27] Smuggling operations went further underground as Yoshy, and many other lesser-known but equally active middlemen continued the lucrative trade in the early 1930s. Worse, from the perspective of the U.S. and Canadian immigration officials, stricter investigation at the northern border redirected greater numbers of Asian migrants to America's less guarded border in the south. Under the tutelage of smugglers, boardinghouse operators, and steamship crews, or on their own, migrants perfected the art of deception. Some Chinese disguised themselves at the Canadian border as local natives wearing Indian garb. Others played on the stereotype of the "drunken Mexican" by singing in Spanish and appearing drunk as they crossed the border to Laredo, Texas. Racial disguise was not limited to the Canadian and Mexican borders. A common strategy for Asian immigrants arriving via Cuba was to paint their faces black and pretend to be part of the steamship crew, allowing them to leave ship without trouble.

As Asians migrated across the land borders, their geographical mobility, legal or illegal, strengthened negative perceptions on the part of U.S. and Canadian authorities, media, and citizens. Erika Lee has illustrated how Chinese immigration from British Columbia and Mexico into the United States became the public symbol of illegality. At the beginning of the twentieth century, media in the United States depicted a stereotypical image of the cunning and evasive "John Chinamen." Wearing loose-fitting pants, "coolie" hats, and distinctive shoes, with ubiquitously long braids of hair, these Chinese men represented "a cultural anomaly that [was] both sexually and racially ambiguous and threatening."[28] Although Chinese were not the only immigrants to enter the United States illegally, a far greater number of others, including Syrians, Greeks, Hungarians, Russian Jews, and "maidens" from other European countries, were assumed to pose little or no threat to U.S. society. Clearly illegality was constructed in racial terms as early as the 1890s.[29]

The highly racialized depiction of Chinese immigrants as illegal also contrasted with the U.S. government's treatment of two major groups of land-border migrants: Canadians and Mexicans. In contrast to the mere seventeen thousand Chinese who entered the United States illegally from 1882 to 1920, approximately one million French Canadians migrated to the United States from 1830 to 1930, and 1.4 million Mexicans did so from 1900 to 1930. Neither Canadian nor Mexican migrants were spared from animosity in the United States, but because they were seen as "long-term residents" of the contiguous border regions (the Southwest and the Northeast) or as temporary sojourners, their U.S. entry before the 1930s was never regulated with the same rigor with which the Chinese, and later Japanese and other Asian migrants, had to constantly struggle.[30] Concerning the imagery contrasting the "Chinese sojourner" with the "European immigrant," it merits reemphasizing that around 1900 about one-third of all labor migrants from Europe stayed in the United States for just a few months or a few years and then returned.[31]

The Mexican-U.S. Border

Like their contemporaries in the north, Asian residents and transients along the Mexican-U.S. boundary lived transborder lives well before the border became the site of close state surveillance. Chinese merchants, *fronterizos* (border residents), commuting farmers, migrant laborers, and journalists moved in both directions across the Mexican border, which was loosely guarded until the onset of the Mexican Revolution in 1910. Together with heightened control along the Canadian-U.S. border and the emigration policies of migrants' countries of origin, political and economic conditions specific to Mexico carved a distinct context for Asian migration to and from it.

Mexico's Welcomed (Contract Labor) Migration

In stark contrast to the exclusionary regimes and racist ideologies of Canada and the United States, President Porfirio Díaz's policy to attract foreign investors, farmers, and laborers to populate and develop the Mexican north lured thousands of Asian migrants to Mexico in the late nineteenth century and early twentieth. Chinese were among the first to arrive in significant numbers after being denied entry into the United States in 1882. Most clustered in the northwest near the Pacific Coast. Japanese headed for Mexico in a considerable number in 1905, largely as a reaction to the flurry of anti-Japanese agitations and exclusionary regulations that enflamed the West Coast from Vancouver to Seattle to San Francisco to Los Angeles, as well as smaller inland communities in Canada and the United States.[32] The incidences and legislation that solidified the anti-Asian movement included, among others, the creation in 1905 of the Japanese and Korean Exclusion Leagues in California, the segregation of Chinese and Japanese pupils in so-called Oriental schools in San Francisco in 1906, the Vancouver riot in 1907, and the Alien Land Laws in California (1913, amended in 1920) and Arizona (1917), among other states, which banned the sale of land to aliens not eligible for citizenship.[33] All pushed Japanese migrants to Mexico.

Mexican civil law granted to the Chinese and Japanese rights equal to those of Mexican citizens. To be certain, such rights did not spare Chinese residents of Mexico from being routinely stopped at the border, whereas Mexicans benefited from free passage in the 1890s. But the claim of citizenship and the privilege accorded to border residents of Chinese and later Japanese origin gave them legal entry, until President Roosevelt imposed a ban on foreign contract laborers, especially Japanese.[34]

In 1889, seven years after the adoption of the Chinese Exclusion Act in the United States, hundreds of Chinese landed in Mexican ports on the Pacific Coast, such as Mazatlán, Guaymas, La Paz, San José, Cabo San Lucas, Ensenada, and Magdalena Bay. They would then travel to Baja California Norte and Sonora and seek entry into the United States. For these Chinese, and many other Asian and European migrants who came to replace the Chinese, landing at the Mexican ports opened a passage not only to the Mexican interior but also to the Mexico-U.S. borderland regions.[35] In the late-1920s the U.S. secretary of labor bitterly recognized the impossibility of preventing illegal entry: "If we had the Army on the Canadian border and on the Mexican border, we couldn't stop them; if we had the Navy on the water-front we couldn't stop them . . . Not even a Chinese wall, nine thousands miles in length and built over rivers and deserts and mountains and along the seashores, would seem to permit a permanent solution."[36]

Another incentive for going to Mexico came from the Japanese government's emigration policies. In 1900 the Meiji government temporarily stopped issuing passports for those bound for Canada and the United States, while it did not restrict the number of passports for other North American destinations and none in South America. The one-and-a-half-year ban was partially revoked in 1902, but the Meiji government continued to exclude the laborer class from emigration.[37] As Japanese entry into the United States and Canada came under harsher restrictions through the passage of the U.S. Immigration Act in 1924 and the Canadian Order-in-Council in 1930, a growing number of Japanese headed for Mexico. Other migrants sought destinations further south, most importantly in Brazil and Peru.[38]

Mexico offered many options to the Japanese, some of whom stayed. According to an inquiry by the U.S. Commission of Immigration, of ten thousand Japanese who had entered Mexico from 1906 to 1907, only a thousand remained there in June 1907; nine thousand had crossed the border into the United States. A Japanese emigration company agent complained in 1906 that 80 percent of the contract laborers for whom the company paid passage to Mexico left for California right after their arrival. Others headed for Canada via the United States.[39] Some deserted transoceanic steamers even before their arrival in Mexico. In October 1906 two-thirds of the fifty-nine Japanese workers on board a steamship bound for the mines in Las Esperanzas disappeared when their vessel called at Seattle. Most others escaped as soon as they arrived in Mexico, leaving just four to be shipped to the coal mines at their final destination.[40] Working and living conditions for Japanese mine workers were difficult, to say the least. Contract-labor migrants commonly suffered from poor pay, dangerous work, and poor living conditions.[41] As workers became increasingly frustrated, those who could afford it returned to Japan. Many others departed for the United States.[42]

Judging from the official statistics, the Mexican route to the United States was a short-lived phenomenon. The number of Japanese who were issued passports jumped to a peak of 5,321 in 1906 and dropped to 3,945 in 1907. In 1908 Japanese migration dropped to a mere trickle of sixteen people, and then to just eleven in 1909.[43] The decrease can be partly attributed to the Ley de 1908, which prohibited the admission of LPCs. Together with Roosevelt's Executive Order and the Continuous Journey Clause, the new restriction made Mexico less attractive.

Finally, the Mexican Revolution closed the period of relative free passage across the Mexican border for U.S.-bound foreigners.[44] Mexican authorities, concerned that the country's own rebels would flee to the northern Republic, placed the southern border under stricter inspection. Equally important, violence and an unreliable railroad service substantially reduced the number of immigrants willing to travel through Mexico. Long at odds with U.S. immigration policy efforts, revolutionary Mexico was far from softening its antagonism toward U.S. soldiers, entrepreneurs, and government officials. The Mexican government, unlike its Canadian counterpart, which tacitly consented to U.S. inspection, persistently refused any agreement with the United States that would permit its immigration authorities to exercise power on Mexican soil. Nevertheless, nationwide turmoil, violence, and xenophobia ultimately pulled Mexico into a new era during which the country closed itself officially to in- and outmigration.

Chinese Fronterizos, Japanese Transborder Residents, and Refugees from the Mexican Revolution

In the years before the Mexican Revolution, Chinese migrants negotiated their passage across the Mexican-U.S. border by claiming their status of *fronterizos*, or border residents. Grace Delgado has studied cases of Chinese merchants who petitioned for entry into the United States from Mexico at the turn of the century. They relied on support from their legal and business contacts among Mexican and U.S. officials, banks, and trading partners. Laborers, on the other hand, faced greater difficulty when crossing the border, but they too were able to maneuver at deportation hearings. The Chinese expatriates' strategic claiming of their membership in Mexican civil society and the legal regime of pre-Revolutionary Mexico that allowed such claims were unique and distinct at the very time when racialized discourses marginalized and excluded co-ethnic contemporaries in the United States and Canada.[45]

Japanese settlers also crossed the Mexican-U.S. border with little difficulty in the early twentieth century. It is essential to underline the oft-overlooked legality of their passage across the border, in contrast to the illegal migration of Asians (and other migrants) that receives far greater attention from contemporary media and state governments as well as historians. The development of an ethnic transborder community sustained regular Japanese crossing and recrossing. One example involved Issei fishermen from Ensenada who traveled legally between Baja California and southern California. Contracted by Japanese firms based in California, many fished tuna and bonito in the deep sea and regularly docked at San Diego and San Pedro to unload their catch. Another group of transborder Issei consisted of farmers in Baja California. They too traveled legally and routinely across the border in both directions. Border-crossing cards allowed these "commuter" farmers, who resided in Calexico, California, to go tend cotton fields in Mexicali. Finally, a third transborder community consisted of large-scale proprietors who typically lived on the U.S. side and hired local Mexicalis to work their farms. Among the landowning Japanese farmers were Issei men such as Inugai Tokujiro, who, increasingly weary of racial harassment and antagonism in the United States, moved south of the border. He had arrived in the United States in 1905, worked as an agricultural field hand in Colorado for eight years, and then responded to a newspaper ad for Japanese workers to establish an agricultural colony in El Naranjo, Sinaloa. He purchased a hundred hectares of land in 1916 and in the following year moved to the region with his family.[46]

The institutionalization of white racism north of the border was certainly a factor, but not the only one that propelled remigrants like Inugai to move to Mexico. The historian Eiichiro Azuma emphasizes the importance of Imperial Japanese expansionist thought to Japanese immigrants' transborder movement. Coupled with the interdependent nature of the ethnic economies on both sides of the border, Issei journalists encouraged those with financial means to go to Mexico for more viable and autonomous agricultural ventures. In addition, some local Japanese associations (*Nihonjin kai*), which functioned as part of the administrative apparatus of understaffed Japanese consulates, served transnational jurisdictions. For instance, the Japanese Association in Los Angeles registered residents in southern California as well as Mexicali, Tijuana, and Ensenada, and issued the necessary certificates when immigrants sent for their family members. This administrative structure of the para-governmental associations reinforced a sense of shared community among the residents in the region.[47]

Further, Azuma alerts us to the danger of romanticized perceptions of contemporary U.S. authorities (and by extension, some of the historical analyses discussed below). They would posit the cross-border movement of Japanese as "Issei resistance to white racism," an expression of "diaspora sensitivity," or "cosmopolitan consciousness that derogated state rules and boundaries." Instead, to many Japanese migrants the pursuit of personal goals was primordial to the heroism of "antiracist fighters, postmodernesque cosmopolitans, or law-abiding citizens-subjects."[48]

Yet another group that entered the United States legally was "Chinese refugees" from Revolutionary Mexico. In 1917 more than five hundred Chinese followed General John J. Pershing and his troops as they marched northward across the Mexican border after their failed hunt for the revolutionary leader Pancho Villa. Many of these Chinese refugees were former shopkeepers who provisioned U.S. soldiers. That their association with counterrevolutionary Americans, or the simple fact of their being Chinese, made them victims of chaos, violence, and persecution by Mexicans propelled them to search for refuge north of the border. Despite the Chinese Exclusion Act of 1882, they were subsequently given permission to enter the United States on condition that they would work for the U.S. Army. Ultimately they were accorded legal resident status; a substantial number came to live in border cities such as

Tucson, El Paso, and San Diego, as well as further inland. The entrepreneurial attitude and friendly demeanor of these recent arrivals provoked one immigration officer in El Paso to comment that they had little in common with older Chinese residents in the city and would never become involved in gambling and opium smoking in Chinatown.[49]

Smuggling across the Southern Border

Asian migrants also moved across the Mexican border without proper documentation. Robert Chao Romero has studied the transnational networks operated by Chinese smugglers through Mexico into the United States during the years from the Chinese Exclusion Law of 1882 to 1916, when that trade came to a halt with the interruption of transpacific steamship service during the First World War.[50] According to Clifford Alan Perkins, a former Chinese inspector who served at Tucson, El Paso, and other localities in the Southwest, the Chinese Six Companies, headquartered in San Francisco, directed the Chinese smuggling traffic from Havana. Some members of the Six Companies were transnational merchants who invested in import-export ventures that extended to lucrative businesses like the opium trade, white slavery, and human contraband.[51] The range of activities engaged in by the Six Companies must have generated additional wealth, which made this association one of the most affluent international commercial networks at the time.

Conclusion

In the late nineteenth century and the early twentieth, with stepped-up efforts for enforcing immigration inspection and border control, the North American governments curtailed significantly the cross-border mobility of Asian migrants. However, state laws and regulations far from sealed the borders. Chinese, Japanese, and East Indian laborers, farmers, and settlers—along with third parties—cooperated and competed to circumvent the states' regulations. In doing so they exploited the lag between the time a law was passed in one country and another, as well as differences in the implementation, regulation, and examination policies of the nation-states. However, some groups of migrants had little or no need to seek surreptitious entry. Chinese refugees, Japanese commuting farmers, and Issei fishermen and proprietors crossed borders daily, seasonally, or once in their lifetime. Their claim for citizenship notwithstanding, cross-border travel of these and other border residents also raised questions about the power and limitations of national governments to regulate, neglect, or exclude Asian immigration.

In lieu of a conclusion, one may suggest future directions for studying Asian land border migration. One possible area of study is the links developed by third parties in migration, as recent scholarship on the transoceanic mobility of European migrants during this period has recently begun to examine.[52] Another approach could incorporate a wider range of actors among non-state and non-migrant parties: in addition to labor contractors, ethnic merchants, and steamship companies, the roles of boardinghouse operators, translators, and emigration companies, among others, deserve exploration. Research in this direction could lead us to rethink the familiar dichotomy that tends to pit Asian migrants against nation-states.

Class, which has emerged prominently in the recent literature on Asian land-border migration, also merits further attention. As Peña Delgado's work on Chinese border residents has shown, merchant and laboring classes alike claimed the legal rights of Mexican citizens as they crossed the prerevolutionary Mexican border freely. Azuma's study illustrates the formation and demise of the transborder Japanese community in the two Californias. But what are the class-specific implications of ideological drives such as Japanese overseas expansionism on southern border residents as well as their lesser-studied contemporaries along the northern border? These questions too call for exploration.

In yet another direction, the glaring dearth of studies on North America's southern borders, other than the Mexican-U.S. one, demands further research. Despite the significant presence of Asians along the Guatemalan-Mexican land border as well as sea borders between the Caribbean and the North American continent, existing histories on cross-border migration in North America largely ignore these migrations. Either as migrants, settlers, transients, or facilitators of migration such as Charlie Sam, men and women of Asian origin, along with North American collaborators, fundamentally transformed the histories of North America's many borders and border regions. Fuller accounts of histories that go beyond the two borders of the United States beg to be told.

Notes

1 *Vancouver Daily Province*, July 24 and July 25, 1907; *Gaimushô Nihon Gaikô Bunsho*, 1906, 740–41. See also Sasaki Toshiji, *Kanada Imin shi* (Tokyo: Fuji shuppan, 1999), 160–61.

2 Clifford Alan Perkins, *Border Patrol: With the U.S. Immigration Service on the Mexican Boundary, 1910–54* (El Paso: Texas Western, 1978), 50–51.

3 Donna Gabaccia, "The 'Yellow Peril' and the 'Chinese of Europe': Global Perspectives on Race and Labour, 1815–1930," *Migration, Migration History, History: Old*

Paradigms and New Perspectives, ed. Jan Lucassen and Leo Lucassen (Bern: Peter Lang, 1997), 177–96.

4 Kornel Suk Chang, "Transpacific Borderlands and Boundaries: Race, Migration, and State Formation in the North American Pacific Rim, 1882–1917" (Ph.D. diss., University of Chicago, 2007); Yukari Takai, "'These Japanese Continuously Violated the Alien-Contract Labour Laws': The Gendered Paths of Labourers, Farmers, and Housewives from Japan Traversing the Canada-U.S. Border in the Early Twentieth Century," *Histoire sociale / Social History* 80 (November 2007), 297–322.

5 Takai, "'These Japanese Continuously Violated the Alien-Contract Labour Laws,'" 307–8; Yukari Takai, "Doing Transnational History at a Canada-U.S. Borderland: Japanese Remigrants and the Rise of the Border" (in Japanese), *American History* 30 (2007), 65–82, esp. 69–71. For South Asians see Chang, "Transpacific Borderlands," 81. See also Patrick W. Ettinger, *Imaginary Lines: Border Enforcement and the Origins of Undocumented Immigration, 1882–1930* (Austin: University of Texas Press, 2009), chapter 4. On the U.S. Border Patrol see Mae M. Ngai, *Impossible Subjects: Illegal Aliens and the Making of Modern America* (Princeton: Princeton University Press, 2004), 64–75.

6 Chang, "Transpacific Borderlands," 80–81.

7 Government of Canada, Royal Commission Appointed to Inquire into the Methods by Which Oriental Labourers Have Been Induced to Come to Canada, Report of W. L. Mackenzie King (Ottawa, 1907), 11, 44–46, cited in Howard H. Sugimoto, "Vancouver Riots of 1907: A Canadian Episode," *East across the Pacific: Historical and Sociological Studies of Japanese Immigration and Assimilation*, ed. Hilary Conroy and T. Scott Miyakawa (Santa Barbara: ABC-Clio, 1972), 112; Ken Adachi, *The Enemy That Never Was: A History of the Japanese Canadians* (Toronto: McClelland and Stewart, 1976), 67–60.

8 Fujioka Shiro, *Ayumi no Ato* (Los Angeles: Ayumino Ato Kankô Kôenkai, 1957), 298; Chang, "Transpacific Borderlands," 70–71.

9 Sasaki, *Kanada Imin shi*, chapter 4, esp. 151–69; Adachi, *The Enemy That Never Was*, 67–68.

10 Dennis M. Ogawa, *Kodomo no tame ni: The Japanese American Experience in Hawaii* (Honolulu: University Press of Hawaii, 1978), 78, cited in Andrea A. E. Geiger, "Cross-Pacific Dimensions of Race, Caste and Class: Meiji-era Japanese Immigrants in the North American West, 1885–1928" (Ph.D. diss., University of Washington, 2006), 197.

11 Willard Jue, "Chin Gee Hee: Chinese Pioneer Entrepreneur in Seattle and Toishan," *Annals of the Chinese Historical Society of the Pacific Northwest* (1983); Paul Yee, "Sam Kee: A Chinese Business in Early Vancouver," *Vancouver Past: Essays in Social History*, ed. Robert A. J. McDonald and Jean Barman (Vancouver: UBC Press, 1986), 91; Gunther Peck, *Reinventing Free Labour: Padrones and Immigrant Workers in the North American West, 1880–1930* (Cambridge: Cambridge University Press, 2000); Chang, "Transpacific Borderlands," 43–51, 74.

12 Chris Friday, *Organizing Asian American Labour: The Pacific Coast Canned-Salmon Industry, 1870–1942* (Philadelphia: Temple University Press, 1994); Chang, "Transpacific Borderlands," 76, 83.

13 Chang, "Transpacific Borderlands," 50, 83.

14 Patricia E. Roy, *A White Man's Province: British Columbia Politicians and Chinese and Japanese Immigrants, 1858–1914* (Vancouver: UBC Press, 1989), 61, 98, 155–56.

15 Hugh Johnston, *The Voyage of the Komagata Maru: The Sikh Challenge to Canada's Colour Bar* (Vancouver: UBC Press, 1989), 4–5 n. 9, 28–33, 58–59.

16 For gendered aspects of land border migration among Asian, European, and Mexican women see chapter 8.

17 Roy, *A White Man's Province*, 212–13; Johnston, *Komagata Maru*. Chang, "Transpacific Borderlands," chapter 5, analyzes South Asian nationalists and their transborder anticolonial activism.

18 Takai, "'These Japanese Continuously Violated the Alien-Contract Labour Laws,'" 303.

19 Erika Lee, *At America's Gates: Chinese Immigration during the Exclusion Era, 1882–1943* (Chapel Hill: University of North Carolina Press, 2005), esp. chapter 5.

20 Erika Lee, "The 'Yellow Peril' and Asian Exclusion in the Americas," *Pacific Historical Review* 76, no. 4 (2007), 537–62; Mae M. Ngai, "Asian American History Forum: Introduction," *Pacific Historical Review* 76, no. 4 (2007), 533–35.

21 Chang, "Transpacific Borderlands," 195.

22 Yukari Takai, "Navigating Transpacific Passages: Steamship Companies, State Regulators and Transshipment of Japanese in Early-Twentieth-Century Pacific Northwest," *Journal of American Ethnic History* 30, no. 3 (March 2011), 7–34.

23 Evelyn Hu-DeHart, "Coolies, Shopkeepers, Pioneers: The Chinese of Mexico and Peru (1849–1930)," *Amerasia* 15, no. 2 (1989), 91–116.

24 James D. Cameron, "Canada's Struggle with Illegal Entry on Its West Coast: The Case of Fred Yoshy and Japanese Migrants before the Second World War," *BC Studies* 146 (summer 2005), 37–62; Ettinger, *Imaginary Lines*, 115–16.

25 Itô Kazuo, *Issei: A History of Japanese Immigrants in North America*, trans. Nakamura Shin-ichiro and Jean S. Gerard (Seattle: Executive Committee for Publication, 1973), 85–87; Geiger, "Cross-Pacific Dimensions," 220.

26 Chang, "Transpacific Borderlands," 236–37.

27 Ettinger, *Imaginary Lines*, 84, 99; Patrick Ettinger, "'We Sometime Wonder What They Will Spring on Us Next': Immigrants and Border Enforcement in the American West, 1882–1930," *Western Historical Quarterly* 37 (summer 2006), 159–81, esp. 177–78; Roy, *A White Man's Province*, 61, 98, 155–56; Lee, *At America's Gates*, 161–62; Cameron, "Canada's Struggle," 56–60.

28 Lee, *At America's Gates*, 162, 165–73.

29 Sauer also discusses this point in her chapter in this volume.

30 Yoland Lavoie, *L'émigration des Canadiens aux États-Unis avant 1930* (Montreal: Presses de l'Université de Montréal, 1972), 45, table 7; Lee, *At America's Gates*, 171; Randy William Widdis, *With Scarcely a Ripple: Anglo-Canadian Migration into the United States and Western Canada, 1880–1920* (Montreal: McGill-Queen's University Press, 1998); Jean Lamarre, *Les canadiens français du Michigan: Leur contribution dans le développement de la vallée de la Saginaw et de la péninsule de Keweenaw, 1840–*

1914 (Sillery, Quebec: Septentrion, 2000); Bruno Ramirez, *Crossing the 49th Parallel: Migration from Canada to the United States, 1900–1930* (Ithaca: Cornell University Press, 2001), chapter 2; John J. Bukowczyk, Nora Faires, David R. Smith, and Randy William Widdis, *Permeable Border: The Great Lakes Basin as Transnational Region, 1650–1990* (Pittsburgh: University of Pittsburgh Press, 2005), esp. chapters 3–4; Yukari Takai, *Gendered Passages: French-Canadian Migration to Lowell, Massachusetts, 1900–1920* (New York: Peter Lang, 2008), 64–66; George Sánchez, *Becoming Mexican American: Ethnicity, Culture and Identity in Chicano Los Angeles, 1900–1945* (Oxford: Oxford University Press, 1993), 18–19; Ngai, *Impossible Subjects*, chapter 4.

31 Dirk Hoerder, "Immigration and the Working Class: The Remigration Factor," *International Labour and Working Class History* 21 (1982), 28–41; Mark Wyman, *Round-trip to America: The Immigrants Return to Europe, 1880–1930* (Ithaca: Cornell University Press, 1993).

32 Hu-Dehart, "Coolies, Shopkeepers, Pioneers," 91. Jerry García, "Japanese Immigration and Community Development in México, 1897–1940" (Ph.D. diss., Washington State University, 1999), 46–47, 86.

33 The Alien Land Laws spread further in the 1920s and 1940s to Washington and Louisiana (1921), New Mexico (1922), Idaho and Oregon (1923), Kansas (1925), and Utah (1943).

34 Grace Peña Delgado, "At Exclusion's Southern Gate: Changing Categories of Race and Class among Chinese *Fronterizos*, 1882–1904," *Continental Crossroads: Remapping U.S.-Mexican Borderlands History*, ed. Samuel Truett and Elliott Young (Durham: Duke University Press, 2004), 183–207, esp. 184–88.

35 Ettinger, "'We Sometime Wonder What They Will Spring on Us Next,'" 174; Ettinger, *Imaginary Lines*, 99–122.

36 Delgado, "At Exclusion's Southern Gate," 185; Ettinger, "'We Sometime Wonder What They Will Spring on Us Next,'" 174; Ettinger, *Imaginary Lines*, 99–122; Constantine Maria Panunzio, *Immigration Crossroads* (New York: Macmillan, 1927), quote p. 282.

37 Migrant laborers who had returned to Japan and wanted to go back to the United States were exempt from the ban. Yuji Ichioka, *Issei: The World of the First Generation Japanese Immigrants, 1885–1924* (New York: Free Press, 1988), 52.

38 Daniel M. Masterson with Sayaka Funada-Classen, *The Japanese in Latin America* (Urbana: University of Illinois Press, 2004), chapter 2.

39 María Elena Ota Mishima, *Siete Migraciones Japonesas en México, 1890–1978* (México: Colegio de México, 1982), 57; Delgado, "At Exclusion's Southern Gate," 186; García, "Japanese Immigration," 116–17; Ettinger, *Imaginary Lines*, 101–3; Geiger, "Cross-Pacific Dimensions," 234–35; Yukari Takai, "Asian Migrants, Exclusionary Laws, and Transborder Migration in North America, 1880–1940," Organization of American Historians, *Magazine of History* 23, no. 4 (October 2009), 35–42. Excluded from entry into the United States, Chinese also went to Mexico intending to move to the northern Republic. Moisés González Navarro, *Los Extranjeros en México y Los Mexicanos en El Extranjero, 1821–1970*, vol. 2 (México: Colegio de México, 1994), 280–81.

40 Daniel M. Masterson with Sayaka Funada-Classen, *The Japanese in Latin America* (Urbana: University of Illinois Press, 2004), chapter 2.

41 Itô Kazuo, *Hokubei Hyakunen Zakura* (Tokyo: Hokubei hyakunenzakura jikkō linkai, 1969), 96–98; García, "Japanese Immigration," 93–98.

42 Iyo Iimura Kunimoto, "Japan and Mexico, 1888–1917" (Ph.D. diss., University of Texas, 1975), 65; García, "Japanese Immigration," 87, 91, 93, 94.

43 García, "Japanese Immigration," 111–12.

44 Ettinger, *Imaginary Lines*, 135–37. See chapter 8 in this volume.

45 Delgado, "At Exclusion's Southern Gate," 183–207.

46 Eiichiro Azuma, "A Transborder Japanese Community in U.S.-Mexican California: A Preliminary Study of Borderland Nikkei Experience," *The World of Transnational Asian Americans*, ed. Daizaburo Yui (Center for Pacific and American Studies, University of Tokyo, 2006), 110–13.

47 Garcia, "Japanese Immigration," 163–64; Azuma, "A Transborder Japanese Community in U.S.-Mexican California," 110–11, 113.

48 Azuma, "A Transborder Japanese Community in U.S.-Mexican California," 108.

49 Perkins, *Border Patrol*, 49–50; Report of Supervising Inspector, U.S. Immigration Service, El Paso, Texas, September 30, 1917, National Archives and Records Administration, Washington, RG 85, entry 9, file 54152, folder 79C. See also Julian Lim, "Stuck at the Border: The Mexican Revolution, Chinese Refugees, and the Exclusion Era United States," paper presented at the American Historical Association, San Diego, 2010.

50 Robert Chao Romero, "Transnational Chinese Immigrant Smuggling to the United States via Mexico and Cuba, 1882–1916," *Amerasia Journal* 30, no. 3 (2004–5), 1–16: Robert Chao Romero, "Dragon in Big Lusong: Chinese Immigration and Settlement in Mexico, 1882–1940" (Ph.D. diss., University of California, Los Angeles, 2003).

51 Perkins, *Border Patrol*, 11–13, 49.

52 "Transit Migration and Crossing Borders in (and between) Europe and North America, 1880–1930," panel at meeting of the Social Science History Association, Long Beach, November 2009.

CHAPTER FIFTEEN

Migration and Capitalism

The Rise of the U.S.-Mexican Border

John Mason Hart

Borders are multidimensional phenomena, with intricate complexities that reflect the deeper nature of the relations between the states that they divide. In the case of the United States and Mexico the area concerned with defining the border extended from the center of Mesoamerica in the Valley of Mexico (and later Mexico City) from pre-Columbian times until the 1830s and 1840s, and from the political center in Washington and the financial center of New York since the early nineteenth century. In addition, the northern states of Mexico, and those that now make up the southwestern United States, have had an intense local history of cultural, economic, migratory, cooperative, and conflictive relationships that have helped to define the region.

Native Peoples' and Europeans' Early Trade

Scholars have long noted the early trade between the more advanced industrial and mercantile center of Teotihuacan (some forty miles north of Mexico City), Chihuahua, and New Mexico. The relationship continued to develop long after the decline of Teotihuacan, with the continued demographic, economic, and cultural growth of the Mexican northwest and its close relationship with the people living in what is now the southwestern United States.

During the fourteenth and fifteenth centuries Paquimé, in northwestern Chihuahua, about 225 miles south of Douglas, Arizona, became an important middle ground in the cultural and economic evolution of the central border region because of its dissemination of advanced technologies and products from Mesoamerica into the cultures to its north. Paquimé, and the "large number of settlements around it," was a major mercantile distribution center for the region, importing tools, architecture, urban design, water control techniques, and seeds.[1] With the decline of the social and cultural matrix of western Chihuahua during the early disruptions caused by the Spanish intrusion, a new wave of migrations began that has gradually increased in intensity to the present day. Spearheaded by Tlaxcalans, who moved to Coahuila in the sixteenth century, people from central Mexico, including mestizos, Europeans, Afro-Mexicans, and indigenous settlers, entered the entirety of the border region. They colonized the rich farmlands of the Lower Rio Grande Valley of Texas, while others occupied a hundred-mile radius around the now abandoned Paquimé, and traveled farther into the more arable regions of Sonora, Arizona, California, and the upper Rio Grande Valley of New Mexico.

During the eighteenth century an influx of European immigrants joined them. They entered the region at the entrepôt of Matamoros on the Gulf Coast. Those newcomers concentrated in settlements along the Rio Grande and Rio Conchos River Basins, with the towns of Paso del Norte in Chihuahua, and Caderyeta and Monterrey in Nuevo Leon, being especially important because of their long-distance trade relationships with Guadalajara, Saltillo, San Antonio, New Orleans, and New York. In Nuevo Leon the newcomers included Sephardic Jewish exiles from Spain, among them the Garza and Sada families, who brought special entrepreneurial skills to the area. Meanwhile a broad spectrum of ethnicities and social classes from central Mexico settled in Tucson, San Diego, and Los Angeles.

The merchants of Matamoros facilitated trade between the interior of the border region and the world. Some two-thirds of all international commerce entering and leaving the northern half of Mexico, preceding the U.S. invasion of Texas in the 1830s, did so via Matamoros, and most of it came from and went to the United States. Capital and manufactured goods entered the region, while raw materials and artisan wares left it. From the inception of these later interactions an almost mystical vision emerged in Mexico of the United States as a materialist cornucopia if not a desirable cultural destination.[2]

Traders, Travelers, and Financiers in the Nineteenth Century

From the early nineteenth century through the late twentieth the people of the border region shared the common experiences of immigration from the south, north, and east; the adoption of varied architecture, including the Mexican "southwestern" style; myriad cuisines; exploration; the discovery and exploitation of strategic resources; the introduction of new technologies by powerful outsiders controlling patents and large amounts of capital; cooperation and competition between various groups; and violence.

The earliest contact of northern Mexicans with the U.S. economy and culture came about because of explorers, traders, and travelers, beginning with unrecorded experiences in the late eighteenth century. This was followed by the direct intrusion of finance capital from the United States. The Brown Brothers Bank, then of Baltimore, established a presence in Tampico as early as the mid-1770s for the purposes of trade with the northern Huasteca region of northeastern Mexico (which had coffee and tropical fruit products) and the consumer market of Monterrey, and to establish a base for activities in agriculture, livestock, and the extraction of strategic resources including precious metals and timber. The Brown Brothers reached the area as a direct result of the growth of early-eighteenth-century trade between the northern and mid-Atlantic colonies on the eastern seaboard of the future United States and their southern counterparts. That activity quickly reached the Caribbean and then Mexico.[3]

The arrival of Charles Stillman at Matamoros in 1828 marked a key moment in the development of the modern U.S.-Mexican border relationship: the introduction of finance capital. Stillman, a dynamic import-export trader from New York, was astonished to see the Mexicans buy out his entire initial cargo in a matter of hours. Then he made an equally high profit on the cargo of mineral ingots, including silver and lead, cotton, and sugar, that he sent back to Manhattan. As a partner in Stillman and Woodward, one of the largest import firms in New York, and as the third-largest investor in the National City Bank, Stillman was well connected in U.S. financial circles. He reported the investment opportunities that he saw in northern Mexico to his partners George Woodward, the founder of the Hanover National Bank, and John Jacob Astor and Moses Taylor, his associates at National City.

Over the next forty years Stillman established a trade and banking empire that extended from Matamoros, the easternmost point in the border region, southwest to Monterrey and San Juan de los Lagos, near Guadalajara, and northwest up the Rio Grande to Paso del Norte. Stillman even owned the riparian rights to the Rio Grande in south Texas, the river that served as the dividing line between the United States and Mexico for the eastern and central areas of the border.

But Stillman's association with the capitalists of National City was the beginning of an even more far-reaching border hegemony. Led by his son James Stillman, who began by managing international investments around Monterrey and then served as bank president from 1892 to 1919, the National City capitalists dominated much of the border region for the next century. The bank director E. H. Harriman managed the Southern Pacific Railroad that connected Chicago, New Orleans, and Los Angeles and that provided transportation infrastructure to southern California, Arizona, New Mexico, Texas, as well as to Sonora, Sinaloa, Chihuahua, Coahuila, and Durango in Mexico. Another director, Henry Huntington, also controlled the rail lines of greater Los Angeles.

Meanwhile, during the late nineteenth century and the early twentieth, firms run by National City directors developed real estate across Southern California, including in Rancho Palos Verdes, Santa Barbara, and the border area between Los Angeles and the "Inland Empire." Another director owned the XIT Ranch in west Texas, claimed to be "the largest Ranch in the World." Other directors—Anson Phelps; Cleveland Dodge; William Rockefeller, the chairman of Standard Oil; and Stillman—dominated the mining industry of northern Mexico and the American Southwest, heading such firms as Phelps Dodge and Amalgamated Copper in Sonora and Arizona. Rockefeller controlled much of the fuel supply for Mexico and the American Southwest.[4] The entire gamut of American capitalists, led by the wider financial community of New York, would become involved in the U.S.-Mexican border region.

In 1861 the appointment of Thomas Scott as undersecretary of war was another key moment in the shaping of Mexico's modern border relationship with the United States. Placed in charge of war materials procurement, Scott was the president of the largest industrial firm in the world, the Pennsylvania Railroad, and already had a well-developed relationship with the nation's leading financiers and industrialists, including Moses Taylor, John Jacob Astor, William Aspinwall, William Dodge, and Anson Phelps of the National City Bank; Junius Morgan and Anthony Drexel of the firm of Morgan and Drexel of Philadelphia; and financiers in New York, including the Roosevelts, Beekmans, and Whitneys, who joined with George Baker to create the First National Bank of New York. These banks became the three most important financial institutions in the United States during the period extending from the Civil War to the 1930s.

The leading financiers and industrialists of the United States were already closely connected with Scott. Steel magnates such as John Griswold, a holder of the Bessemer patent, and locomotive and machinery manufacturers such as Charles Morgan of the Morgan Iron Works of New York, the leaders of the duPont Company of Wilmington, and the bridge builder James Eads of St. Louis had vast experience in meeting the demands of the expansive railroad industry. Their manufacturing complex demonstrated its capacity by undertaking the construction of fifty-four iron and steel *Monitor* warships during the Civil War. Scott widened his interactions to include the firearms divisions of the companies with which he had contacts, while also adding to his contacts to include the arms company Remington. That contact would be important to events along the U.S.-Mexico border.

The elite U.S. financial houses sold Union bonds for the Civil War effort throughout the Northeast and Great Britain to underwrite the government's arms orders, creating an unprecedented cohesion of capitalist interests between the Anglos and the Americans, and between regional capitalists in the Northeast and Midwest. The manufacturers in turn needed financing to expand sufficiently to meet wartime demand. The northern financial elites were also buying shares in Remington, Union Metallic Cartridge, and the other arms companies, enabling the larger firms to acquire the smaller ones as the war went on. They would demonstrate that cohesion immediately after the war, when they financed and provided the necessary arms for the Mexican resistance to expel the French invaders from their country by 1867. The success of the Mexican resistance was greatly enhanced by the delivery of arms by prominent U.S. officers. General William Tecumseh Sherman ceremoniously turned over artillery and modern rifles to President Benito Juarez at Paso del Norte. Those weapons were part of a stream of U.S. military supplies given to the Mexicans by the leading American banking capitalists and by the U.S. government. These weapons armed the men of General Luis Terrazas, who in 1866 crushed a strong French force between Chihuahua City and Paso del Norte.

General Mariano Escobedo received thousands of rifles and artillery from General Lew Wallace that were used to defeat the strongest French force in the northern half of Mexico, forcing the Europeans to retreat to a line far to the south extending from San Luis Potosi to Zacatecas. Later that year, at Chihuahua City, General Wallace presented a contract to President Juarez on behalf of the bondholders of Mexican debt in New York. The agreement offered to forgive the now enormous Mexican national debt in return for a national telegraph and railroad concession that would have given ownership of Mexico's transportation and communications infrastructure to the largest capitalists in the United States. Juarez refused the offer.

The closeness of the U.S. financial elites who came to dominate the border after the Civil War had a social dimension as well. Using Phelps Dodge and Remington as an example, we find a Dodge marrying a Hartley, the coupling that brought the Remington Arms president Marcellus Hartley Dodge into the world. Notably, leading guests at the wedding included Taylor, the president of National City, and Charles Stillman, the leading U.S. investor in Mexico and the third-largest investor in City Bank.

Since 1828 Stillman had marketed U.S. products at the annual trade fairs at San Juan de los Lagos, exchanging U.S. and Mexican exports and employing

Mexicans to haul the goods between Guadalajara, Saltillo, Monterrey, Matamoros, Brownsville, Laredo, and Corpus Christi, Texas. He also bought more than two million acres of land in the Rio Grande Valley of Texas and worked the properties with Mexican crews, some of whom learned to migrate from Mexico to Texas yearly. During the Civil War Stillman earned the modern-day equivalent of approximately $18 billion shipping cotton from Texas, Arkansas, and Louisiana to Monterrey, Mexico, for the production of Confederate Army uniforms at the La Fama textile mills and to New York, where his largest customer was Scott's Union Army. It was a triumph of capitalism and tied American expansion and profits directly to Mexico and to Mexican workers in the garments industry.

U.S. Investments in Mexico: Railroads to Oil

After the Civil War Scott and the three largest financial interests that had supported the Union—the directors of the Morgan, First National, and National City banks—joined Generals Grenville Dodge, William Jackson Palmer, William Rosecrans, Ulysses S. Grant, James Garfield, and Rutherford B. Hayes in the development of western U.S. and Mexican railroads, while Generals Luis Terrazas of Chihuahua and Phillip Sheridan led campaigns to control the region against the Native Americans who claimed it. In Mexico and the Southwest, Mexican workers joined their Asian counterparts in the laying of the rails.

General Philip Sheridan led his forces westward against the hopelessly outgunned Native Americans and the railroaders followed him. In this chapter we take the southern route toward Mexico to underscore the modern origins of Mexican-U.S. immigration. In 1865 Charles Stillman financed George Brackenridge with $100,000 for the creation of the San Antonio National Bank, an institution that worked with National City in support of the industrialization of Monterrey and with Brown Brothers to develop commercialized agriculture in the neighboring "Laguna" region around Torreon. Those workers soon began a yearly migration pattern that continued into the mid-twentieth century from La Laguna to Texas, then Oklahoma, and then Kansas, before returning to the "Laguna." That practice did not end until the workers were replaced by the braceros during the 1950s.

Bankers in Texas played a critical role in the development of trade with the border region and Mexico. In the early twentieth century James Stillman, chairman of the National City Bank and protégé of Moses Taylor, who financially pioneered the northwestern United States, owned nineteen banks in Texas alone, while his bank financed the operations of copper companies including Phelps Dodge, Amalgamated Copper, Towne, and American Smelting and Refining. These companies depended on transnational Mexican workers who crossed the border between sites such as Nacozari, Cananea, San Luis Potosi, El Paso, Douglas, Bisbee Jerome, and Silver City and refineries in El Paso, Silver City, and Arizona.

But an even higher level of capital involvement took place earlier in the border region. During the 1870s and 1880s Scott, Anson Phelps, William Dodge, and others pushed the Texas and Pacific Railroad from Dallas toward El Paso, while National City and other New York financiers bankrolled the construction of the Southern Pacific from New Orleans to Los Angeles. They did so while George Baker, Junius Morgan, and J. P. Morgan took control of the Northern Pacific and joined Stillman, William Rockefeller, and other National City Bank leaders to share control of the Union Pacific, which crossed the nation at its geographic center, between the Northern Pacific and Southern Pacific. A small national financial elite emerged in control of the entire U.S. transportation infrastructure, and it would extend its success across the border into Mexico. That step provided Mexican workers with easy access to higher-paying jobs in their neighboring country.[5]

The American financial engagement with Mexico reached an unprecedented level of intensity between 1865 and 1867, when the victorious northern financiers emerged from their Civil War to become "the New York Bondholders of the Mexican National Debt." They had given loans and arms grants to Mexico's government during its struggle against French imperialism. By the end of the struggle the Mexican government had incurred debts beyond reckoning with the leading U.S. capitalists who headed the American banks, strategic resource companies, industries, and agribusinesses. After years of negotiations with the Mexican presidents Benito Juarez and Sebastian Lerdo de Tejada, who feared close ties with the expansive U.S. elites, various railroad concessions were finally agreed to between 1872 and 1875. The leading New York financiers, who were financing the Pennsylvania Railroad and already creating the New York Central Railroad and the Mexican Telegraph Company, along with secondary banking interests who included the Beekmans and Roosevelts, were poised to take over Mexico's transportation and communications infrastructure.

Díaz's Regime and American Capitalists

In late 1875, however, after Lerdo's election to a second term as president, he announced the cancellation of all the contracts that allowed railroads to cross the border into Mexico, with the admonition "Better a desert between strength and weakness." At that point General Porfirio Díaz emerged — the prototype of the third world general deemed worthy of support by American elites. His dictatorship would extend from 1876 to 1910 and set the standard for the Duvaliers, Batistas, Marcoses, Rhees, Pinochets, Pahlevis, and others who followed during the next century.

During 1876 Díaz lived in the Stillman residence at Brownsville, Texas, and received two million recharging cartridges and other weaponry from Remington and the Whitney Arms Company. The supplies were delivered by the Morgan Steamship line of New Orleans and New York, which during the 1830s had rushed supplies to Sam Houston one day before the Battle of San Jacinto. Díaz armed sixteen hundred men, divided equally between Mexicans and Americans, and attacked across the border repeatedly in the first half of 1876 until Matamoros was taken. Later that year he seized the presidency in triumph from a militarily defeated and bankrupt government unable to secure the loans it had sought in New York.

Over the next two decades a handful of American elites, a virtual foreign policy oligarchy, gained control of the transportation and communications infrastructures of both countries and was ready to expand to the rest of the world. By 1910, after thirty-five years of Díaz's brutal regime, the leading financiers and industrialists of the United States controlled 90 percent of the land directly on the Mexican side of the border. They extended their power to include more than 70 percent of remaining coastlines and frontiers, most port facilities, and 23 percent of the nation's surface area, including enormous oil, timber, and mineral properties. About eight thousand American colonists and proprietors, holding less than 100,000 acres each, held another 5 percent of Mexico's land surface. Meanwhile U.S. businessmen owned an estimated 80 percent of incorporated enterprises on the Mexican side of the border area and an even higher percentage of active capital. Sir Weetman Pearson, a close friend of Stillman and Morgan, owned the principal non-American oil property in Mexico, while other British capitalists owned two-thirds of the non-U.S. capital. That pattern was replicated on the border, where one French mining interest and one British landholding interest, both in Baja California Norte, depended on American shipping and railroad lines. European investors held about 3 percent and the Mexicans only 7 percent of incorporated assets on the border and across the nation.

On the American-owned estates on the Mexican side of the border, the socioeconomic order, imposed from the outside, included a labor regime characterized by debt peonage, a ban on unions not approved by the government, segregated housing and workplaces, and even slavery at U.S.-owned properties on the southern periphery,[6] the Rascon Hacienda in the Huasteca Potosina and the Batopilas silver mines in the Copper Canyon. In the late nineteenth century the border experienced extremes of wealth, power, poverty, and hopelessness. The U.S. capitalists who went there quickly enveloped all of Mexico before spreading out across Latin America, the Pacific, and then the world. The hopes, inequalities, and abuses of the border became global. In the 1840s Moses Taylor had envisioned the Pacific Ocean as an "American Lake," and he started the Pacific Mail Steamship Company, with headquarters in San Francisco and ports of call that included Ensenada and Mazatlan.

Then during the 1880s J. P. Morgan, George Baker, James Stillman, and Jacob Schiff of Kuhn Loeb adopted the name South America Group as they aligned themselves as junior partners with the leading capitalists of the British Empire for investments throughout Latin America. At the same time Morgan, Baker, and Stillman, calling themselves "the Trio," made global investments with their British imperial banking partners. The group would include Lord Balfour, Sir Ernest Cassell, John Jacob Astor, Cecil Rhodes, and probably Pearson. Stillman, Baker, and Morgan each took 5 percent on behalf of their investors' syndicates for a total of 15 percent of British imperial business undertakings in Asia, the Middle East, and Africa. The Trio and the South American Group included America's wealthiest men as partners in the venture. The cooperation, competition, and interactions that began on the Mexican-U.S. border between U.S. elites and Mexicans resulted in a social mixture that continues in the region as well as on a global scale.

In the late nineteenth century the nation's leading financial heavyweights hired Mexican workers for their enterprises on the border: Cyrus McCormick, William Rockefeller, John D. Rockefeller, Andrew Carnegie, James Ben Ali Haggin, William Salomon, August Belmont (representing the Rothschilds), Collis Huntington, Ford Frick, Elbert H. Gary, Henry Phipps, William Dodge, Cleveland Dodge, Anson Phelps, W. S. Valentine, John Stewart, the Barney brothers, and members of the Converse, Dodge, Doheny, duPont, Conant, Fargo, Grace, Guggenheim, Harriman, Pullman, Mills, Hyde, Drexel, Hearst, Tevis, Vanderbilt, Whitney, and Wrigley families. Their power was hegemonic. While there was virtually no Mexican capitalist capable of offering employment in the exploitation of strategic resources, several hundred U.S. mining engineers in northern Mexico joined an even larger number of skilled U.S. workers in the timber and cattle industries throughout the country in the last two decades before the Revolution of 1910.

The movement into Mexico had a logical consistency with the elites' experience on the U.S. side of the border. Tevis, Hearst, and Ben Ali Haggin, partners in the Anaconda mines, purchased the Kern County Land Company that dominated the San Joaquin Valley in California. Their company and others soon engaged thousands of Mexican agricultural workers. Before entering Mexico, Hearst bought the land around Silver City and the extension from Deming to Columbus. Haggin and Tevis simultaneously took part in the silver industry at Batopilas and in the Sierra Madre. At Batopilas they employed eighteen mining engineers, a schoolteacher, a doctor, and two nurses, all from the United States. Nearby Hearst purchased gold mines at El Oro in Durango and the Babicora cattle ranch in Chihuahua, where he too brought in American foremen and their families.

Converse, a chief railroad construction engineer, built the Southern Pacific from Houston to Eagle Pass before taking over construction of the Mexican National Lines from the border to the interior of Mexico, a project which involved many skilled American workers. He then invested in the Intercontinental Rubber Company of Zacatecas, a company which included major Rockefeller and Guggenheim participation as well as skilled American personnel, who worked in supervision and guided major projects such as planting. Its guayule product—latex from the guayule bushes—entered the United States on trains running on the railroad lines that Converse engineered.

At the end of the nineteenth century Phelps, Dodge, Stillman, Harriman, Huntington, and the Rockefellers then joined in the creation of the Amalgamated Copper Trust, an attempt to monopolize copper production around the world. They began with their mines in Arizona, Sonora, and Montana, which included those at Cananea and Nacozari. In competition with them Morgan supported the Guggenheims and their American Smelting and Refining Company (ASARCO), the operations of which extended from Colorado to El Paso to central Mexico. Mexican and U.S. workers regularly crossed the border to work in the Amalgamated Copper and ASARCO mining camps.

During the 1890s Stillman, William Rockefeller, and John Stewart, head of the United States Trust Company of New York, created the Monterrey Belt Railroad which girded the city and dominated its economy. On a grander scale they joined Baker and Morgan in the ownership of the National and Central railways of Mexico and the Mexican Telegraph Company. Stillman, William Rockefeller, and W. H. Harriman of the City Bank also controlled the Sud Pacifico of Mexico, which connected Guadalajara, Sinaloa, and Sonora with the Southern Pacific at Nogales and Yuma, providing access to Arizona and California for tens of thousands of Mexicans yearly.

At sea, beginning in the 1860s, William Aspinwall and Stillman of City Bank, followed by J. P. Morgan and others of the Pacific Mail Steam Company, had begun bringing Mexicans from Mazatlan, Manzanillo, Acapulco, and Salina Cruz, along with their products—silver, cotton, fruits, and sugar—to northern Baja California, southern California, San Francisco, and Asia.

In the early twentieth century duPont established a munitions factory at Dinamita, Durango, on Huntington's Mexican International railroad which ran from Eagle Pass to Torreon to Durango. Earlier Huntington had created the Durango Iron Company, while the Cudahy cattle products company began ranching operations in Durango and American timber interests bought several million acres of forest in the Sierra Madre Mountains of Durango and Chihuahua. All these enterprises involved the introduction of skilled American personnel.[7]

At the end of the nineteenth century the agricultural industry on the Nazas River near Torreon became enormous and engaged many thousands of Mexican laborers. William Potter of the Brown Brothers Bank of New York managed the Tlahuallilo Estates, the largest of these enterprises. The company provided the United States with fresh vegetables in the winter delivered by the International Railroad, owned by the Southern Pacific Group.[8] Meanwhile U.S.-owned railroads and lumber companies accessed the vast timber and mineral resources of the Sierra Madre through shorter lines known as *minerales*. By the late 1880s Mexican lumberjacks had joined their mining and agricultural counterparts, regularly moving between northern Mexico and the American Southwest.

Finally, the Mexican oil industry began with a series of bonanzas in the first decade of the twentieth century and provided yet another dimension of the border relationship. Financed through competitive bidding between banks, the industry required the financiers in New York to have an easy familiarity with the region. William Salomon advanced Edward Doheny with millions of dollars after Doheny was able to demonstrate the enormous extent of his discoveries near Tampico. Then thousands of skilled U.S. oilfield workers from Louisiana, Texas, and Oklahoma flooded into the region between Tampico and Tuxpan. Once again the shipping and railroad lines provided a rapid transportation of goods and people to Houston, New Orleans, and New York. In the two decades before and during the revolution of 1910, Mexican businessmen made regular trips to Houston and New York State.[9]

Conclusion

U.S. capital sought strategic resources in Mexico as the first step in what became a global expansion, in the process developing a close and unequal relationship with the Mexican working class. That process began with the creation of an extensive travel and communications infrastructure that led to a transformation of Mexico's economy and culture and that introduced technology and higher levels of production and consumption. Yet the inequalities between Mexican workers and their elites, and between American capitalists and Mexico, created a condition of economic dependency and extreme inequality. The actions of U.S. elite capital and Mexico's continuing weakness introduced and continued a transformation of the demographics of the American Southwest, as infrastructure and strategic resource companies sought the financial advantages offered by cheap Mexican labor at points of extraction in Mexico and at processing centers in the United States. Well before the Revolution of 1910 Mexican workers were emigrating to Los Angeles, San Antonio, Kansas City, and Chicago in search of employment and better housing, diets, healthcare, and schools. Their pioneering efforts prepared the way for the waves of immigrants who followed.[10]

Notes

1 "Archeological Zone of Paquimé, Casas Grandes," Decision of the World Heritage Commission, UNESCO (Mexico City, 1991), 40.

2 To begin study of the vast literature treating northern Mexico during the Spanish colonial era and the American Southwest see David J. Weber, *The Spanish Frontier in North America* (New Haven: Yale University Press, 1992).

3 For an analysis of the process of U.S. expansion see James A. Henretta, *The Origins of American Capitalism* (Boston: Northeastern University Press, 1991).

4 For an extended discussion of Charles Stillman on the border see John Mason Hart, *Empire and Revolution: The Americans in Mexico since the Civil War* (Berkeley: University of California Press, 2002), 22–28; and Hart, *Revolutionary Mexico: The Coming and Process of the Mexican Revolution* (Berkeley: University of California Press, 1987), 107–24.

5 Hart, *Empire and Revolution*, 33–51.

6 Slavery had been abolished in Mexico at the time of independence and again, with regard to the state of Texas, when immigrant U.S. planters in contravention of the law brought slaves with them in 1829.

7 Hart, *Empire and Revolution*, 261–418.

8 For the best discussion of Mexican migratory labor see Emilio Zamora, *The World of the Mexican American Worker in Texas* (College Station: Texas A&M Press, 1993).

9 Hart, *Revolutionary Mexico*, 105–24, 247–49.

10 Gilbert G. Gonzalez, Guest Workers or Colonized Labor? Mexican Labor Migration to the United States (Boulder: Paradigm, 2006).

PART FOUR

Contemporary and Applied Perspectives

CHAPTER SIXTEEN

Central American Migration
and the Shaping of Refugee Policy

María Cristina García

A quarter-million people died during the political upheavals in Nicaragua, El Salvador, and Guatemala in the last decades of the twentieth century, and more than a million were internally displaced. Many of those who survived the warfare and the human rights abuses chose temporary refuge in neighboring countries such as Costa Rica and Honduras, living anonymously as undocumented immigrants or refugees in government-run camps. When the camps filled up, or when the survival of the refugees was again threatened, Nicaraguans, Salvadorans, and Guatemalans traveled farther north to Mexico, the United States, and Canada (see chapter 17).

This chapter examines the impact that nongovernmental actors had on refugee policy during the refugee crisis of 1974–96. The policies of three receiving nations—Mexico, the United States, and Canada—are examined. An estimated two million of the Central Americans who fled the region during this period settled in one of these three countries, and it was the pressure exerted by nongovernmental actors that forced these states to address the refugee crisis. This chapter examines how these actors reframed national debates about immigration, pressed for changes in policy, met the needs of refugees, and ultimately provided a voice for the displaced.

The Refugees

The revolutions in Nicaragua, El Salvador, and Guatemala were each the product of decades of struggles over land and resources, but the violence escalated during the 1970s and 1980s. In Nicaragua the *contras*, backed by Washington, waged war against the Sandinista government that overthrew the Somoza dictatorship in 1979. In El Salvador the *escuadrones de la muerte* (the paramilitary "death squads"), with ties to the country's civilian-military juntas, silenced through rape, torture, and assassination all those perceived to be enemies of the state, including journalists, labor organizers, and priests and nuns who espoused liberation theology. In Guatemala a series of right-wing military dictatorships waged war against the guerrilla groups associated with the Guatemalan National Revolutionary Unity (URNG). Through their "scorched earth" policy the Guatemalan army burned hundreds of Mayan villages to eliminate the guerrillas' support base, and slaughtered thousands.[1]

Central Americans displaced by the turmoil in their countries traveled wherever they had networks of family, friends, or countrymen. Some moved within their own country; others crossed borders, following established patterns of migration. Salvadorans traveled to Honduras and Guatemala, and Guatemalans to Chiapas, because they had done so for decades as migratory labor.[2] But with each passing year populations emerged in less traditional areas: Salvadorans in Mexico, Guatemalans in Belize, and Nicaraguans in Costa Rica.[3] The clustering of several Spanish-speaking countries in a small geographic territory made it comparatively easy for refugees to seek safer opportunities elsewhere.

The international press commonly referred to these migrants as refugees because political upheaval played a role in their migration, but their legal status varied from country to country. According to article 1A(2) of the 1951 UN Convention Relating to the Status of Refugees, a refugee is a person who, "owing to a well-founded fear of persecution for reasons of race, religion, nationality, membership of a particular social group or political opinion, is outside the country of his nationality and is unable, or owing to such fear, is unwilling to avail himself to the protection of that country; or who, not having a nationality and being outside the country of his former habitual residence as a result of such events is unable, or owing to such fear, is unwilling to return to it."[4] Even though most Central American countries were signatories to the UN Convention, its 1967 Protocol, or both, as well as to several regional conventions on refugee issues,[5] most did not have formal procedures through which to grant asylum. They also demonstrated varying levels of commitment to the convention's principle of *non-refoulement* (no forced return).

Most Central American migrants did not meet the UN definition of refugee status, having fled their countries because of a generalized climate of violence. By 1980 the United Nations High Commissioner for Refugees (UNHCR) readily admitted that the convention and protocol were too restrictive and advocated a more lenient response toward those who did not meet the strict definition of "refugee." In 1984 the nonbinding Cartagena Declaration on Refugees tried to offer further guidance in dealing with the Central American refugee crisis. It stated that refugees were "persons who have fled their country because their lives, safety, or liberty have been threatened by generalized violence, foreign aggression, internal conflicts, massive violations of human rights or other circumstances which have seriously disturbed public order."[6] However, each country conducted its own domestic debate on what constituted a refugee, and what types of programs should be made available to those so designated (e.g. asylum or temporary safe haven, work authorization, social services, etc.). Most governments preferred to view the Nicaraguans, Salvadorans, and Guatemalans as economic migrants because doing so freed them from any responsibility. Human rights organizations and other NGOs were at times the migrants' only advocates, urging a broader definition of their status that would facilitate their accommodation.

Despite a migratory tradition within the region, the Central American nations were ill prepared for the refugee crisis. Even refugee-producing nations were forced to accommodate refugees from other countries (Nicaragua hosted displaced Salvadorans; El Salvador hosted displaced Guatemalans).[7] By 1989 six nations—Costa Rica, Honduras, Nicaragua, El Salvador, Guatemala, and Belize—reported an aggregate 800,000 immigrants, of whom only 10 percent were officially documented as refugees and received assistance. The UNHCR advocated resettlement within the region because such an arrangement would facilitate eventual repatriation, and it provided millions of dollars in funding to local government agencies to establish camps and provide emergency food and medical care. But camps filled up quickly, and opportunities for wage-earning labor and for education were limited in these facilities. Not surprisingly, many refugees continued moving north to Mexico, the United States, and Canada in search of better opportunities.

Guatemalans in Mexico

For the first time in its history Mexico was forced into the role of country of first asylum for hundreds of thousands of people. Mexican legislation recognized the category of "persons granted asylum," but asylum was rarely granted—and then only to those who applied from outside the country and could demonstrate political persecution. Central Americans fleeing a general climate of violence did not meet that category. In the early 1980s, for example, only one hundred Central Americans were granted the F.M. 10 visa (asylee), and none were granted this status from 1986 to 1990.[8]

Nicaraguans and Salvadorans migrated illegally to Mexico in large numbers, but it was the Guatemalan migration that provided the greatest challenge for both state and nongovernmental actors in Mexico. According to UNHCR sources, the Guatemalan refugee migration to Mexico began in 1980. The refugees were mostly Maya Indians, especially Kanjobal, Chuj, Jacalteca, and Mam, largely from the heavily populated departments of El Quiché and Huehuetenango, targeted by the government during its counterinsurgency campaign. Thousands of Maya fled across the Guatemalan-Mexican border and established settlements in Chiapas, creating a type of "refugee zone."[9]

In July 1980 López Portillo's administration established a new interdepartmental office, the Mexican Committee for Refugee Assistance (COMAR), to oversee UNHCR assistance to the Central American refugees. Mexico agreed to accept Guatemalans as long as they were approved and registered by COMAR and remained in government-supervised camps and settlements in Chiapas. Those who were approved were granted ninety-day renewable visas (the F.M. 8), which offered them the temporary, nonimmigrant status of "border visitor." If the Guatemalans traveled beyond the 150-kilometer refugee zone they forfeited their rights to protection.[10] Despite the continual arrival of refugees each week, the administrations of José López Portillo and his successor Miguel de la Madrid (1982–88) resisted drafting new refugee or asylum legislation, arguing that the Mexican constitution offered its "border visitors" sufficient rights and guarantees.

By 1984 ninety-two camps and settlements housed 46,000 refugees in Chiapas. Access to the camps was restricted: armed agents of the Servicios Migratorios patrolled each camp, and only church and UNHCR representatives were granted permission to enter the area. Conditions in all the settlements and camps were poor, reflecting the poverty of Chiapas, the UNHCR's stretched budget, and to some extent government policy. The refugees provided aid workers with a number of challenges. They arrived malnourished and with a host of gastrointestinal and respiratory illnesses. Infant mortality was estimated at two hundred deaths per thousand live births. To halt the spread of disease, aid workers worked around the clock to build wells, sewers, and latrines in settlements that seemed to spring up virtually overnight. Camps and settlements offered few opportunities for wage-earning labor, land cultivation, or vocational training, and most refugees did not qualify for work permits outside the settlements.[11] Not surprisingly, the majority of Guatemalans who arrived in Mexico preferred to remain outside the government's reach: by 1992 an estimated 150,000 Guatemalans lived without authorization in Chiapas.

The refugee crisis also presented the Mexican government with one of its most serious diplomatic challenges. In Guatemala the governments of Romeo Lucas García (1978–82), Efraín Ríos Montt (1982–83), and Oscar Mejía Víctores

(1983–86) charged that guerrillas channeled weapons, food, and medicine to their compatriots-in-arms through these refugee camps, and demanded that Mexico repatriate the refugees or at the very least relocate them farther from the border zone. When the Mexican government failed to act decisively either way, the Guatemalan army expanded its counterinsurgency campaign into Mexico. From 1982 to 1984 units known as the *kaibiles* crossed the border to kidnap, interrogate, and murder alleged guerrillas and their supporters, and Guatemalan planes and helicopters strafed and bombed refugee camps and settlements to intimidate the population.[12] In 1984 the Mexican government announced that in the interest of national security and the refugees' own protection the refugees would be relocated to the states of Campeche and Quintana Roo. In response refugee advocates launched an intensive media campaign to discourage the relocation, arguing that it would undermine the refugees' families, communities, and networks. The pressure from church workers, journalists, scholars, and NGOs ultimately forced the Mexican government to allow the majority of the refugees to remain in Chiapas. Between 1984 and 1987 only 18,000 of the 46,000 refugees were relocated.[13]

Throughout the 1980s and 1990s a number of actors played a role in defending rights of Central Americans in Mexico. "Solidarity committees" such as the Movimiento Mexicano de Solidaridad con el Pueblo de Guatemala and the Comité Mexicano de Solidaridad con el Pueblo Salvadoreño represented the refugees' interests before government agencies. Four of Mexico's political parties made pronouncements in defense of refugee rights, and the moderate-to-liberal press, especially *La Jornada* in Mexico City, published sympathetic articles and editorials reminding the government of its humanitarian responsibilities.

The more liberal sectors of the Roman Catholic Church played the most visible role in refugee assistance. Clergy, nuns, and lay church workers in southeastern Mexico were among the first to notice the steady influx of Central Americans into their communities. Through parish aid offices they organized networks of volunteers who visited the refugees in their settlements and provided them with medical care, food, and clothing. UNHCR personnel remarked at the generosity of Mexican *campesinos* who, though living at subsistence levels themselves, shared their land and resources with those they considered even needier. The Roman Catholic dioceses of San Cristóbal de las Casas and Tapachula created organizations to oversee the distribution of aid: its Comité Cristiano de Solidaridad (CCS) targeted the Guatemalan refugees in government-run camps, while the diocese of Tapachula's Comité Diocesano de Ayuda a Inmigrantes Fronterizos (CODAIF) assisted Central Americans who did not receive government recognition or assistance. Other Catholic dioceses, among them those of Tehuantepec and Cuernavaca, collected and transported material aid for the refugees in Chiapas. At first these organizations concentrated on meeting the refugees' immediate housing, food, and medical needs, as well as providing pastoral counseling. As the refugee migration became a seemingly permanent aspect of life in the southeast, they concentrated on "durable solutions" to help the refugees become self-supporting.

Bishop Samuel Ruiz García of the Diocese of San Cristóbal emerged as the most visible defender of refugee and indigenous rights in Mexico. When the Guatemalans began settling in his diocese Ruiz recorded the *testimonios* of the refugees and documented the Guatemalan army's attacks on settlements, as well as the failure of the Mexican government to respond to the crisis. Excerpts from his reports were published in newspapers, newsletters, and church bulletins throughout Mexico and abroad; the diocesan newsletter, *Caminante*, circulated widely and gave up-to-date information on conditions in Central America as well as in the camps and settlements. This information attracted donations from international NGOs. By the mid-1980s Ruiz was raising over a million dollars in emergency aid each year, and his CCS coordinated the work of hundreds of international volunteers. His diocese worked with local Mexican landowners to create a land-lease program so that some of the refugee communities could produce their own food. Working with advocacy networks in Europe, Canada, and the United States, the diocese also found international markets for the refugees' crafts so they would have another vehicle for self-sufficiency.[14]

The Catholic Church in Chiapas respected the refugees' rights to seek safe haven outside the UNHCR camps and settlements. Churches helped to hide undocumented Central Americans from local police and often arranged their transportation to safer locations. By 1981 a network of "sanctuaries" had emerged throughout the country, as far north as Matamoros and Nogales on the U.S.-Mexican border, that helped undocumented Central Americans avoid detection by police, find housing and employment, or cross over into the United States. When a sanctuary movement emerged in the United States in 1981, American volunteers worked with church workers in Tapachula, Ciudad Hidalgo, and other border towns to inform refugees of the opportunities for safe haven north of the border.[15] Later, when the peace accords were signed in 1996, Catholic relief workers also played a central role in the repatriation efforts, and they helped tens of thousands of refugees to reintegrate into Guatemalan society.

On July 17, 1990, after years of lobbying and advocacy from different groups, the Mexican Congress agreed to amend the General Population Law and provide new guidelines for the recognition and admission of refugees. Refugee status, as delineated by article 42, section 6, of the new law, drew on the definition offered by the Cartagena Declaration and marked the first time a state had included this more liberal definition into its legislation. Mexican law now recognized that a climate of "generalized violence" was sufficient grounds to offer protected status. In 2000 Mexico finally became a signatory to the UN Convention and Protocol.

Salvadorans in the United States

Mexican refugee policy affected the character and flow of migration to the United States and Canada. Since Nicaraguans and Salvadorans had little chance for government recognition and assistance in Mexico, they were more likely to continue migrating northward. A number of them entered with some type of temporary visa such as a student or tourist visa, and simply stayed once their visas expired, but the majority arrived without documents across the U.S.-Mexico border. The Central Americans who came to the United States were a cross-section of their societies: urban and rural dwellers, factory and agricultural workers, students and professionals, young and old.[16]

Officials of President Reagan's administration argued that there was little need for Central Americans to travel all the way to the United States. That many chose to come to the United States when there were opportunities for safe haven elsewhere suggested to administration officials that these migrants were economically rather than politically motivated. However, the administration's assumption that refugees' needs could be satisfactorily met in other countries was unrealistic. Likewise, members of the administration seemed unwilling to recognize their own role in destabilizing the region. But to admit that these migrants were bona fide refugees would have been to acknowledge that the groups and governments supported by Washington with millions of U.S. tax dollars violated human rights.

The majority of Central Americans did not qualify for asylum in the United States under the terms of the Refugee Act of 1980, which adopted the stricter UN definition of refugee. A petitioner for asylum now had to provide evidence of a well-founded fear of persecution. In a letter to the *New York Times*, a spokesperson for the State Department's political asylum division wrote: "It is not enough for the applicant to state that he faces the same conditions that every other citizen faces. [Under the terms of the Refugee Act we ask:] Why are you different from everyone else in your country? How have you been singled out, threatened, imprisoned, tortured, harassed?"[17]

In October 1981 the UNHCR charged that the United States was not living up to its responsibilities as a signatory to the UN Protocol, specifically its commitment to non-refoulement, or forced return. According to the UNHCR, the United States had engaged in a "systematic practice" of deporting Salvadorans to their country regardless of the merits of their claims to asylum.[18] Throughout the 1980s the UNHCR urged the United States to legislate a temporary status other than asylum as a compromise, offering protection to a group of people who temporarily needed it while allowing the United States to maintain its immigration priorities. Such a status would also protect Central Americans from deportation to a war zone and possible death.

Immigration legislation in the United States allowed for such a temporary status. Eventual Voluntary Departure, or EVD, was a discretionary status given by the State Department when it determined that conditions in a sending country made it dangerous for refugees to return. But Reagan resisted the idea of EVD for Central Americans on the grounds that the violence in El Salvador (as well as Nicaragua and Guatemala) was not sufficiently intense or widespread. State and Justice Department officials also worried that the promise of EVD would lure even more people to the United States who would then find a way to remain permanently. Thus while the United States publicly supported safe haven for non-convention refugees in theory, Reagan and his successor George H. W. Bush excluded the Central Americans from any such consideration. From 1983 to 1990 only 2.6 percent of Salvadoran asylum applications and 1.8 percent of Guatemalan applications were successful.[19]

The Justice Department instructed the Immigration and Naturalization Service (INS) and its Border Patrol to increase its surveillance of the border and expedite the deportation of the undocumented. Bail bonds were raised to as much as $7,500 per person in some INS districts to prevent release into society. Detention centers along the border filled to capacity with people the Border Patrol called "OTMs" ("Other Than Mexicans"). Abuses at detention centers in Texas and California, especially Port Isabel, Los Fresnos, and El Centro, prompted several lawsuits against the INS in the early 1980s. U.S. judges hearing these cases ruled in favor of the plaintiffs, ordering the INS to inform detainees of their right to petition for asylum and to meet with legal counsel. According to the courts, no one could be deported or coerced to sign voluntary departure forms without being informed of these rights. But over the next few years these rights were repeatedly violated.[20]

A vocal segment of the U.S. population kept Central America—and the plight of its refugees—on the front pages of U.S. newspapers. They challenged U.S. refugee policy as a means of protesting its foreign policy in Central America. These Americans argued that the United States had a legal obligation to protect the refugees based on the international conventions to which it was a signatory, and a moral obligation to do so because of its role in supporting the corrupt military regimes and death squads that had displaced the refugees.

Community groups along the border were at the frontlines of the refugee assistance network and mobilized to provide the Central American refugees with shelter, medical attention, and legal and psychological counseling. The Border Association for Refugees from Central America (BARCA) provided food, shelter, and clothing; raised funds to pay the bail bonds of detainees; and located sponsor families for refugee children who were alone in the United States. Groups such as Proyecto Libertad, El Rescate, the Central American Refugee Center (CARECEN), the Rio Grande Defense Committee, Texas Rural Legal Aid, and the Immigrant and Refugee Rights Project provided legal counseling and representation. Shelters for the refugees opened throughout the Southwest. In the border town of San Benito, Texas, just outside the Brownsville city limits, the Roman Catholic diocese operated Casa Oscar Romero (named for the Salvadoran archbishop assassinated by death squads in 1980), which became one of the most important symbols of popular resistance to INS policy during this period. Not surprisingly, most of these groups and shelters came under FBI surveillance.[21]

As in Mexico, religious groups played a central role in assisting the refugees and as part of a broader movement that lobbied to change immigration policy and foreign policy. Prominent theologians and peace activists, representing a variety of religious traditions and denominations, wrote and spoke out against U.S. policy, among them Daniel Berrigan, Elie Wiesel, and William Sloane Coffin. Roman Catholic religious orders such as the Maryknolls, the Paulists, and the Jesuits underwrote films and documentaries about Central America, published biographies of church workers assassinated by the death squads, and used their newsletters and periodicals to provide alternative interpretations of events in the region. Religious groups organized letter-writing campaigns and sent representatives to testify before Congress. Much of their energy focused on the campaign to win EVD status for Central Americans, especially for the Salvadorans who were believed to be in the most desperate situation.

Religious groups were also at the forefront of one of the most important acts of civil disobedience of the late twentieth century—the sanctuary movement—a resistance movement that protested U.S. foreign policy by harboring and transporting refugees in violation of immigration law. Reagan's administration tried to discourage the growth of the movement by dismissing this civic tradition and reminding activists that the principle of sanctuary was not recognized in common or statutory law. Violators faced hefty fines and imprisonment. The Justice Department began its surveillance of the sanctuary movement in 1982, and a number of activists were indicted soon after. The biggest sting against the movement occurred in 1984–85 in Tucson, where a covert operation called Operation Sojourner led to the indictment of sixteen sanctuary workers. These actions did not halt the spread of the movement. By the end of 1987 the number of sanctuaries had reached 450 and the movement involved 2 states that had made official pronouncements in support of sanctuary, 28 cities, 430 distinct religious bodies in 39 states, and more than 70,000 active participants.[22]

None of the lawsuits filed during the 1980s to protect the civil liberties of detainees halted the deportation of Central Americans; it just delayed the inevitable. However, the decisions handed down in various lawsuits did buttress a larger class-action lawsuit against the U.S. government in 1985, filed by eighty religious and refugee assistance groups with the goal of securing asylum for Salvadorans and Guatemalans: *American Baptist Churches in the USA v. Meese* (popularly known as the ABC lawsuit). In January 1991 a settlement was reached which granted new trials to Salvadorans who had entered the United States before September 19, 1990, and all Guatemalans who had entered before October 1, 1990.

As a parallel development, Congress passed the Immigration Act of 1990, which provided the statutory basis for safe haven through a status called temporary protected status (TPS). Over 200,000 Salvadorans living in the United States registered for TPS, and once it expired they became ineligible for Deferred Enforced Departure (DED), which delayed deportation for an additional period. Under the terms of the ABC settlement Salvadorans were eligible to apply for asylum once their DED status expired.

Through TPS, DED, and the new asylum adjudication process, Salvadorans had more vehicles through which to negotiate their legal stay in the United States. In 1997 Congress passed the Nicaraguan Adjustment and Central American Relief Act (NACARA), which allowed Nicaraguans present in the United States as of December 1, 1995, to adjust their status to that of legal permanent resident. Although the law primarily benefited Nicaraguans, Cubans, and nationals of the former Soviet bloc countries, Salvadorans and Guatemalans benefited to some extent as well, qualifying for "cancellation of removal" in some circumstances. By 2000 the Census Bureau reported that there were 655,000 Salvadorans, 372,487 Guatemalans, and 177,684 Nicaraguans living in the United States. The great majority were first-generation immigrants and their children.

Central Americans in Canada

Overland migration to Canada increased as the violence in Central America escalated, refugee camps filled up, and restrictive policies were enacted in Mexico and the United States. In general Canada received fewer Central American immigrants than Mexico and the United States did, in large part because of its more distant geographic location, but it granted asylum to a larger proportion of those who crossed its borders. From 1980 to 1986, for example, the approval rate for Salvadorans' asylum applications ranged between 21 and 60 percent, and for Guatemalans between 28 and 71 percent.[23] In all, 85,545 Salvadorans, Guatemalans, and Nicaraguans migrated to Canada between 1971 and 2001; Salvadorans accounted for close to two-thirds of that number.[24]

Just as Mexican policies affected the flow of migration to the United States, changes in U.S. policy forced the Canadian government to adjust its own policies reciprocally. In 1986 the U.S. Congress passed the Immigration Reform and Control Act (IRCA), which created a series of measures to restrict the number of undocumented workers in the country, among them an expanded border patrol and penalties on employers who knowingly hired undocumented workers. Consequently, Canada experienced a dramatic rise in the number of petitions for asylum, as immigrants of many countries left the United States and traveled northward in search of work and safe haven. In response the Canadian government imposed a series of new restrictions to discourage the increase in overland migration. Immigration officials at the Canadian border were instructed to send asylum applicants back to wait in the United States; the applicants were given a preliminary hearing date, usually many months away, and told to return at that time. Many of those forced to wait in the United States were then obliged by the INS to sign the voluntary departure form, to facilitate automatic deportation by the United States if Canada rejected their petition.[25] Those who were allowed to stay pending a review were left waiting in halfway houses, homeless shelters, gymnasiums, and churches on the U.S. side of the border in cities such as Detroit, Great Falls, Plattsburgh, Rochester, Buffalo, and Lackawanna.

Two bills were introduced in Parliament to address Canadian concerns about the burdens on their immigration system. Bill C-55, which passed in 1988, established a new independent tribunal, the Immigration and Refugee Board (IRB), and a more streamlined system of processing asylum claims to eliminate the backlog of applicants.[26] Much more controversial was Bill C-84, which introduced new measures for "detention and deterrence," including criminal penalties on those assisting unauthorized immigrants, designed to target sanctuary workers. C-84 passed despite vocal opposition from Canadian

NGOS. Over the next decade several other bills were passed by Parliament that established tougher criteria for asylum, resettlement, and detention. Among the most controversial policies enacted was the "safe third country" provision that allowed immigration officials to return asylum seekers to a third country—usually the United States—for adjudication if the claimant had passed through that country on the way to Canada. Because the United States had a much lower approval rate than Canada, refugee advocates argued that deportation to the United States was inhumane.[27]

As in the United States and Mexico, a small but vocal segment of the population affiliated with churches, charitable organizations, universities, labor groups, and other NGOs used their moral authority to remind the state of its humanitarian commitments. They lobbied to keep Canadian borders open and the refugee determination system fair and accessible. While not successful in shelving legislation, they were often instrumental in softening (and in some cases eliminating) the most restrictive measures.

Canadian labor groups generally advocated a generous state response to the refugee crisis. For example, when Canadians complained that the new immigrants took away jobs from citizens, labor groups disputed these claims. In 1987, when bills C-55 and C-84 were under discussion in Parliament, the president of the Canadian Auto Workers was among those who criticized the proposed legislation.[28] Likewise, Canadian scholars and policy analysts tried to influence state policies through conferences and symposia on asylum issues. The Latin American Working Group (LAWG), founded in the late 1960s, criticized what it perceived as the Canadian government's tacit support of human rights abuses. The Centre for Refugee Studies at York University founded its publication *Refuge* in 1981 as a forum for discussing such issues as the determination of refugee status, sponsorship, and resettlement programs. In 1985 the Canadian Institute for International Peace and Security (CIIPS) and the Canadian-Caribbean-Central American Policy Alternatives (CAPA) discussed ways that Canada might initiate durable solutions projects in the region. And the Canadian Council for Refugees, which represented 180 agencies and organizations, advocated for the rights of refugees in a variety of forums.

Church groups in Canada played a central role in challenging state policies. Using information from Canadian missionaries in the field, coalition groups such as the Inter-Church Committee on Human Rights in Latin America (ICCHRLA) and the Inter-Church Committee on Refugees published information on military maneuvers, death squads, human rights abuses, and refugees and displaced persons—information which some considered to be far superior to that of government sources. Church groups vocally opposed aid to repressive regimes in El Salvador and Guatemala, demanding that it be contingent on substantive improvements in human rights.

Speaking against the immigration policies of the late 1980s were influential mainline denominations and religious groups such as the Anglican Church, B'nai B'rith, and the Conference of Catholic Bishops. Some religious groups chose to litigate: in 1987 the Toronto Refugee Affairs Council, representing twenty-eight church and refugee aid groups, threatened to sue the federal government over the new legislation, claiming that it violated the Canadian Charter of Rights and Freedoms.[29] The Inter-Church Committee on Refugees (ICCR) submitted a brief to the UN Committee for Human Rights, charging that Canada's asylum determination system subjected asylum seekers to "cruel, inhuman, and degrading treatment."[30]

At the local level, individual churches established their own "refugee committees" and assumed financial responsibility for hundreds of immigrants. By the mid-1980s Canadian church workers were also active in the transnational "sanctuary work," transporting refugees across the U.S.-Canadian border, hiding them in safe houses, and securing legal and material assistance. Working with their counterparts in Mexico and the United States, Canadians traveled to detention centers, churches, shelters, and halfway houses to assist refugees in their asylum efforts. Their network on both sides of the border was particularly well developed. The Windsor Central American Refugee Sponsorship Network worked with churches and other groups in Detroit; *La Casa*, a refugee shelter in Buffalo, New York, worked with a sister shelter, *la Casa del Norte*, in Fort Erie, Ontario; clergy in North Dakota transported refugees across the border to their contacts in Manitoba.[31] As Canada was the final option for these refugees, their supporters helped them navigate the Canadian legal system.

Conclusion

After the Nicaraguan elections of 1990, the Salvadoran peace accords of 1992, and the Guatemalan peace accords of 1996, tens of thousands of Central Americans returned home to rebuild their lives and their countries. However, the majority of those who fled the region during the 1980s chose to remain in North America, especially as opportunities to normalize their status became available. They began to influence their countries of birth from abroad through millions of dollars in annual remittances. By 2003, for example, the Salvadoran immigrant community in the United States alone sent more than $2 billion in remittances each year, far exceeding the amount of money the United States spent in foreign aid to El Salvador.[32]

Despite the negotiation of peace accords, the migration from Central America has continued. During the late 1990s a series of natural disasters devastated the agricultural economies of this region and again forced thousands to seek wage-earning opportunities in the immigrant communities of *el norte*. These newer immigrants follow *la cadena*—their networks of family and friends who have already settled abroad. Consequently, in Central American communities today—in cities as diverse as Mexico City, Los Angeles, Miami, Washington, Toronto, and Montreal—it is not unusual to find households where members are both foreign and native-born, immigrant and sojourner, "legal" and unauthorized, monolingual and bilingual. As a result of the growing influence of these Central American communities abroad, it is also not unusual to find that homeland political candidates make campaign stops in these cities, with the hope that the migrants might influence family members' political choices back home.

The political and economic realities in Central America continue to produce a large migration of unemployed workers and asylum seekers, but today it is easier to remain an unauthorized immigrant in the underground economy of Mexico, the United States, or Canada than to secure an immigration visa or to secure safe haven, asylum, or some other protected status. Mexico, the United States, and Canada are committed to the free movement of trade and capital, but they are not equally committed to the free movement of labor.

One legacy of the refugee crisis is that it has encouraged greater cooperation in immigration matters between Mexico, the United States, and Canada, as well as other countries in the region. Since 1996 representatives from the Americas have met regularly at the Regional Conference on Migration (also known as the "Puebla Process") to exchange information and discuss such issues as transborder cooperation in surveillance, sanctions against trafficking, detention and deportation procedures, the integration of immigrants in host societies, migrant health, and the problems of women and minors.[33] Representatives from nongovernmental organizations have played a key role at these conferences, and increasingly governments are turning to NGOs not only as a reliable source of field data but as the source of creative solutions to complex problems.

Notes

1 Walter LaFeber, *Inevitable Revolutions: The United States in Central America* (New York: W. W. Norton, 1993); William M. LeoGrande, *Our Own Backyard: The United States in Central America, 1977–1992* (Chapel Hill: University of North Carolina Press, 1998); H. Rodrigo Jauberth et al., *The Difficult Triangle: Mexico, Central America, and*

the United States (Boulder: Westview, 1992); Jonathan Lemco, *Canada and the Crisis in Central America* (New York: Praeger, 1991); and Peter MacFarlane, *Northern Shadows: Canadians and Central America* (Toronto: Between the Lines, 1989).

2 Cecelia Menjívar, *Fragmented Ties: Salvadoran Immigrant Networks in America* (Berkeley: University of California Press, 2000); Germán Martínez Velasco, *Plantaciones, trabajo guatemalteco y política migratoria en la frontera sur de México* (Tuxtla Gutiérrez: Goberino de Chiapas, 1994); Sergio Aguayo, *El éxodo centroamericano: Consecuencias de un conflicto* (Mexico City: Consejo Nacional de Fomento Educativo, 1985).

3 UNHCR, Information Paper, International Conference on Central American Refugees (CIREFCA), Guatemala City, May 29–31, 1989; Gilda Pacheco, *A Decade of Ambiguity: Approaches to Central American Refugee Assistance in the 1980s* (Washington: Center for Immigration Policy and Refugee Assistance, Georgetown University, 1991); Tanya Basok, "How Durable Are the 'Durable Solutions' Projects for Salvadoran Refugees in Costa Rica?" *Refuge* 5 (May 1986).

4 "Convention Relating to the Status of Refugees Adopted on July 28, 1951, by the United Nations Conference of Plenipotentiaries on the Status of Refugees and Stateless Persons . . . ," http://www.unhchr.ch/html/menu3/b/o_c_ref.htm.

5 Four regional conventions address the issue of asylum: the Havana Convention of 1928; the Montevideo Convention of 1933; the 1954 Caracas Convention on Diplomatic Asylum; and the San Jose Pact of 1969.

6 The Cartagena Declaration resulted from the "Coloquio sobre la proteccíon internacional de los refugiados en América Central, México y Panamá" held at Cartagena, Colombia, November 19–22, 1984.

7 U.S. Department of State, Bureau for Refugee Programs, *World Refugee Report* (September 1991); Augusto Morel, *Refugiados Salvadoreños en Nicaragua* (Managua: Asociación de Colectivos de Refugiados Salvadoreños, 1991); UNHCR, Information Paper; Patricia Weiss Fagen, *Refugees and Displaced Persons in Central America*, Report of the Refugee Policy Group, Washington, March 1984.

8 Bill Frelick, *Running the Gauntlet: The Central American Journey through Mexico* (U.S. Committee for Refugees, January 1991), 6; Sergio Aguayo and Patricia Weiss Fagen, *Central Americans in Mexico and the United States: Unilateral, Bilateral, and Regional Perspectives* (Washington: Hemispheric Migration Project, Center for Immigration Policy and Refugee Assistance, Georgetown University, 1988), 11, 47–48.

9 Luis Raúl Salvadó, *The Other Refugees: A Study of Non-recognized Guatemalan Refugees in Chiapas, Mexico* (Washington: Center for Immigration Policy and Refugee Assistance, Georgetown University, 1988), 15.

10 Aguayo and Fagen, *Central Americans*, 5–7; Adolfo Aguilar Zinser, "Repatriation of Guatemalan Refugees in Mexico," *Repatriation under Conflict in Central America*, by Mary Ann Larkin et al. (Washington: Center for Immigration Policy and Refugee Assistance, Georgetown University, 1991), 62; Elizabeth Ferris, "The Politics of Asylum: Mexico and the Central American Refugees," *Journal of Inter-American Studies and World Affairs* 26 (August 1984), 369.

11 César Pastor Ortega, "Emergencia en Chiapas," *Presencia de los refugiados guatemaltecos en México* (Mexico City: COMAR and UNHCR, 1999), 58–60.

12 "Bombardeo de Campamentos," *Caminante* 31 (February 1984), 10–12.

13 Rosa Elvira Vargas, "Partió de México el último grupo de los repatriados," *La Jornada*, July 29, 1999, http://www.jornada.unam.mx/1999/jul99/990729/retorno.html; Laura Carrera Lugo, "Creación de nuevos asentamientos en Campeche y el programa multianual," *Presencia de los refugiados guatemaltecos en México.*

14 Edelberto Torres-Rivas, *Report on the Condition of Central American Refugees and Migrants* (Washington: Center for Immigration Policy and Refugee Assistance, Georgetown University, July 1985). See also Larkin et al., *Repatriation under Conflict*; and Carlos Fazio, *Samuel Ruiz, El Caminante* (Mexico City: Espasa Calpe, 1994).

15 Ann Crittenden, *Sanctuary: A Story of American Conscience and the Law in Collision* (New York: Weidenfeld and Nicolson, 1988); see also *Refugee Reports*, May 19, 1989.

16 Aurora Camacho de Schmidt, "US Refugee Policy and Central America," *Christianity and Crisis* 49 (September 25, 1989), 283.

17 Laura Dietrich, "Political Asylum: Who Is Eligible and Who Is Not," *New York Times*, October 2, 1985, § A, 26.

18 Sid L. Mohn, "Central American Refugees: The Search for Appropriate Responses," *World Refugee Survey* (1983), 44.

19 "Asylum Cases Filed with INS District Directors Approved and Denied, by Selected Nationalities," *Refugee Reports*, December 21, 1990, 12.

20 Robert S. Kahn, *Other People's Blood: US Immigration Prisons in the Reagan Decade* (Boulder: Westview, 1996), 14–18; Mohn, "Central American Refugees," 45.

21 "Break-ins at Sanctuary Churches and Organizations Opposed to Administration Policy in Central America," *Hearings before the Subcommittee on Civil and Constitutional Rights.* Committee on the Judiciary, House of Representatives, 100th Congress, 1st session, February 19–20, 1987.

22 David Kowalewski, "The Historical Structuring of a Dissident Movement: The Sanctuary Case," *Research in Social Movements, Conflicts, and Change* 12 (1990), 103; Miriam Davidson, *Convictions of the Heart: Jim Corbett and the Sanctuary Movement* (Tucson: University of Arizona Press, 1988), 85.

23 R. A. Girard, "Canadian Refugee Policy: Government Perspectives," *Refuge or Asylum: A Choice for Canada*, ed. Howard Adelman and C. Michael Lanphier (Toronto: York Lanes, 1990), 119.

24 María Cristina García, "Canada: A Northern Refuge for Central Americans," *Migration Information Source*, April 2006, http://www.migrationinformation.org.

25 Tom Clark, "Human Rights versus Immigration Controls: A Canadian Profile," *World Refugee Survey: 1988 in Review* (Washington: U.S. Committee for Refugees, 1988), 84; Marita Hernández, "Many in US Turn to Canada," *Los Angeles Times*, March 9, 1987, 1.

26 "Canadian Asylum Rates at 75 Percent, Government Seeks to Streamline Process," *Refugee Reports* (October 26, 1990), 15.

27 Arch Mackenzie, "Refugees' Lives Threatened by New Bill, MPs Warned," *Toronto Star*, August 19, 1987, § A, 1; M. Rose and S. Aikenhead, "New Policy, New Protests,"

Maclean's, May 18, 1987, 16; see also David Hatter, Matthew Horsman, and Philip Mathias, "Refugees: Tough Choices," *Financial Post*, July 20, 1987, 1.

28 Janice Turner, "Hundreds Condemn 'Draconian' Policies to Thwart Refugees," *Toronto Star*, March 9, 1987, § A, 13.

29 Dale Brazao, "Church Groups May Go to Court over Refugee Curbs," *Toronto Star*, February 21, 1987, § A, 4.

30 "Canadian Asylum Rates," 15.

31 Rosie DiManno, "Crackdown on Refugees Protested," *Toronto Star*, February 23, 1987, § A, 3; Ann Finlayson, "The Underground Railroad to Canada," *Maclean's*, May 13, 1985, 44; Agnes Bongers, "For Isaac, It's like Being Born Again," *Hamilton Spectator*, November 26, 1991, § C, 4.

32 Susan Bibler Coutin, "The Odyssey of Salvadoran Asylum Seekers," NACLA *Report on the Americas* 37, no. 6 (May–June 2004).

33 Since the first meeting in Puebla in 1996, the RCM has met in Panama City, Ottawa, San Salvador, Washington, San José, Antigua, and Cancún. See http://www.crmsv .org. Since 1999 the South American Migration Dialogue, sponsored by the International Organization for Migration (IOM), has brought together representatives from twelve South American nations as well as NGOS to discuss migration issues.

CHAPTER SEVENTEEN

Central American Transmigrants

Migratory Movement of Special Interest to Different Sectors within and outside Mexico

Rodolfo Casillas-R.

The southern border of Mexico has been the destination of much established international migration as well as the site of significant transmigratory activity over the last twenty years. More recently it has also been the origin of a growing amount of international emigration. International immigration relies upon easy entry into the country. The border is porous, which has both advantages and disadvantages. The chief advantage is that Central American immigrants provide stability and social cohesion along the length of the border, with benefits on both sides. Mexico can thus depend in the south on stable national borders, with dynamic border societies and multiethnic, multinational populations. The disadvantages include different levels of negative impacts and deleterious effects on relations with the United States and Central America.

Longstanding shortages and limitations characteristic of Central American patterns continue to encourage emigration to the United States and money transfers from it. Passing through Mexico has become ever more important for transmigrants and impacts strongly on the limited number of social groups that provide support. It involves the expanding criminal organizations that get rich from exploiting transmigrants, banking institutions and their extended network of financial services, and inconsistent public authorities charged with enforcing laws and regulations. The current spectrum of immigration policy is shaped by national security concerns, the wars against drugs and human trafficking, the promotion of trade with the Central American isthmus nations, and regulation of the regional labor market encompassing southern Mexico,

Guatemala, and Belize. These diverse interests, interventions, and expectations as well as the concurrent existence of different social and institutional processes defy clear-cut agendas and time frames to implement them. This chapter offers an account of the present-day situation.

Assessments of the Magnitude of the Movement

Along Mexico's southern border, movement of six categories of international migrants takes place: local visitors; regional workers;[1] refugees; border residents; tourists; and transmigrants. Of these the transmigrants have the largest and most complex international impact. However, it is the involvement of other actors in their journey that makes their movement appear to have negative effects on public safety and possibly even on national security. The tangled interests of the multiple actors and negative images emerging from them lead to varying degrees of vulnerability for undocumented transmigrants and immigrants.

Increased involvement of the state and international pressures are reflected in the increase of the total number of undocumented migrants in custody since the 1990s. However, since the end of 2005 official records point to a marked decrease in detentions (table 1). This does not necessarily correspond to a decrease in movement, as there are no indications of improvement in the Central American economies. Nor is it due to successful implementation of a policy of containment of transmigration. The high turnover of appointees in the Secretary of the Interior (Secretario de Gobernación), relevant undersecretaryships, and the National Institute for Immigration (Instituto Nacional de Migración, or INM),[2] and of regional directors, the great majority of whom have lacked experience in matters of immigration, has prevented the elaboration and implementation of coherent approaches to transmigration and their implementation.

The decrease in the number of detainees, along with a decrease in transmigratory movement, is a result of changed numbers of migrants, their means of travel, and the routes they have selected, adjustments which have been caused by hurricanes and other natural disasters that over the past three years have affected transit routes and places of stopover as well as by traffickers' capacity for innovation and adaptation. It is not yet possible to determine the effect of the U.S. policy of containment and the shrinking Mexican economy on the relative decline in the movement of immigrants.

Since the close of the twentieth century the most heavily represented have predominated. Since the 1990s, when Mexican immigration authorities in-

Table 17.1 Instances of Detention of Undocumented Foreigners in Mexico According to Nationality, 2001–2008

	Guatemala	Honduras	El Salvador	Nicaragua	Others	Totals
2001	67,522	440,105	35,007	21,582	7,896	152,412
	44.9%	26.6%	23.3%	1.1%	4.1%	100%
2002	67,336	441,801	20,800	1,609	6,515	138,061
	48.8%	30.3%	15.1%	1.2%	4.6%	100%
2003	86,023	61,900	29,301	2,150	8,240	187,614
	45.9%	33.0%	15.6%	1.1%	4.4%	100%
2004	94,404	72,684	34,572	2,453	11,582	215,695
	43.8%	33.7%	16.0%	1.1%	5.4%	100%
2005	100,948	78,326	42,674	3,980	14,341	240,269
	41.0%	33.0%	18.0%	2.0%	6.0%	100%
2006	84,523	58,001	27,287	3,590	1,104	182,705
	46.3%	31.7%	14.9%	2.0%	0.6%	100%
2007	15,143	22,989	5,837	862	795	50,598
	29.9%	45.4%	11.5%	1.7%	1.6%	100%
2008*	10,000	14,226	3,547	544	5,538	33,312
	30.0%	42.7%	10.6%	1.6%	16.7%	100%

* Preliminary data as of September 2008.
Source: Prepared by the author based on Instituto Nacional de Migración, *Datos estadísticos migratorios de México* (statistical data on immigration in México).

Table 17.2 Percentage of Deportation of Foreigners from Mexico According to Nationality, 1990–2000

	Guatemalan	Salvadoran	Honduran	Nicaraguan	Others	Total	Number
1990	46.5	36.1	11.8	2.4	3.2	100	126,440
1991	52.5	30.3	13.8	0.9	2.4	100	133,342
1992	53.1	21.7	20.8	1.4	3.1	100	123,046
1993	48.3	23.5	21.9	2.8	0.5	100	122,005
1994	38.0	20.2	28.7	10.9	2.3	100	113,115
1995	49.1	18.4	25.7	2.4	0.3	100	105,940
1996	47.1	19.5	29.0	1.8	2.6	100	107,118
1997	44.2	22.0	29.1	1.4	0.3	100	85,588
1998	41.3	23.1	31.5	1.7	2.4	100	111,572
1999	40.3	20.7	25.4	1.1	0.5	100	126,498
2000	45.9	21.7	26.5	1.1	0.8	100	172,935
Total	46.2	23.6	24.6	2.5	3.2	100	1,327,599

Source: Prepared by the author based on Instituto Nacional de Migración, *Datos estadísticos migratorios de México* (statistical data on immigration in México).

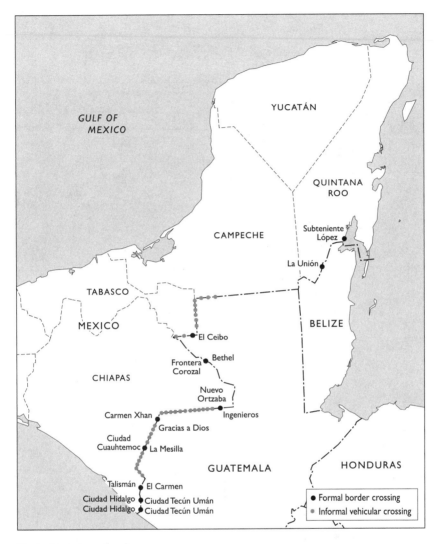

Mexico's southern border

creased their efforts to contain undocumented immigration, Guatemalans, Hondurans, Salvadorans, and Nicaraguans were the most heavily represented undocumented foreigners detained by INM (table 2).

The emphasis on detention in the 1990s was reflected in the construction and adaptation of buildings for the imprisonment of undocumented foreigners pending deportation to their country of origin. Their number increased from one detention center in the Federal District and twenty-four holding centers in 2000 to to fifty-two centers by 2005. Some of these subsequently had to

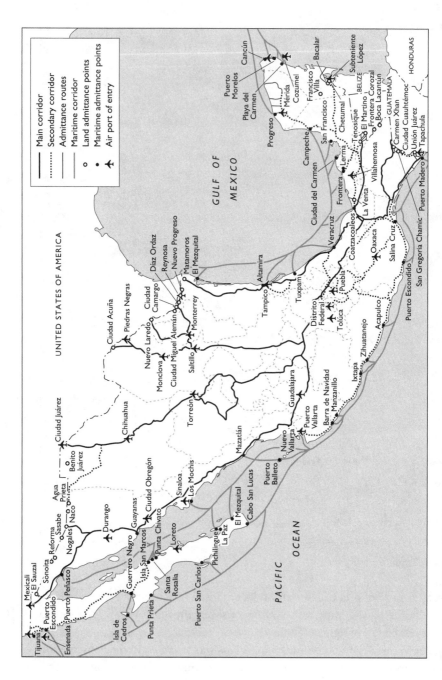

The main routes followed by Central American and other transmigrants in Mexico, 2001–2005

be closed because they did not meet minimum operational requirements and had been publicly criticized by the National Commission on Human Rights (NCHR, or Comisión Nacional de los Derechos Humanos de México).[3] The holding centers were located primarily in cities that connected main arteries of movement and in strategic maritime and aerial points of entry in Mexico's south and central regions, especially in the south-southeast to contain the mainly undocumented migration along the border shared with Guatemala and Belize; some are in important northern cities and at U.S. border crossings. The *diversification* of detention centers did not contain the transmigratory movement. It merely served to increase the detainees nationwide before 2005.

Some Obstacles along the Way

U.S.-bound Central American transmigration through Mexico has a long history, but until the 1980s the Mexican government showed little interest. And for the United States the small number of Central American migrants presented no problem. When, because of the military and political conflicts ravaging the main isthmus countries, these became refugee-exporting countries and the number of migrants grew, the United States decided to tolerate the influx. Politicians were reluctant to complicate the efforts of the weak Central American governments in combating leftist and indigenous movements. These efforts had the backing of the United States governments and, at the same time, made the United States the recipient country for ever larger numbers of refugees.[4] But after the peace accords of the 1980s the situation changed. The United States introduced stricter visa requirements and border patrols (see chapter 16). The implementation of security measures along its southern border combined physical barriers (fences in strategic locations),[5] manpower (more personnel for the Border Patrol, now part of the Department of Homeland Security, or DHS), and sophisticated equipment and technology. This new emphasis since 9/11, continuing to the present, is on fighting terrorism, a policy unconnected to developments in Central America and Mexico.

To circumvent these new obstacles Central American transmigrants through Mexico established a diversity of routes and dynamics, first rather loosely, then under pressure, and finally at increasingly great risk—and kept coming, by sea; by air; and by land (using rail lines, foot trails, passenger buses, freight buses, and privately owned cars).[6]

In itself Central American transmigration has never been a problem for Mexico. It became a problem only when the United States changed its immigration policy toward Central America. On the one hand the United States began a new cycle of deportations to the south (which because of the sheer numbers of people involved had a greater and more direct effect on Mexico); at the same time these deportations forced Mexico to exert greater control along its southern border. Thus the government initiated a new immigration and transmigration policy with intent to control the south-to-north movement. Thus the increased enforcement, from the 1990s to 2005, and the expansion of administrative structures, personnel, and detention centers have been focused on efforts to contain Central American transmigration as well as undocumented immigration.

A Plurality of Routes

Transmigrants, relying on an accumulation of social experiences, have responded by diversifying their routes and broadening the social spectrum of aid. They distinguish between major and secondary routes, depending on length, cost, safety, the availability of alternatives, and other factors. A route may contain stretches of major highways but usually cannot consist of major highways alone. And a route may be considered major in one part and secondary in another, depending on the presence of new checkpoints or crime networks, or the availability of a more convenient route. Evaluation of a route depends on information gathered by migrants and networks of aid or traffickers, and on experience.

Roads, highways, and railroad tracks serve many functions, legal and illegal. Routes are considered either autonomous, when used solely for migration, or shared, when used for other means as well (for instance, drug and human trafficking, or the transport of food products). Based on their perception of risk, some transmigrants choose roads that are heavily traveled while others prefer less heavily traveled ones. Some transmigrants believe that in more populated areas the border will be more porous, making their movement easier. Others believe that in the less densely populated countryside it is easier to have early warning of and evade migration controls and government officials, because law enforcement usually barely reaches main roads and only occasionally secondary ones. Transmigrants will consider some such routes autonomous, perhaps not accurately but because they are unaware of parallel usages—the trafficking of people, goods, and drugs. Perceptions explain why some migrants follow one route, then branch off onto another, only to later return to the first. The sinuous nature of the routes corresponds more to the logic of assumptions than to actual curves in the network of highways and rail lines. Air passage follows a different kind of logic, given the greater security measures at airports, which hinder the movement of large numbers of people and increase cost. Transmigrants do not construct passageways: they take possession of those that exist and they do not ask for permits but practice free transit. Since childhood and over the course of generations, transmigrants have learned how to migrate north. At home they listen to conversations about the experiences of past generations and of members of their own generation who have gone ahead of them. They experience the problems caused by the social and economic structures of the states into which they were born. And, most important, by their own experiences, transmigrants learn how to negotiate the ups and downs of life on the road. Emigration is one way to avoid hunger; it is a way of life.

Land routes are the ones most heavily used, and among them the railroad has been the most useful in recent years. Migrants may engage in hitchhiking, especially in vehicles transporting freight from strategic locations throughout Mexico, such as the main wholesale market for Mexico City. Freight trains are the preferred means, especially for those with the fewest resources, though even stowaways need to pay for their "right of way." Railroad employees, private security guards of the companies, and officials thrive on bribes obtained from undocumented transmigrants. Payment of a fee allows transmigrants to board trains and guarantees that they will not be taken off by guards, that they will be dropped off before the train reaches a police or military post, or that the train will not slow down while passing an immigration checkpoint. Checkpoints are obstacles but not necessarily insuperable ones. Transmigrants seek means of avoiding the officials and, when asked for papers, of obtaining (often through a request from the interested party) a particular public servant's goodwill to clear their way. For Central American transmigrants the trip entails the disbursement of money and sometimes of favors (especially from women).

Some places are considered boarding platforms (areas where groups of migrants arrive, regroup, take shelter, and depart); others are points of junction or nodes (places where alternative routes are provided and where migrants are redirected); still others are stops along the way (places where migrants replenish supplies or rest). In the places en route transmigrants find houses providing support from individuals or social networks;[7] safe houses and humanitarian shelters; and public spaces like plazas,[8] markets, bus stations, railway stations,[9] and waiting areas. In general such spaces are used almost exclusively by people who have the least support and fewest resources. At the same time, these spaces are put to equal use by traffickers, whether to disguise their groups, get migrants into their clutches, find people who will help move illegal goods, give their groups a rest, or get rid of their groups. Humanitarian shelters and safe houses may, against the will and vigilance of the people responsible, be used by trafficking networks.

Routes of Crime, Solidarity, and Business

Undocumented migrants are the targets of robbery, abuse, and violations of their human rights. Women, adolescents, and children—girls and boys—confront the greatest risk of physical abuse and rape. Even though these crimes occur throughout the country, there are places where they occur more frequently, and this has been the subject of recent public debates.[10] As trans-border movement has been pushed from the coast to the central region, migrants and, not far behind them, traffickers of foreign nationals have increasingly congregated in places such as San Luis Potosi. Empirical evidence points to a growing number of violations of the human rights of these migrants as they stay or pass through Mexico. Usually the victims do not file grievances with the appropriate state authorities.[11]

Transmigration has increasingly high costs, and there is a direct relationship between stateside obstacles and costs. The immigration policies of the countries in the northern part of the continent have had two secondary negative effects: an increase in trafficking networks and a rise in the price of transmigration. Together these effects have caused the assets of migrants to dwindle even faster during their travels through Mexico. The assets may include savings, loans, proceeds from the sale of worldly goods, resources from the United States, and payments for seasonal or temporary work (especially for women, whose work may also include providing sexual services). Transmigrants also avail themselves of humanitarian aid, such as that provided at shelters.

The increasing flow of international migrants to and through Mexico, especially of undocumented migrants from the southern part of the continent, cannot be fully explained without discussion of distinct networks of traffickers. These networks, if operating from the migrants' point of origin or residence, throughout the journey, and at the point of destination, actively facilitate the movement of large groups of people. Within the trafficking networks functions, some of necessity visible while others remain in the shadows, are stratified.[12] They span recruiting, organizing, caring for, guarding and escorting, guiding, and charging the immigrants. Each person involved in human trafficking has only limited functions, whether as part of a formal structure or not. Actors in the criminal networks show different levels of competence and have different levels of access to the network's human and material resources. Many of the actors, both public and private, farm out delivery of services to others, and networks continue to intertwine. Success depends on a highly fragmented set of collaborators, so that if one collaborator is caught by the authorities, all that the organizations lose is one of numerous intermediaries, leaving the organization intact.

Elements of the trafficking network range from individuals connected to the goods and services sector, private agents (such as families with roots in localities removed from trafficking), young people, farm workers, and public officials—especially members of municipal police forces and local immigration officials. This multisector participation is what enables us to speak of different kinds of structured collaboration. It is possible to point out the longstanding practice of social initiation, training, and development of participants in this set of criminal practices which have long since invaded and corroded institutions and different social sectors and continue to do so unpunished to the present.

Over the past several years one of the most effective protective strategies of the transmigrants as they pass through Mexico has been the staggered receipt of funds for the next leg of the trip through electronic remittance, whether to continue the journey northward or to return after having given up.[13] This strategy has generated new mechanisms of social cohesion, until now hardly studied, among Central American transmigrants as they cross Mexican territory and the border, between them and social support groups at the point of origin, in transit, and at the point of destination in the United States. These mechanisms of social cohesion have strengthened the social fabric of the transmigrants, with effects limited neither to their world nor to the national territorial spaces they call home.

Staggering the shipment of remittances creates multiple benefits for different parties. *Senders* are able to ship smaller sums in designated installments. *Recipients* can count on the cash needed to cover a specific stage of the trip, giving them the ability to cover the desired distance as well as a guaranteed lifeline. *Criminal networks* have a secure source of income without having to resort to extreme violence, even though the fragmented set of tasks entailed by staggered remittances requires more time and effort.[14] They have the additional benefit that their criminal behavior, now broken up into smaller tasks, makes it harder for government officials, humanitarian organizations, and immigrants to trace their activities. *Government* benefits from the existence of an ad hoc mechanism free of governmental control that prevents, eases, or postpones social conflict, and at least in the short term lessens the societal pressure on the state, and on the executive branch in particular, to take a clear stand on migration, labor, justice, and other social issues. Some but not all *humanitarian social organizations* find it easier to offer aid as part of a broader strategy to increase undocumented migration—in many cases without intending to do so. Finally, *financial companies* are able to increase their transnational clientele and services thanks to the international means by which remittances are sent: they have increased their presence and their profits in a promising international market.

It may be concluded that remittances to transmigrants provide an intangible cohesive bonus which is effective in counteracting activities harmful to transmigrants in general but which may also encourage extreme violence. Further, when remittances effect a redistribution that is real and satisfactory for all those involved in the transmigration process, remittances contribute toward easing social conflicts.

Shared Space

Transmigratory movement from Central America to the United States has transformed Mexico into an international corridor in a strategic space. In it a diversification of movements and routes may be observed that are marked by the growing participation of distinct types of participants and institutions, which may function legally or illegally. Changes in the national, regional, and local spheres in Mexico have produced tensions and crucial contradictions in national immigration policy. On the other hand, social organizations working with transmigrants have taken action to confront emerging problems with a good measure of pragmatism. Even so, humanitarian social networks have yet to come to large-scale agreements that may allow them to combine their energies without being hindered by their ideological and conceptual differences.

The hurricane and other natural disasters of 2005 and beyond tested the capacity of many of the people and institutions involved in Central American transmigration to respond. The convergence of electoral politics and a change in administration at the federal level had additional effects on institutional behavior. It is compelling to note that criminal networks were again quicker to put innovations in place and adapt to changes in railway and overland routes, as well as to capitalize on the transmigrants' needs. These networks, with a modicum of financial support, have the means to meet the new challenges. It was prudent on the part of the INM to suspend operations against undocumented migrants and provide opportunities for their return. At the same time, some shelters became victims of the overflow of transmigrants and struggled to stay afloat, while others were overwhelmed by the extraordinary circumstances.

International transmigration along the southern border of Mexico is not in itself a public or national security problem for the country. The migrations have a variety of meanings for society and for public institutions. The confused interventions by the people involved at close hand, as well as the incompatible and insufficient steps taken by governmental agencies, may do more harm than good. The results, often achieved inadvertently, may create public dangers that are difficult and costly to solve. Only by making analytical distinctions between different types of migration will it be possible to establish public policies that will strengthen the social fabric and discourage developments that weaken it.

Notes

The author's research project, "The Present and Future of Central American Transmigrants in Mexico" (August 2005 to December 2006), took place under the auspices of the Fondo Sectorial Segob-Conacyt (Sectorial Fund of the Department of the Interior—Segob, or Secretaría de Gobernación) and the National Council for Science and Technology (Conacyt, or Consejo Nacional de Ciencia y Tecnología).

1 The nature of labor markets along the southern border of Mexico requires further research. Case studies of the mid-1990s are insufficient to satisfactorily determine the sociodemographic characteristics and volume of the present-day international labor force. The Emif-Guamex survey (Emif Sur, from 2008; the same survey with some changes), a recent attempt to periodically match the volume of agricultural workers with a certain area along Mexico's southern border, is not unbiased, not easily accessible to the general public, and methodologically unreliable because of multiple changes that have undermined its trustworthiness as regards comparisons over time.

2 From October 1993 to December 2006 the INM was directed by twelve different officials. Since December 2006 Lic. Cecilia Romero Castillo has stayed in office, but it is unclear whether the tendency to longer tenure will continue. Most members of the top leadership did not, according to their curricula vitae, have knowledge of the field of migration before their commission.

3 See for example the Special Report of the NCHR of September 1, 2006, "Status of Human Rights in Immigration Stations and Adapted Locales of the National Institute of Immigration in the Mexican Republic (Situación de los Derechos Humanos en las Estaciones Migratorias y Lugares Habilitados del Instituto Nacional de Migración en la República Mexicana).

4 Timothy Dunn, *The Militarization of the U.S.-Mexican Border, 1978–1992: Low Intensity Conflict Doctrine Comes Home* (Center for Mexican American Studies, University of Texas, 1996), 35–102.

5 The new U.S. strategy involved building a fence in California across the area adjoining the city of Tijuana (1991, 1993); Operations Blockade and Hold the Line (1993); Operation Gatekeeper (1994); and Operation Safeguard (1995). In 1996 the current law, the Illegal Immigration Reform and Immigration Responsibility Act (IIRIRA), was approved, and in 1997 Operation Río Grande went into effect.

6 For a graphic representation of transmigration see Casillas, *Una vida discreta, fugaz y anónima. Los centroamericanos transmigrantes en México*, published in 2007 by the Mexican NCHR and the International Organization for Migration (Organización Internacional para las Migraciones).

7 Different support organizations for Central American migrants have been estab-

lished along the routes, according to el Foro Migraciones, a registry that incorporates a network of civil associations, human rights centers, and shelters in Mexico. These organizations emerge and disband. Some offer humanitarian aid but do not pay particular attention to violations of rights. See Foro Migraciones, mimeographed list (Mexico City, 2006).

8 The main square of the city of Tapachula is one of the most popular places for contacting migrating adolescents and women, be it for domestic work, informal services, or human trading and trafficking. See R. Casillas, *Trading in Women, Adolescents and Children in Mexico: An Exploratory Study in Tapachula, Chiapas / La trata de mujeres, adolescentes, niñas y niños en México. Un estudio exploratorio en Tapachula, Chiapas* (2006), edited by the Inter-American Commission of Women (CIM), Organization of American States (OAS), International Organization for Migration (IOM), National Institute for Women (Inmujeres), and National Institute for Immigration (INM).

9 Until mid-2005 Tapachula's train station was a meeting place and information node of great importance for undocumented Central American transmigrants. After the natural disasters of 2005 the transmigrants had to walk or use public transportation for some three hundred kilometers to reach the closest train station, in Arriaga in northern Chiapas.

10 National Commission for Human Rights, "Special Report on Kidnappings" (Mexico City, June 15, 2009).

11 One noteworthy case is the ongoing effort of the Belén Shelter in the city of Saltillo, where under the direction of Frontera con Justicia, A.C. (Borders with Justice, a civil association), methodical on-target documentation has produced important reports for 2006 and 2007.

12 Emphasis is only on networks operating in open spaces in the south-southeast of Mexico. Other kinds of networks, often institutional ones, commit more covert crimes, with legal immigrants as their primary target.

13 At Elektra appliance stores (partners with Western Union) and other local businesses, international migrants and their families can send and collect remittances. By October 2006 Elektra had a widespread network of 1,569 branches throughout Mexico, 74 in Guatemala, 70 in Honduras, 30 in Panama, and 81 in Peru. It had ambitious plans to expand operations.

14 "Express" kidnappings of undocumented migrants are an example of this extreme violence. The sending of remittances has encouraged criminal activity and its spread to locations in southern Mexico and towns and cities bordering the United States. The expectation is that the ransom demanded can be transmitted electronically to any location and any account. "Express" kidnappings have become commonplace, according to the NCHR's "Special Report on Kidnappings"; almost ten thousand occurred during the first half of 2009. See R. Casillas, "L'enlèvement, un nouveau visage de la vulnerabilité du migrant centramericain au Mexique," *Problèmes d'Amérique latine* 76 (2010).

CHAPTER EIGHTEEN

Interrogating Managed Migration's Model

A Counternarrative of Canada's Seasonal Agricultural Workers Program

Kerry Preibisch

Temporary migrant worker programs (TMWPs) for less-skilled workers are on the rise throughout high-income countries, with new programs emerging and older versions experiencing renewed growth. Amid the growing securitization of borders and restrictive immigration policies by high-income states, TMWPs hold their attractiveness. These guest-worker programs seek to solve labor shortages by issuing temporary entry and work permits to migrants from lower-income countries who are offered jobs but not permanent residence. Within policy circles the resurgence of guest-worker policies has been accompanied by a search for models and codes of practices for implementing managed migration programs effectively. Internationally, Canada's Seasonal Agricultural Workers Program (SAWP) has often been regarded as a model. This chapter describes and interrogates the narrative of the model Canadian guest-worker program. Among the questions that it seeks to answer: Why is the Canadian SAWP considered a model TMWP? What evidence contradicts this image? How does this narrative, while contributing to pragmatic solutions within the contemporary immigration policy environment, in practice legitimize discrimination against migrants and the denial of their rights?

The Canadian Program as Model

In 2007 the SAWP was called "a model despite flaws" by a well-known Canadian scholar, an "example of best practices" by a Mexican academic, and a source of "useful lessons" for Australia by the World Bank. These endorsements of the SAWP contribute to an increasingly established international discourse regarding Canada's employment of foreign workers in less-skilled sectors of the labor market as a model of best practices.[1] This narrative is significant given the current historic moment of increasingly restrictive immigration policies and heightened border controls within high-income nations. In this context labor-receiving states find it highly desirable to have managed migration schemes that allow them to move migrant workers into jobs and yet retain control over the conditions of their entry, work, and residence. For labor-sending countries and households dependent on remittances, these schemes represent a much safer alternative to undocumented passage and the promise of secure remittances. TMWPs have expanded significantly in many high-income countries, particularly in occupations requiring lower-skilled workers. Although the U.S. economy depends heavily on irregular migrants, the increased securitization of the border has contributed to the re-opening of the guest-worker debate. Europe is currently experiencing a return to guest-worker policies, including in former labor-sending countries such as Spain.[2] Nonwestern high-income countries, such as those in the Persian Gulf, also employ many migrants, while Australia and New Zealand recently instituted TMWPs for agriculture. In Canada the trend toward temporary migration is unmistakable. In 2006 the province of Alberta received more temporary migrant workers than permanent immigrants—triple the number since 1997.

As countries increasingly turn to mechanisms for incorporating migrant workers into their economies, existing programs are scrutinized, compared, and imitated. The "best practices" or "model" elements of the Canadian SAWP have assumed greater relevance in policy circles. In 2003 the program became the subject of extensive consultation by the Australian government as a result of pressure by the National Farmers Federation and the World Bank to allow Pacific Islanders to fill seasonal farm jobs.[3] The Australian examination of the SAWP illustrates the weight that this migration narrative carries in policy circles and ultimately its material impact on the lives of thousands of migrant workers and their households across the globe. Each year the SAWP grants temporary employment authorizations to some 28,000 migrants. The program, which began in 1966, operates under bilateral frameworks of agreement signed between the government of Canada and several migrant-sending countries: Barbados, Jamaica, Mexico, members of the Organization of Eastern Caribbean States, and Trinidad and Tobago. This highly managed program involves a significant amount of administration. The Canadian federal government is involved primarily in approving eligible employers to receive hires from abroad and processing visas for eligible migrants. Regional growers' organizations undertake day-to-day management of the program, including processing employer requests and communicating policies and procedures to growers. Further, migrant-sending states shoulder a considerable share of the administrative burden, managing the selection, recruitment, and documentation of workers. They also operate offices in Canada, whose agents serve as liaisons between migrants and employers. With the exception of workers, all parties—the Canadian government, sending countries, and employers—participate in annual negotiations of the bilateral agreement, including wage rates. This high level of government involvement distinguishes the SAWP from its U.S. equivalent, the H2A visa program.[4]

Canada issues visas to migrants for an eight-month period, and work permits are valid with a single, designated employer. On average, migrants have six-month contracts, after which almost all leave the country. They are unable to work legally for another employer without negotiating an official contract transfer, and their continued placement in the SAWP is contingent on their return. Further, sending countries and employers exert considerable pressure for migrants to leave Canada at the end of their contracts (or when they are injured or sick), to avoid visa overstays. The remarkable success of the SAWP in moving workers back home after their jobs are finished—referred to in policy circles as "circularity"—is considered one of the program's strengths; an estimated 98.5 percent finish their contracts each year.[5] Since employers can request their workers by name, most migrants return to the same farm each year. This saves employers training costs and provides workers with some stability in terms of estimated earnings and length of stay. Another feature of the SAWP that is considered a model element is the use of standard, rather than individual, contracts.

The SAWP's four decades of operation and high return rates of migrants are considered indications of its success, as is the range of recognized benefits for the program's stakeholders. For migrants the SAWP provides an opportunity to earn higher pay rates than those available within their home country *through legal channels*. Unlike the bulk of U.S.-bound migrants, SAWP participants avoid smugglers' fees and the dangers of crossing increasingly militarized borders. Interviews with migrants in Canada and the United States suggest a strong preference for migrating legally.[6] Since SAWP workers return year after year, they endure shorter separations from their families than those suffered by most undocumented workers. Importantly, the SAWP links workers to employers through government agents, reducing the fees and abuses linked to private intermediaries that plague the H2A program in the United States. Finally, the SAWP's relatively low entry costs make it more accessible to poor applicants.

The earnings differential is substantial. A survey of Mexican farmworkers in Canada in 2006 found that almost half earned between CAD $6,501 and $9,500 per season after deductions, significantly more than their projected earnings in Mexico.[7] Through their employment abroad SAWP migrants are able to invest in their families' nutrition, housing, healthcare, and education. Some migrants are able to use their Canadian earnings to invest in land or build small businesses. Another study found evidence that the longer migrants participate in the program, the greater the likelihood that their children will attain a higher level of education and find nonagricultural employment. Some 93 percent of respondents felt that the SAWP had improved their well-being and that of their family.[8]

Migrants' remittances accrue benefits for the sending countries. The Mexican government estimated that the SAWP generated some CAD $67.5 million in remittances in 2004.[9] While this figure is slight relative to U.S. remittances, money remitted to Mexico by SAWP workers supports some ten thousand households.[10] The importance of remittance income for the participating Caribbean countries, which have far less diversified economies, is probably greater. Furthermore, migration to Canada holds more weight for the Caribbean than it does for Mexico: less than 1 percent of Mexican remittances originate in Canada, while for Jamaica, SAWP migrants generate remittances comparable to those of H2A migrants.[11] Migrants' investments in housing, education, and healthcare contribute to broader development outcomes in sending countries. They also reduce political pressure on states facing challenges in public service delivery, job creation, and rural development. Indeed, the mechanisms that migrant-sending governments have put in place to capture and channel migrant remittances testify to their economic importance.

The SAWP also has significant benefits for Canadian producers and the economy. Producers gain access to a reliable workforce, allowing them to plan production with greater confidence and freeing them from the threat of immigration raids and fines. Employing the same workers each year also provides benefits in terms of training, workplace health and safety, and productivity. The availability of migrant workers has had economic benefits for agribusiness in general, allowing for the dynamic growth of some industries while enabling more marginal ones to survive. Further, migrant expenditures also sustain and fuel rural businesses and services. Although some residents express xenophobic attitudes toward migrants, the impermanence of their settlement mitigates some of the political pressure.

Flawed, despite the Model

Despite these benefits the SAWP has less-than-exemplary features. One of the key areas of contention among SAWP critics has been the well-documented abuse of workers' rights and dignity. These problems occur largely because employers have disproportionately more power than migrants and because Canadian authorities have generally failed to monitor and ensure employers' compliance. In the following discussion I systematically review how the operation of the SAWP creates these power differentials, not only through established mechanisms but through a failure to create appropriate safeguards.

Migrant workers' immigration status is among the principal power dimensions. Employer-specific worker permits prevent migrants from circulating freely in the labor market, setting them apart from citizens, landed immigrants, and even undocumented workers who can "vote with their feet" and move to better worksites. One worker told me that if he could make one change in the SAWP, it would be to abolish employer-specific work permits: "that way, bosses who offered good working conditions and housing would have people lining up at their farm looking for work, while those offering poor working and housing conditions would have to improve them in order to attract workers." This feature of the SAWP has led scholars to refer to participants as a "captive" or "unfree" labor force. Moreover, as noncitizens, migrant workers are ineligible for the range of services and protections associated with landed immigrant status that facilitate social integration, such as government-funded English classes. Furthermore, SAWP migrants do not have the opportunity to apply for landed immigrant status, regardless of how many years (or in some cases decades) they have worked in Canada.

The social, economic, and political conditions within the sending countries add to migrants' vulnerability. The SAWP's bilateral partners are low- and middle-income countries experiencing high rates of poverty, growing income inequality, and a deficit of higher-paying jobs. Since migrants' Canadian wages are often considerably more than their projected earnings at home, they greatly value the opportunity to work in Canada. This dual frame of reference induces migrants to overperform relative to Canadian workers and to suppress any criticisms they might have of working conditions.

Employers' power is enhanced by their ability to indicate the nationality and gender of the migrants they seek to hire. If an employer is dissatisfied with the performance of a group of migrants or the government agents of a particular sending country, it has the option of choosing a different group the following year. The threat and actual practice of labor substitution dampen the power of workers and migrant-sending governments to negotiate for better wages and working conditions. The representation of migrants' interests is further compromised by serious obstacles to unionizing. Two-thirds of SAWP migrants are employed in Ontario, a province which denies agricultural workers the right to bargain collectively. Even in provinces where agricultural workers can unionize, migrants fear reprisals. Research on the H2A program in the United States found that workers who ally themselves with unions have put their jobs at risk and have sometimes been blacklisted from future participation in the program. The policy that allows employers to request their migrants by name also fosters self-discipline among workers, who perceive that failure to be renamed jeopardizes their continued participation in the SAWP.

Nationality and race form additional layers of power differential. SAWP workers are negatively racialized next to predominantly white employers and rural communities. Racial discrimination is a fundamental factor in the class formation of Canadian society, to the extent that scholars have identified a "color-coded vertical mosaic," or social hierarchy of race.[12] Thus despite commitments to diversity and multiculturalism, racialized groups are subject to social marginalization and persistent expressions of xenophobia. Within rural areas perceptions of migrants often conform to racial stereotypes, and some migrants have been subject to racially motivated aggression. Colby found that 75 percent of Mexican SAWP workers who had previously worked in the United States felt more racism in Canada, a finding that she attributes to the absence of a Hispanic population.[13]

The SAWP has a number of characteristics that reduce workers' agency, notably recruitment norms. Historically recruitment has shown preferences on the basis of family status (favoring applicants with dependents over singles), gender (favoring men over women), class (favoring small-scale farmers or farmworkers), and rural-urban location (favoring rural dwellers over urbanites). The recruitment bias toward applicants with dependents is an attempt to reduce visa overstay, premised on the assumption that migrants who are married with children are more likely to return home and less likely to seek permanent immigration status through marriage to a Canadian citizen. That workers are compelled to migrate without their families also means that they are more willing than Canadians to accede to employers' requests to work longer hours and over weekends. Indeed, migrants' limited social commitments within Canada make them particularly reliable employees.

The male bias in recruitment reflects cultural norms that consider men more suitable candidates for farm work. The vast majority of SAWP workers are male; in 2008 the ratio was one female worker per thirty men. The program's masculinized nature has translated into greater restrictions on women migrants and their sexual stigmatization within the migrant community. Sexual harassment of migrant women is commonplace.[14] Finally, recruitment preferences for land-poor farmers or landless farmworkers and for rural location (where poverty in migrant-sending countries is concentrated) further ensure that migrants will highly value their Canadian earnings. Because wage rates are relatively low and subject to a range of deductions,[15] however, migrants have to return to Canada for several years before they are able to accumulate savings to finance investments back home.

An additional mechanism in the sawp that skews power in employers' favor is the presence of repatriation provisions that permit employers to dismiss workers for "non-compliance, refusal to work, or any other sufficient reason."[16] Sending-country governments facilitate migrants' deportation in these cases largely to prevent visa overstays, one of the most politically sensitive features of guest-worker programs. Migrants usually comply with their deportation, often because they seek to return to Canada under the sawp in the following year. Moreover, few migrants are aware that they can legally remain in the country until their visa expires. Regardless, financial and logistical obstacles ensure their compliance; since migrants are housed on their employer's property, loss of work is accompanied by loss of residence. While rates of forced return are low, because migrants have been repatriated unfairly, the threat of repatriation itself is an effective mechanism of control.[17]

Housing arrangements which require employers to provide accommodation at no cost (often on their property) also shape power relations. While such arrangements hold benefits for migrants given the scarcity and quality of low-cost rural housing, they also extend employers' control over farmworkers' behavior beyond the workplace, restricting workers' mobility off the farm. The arrangement also fosters paternalistic, personal labor relations.[18] The extra level of control accorded by housing workers on employers' properties is reinforced through "farm rules" that employers have the right to establish. Intended as guidelines regarding care of the property, some employers have instituted curfews, prohibited visitors of the opposite sex, or obliged workers to inform them of their whereabouts when outside the farm.

Other dimensions that disempower migrants relative to their employers include the occupational status that farm labor occupies in Canada, the rural settings in which most of it takes place, and the hours that migrant workers invest in their jobs. First, farm labor is near the bottom of the occupational hierarchy in Canada; it is among the lowest-paid, least protected, and most dangerous work in the country. In many provinces farmworkers enjoy fewer legal rights than other workers. Second, migrant farmworkers remain largely invisible to the greater part of Canadian society that resides in cities. Even in regions of labor-intensive agriculture, farms can be at great distances from towns. Migrants face additional constraints to exercising civic engagement. Physically demanding jobs and hours, six to seven days a week, leave migrants with little time or energy for socializing. Finally, workers often agree to employers' requests to work long hours, in part because doing so is the only way they are able to increase their earnings.

As this chapter has shown, even though migrants are in theory subject to many of the same employment standards protecting all workers in Canada, in practice they cannot exercise their labor rights in the same way as citizens. The Canadian government has failed to put in place adequate safeguards to protect migrant workers' rights and has failed to sanction those who seek to violate these rights. At the federal level there is no system in place to monitor the employment of migrant workers. Although the government claims to be working on this area, the pace of policy development pales in comparison to the alacrity with which measures have been instituted five years into the program to facilitate and expedite the hiring of migrant workers, including extending the length of the work permits, widening the pool of worksites eligible to hire migrant workers, and providing additional assistance to employers. Part of the problem lies in the SAWP's governance structure. Accountability is a key issue. Although the program is implemented at the federal level as part of the country's immigration policy, federal officials often defer the onus of responsibility to provincial governments (responsible for employment standards, labor, and health) or migrant-sending country officials, who in turn deflect accountability upward. The absence of effective, transparent governance of the SAWP has compelled pro-migrant groups to invest considerable effort in navigating the various levels of government bureaucracy. Employers also enjoy a prominent role in the SAWP's governance structure. As mentioned, employer organizations coordinate the day-to-day administration of the SAWP, and their representatives participate in the program's annual negotiations, a forum closed to workers and unions. The high level of employers' involvement reflects the employer-driven nature of the SAWP, a program whose creation and expansion are a direct result of sustained and influential private sector lobbying.

Legitimizing Discrimination, Endorsing Disentitlement

A common response to critiques of the SAWP is to compare it to undocumented migration or guest-worker programs dominated by private recruiters. A second common response of the SAWP's proponents is to compare labor conditions in Canada to the broader North American region, with particular reference to abusive practices in labor camps in California and agribusiness operations in northern Mexico. Such comparisons of differential levels of exploitation are often evoked in discussions featuring the SAWP, particularly among Canadian rural residents and employers. One grower claimed that "what [the workers] get here is 100 per cent better than in Mexico."[19] Similarly, a resident whom I interviewed in 2003 stated that "the people in the community think the workers here are treated like slaves . . . but we have to remember that the countries that these people come from, the conditions they come from, are ten times worse than what they are living in here." Emphasis on the disparities between migrants' home countries and Canada is also a common discourse framing other TMWPs, such as the Live-in Caregiver Program. Canadian benevolence figures prominently in these arguments, a discourse used by the federal government itself, which casts TMWPs as part of the country's efforts to aid "third world" countries and ameliorate unemployment abroad.[20] Recently the Canadian High Commissioner to Jamaica called the SAWP the island's "golden egg."[21]

Like the narrative of the "model" program, discourses that rely on comparisons of relative exploitation legitimize discrimination against international migrant workers in the labor markets and societies of high-income countries and do nothing to raise the bar in terms of positive and fair treatment of farmworkers and migrants. As Sharma has convincingly argued, TMWPs are one mechanism in a system of border controls that seeks not to physically exclude people classified as foreigners from national space but legally *differentiate* them in order to position them in inferior categories of entry, work, and residence in Canada: "what restrictive immigration policies restrict, then, is not necessarily the mobility of people but the rights and entitlements migrants are able to lay claim to."[22] This feature of TMWPs has implications not only for migrant workers but for all workers who share a national space, as the import of a vulnerable group of workers functions to infuse competition throughout the domestic labor market.

Moreover, while queries into the relative level of exploitation of farmworkers across countries and programs might be useful, they distract from a set of other questions: Which characteristics common to all TMWPs are exploitative? Why are some workers less deserving of permanent residency than others? How can we characterize the jobs that temporary migrants are filling, and how sustainable are these jobs within high-income countries? In terms of TMWPs for agriculture, how do poor labor standards in agricultural systems globally threaten model elements of protection for farmworkers enacted locally? And ultimately, how does international labor migration contribute to capital accumulation in high-income countries and underdevelopment in labor-sending countries?

These questions merit careful consideration, but they are not in vogue in policy circles. For example, the broader labor market advantages that TMWPs afford to high-income countries are rarely mentioned, nor are the ways in which immigration policy in high-income countries is overly restrictive, ethically questionable, and even economically shortsighted. The emphasis in development policy debates is squarely on how migration can fuel development in migrant-sending countries, in this case the Caribbean states and Mexico, rather than on how international labor migration may engender underdevelopment and global inequalities between countries. There has been little attention paid to how international labor migration acts as a hidden subsidy to agriculture in high-income nations, allowing them to compete in international markets, including ones in which the migrant-sending countries are fighting to find a foothold. In Canada the SAWP has maintained flagging industries and stimulated more dynamic ones. Without migrant workers some sectors would struggle; indeed, labor shortages in industries such as agriculture that rely on lower-skilled workers are to a large extent socially constructed by poor wages, working conditions, and social statuses in those industries.[23] All of these make them undesirable to workers with other employment opportunities. This is why agricultural producers cannot retain new immigrants, who stay in these jobs only long enough to find better wages and working conditions elsewhere.[24] In essence, the availability of migrant workers provides a highly disciplined labor force across the sector, including to marginal performers, and dampens incentives to improve productivity through labor-saving technology.[25] Further, there is evidence that the availability of migrants has a negative effect on agricultural production in farmworkers' countries of origin.[26] Clearly TMWPs need to be seen not merely as sources of employment opportunity provided by benevolent states and employers but as powerful instruments of labor market policy at the disposal of high-income states that strengthen their ability to compete for dominance in globalized supply chains.

Model Deviations

In a time of restrictive immigration policies and tighter border controls, Canada's SAWP is considered a model among temporary migrant worker programs. Given the weight of this narrative internationally, it is paradoxical that in 2002, when the Canadian federal government broadened the eligibility of employers to hire migrant workers in a range of low-skilled positions beyond agriculture, the "model" was not replicated. Rather than create a twin program structured on bilateral agreements, Canada introduced a new TMWP, now known as the Pilot Project for Occupations Requiring Lower Levels of Formal Training (National Occupations Code C&D) or the NOC C&D Pilot. Although a thorough comparison between the SAWP and the new pilot is beyond the scope of this chapter, the main point of divergence is the level of government involvement and cooperation. Three key differences in this respect are noteworthy. First, the new program does not bind the Canadian government to bilateral agreements signed by participating labor-sending countries. Second, it requires less government involvement in linking workers to employers, which has created a new role (and market) for private intermediaries. Third, the program does not require the same level of consultation between Canada, the migrant-sending governments, and the private sector. It is unsurprising, therefore, that problems are already emerging, involving private recruiters exploiting migrants by charging extortionate fees, discrepancies between the contracts that workers sign in their home countries and the ones they receive in Canada, and labor rights violations. It has also resulted in a number of visa overstays, as migrants leave their designated employers to join the undocumented working class or apply for refugee status until they can earn enough money to justify the inordinate costs of their migration and return home to their families. Thus rather than strengthen cooperation between sending and receiving countries—considered a key dimension of any alternative model to current migration policies that continue to exploit, discriminate against, and marginalize migrant workers—Canada appears to be going in the opposite direction. Rather than assume greater responsibility for ensuring the protection of migrants' human rights, the Canadian government would prefer to assume less. The recent deviation from the (already flawed) model strengthens the argument that TMWPs are first and foremost a tool for using citizenship status to differentiate the labor market as part of Canada's restructuring in response to global pressures, while allowing it to maintain a restrictive immigration policy that denies citizenship opportunities and equality to certain groups of workers.

Conclusions

Canada's SAWP is internationally regarded as a model of managed migration, a "best practice" among temporary migrant worker programs. For receiving states the program's principal feature is its exceptional rate of circularity, as almost all participants return home. Given the history of TMWPs across the globe, it is remarkable that in a single year the Canadian state is able to move 28,000 people across the border to meet variable labor demands and back again. For sending countries, circularity (within the legal framework which makes it possible) is also a virtue, ensuring that most participants will not establish themselves permanently abroad and will instead continue the circular flow of remittances southward. For migrants the program permits them to legally cross borders and earn higher wages, at relatively low cost. It is no surprise that participating countries have no shortage of applicants. The principal North American migratory alternatives to the Canadian program involve crossing the increasingly militarized U.S. border and joining the ranks of the undocumented, or paying substantial intermediary costs to obtain an H2A visa.

Discussions of the relative merits of TMWPs and undocumented migration, or the benefits of one program over another (e.g. the SAWP over the H2A) are important and useful when examining legal and protected international labor migration in general and in North America in particular. In these debates, however, it is critical not to scuttle other questions that demand thorough exploration, such as why we accept the further militarization of borders or why the path to permanent immigration for less-skilled workers is so elusive. Furthermore, we should be mindful of how comparing levels of exploitation contributes to making more palatable the denial of rights to migrant workers and discrimination against them, in effect sanctioning the disentitlement of a growing segment of workers in high-income countries. Indeed, while the Canadian program may be better than its alternatives, this should not justify the subordination of migrants within the domestic labor market or the failure of migrant-receiving governments to monitor and enforce the rights of all workers.

Notes

1 Tanya Basok, "Canada's Temporary Migration Program: A Model despite Flaws," *Migration Information Source* (Washington: Migration Policy Institute, 2007), www .migrationinformation.org; Gustavo Verduzco, *The Impact of Canadian Labour Experience on the Households of Mexicans: A Seminal View on Best Practices* (Ottawa: Canadian Foundation for the Americas, 2007); World Bank, *At Home and Away: Expanding Job Opportunities for Pacific Islanders through Labor Mobility* (2006), report no. 37715-EAP.

2 Stephen Castles, "Guestworkers in Europe: A Resurrection?," *International Migration Review* 40, no. 4 (2006), 741–46.

3 Peter Mares, "Inquiry into Pacific Region Seasonal Contract Labour," Submission to Senate Employment, Workplace Relations and Education References Committee, Parliament of Australia (2006), http://www.sisr.net; World Bank, *At Home and Away.*

4 David Griffith, *The Canadian and United States Migrant Agricultural Workers Program: Parallels and Divergence between Two North American Seasonal Migrant Agricultural Labour Markets with Respect to "Best Practices"* (Ottawa: North South Institute, 2003).

5 *FARMS 2002 Harvest System Ontario: Workers by Country and Repatriation*, report F39, 11/11/03 (Mississauga: FARMS, 2003).

6 Tanya Basok, *Tortillas and Tomatoes: Transmigrant Mexican Harvesters in Canada* (Montreal: McGill-Queen's University Press, 2002); Leigh Binford, "Contract Labor in Canada and the United States: A Critical Appreciation of Tanya Basok's *Tortillas and Tomatoes: Transmigrant Mexican Harvesters in Canada*," *Canadian Journal of*

Latin American and Caribbean Studies 29, nos. 57–58 (2004), 289–308; David Griffith, Monica Heppel, and Luis Torres, "Guests of Rural America: Profiles of Temporary Worker Programs from U.S. and Mexican Perspectives," Report to the Ford Foundation (New York, 2002).

7 During the period of her study the Canadian dollar was worth between USD $0.85 and $1.10. Lidia Carvajal, *The Farm-Level Impacts in Mexico of the Participation in Canada's Seasonal Agricultural Workers Program (CSAWP)* (Ph.D. diss., University of Guelph, 2008).

8 Verduzco, *The Impact of Canadian Labour Experience on the Households of Mexicans.*

9 Approximately USD $56 million. Carvajal, *The Farm-Level Impacts in Mexico of the Participation in Canada's Seasonal Agricultural Workers Program.*

10 Secretaría de Trabajo y Previsión Social, Dirección General de Empleo (2006), http://www.dgec.df.gob.mx/programas/snedf/capacitacion.html#migratorios.

11 Janet McLaughlin, "Seeking Rough Hands and Rough Lives: Recruitment, Selection, and Screening of Canada's Temporary Foreign Workers in Jamaica and Mexico," paper presented at the Canadian Sociological Association Annual Meetings, Vancouver, June 3–6, 2008.

12 Grace Edward Galabuzi, *Canada's Economic Apartheid: The Social Exclusion of Racialized Groups in the New Century* (Toronto: Canadian Scholars' Press, 2006).

13 Catherine Colby, *From Oaxaca to Ontario: Mexican Contract Labor in Canada and the Impact at Home* (Davis: California Institute for Rural Studies, 1997).

14 Kerry Preibisch and Evelyn Encalada, "The Other Side of 'El Otro Lado': Mexican Migrant Women and Labor Flexibility in Canadian Agriculture," *Signs: Journal of Women in Culture and Society* 35, no. 2 (2010), 289–316.

15 Federal government deductions that apply to all workers in Canada include those for the pension plan, employment insurance, and the income tax. SAWP workers pay program-specific fees, including for their visa, medical exams, a portion of their airfare (except in British Columbia), and housing (only in British Columbia).

16 Veena Verma, *The Regulatory and Policy Framework of the Caribbean Seasonal Agricultural Workers Program* (Ottawa: North-South Institute, 2007), 11, http://www.nsi-ins.ca/english/pdf/Regulatory_Policy_Verma.pdf.

17 Workers have been deported for becoming injured or sick, refusing unsafe work, complaining about housing or working conditions, challenging abusive employers, and refusing to have sex with an employer.

18 Robert Cecil and G. Edwards Ebanks, "The Human Condition of West Indian Migrant Farm Labour in Southwestern Ontario," *International Migration* 29, no. 3 (1991), 389–404; Ellen Wall, "Personal Labour Relations and Ethnicity in Ontario Agriculture," *Deconstructing a Nation: Immigration, Multiculturalism and Racism in 90s Canada*, ed. Vic Satzewich (Halifax, N.S.: Fernwood, 1992).

19 Roger Varley, "Workers 'at Mercy' of Farm Owners," *Era Banner* (Newmarket), October 7, 2004, 1 (retrieved March 28, 2009, from Canadian Newsstand Torstar database).

20 Sedef Arat-Koc, "Immigration Policies, Migrant Domestic Workers and the Defini-

tion of Citizenship in Canada," *Deconstructing a Nation*, ed. Satzewich, 229–42, and Wall, "Personal Labour Relations and Ethnicity in Ontario Agriculture," *Deconstructing a Nation*, ed. Satzewich.

21 "Jamaican Jobs Scheme Jeopardized," Toronto Globe and Mail, December 2, 2003.

22 Nandita Sharma, *Home Economics: Nationalism and the Making of Migrant Workers in Canada* (Toronto: University of Toronto Press, 2006), 133.

23 Castles, *Guestworkers in Europe*.

24 When the United States granted an amnesty to thousands of undocumented farmworkers under the Special Agricultural Worker legislation, many of these workers exited agriculture for higher wages and improved benefits outside the sector. P. Martin, M. Abella, and C. Kuptsch, *Managing Labor Migration in the 21st Century* (New Haven: Yale University Press, 2006).

25 Richard Mines, "Family Settlement and Technological Change in Labour-intensive U.S. Agriculture," *The Dynamics of Hired Farm Labour: Constraints and Community Responses*, ed. J. L. Findeis, A. M. Vandeman, J. M. Larson, and J. L. Runyan (Wallingford, Oxfordshire: CABI, 2002), 41–53; David Griffith, *American Guestworkers: Jamaicans and Mexicans in the U.S. Labor Market* (University Park: Penn State University Press, 2006); Keith Hoggart and Cristóbal Mendoza, "African Immigrant Workers in Spanish Agriculture," *Sociologia Ruralis* 37, no. 4 (1999), 538–62; Sam Scott with Ashley McCormick and Maja Zaloznik, *Staff Shortages and Immigration in Agriculture* (London: Migration Advisory Committee, 2008).

26 Jill Findeis, "Hired Farm Labour Adjustments and Constraints," *The Dynamics of Hired Farm Labour*, ed. Findeis, Vandeman, Larson, and Runyan, 3–14.

CHAPTER NINETEEN

1867 and All That . . .

Teaching the American Survey as Continental North American History

Angelika Sauer and Catherine O'Donnell

Now that we have learned so much and unlearned, perhaps, even more—shedding nationalist frameworks and cultural myths on our way to an analytically powerful form of transnational scholarship—we are left with a question: How much of this can we share with our students? Specifically, how much can we productively share with students in our introductory surveys? "Why, all of it!," cries the good teaching angel on one shoulder. "For heaven's sake, they can hardly keep straight the simple story, must I really complicate it?," sighs the tired teaching angel on the other. In this chapter we will try to heed both voices, positing ways to bring new frameworks into our survey classrooms without stretching the canvas, and ourselves, too thin.

The scholarship of Nora Faires, Dirk Hoerder, and the many contributors to this volume makes clear that a continental perspective requires thinking at once bigger and smaller. The need to think bigger is readily apparent in any number of ways: rather than focus only on the British colonies and on the United States as it forced its way east to west, we must consider Canada, Mexico, and the Caribbean. Rather than begin with European settlement in North America, we must explore the expanse of time in which the land was known only by First Peoples. Rather than only English-language sources, we must work with French, Dutch, Spanish, and Russian, as well as with indigenous American languages and with anthropological sources. But these scholars are also adamant that we must think smaller: we must set aside the baggy term "Indians" and attend to diverse tribes; we must look inside Spain and see Andalusia, Catalonia, and Galicia; we must look within individuals to view their myriad allegiances to polities and cultures that are themselves both larger and smaller than nations. In that movement from large to small and back—an intellectual migration that accompanies the literal migrations traced in this volume—rests a way to make sense of a "continental" survey.

The freshman survey in the United States has been perhaps the last bastion against attempts to close the gap between postnational historical scholarship and the teaching of history in the undergraduate curriculum. For over a century the survey course has had unabashedly civic goals and, as its critics claim, it has done much to promote the inward-looking, exceptionalist orientation of the average American student. In its report to the American Council on Education in 2005, a committee of the American Historical Association on internationalizing student learning outcomes in history suggested that American survey courses held the greatest potential for being reconstituted in ways that would allow twenty-first-century students entry points into the analysis of larger global forces.

To teach American history as North American history is one possible way of achieving that reconstitution. Like other units of analysis, North America—analyzed in a new North American textbook by Michael Brescia and John Super as the territory covered by the modern states of Mexico, the United States, and Canada, to which we would add the Caribbean—is a flawed geographical or economic construct and must be presented as such to the students. Critics might dismiss this approach in favor of the hemispheric history so eloquently outlined by Felipe Fernández-Armesto, or simply surround the United States with larger world-history themes and encase its traditional national keynotes in global developments. Both approaches have undoubted merit but both face practical roadblocks, starting with the specialized training of faculty and the daunting information deficit of any student venturing outside the traditional national narrative. Students are more responsive to concrete realities than to intellectual constructs, whatever the latter's superior merits. In our experience American students respond to the power of contiguity, recognizing Canada and Mexico as continental neighbors. If they live in northern or southern borderlands regions, they may also be aware of the fluidity, yet salience, of the political boundaries that separate the neighbors. Here then are the natural entry points to probe perceived national differences and to historicize not only the three North American nations and the Caribbean but the concept of nation making itself.

We propose first a small adjustment in the way the survey is divided. Let's make the pivot point 1867, rather than 1865 or 1877. If we say, "1867 was an important turning point in North American history," what might this mean to survey students? Historical dates, anchored as they tend to be in political events of alleged national significance, do not mean much to most young people, and even less if they are not part of the accepted national narrative.

But students in our reimagined survey course will learn that 1867 was the year of Confederation and hence the beginning of Canada's history as a country, and that the year also marked the final defeat of European intervention and the victory of La Reforma, hence the starting point of modern liberal Mexico, symbolized by Benito Juárez's presidency. In the Caribbean, 1867 saw the imposition of harsh Spanish laws in Cuba, laws that would in 1868 spark the Ten Years War. In the United States 1867 saw the purchase of Alaska, thus the end of continental expansion, as well as being an important year in Reconstruction and thus in the creation of the modern American nation-state. A course that begins or ends in 1867 is thus a course that begins with questions, not answers. Why 1867 and not 1865, students in and of the United States would wonder? From there the class easily moves to the following inquiries: How were the different events of 1867 relevant to people across the continent? How, that is, might the start of modern Mexico have affected those who would inhabit Mexico's northern neighbors? And we will also ask: How were these events that we now consider of national significance probably invisible to people who lived through them—even to people who lived through them within the nation in which they occurred? The students' own uncertainty (before the course) about the historical meaning of 1867, that is, probably overlaps with the uncertainty of people whose lives they will be studying. Even as we point out to students this unexpected communion with their subjects, we remind them that the events of 1867 of course truly did matter, both to the past and to the present that the past helped to shape. And so we have begun the course acknowledging both the relevance of nations and their traditional political narratives, and their insufficiency.

Let's turn now to the separate halves of the survey. How might each benefit from the kind of scholarship in this volume? On the one hand, broadening the early part of the survey simply makes sense. The handwringing over the need to internationalize the survey has seemed to many early Americanists somewhat overdone. There was no United States for the majority of years covered in this part of the survey, but rather myriad First Peoples and a collection of colonies so patently part of a transatlantic system that early Americanists have simply never had the temptation or the luxury of ignoring the rest of the world. Moreover, Atlantic history, and its assiduous attention to the Caribbean's importance as the site of clashing empires and burgeoning slave societies, has begun to permeate not only monographs but textbooks. That admirable breadth, however, often appears only in flashes—for instance, during discussions of first encounters, the slave trade, and the War of 1812— while much of the survey still collapses into a focus on the British colonies and the young nation. A North American survey can incorporate many of the important contributions of comparative empires and Atlantic world approaches, while not entirely abandoning the national history that orients students and so makes possible the more ambitious moves from large to small.

What do we mean by this? A North Americanized survey can attend to a political chronology familiar to those of us who teach the American survey—encounters between settlers and indigenous peoples, imperial contestations, the emergence of chattel slavery, demographic and political revolution, the rise of the powerful nation-state, wars with indigenous peoples and with Mexico, fragmenting domestic politics, Civil War. But the survey embeds that chronology in a comparative framework encompassing empire and the Atlantic world, and brings it to life with attention to change over time in individual borderland communities. A continental perspective, imperfect as it is, offers the hope of a more consistent—and insistent—international perspective and comparative analysis, without promising to study everything everywhere. The Caribbean, Canada, and Mexico will appear not only when conflicts briefly make their territory visible through a nationalist periscope (French and Indian War, Mexican-American War) but throughout the survey, and they will appear not only as contested land masses but also as the complex and interrelated societies and polities that they of course are. The framework immediately introduces students to a far wider array of economies, political structures, religions, and indigenous societies. The *pays d'en haut* of Richard White's *Middle Ground* and the New Mexico of James F. Brooks's *Captives and Cousins*, these regions, seen through new historical lenses, allow students to understand areas and systems that straddled eventual national boundaries (and to understand that areas and systems did indeed straddle national boundaries). They also offer illuminating contrasts to the farming and plantation societies that developed in the thirteen colonies and that interacted in their own distinctive ways with indigenous societies.

A concrete example, drawn from this volume, is scholarship on what is now the American Southwest that makes it possible to glimpse the region as it existed in the sixteenth, seventeenth, eighteenth, and nineteenth centuries. A survey teacher might introduce the region in the first week of class, then return to it periodically throughout the semester, each time attending to the ways the Southwest fits into both our larger and our smaller (supranational and subnational) frameworks. Our first visit would be to the area before the arrival of the Spanish, and would explore its cultural, political, linguistic, and environmental characteristics. We would return to the region in the seventeenth century, witnessing its changed physical environment and learning how Apache, Comanche, and Ute peoples struggled and cooperated with each other, with Spanish conquistadores and settlers, with creoles, and with those whose mixed ancestry bore testament to the region's history of violence, adaptation, and improvisation. Large and small are immediately evident: the Spanish empire, in its reach and its limitations, necessarily forms a part of understanding that story, and so too do the intricate family histories unearthed by authors such as James Brooks. When the class revisits the area after 1821, revolutions in both Mexico and the United States—as well as changing views and uses of slavery—will have reshaped the area's culture and politics and will be slowly rendering it more visible to the new national capitals. Finally, when we emerge at the Mexican American War, that war is more than simply an expected stopping point on the conventional timeline of United States history. It emerges from centuries of imperial and national development, and its progress is as much affected by the depopulating effects of Comanche power in the region as by the American ideal of Manifest Destiny. The aftermath of the war, moreover, will be readily seen as shaping the lives of individuals and communities, not simply as helping to fill in the map of the present-day United States.

In addition to both humanizing and internationalizing students' view of history, a broadened perspective offers the possibility of revealing that processes such as slavery, emancipation, and the dispossession of Native Americans are the product of circumstances and decisions, not simply the natural state of things. The parameters of political and economic possibility are also broadened. Church and state relations developed differently in Mexico than in the United States, differently in the United States than in Anglo-Canada, and differently again in Quebec. In Quebec, in fact, the toleration that Great Britain extended to the Catholic Church after 1763 helped to spur colonial Americans' decision to declare independence, illuminating a linkage between religious mistrust and political liberty that challenges students to think more deeply about the Revolutionary era. The abolition of slavery, for its part, occurred in Mexico, Canada, and Spanish and Danish possessions in the Caribbean before it occurred in the United States, a fact which many students find startling. The Haitian Revolution began as the most broadly successful slave revolt in the western hemisphere, and it both inspired and terrified other inhabitants of North America for decades. In short, a "North Americanized" early American survey, like the chapters in this volume, disrupts the traditional view of "American" history just enough to make us see it more clearly.

The task of "continentalizing" the post–Civil War or post-1867 portion of the survey seems to confound instructors more than the earlier periods. Is it not obvious that self-consciously distinct and independent nations took shape from the late 1860s onward, and that whatever continental trends existed in the histories of Native American interactions or European empires in North

America now have to take a backseat to narratives of nation building? Indeed a compare-and-contrast approach, outlining how history and geography produced distinct, nationally defined issues that were confronted with distinct national solutions, can fruitfully be part of this section of the survey, if it is layered with examples of how both regional and continental dynamics subverted the story of national distinctiveness. Thus, for example, the stories of an old order disappearing in violent civil war, and being replaced by a vision of the future that remained largely unrealized, can be told in both Mexican and U.S.-American examples, and contrasted with the political conflict and no less flawed compromise solutions of the new Dominion of Canada. At the same time, the respective frontier stories of the three countries—two "Wests" and "el Norte"—will reveal the common trend of removing First Peoples by destroying Native political and economic structures, while regional migration patterns can demonstrate that family trajectories—which might have begun in Europe and Asia—were built around the search for land or jobs and easily crossed the northern and southern borders of the United States in both directions. The expansionist history of the United States cannot be fully understood without attending to debates over the possible annexation of Cuba, debates that exposed the racial and religious frameworks in which policymakers understood Manifest Destiny. A section on the growth of the industrial order in the later part of the nineteenth century can be focused on the resulting regional inequalities, with a closer look at railroad building quickly revealing the emerging patterns of the continental economy, as its north-south connections directly fed into national networks of transportation and communication. A focus on growing social inequality as the concomitant to modernization can lead to a discussion of the full range of reform and revolutionary ideas that played out across the continent into the twentieth century.

Much of the twentieth-century part of the traditional survey deals with the rise of the United States to world power status and its interactions with the world. This approach has contributed to seeing the United States and "the world" as distinct and separate. Again, the continental approach can help students to understand how the United States participated in, created, and reacted to global issues. Starting with the age of imperialism in the first decades of the twentieth century, its activities in the Caribbean and Central America can be embedded in a story that includes Mexico's struggle with Guatemala over the Chiapas region and Canadian imperialists' attempts to turn trading and banking interests in the West Indies into some form of political union. The 1920s can be presented as a decade of North American culture wars in the broadest sense, ranging from strident anti-Asian sentiments that were common to the entire North American Pacific Coast, to harsh internal and external boundaries for groups that challenged the claims of a dominant culture to sole national status, to conservative and progressive tugs-of-war, and to the struggle of Mexico and Canada for their cultural, economic, and political distance from an increasingly overwhelming neighbor. Similarly, the 1940s can be used as an example of cooperation among countries of unequal sizes and capabilities but also provide examples of economic and political integration on a new and unprecedented scale, represented by the Mexican-American *bracero* program and Canadian-American defense cooperation. Finally, the 1960s can be presented in the context of global decolonization as a period when the previously oppressed and disadvantaged demanded the fulfillment of promises made a century earlier. Thus the civil rights movement stands alongside Quebec separatism and the Tlatelolco massacre of demonstrating students in Mexico City in 1968 as an example of protest and backlash. In this way different historical approaches — social, political, economic, cultural and military — are given their due.

Why complicate the survey course, one might ask? What are the rewards for students and instructors, and what are the pitfalls? Students in our experience are surprisingly open to learning something that seems entirely new, as opposed to retreading the ground of high school boredom. In the process of learning about what might be to them the "other" of an unknown neighbor, they naturally slip into relearning the story about themselves. The results are often rewarding to all parties involved. The risk of a continental approach is the oversimplification of complicated histories, along with the creation of an illusion of North American convergences or a teleology of integration. The rewards are new ways of looking at gender, race, and class, and at conflict and cooperation, along with many opportunities to unravel the "natural" narratives of exceptional countries that are present not only in the United States but also in Canada and Mexico. North American history allows students and instructors to think, as Antoinette Burton has said, "with and through the nation."

Further Reading

American Historical Association. "Internationalizing Student Learning Outcomes in History: A Report to the American Council on Education," presented September 2005, http://www.historians.org.

Bender, Thomas. *A Nation among Nations: America's Place in World History*. New York: Hill and Wang, 2006.

Brescia, Michael M., and John C. Super. *North America: An Introduction*. Toronto: University of Toronto Press, 2009.

Brooks, James L. *Captives and Cousins: Slavery, Kinship, and Community in the Southwest Borderlands*. Chapel Hill: University of North Carolina Press, 2002.

Burton, Antoinette, ed., *After the Imperial Turn: Thinking with and through the Nation*. Durham: Duke University Press, 2003.

Elliott, John H., *Empires of the Atlantic World: Britain and Spain in America, 1492–1830*, New Haven: Yale University Press, 2006.

Fernández-Armesto, Felipe. *The Americas: A Hemispheric History*. New York: Modern Library, 2003.

Hijiya, James, et al. "How the West Is Lost." *William and Mary Quarterly*, 3rd series 51 (1994), 717–54.

Laing, Annette. "Exploring the Atlantic World: An Experiment in Teaching an Emerging Paradigm." *Teaching History: A Journal of Methods* 28, no. 1 (2003), 3–13.

Meinig, D. W. *The Shaping of America: A Geographical Perspective on 500 Years of History*, vol. 3, *Transcontinental America, 1850–1915*. New Haven: Yale University Press, 1998.

Meyer, Michael C., William L. Sherman, and Susan M. Deeds. *The Course of Mexican History*., rev. ed. New York: Oxford University Press, 2007.

Reichard, Gary W., and Ted Dickson, eds. *America on the World Stage: A Global Approach to U.S. History*. Bloomington: Organization of American Historians, 2008.

White, Richard. *The Middle Ground: Indians, Empires, and Republics in the Great Lakes Region, 1650–1815*. New York: Cambridge University Press, 1991.

Wigen, Kären E., and Martin W. Lewis. *The Myth of Continents: A Critique of Metageography*. Berkeley: University of California Press, 1997.

About the Contributors

JAIME R. AGUILA is an assistant professor of Mexican history in the School of Letters and Science at Arizona State University.

RODOLFO CASILLAS-R. is a member of Facultad Latinoamericana de ciencias sociales (Flacso), Mexico City.

The late NORA FAIRES was a professor of history and of gender and women's studies at Western Michigan University.

MARÍA CRISTINA GARCÍA is a professor of history at Cornell University.

DELIA GONZÁLEZ DE REUFELS is a professor for Latin American history at the University of Bremen.

BRIAN GRATTON is a professor of history at Arizona State University.

SUSAN E. GRAY is an associate professor of history at Arizona State University.

JAMES N. GREGORY is the Harry Bridges Endowed Chair of Labor Studies and professor of history at the University of Washington.

JOHN MASON HART is a professor of history at the University of Houston.

DIRK HOERDER teaches North American social history, the history of global migrations, borderland issues, and the sociology of migrant acculturation at Arizona State University.

DAN KILLOREN is a Ph.D. student in the public history program at Arizona State University.

SARAH-JANE (SAJE) MATHIEU is an associate professor of history at the University of Minnesota.

CATHERINE O'DONNELL teaches early American history and the Atlantic world at Arizona State University.

KERRY PREIBISCH teaches in the Department of Sociology and Anthropology, University of Guelph, Canada.

LARA PUTNAM is an associate professor of history at the University of Pittsburgh.

BRUNO RAMIREZ is a professor of history at the Université de Montréal.

ANGELIKA E. SAUER is a professor of history at Texas Lutheran University.

MELANIE SHELL-WEISS is an assistant professor of liberal studies at Grand Valley State University.

YUKARI TAKAI is an assistant professor at the Department of History at Glendon College, York University.

OMAR S. VALERIO-JIMÉNEZ is an assistant professor of borderlands history at the University of Iowa.

CARLOS G. VÉLEZ-IBÁÑEZ is the Motorola Presidential Professor of Neighborhood Revitalization and a professor of transborder Chicana/o and Latina/o studies at the School of Human Evolution and Social Change at Arizona State University.

Index

Page numbers in *italics* refer to figures, maps, and tables.

Canadian-born migrants in U.S. and, 89–90, 92–93; Central American refugee policy and, 319, 357–60, 363; Chinese migrants in, 15, 22; circular migrations between Caribbean and, 16, 19, 25, 30, 108–9, 181, 183, 301, 305–6, 308, 310 n. 13, 378, 380, 385; civil rights for migrants in, 380–82, 384, 389 n. 17; as cultural-political region, 4–5, 10, 172 n. 12; deportations and, 31; East Indian migrants in, 22, 317–18; economics and, 14, *24*, 31, 41 n. 19, 215, 380, 386; Europeans' migration to, 4–5, *7, 8, 9*, 23, 27, 41 nn. 10–11, 86–89, 97 n. 35, 132, 136, 314; federal governments and, 384; geographic regions and, 4–5, 10, 23, 26; German migrants in, 13, 14; during Great Depression, 63, 82; Guatemalan migrants in, 202, 357; illegal alien category and, 213; inequalities between nations and, 341, 343–44, 381, 385–87; internal regulatory systems and, 212; international and regional refugee policies and, 360, 363 n. 33; intra-continental migration and, 23, 31, 305; Italian migrants in, 21, 26, 86; Japanese migrants in, 22, 32; labor unions in, 216, 384; literacy tests in, 222; logging industry in, 35, 79, 91, 315, 316; Loyalist migrants in, 27, 35, 89, 134–35, 298, 299–300, 302–3, 309; macro-level studies and, 4–5, *7, 8, 9*, 41 nn. 10–11; medical criteria for migrants and, 217–18; migrant populations in, 136, 189; migration from, 82–85; national identities in, xvi, 1, 17, 133–36, 142; nation-states' emergence and, 15, 16; nativism and, 133; NGOs and, 357–59; NOC C&D Pilot project in, 386–87; passports and, 139–40; public safety and, 216, 217; quota systems and, 178, 318; railroads in, 22, 23, 26, 35, 78, 87, 214, 306, 315; repatriation for Canadians and, 89–90, 92–93, 134; repatriation for guest workers and, 383, 389 n. 17; repatriation of Europeans from, 23, 86–89, 97 n. 35; repeat migrations and, 83, 84, 92; segregation in, 298, 306–7; social hierarchies in, 383; subsidies for agriculture in, 386, 390 n. 24; transmigration routes for Mexicans to, 206; transnational perspectives on, 32, 34–35, 44 n. 48; transpacific migration and, 15, 22; U.S.-born residents of, 25–26, 76, 93; U.S. migration to, 134–35; visas and, 178, 360, 378–79, 382–83, 387–88, 389 n. 15; wheat crop in, 80–81. *See also* Africans' experience in Canada; Anglo-Canada; Canada-U.S. border; First Peoples (Canada); French Canada; immigration regulations in Canada; racism in Canada; Seasonal Agricultural Workers Program (SAWP)

Canada-U.S. border, *11*, 95, 129–31; agriculture and, 81, 83, 90–91; American Revolution and, 132; Anglo-Canadians and, 76, 82, 84; Asian migrants and, 22, 213–16, 213–18, 220–21, 315–16, 317–22; border diplomacy and, 213–14, 319; Canadians and, 27, 79–86; Canadians' circular migration and, 83, 84, 89–94, 134–35, 136–37; Canadians' repatriation with U.S.-born children and, 89–90, 92–93; Catholic missionaries and, 255, 275; child migrants and, 76, 78–79, 84; Chinese circular migration and, 315; Chinese migrants and, 213–14, 320–21; cross-border lives and, 77–78, 136–38; cross-border migration and, 14, 26–30, 77, 78; doors to migration discourse and, 20, 218; East Indian migrants and, 143, 315, 320–21; economics and, 215–16; Euro-American raiding parties and,

Dirk Hoerder teaches North American social history, the history of global migrations, borderland issues, and the sociology of migrant acculturation at Arizona State University.

The late Nora Faires was a professor of history and of gender and women's studies at Western Michigan University.

Library of Congress Cataloging-in-Publication Data
Migrants and migration in modern North America :
cross-border lives, labor markets, and politics /
Dirk Hoerder and Nora Faires, eds.
p. cm.
Includes bibliographical references and index.
ISBN 978-0-8223-5034-7 (cloth : alk. paper) —
ISBN 978-0-8223-5051-4 (pbk. : alk. paper)
1. North America—Emigration and immigration—
History. 2. Immigrants—North America. 3. Cultural
pluralism—North America. I. Hoerder, Dirk.
II. Faires, Nora Helen.
JV6351.M547 2011
304.8'7—dc22
2011015531